SOLANO

COMMUNITY COLLEGE

★★★★ RUNNING ON RACE ★★★★

RUNNING
ON RACE

★ ★ ★ ★ ★ ★ ★ ★ ★ ★ ★ ★

Racial Politics in Presidential Campaigns,
1960–2000

JEREMY D. MAYER

 RANDOM HOUSE ★ NEW YORK

All rights reserved under International and Pan-American Copyright Conventions. Published in the United States by Random House, Inc., New York, and simultaneously in Canada by Random House of Canada Limited, Toronto.

RANDOM HOUSE and colophon are registered trademarks of Random House, Inc.

Library of Congress Cataloging-in-Publication Data

Mayer, Jeremy D.
    Running on race: racial politics in presidential campaigns, 1960–2000 / Jeremy D. Mayer
        p. cm.
    Includes bibliographical references and index.
    ISBN 0-375-50625-X (acid-free paper)
    1. United States—Politics and government—1945–1989.   2. United States—Politics and government—1989–   3. United States—Race relations—Political aspects.   4. Racism—Political aspects—United States—History—20th century.
5. Presidents—United States—Election—History—20th century.   6. Political campaigns—United States—History—20th century.   I. Title.
E839.5 .M39 2002   324.973'092—dc21   2001048986

Printed in the United States of America on acid-free paper

Random House website address: www.atrandom.com

98765432

First Edition

Book design by Casey Hampton

THIS BOOK IS FOR K.I.M. AND J.R.M.

★ ★ ★ ★ Hands that once picked cotton can now pick presidents.

JESSE JACKSON, 1984

★ ★ ★ ★ Let's forget about race and be one nation again.

BILL CLINTON, 1992

ACKNOWLEDGMENTS

Many people helped me write this book.

Bob Stauffer and David Strauss read every word and provided immensely helpful support and encouragement. I am also grateful to those who read smaller portions of the manuscript: David Barclay, Karen Struening, John Dugas, Clyde Wilcox, Jason Owens, Ashlyn Kuersten, Shana Alexander, Gordon Agress, Sara Thom, Walter Palmer, and James and Marjorie Mayer. Amy Sullivan read the first six chapters, and the manuscript benefited greatly from her editorial insights, constructive criticism, and enthusiastic response. John Wickstrom and Ken Mayer provided insight into race in the ancient world.

This book relied on interviews with many wise people who worked on or covered presidential campaigns. As I wrote the more modern chapters, interviews became even more crucial, as archival resources were either closed or nonexistent. It gave me a sense of the closeness of history, to meet men who talked civil rights with Eisenhower and Kennedy, who were in the room when Reagan decided to go to Neshoba, who debated with Bobby Kennedy about integration days before he was killed, who saw Clinton attack Sister Souljah. To all of the mighty and powerful who agreed to talk to an unknown professor at a small midwestern college, I am very grateful, especially to David Broder, Eugene McCarthy, George McGovern, Lawrence Walsh, Arthur Schlesinger, Rene Amoore, Charles McWorter, Rich Bond, Theodore Sorensen, Martin Anderson, Ed Meese, Doug Bailey, Richard Wirthlin, and Ron Walters.

Documents used in this book reside at the Kennedy Library in Boston; Johnson Library in Austin; Eisenhower Library in Abilene, Kansas; Nixon Library in Yorba Linda, California; Nixon Project in Bethesda, Maryland; Ford Library in Ann Arbor, Michigan; Carter

Library in Atlanta; and the Reagan Library in Simi Valley, California. In particular, David Haight of the Eisenhower Library pointed me to the crucial postelection memo mentioned in Chapter 5. I'm also grateful to the following paper collections: Goldwater Papers in Tempe (Arizona State University); Humphrey Papers (Minnesota Historical Society); Wallace Papers (Alabama Department of Archives and History); McGovern Papers (Mudd Library, Princeton University). Those who curate the papers of failed presidential candidates do so without the big budgets of the presidential libraries, but they persevere with admirable verve. The archives of the Fair Campaign Practices Committee kept at Georgetown University were also useful.

I acknowledge my debt to all of the authors who came before whose accounts of the campaigns and the politics of the period were crucial to my own understanding. In particular, I should mention the late Theodore White, whose 1960 book changed journalism and eventually presidential politics, and political scientists Ed Carmines and Jim Stimson. I'm also duty bound to acknowledge the work of political scientist Hanes Walton Jr. and historian Dan Carter.

Several people put me up during my many visits to presidential libraries and paper collections. As a relatively destitute assistant professor at a small liberal arts college, I appreciated their generosity, but their company was even more valuable. Pam and Rob Hitchcock in Boston; Jason Boehk in Boston; my aunt and uncle Barbara and Doug Henderson in Beverly, Massachusetts; Lauren Hale in Princeton, New Jersey; Elysa Marden in New York City; Tony and Carol Tether in Corona Del Mar, California; Colleen Hobbes and David Woodruff in Austin, Texas; Lena Gavruseva in Iowa City. The Novel Café in Santa Monica, and the Fourth Coast and Water Street Cafés in Kalamazoo, Michigan, provided sanctuaries for writing, and caffeinated fuel.

A very special thanks to a great writer, Shana Alexander. Shana's willingness to read a manuscript by a distant cousin is something I will always remember with gratitude. I should also thank my editor, Bob Loomis, whose faith in this manuscript came at just the right moment. Thanks also to Dominique Troiano, Jeff Shesol, Larry Mayer, Clyde Wilcox, and Mark Rozell.

My students at Georgetown University and Kalamazoo College I thank for always keeping me on my toes. Special thanks to Tracy

McCollum, Dawne Bell, and Kyle Reynolds for help with the bibliography and photos.

The seven-thousand-mile summer trek to the paper collections and presidential archives was partially supported by a grant from the Faculty Development Committee of Kalamazoo College. The college was also generous with sabbatical time in the winter and fall quarters of 2000.

Portions of Chapter 2 were presented in a paper at the American Political Science Association's annual meeting in Atlanta, in 1999, as well as in a public lecture in honor of Martin Luther King Day at Kalamazoo College, subsequently broadcast on WMUK. Chapter 3 appeared in a very different form in *Prologue: The Journal of the National Archives and Records Administration*. A version of Chapter 4 was published in *The Historian*. A version of Chapter 12 also appeared in a volume on the 2000 elections edited by Steve Wayne and Clyde Wilcox.

Thanks to all the teachers who encouraged my love of politics, history, and writing: Mary Martin, John Harocopos, Anne Ledyard, Kathy Holcombe, Ann Eckbreth, Tom Schelstrate, John Smith, Sally Bassler, Ann Whitten, Stephen Graubard, and Ed Beiser.

Thanks of course to Ken and Jen, my brother and sister, who share my love of politics and have always been my toughest critics, much to my benefit, and to my parents, who have been there for me at every step of the road. As partisan Democrats, they may not be pleased by everything they read herein, but that's what happens when you raise a son to think for himself. They won't make that mistake again!

Washington, D.C., December 6, 2001

CONTENTS

★ ★ ★ ★ RUNNING ON RACE ★ ★ ★ ★

THE IMPORTANCE OF RACE
IN PRESIDENTIAL ELECTIONS

The problem of the Twentieth Century is the problem of the color line.

W. E. B. DU BOIS, 1903

At the opening of this century, W. E. B. Du Bois boldly predicted that the story of the next hundred years would be the problem of the color line, the tortured divide between black and white. For at least fifty years, Du Bois was wrong; politicians of both parties worked to keep race off the nation's agenda until 1948, and the issue would not dominate our politics until 1963–65. Yet the last decades of this century confirm Du Bois's prescience, for the upheavals and changes that have been wrought in the matter of race have been the dominant narrative of American history in this era. Beneath the surface of American politics, the pressure for change in America's racial caste system had been building and exploded in the tumult of the 1960s. Much of the battle over racial equality revolved around the presidency. Just as slavery and Reconstruction shaped sixty years of presidential politics and policies, so too with the admission of blacks into the sunlight of de jure equality.

Race and the array of issues surrounding it have been crucial to every presidential election since 1960. Every presidential candidate during this period has had to take positions on racial matters, and each campaign's strategic choices were influenced by the racial environment of the election year. Moreover, decisions about racial issues played a role in each party's nomination fights. Race affected the presidential contest in years when race was central to the nation's agenda and in years when race was submerged by a host of other issues. Race always mattered in presidential campaigns, whether the candidate was liberal or conservative, Democratic, Republican, or independent.

CONTINUITY AND CHANGE IN THE RACIAL POLITICS OF CAMPAIGNS, 1960–2000

At the midcentury, the politics of race underwent tremendous change. African Americans, who had tended to vote Republican out of loyalty to the party that brought Emancipation and the brief period of Reconstruction, had shifted to Roosevelt in 1936 in response to his economic populism. FDR maintained their loyalty in each of his subsequent elections, and blacks became a key part of the New Deal presidential coalition that dominated American politics from 1932 to 1968. However, the coalition was inherently unstable, because segregationist southern whites were an even larger component of the Democratic majority. FDR successfully kept race from emerging on the national scene during his presidency, but by 1960, the issue was becoming unavoidable. In 1956 blacks had voted Republican at a higher rate than at any point since 1932, because of Stevenson's studied vagueness on race and Eisenhower's halting moves toward racial equality. Thus, the black vote was up for grabs in 1960, as it has never been at any time since.

On the surface, there is a great deal of stasis to the racial politics that followed 1960. Blacks would vote Democratic by overwhelming margins, outpacing any other ethnic or occupational group in their loyalty to Democrats. Indeed, in most years blacks would vote Democratic at higher levels than all professed Democrats. At the same time, majorities or pluralities of whites voted Republican in ten of the eleven presidential elections from 1960 to 2000, turning Democratic only in the Johnson landslide of 1964. Also, the competitive policy positions of the two parties did not change during this period; in every election after 1960, the Republicans were more racially conservative.

Yet change was also vast and far-reaching. The most obvious and significant change during this period was the growth in black electoral power. In 1960, only a fraction of eligible blacks were registered in the

South, the region where the majority of African Americans lived. In the North, blacks voted in great numbers but frequently saw their political leadership co-opted by urban machines. The 1965 Voting Rights Act (VRA) succeeded, after much blood and struggle, at enfranchising blacks almost a century after the Fifteenth Amendment ostensibly gave them the right to vote. The majestic realization of this overdue promise signaled the end of the one-party white South, indirectly helped bring down the last urban machines, and forever altered the electoral land-scape. Blacks were no longer passive observers to the political process; they could be defeated, but they could not be easily ignored. The only comparable electoral shift in American history was the 1919 awarding of the franchise to women. However, the full enfranchisement of African Americans was more significant because blacks shared a common economic and ethnic history, a cohesive set of political goals, and a great tendency to cohere as a voting bloc, none of which character-ized women in the decades after they won the vote. Because of their unequal distribution around the nation, and their nearly monolithic voting in presidential elections, blacks elected every Democratic presi-dent since 1944 except Johnson, just as declines in their turnout helped defeat Hubert Humphrey and others. As important, the introduction of black suffrage radically altered white voting behavior in the South and in parts of the North. As black registration rose, so too did white registration. As blacks voted monolithically Democratic in response to Kennedy's and Johnson's civil rights moves, many whites eventually shifted their allegiance to the GOP in response. In many ways, the American political order is still shaking with the aftershocks of the 1965 electoral earthquake of black enfranchisement.

Racial issues also changed greatly from 1960 to 2000.* The racial debates of 1960 revolved around ending the most egregious examples

---

* One of those changes was the increasing ethnic diversity of the country, due to His-panic and Asian immigration. This book focuses on the black-white divide in pres-idential politics. From 1960 to 2000, this was the most enduring, and most influential, racial fault line in our political system. While the scope of this study is limited to a particular aspect of racial politics, the others are surely worthy of examination. Some of the implications of our increasing ethnic diversity will be raised in the conclusion.

of Jim Crow segregation in the American South. By 1964, the desegregation of all public accommodations was on the agenda, as well as the looming prospect of full voting rights. In 1968, the focus shifted to the North, as the ghettos burned amid advances in the legal and socioeconomic standing of African Americans. By 1972, no major political figure would endorse segregation, not even George Wallace, who had proclaimed in 1963, "Segregation today, segregation tomorrow, segregation forever!" Yet how to end segregation, as well as what to replace it with, bedeviled political elites, as candidate after candidate responded to the white backlash against busing. Indeed, busing was the pivot for the most radical change in the rhetoric of racial politics. Up until that point, racial liberals typically argued for color blindness, and racial conservatives pined for a government that at least tolerated traditionally color-conscious social structures. With busing and affirmative action, the terms of the debate upended to the point where racial conservatives hijacked the rhetoric of the slain Martin Luther King Jr., and advocated a society that judged individuals on their individual character, not the color of their skins. De jure equality was now the stated goal of racial conservatism. Racial progressives, on the other hand, argued for the benign use of race to eradicate remaining inequalities. In 1960, an all-black dormitory on a majority white campus was an obscene symbol of racial intolerance; nine years later, such a dorm was an emblem of racial progressivism. In 1964, the colorblind language of the Civil Rights Act (CRA) ignited the fervent opposition of millions of segregationists; in the 1990s, racial conservatives in a number of states worked to put that exact language into statute and state constitutions, fiercely opposed by modern racial liberals. Even while the partisan loyalties of blacks and whites did not change much during 1960–2000, racial issues were radically transformed.

As blacks gained voting strength, and the racial agenda shifted, political elites also adapted, sometimes with surprising speed. No one could look at the careers of Richard M. Nixon, Hubert H. Humphrey, and George C. Wallace, three inveterate presidential hopefuls of the 1960s and 1970s, without grasping how radically and rapidly the terms of the racial debate changed. Nixon, a member of the National Association for the Advancement of Colored People

(NAACP) and a leading Republican advocate of civil rights for much of the 1950s, would mastermind the creation of a Republican majority based in part on white backlash. Humphrey, the civil rights radical of 1948 who precipitated the walkout of the Dixiecrats with his fearless endorsement of civil rights in a fiery convention speech, would end his career three decades later wooing Wallace voters by opposing busing. Wallace, whose gubernatorial campaigns of 1962 and 1970 and presidential campaigns of 1964 and 1968 often trafficked in the most heinous racial caricatures, gradually rejected his racist past until he was reelected governor of Alabama with overwhelming black support.

Such evolutions should not astonish us. A political party can be defined as a group of political elites who share an ideological viewpoint or who share an interest in gaining power through electoral triumph. During a campaign, the second definition predominates. When parties compete for the highest office in the land, the first goal is victory. If political scientist David Mayhew is right that there are few selfless angels in Congress who put policy over reelection, there are perhaps even fewer on the presidential campaign trail. However, regardless of personal morality, a campaign strategist must take particular care when considering racial issues. Appealing to racial divisions in our society attracts more opprobrium than any other political tactic. "Playing the race card" is the strongest pejorative in modern political parlance, because of the sense that race should be viewed as a moral issue. That appeals to racial fears or tensions persist despite the prospect of harsh criticism illustrates the effectiveness of these tactics, as well as the enduring nature of America's racial divide.

In studying the effect of racial strategies on presidential campaigns, this book takes a firm position in an ongoing debate within electoral studies. Some have argued that because macroeconomic factors predict presidential election outcomes effectively up to a year before any ballots are cast, presidential campaigns cannot matter, or matter only at the margins. Presidential elections are in fact surprisingly obedient to economic trends, and the best-run campaign may be unable to dislodge an incumbent in boom times or stop a challenger when the economy is sickly. Similarly, war and national security issues may overwhelm campaign strategies, particularly those that focus on domestic issues. Yet there is persuasive evidence that campaigns matter and are worthy of study. For example, George Bush in 1988 did substantially better than economic models predicted, probably because of the cunning campaign his staff ran (or, alternatively, because of the ineptitude of the Dukakis campaign). That Bush's campaign featured a textbook example of a coded appeal to the politics of race (the Willie Horton ads and speeches) suggests that race may be a particularly potent campaign strategy, presenting perhaps the strongest case that campaigns matter. Many have argued that race was central to the collapse of the New Deal Democratic coalition, which dominated U.S. politics from 1936 to 1968. That coalition first crumbled at the presidential level; the presidential campaigns of this era both reflected and affected the gradual collapse of FDR's coalition of northern urban ethnics, unionists, African Americans, and southern whites. Voters are not simply utility maximizers who vote according to their pocketbooks, but vivid human beings who often respond to emotional appeals to group identity and threat. Perhaps no other issue shows the limitations of economic analyses of elections better than racial politics does.

This study begins in 1960, a year in which race was not prominent on the nation's agenda. Yet the 1960 race is far more typical of American elections since FDR than, for example, the 1964 contest. While race is always present, it is rare for civil rights and race to dominate the domestic agenda as they did in 1964, 1968, and 1972. The 1960 race is the crucible in which the pattern of modern racial politics was forged. It was the last year the Republicans attempted to equal the Democratic commitment to civil rights. It was the last time that a racial conservative could imagine that the national Democrats were more sympathetic to his views than the Republicans were. In the election of 1960, the racial tensions building within FDR's coalition were almost exposed; only the extraordinary skill of the Kennedy campaign kept them somewhat submerged. The 1960 race also is a crucial archetype for Democratic victory. Democrats won after 1960 only when they emulated Kennedy's calculated and symbolic outreach to racial conservatives. In the 1960 race, the end of the old electoral order as well as the birth of the new can be seen.

A TALE OF TWO STRADDLES

The Subterranean Racial Politics of 1960

There are moments when the politically expedient can be morally wise.

MARTIN LUTHER KING JR., 1960

A key to the new strategy of the Democratic party is the current behavior of a presidential hopeful, Sen. John Kennedy, Massachusetts. Kennedy has been assiduously wooing Southern votes by making speeches in Georgia and Arkansas. He recently delivered the commencement address at the University of Georgia. . . . Kennedy joined a runaway faction of self-styled liberals in voting against civil rights on two roll calls in the Senate. . . .

ETHEL PAYNE, BLACK COLUMNIST, JULY 25, 1957

When John Fitzgerald Kennedy defeated Richard Milhous Nixon by the narrowest margin in the postwar era to become the thirty-fifth president, many attributed Kennedy's success to his decision to telephone the wife of imprisoned civil rights leader Martin Luther King Jr. However, racial politics were crucial to the 1960 contest long before the state of Georgia sentenced the Reverend King to hard labor for a traffic violation. Moreover, the 1960 election revealed in embryo the racial politics that would shape presidential elections for the rest of the century. Although most analysts point to 1964 as the watershed election for black-white politics, the 1960 campaigns were crucial in establishing the patterns of racial strategizing that have characterized the next ten presidential elections. The story of Kennedy's successful navigation of the tricky straits of racial animus and Nixon's maladroit fumbling of the same served as a cautionary tale for all future candidates.

1960: THE PRECAMPAIGN SETTING

What is perhaps most surprising about the political landscape of the nation in January of 1960 is how low civil rights was on the agenda. Six years after *Brown* v. *Board,* the vast majority of southern states still maintained Jim Crow segregation. De facto segregation and rampant discrimination characterized much of the urban North. Yet these injustices only intermittently pricked the conscience of the nation. But if civil rights did not occupy the top position on the domestic agenda, the importance of the black vote was certainly apparent to political insiders. The stakes were quite high: a candidate who moved too far toward integration would lose the white South, while too much appeasement of Jim Crow would lose the northern black vote. This was the Gordian knot that racial politics presented to both parties in January of 1960. The black vote was of particular interest because the election in the North might be quite close. Three years before the contest, Martin Luther King Jr. argued in a letter to Nixon that "[t]he Negro vote is the balance of power in so many important big states that one almost has to have the Negro vote to win a presidential election."

Going into the 1960 election season, neither party had a lock on the black vote. In 1956, Eisenhower had done better among blacks than any Republican since 1932, receiving at least 40 percent of their votes, with estimates ranging much higher. A majority of black newspapers had endorsed Eisenhower, with only 15 percent endorsing Stevenson. The leading black politician, Congressman Adam Clayton Powell, abandoned his own party's nominee to endorse Eisenhower. Given this recent history, the Negro vote was apparently up for grabs in 1960. But as one black voter put it: "What have the two parties really done on civil rights for the Negro? They seem more interested in grabbing off the Southern white vote."

The anonymous respondent identified the dilemma; at the same moment that blacks were contemplating moving out of the New Deal coalition and back to the party of Lincoln, southern whites were similarly questioning their firm Democratic roots. Since the 1948 Dixiecrat challenge of Strom Thurmond, the myth of the solid Democratic South had been exposed. Just as blacks wondered which party would work for their agenda, southern whites had a similar problem in regard to race. Was the Republican Party to "blame" for the insertion of federal troops into Little Rock in 1957? Was it significant that Earl Warren, author of the *Brown* v. *Board* decision, was a moderate Republican? Or should southern whites rather fear the national Democrats, who included in their ranks such strident advocates of desegregation as Hubert Humphrey and Eleanor Roosevelt? The choice between the two national parties offered as little clarity to southern whites as it did to blacks nationally. Southerners also knew that they would have a third option, as Senator Harry Byrd of Virginia planned a quiet third-party campaign. Both parties had to worry about Byrd's potential to steal much of the region, as Thurmond had in 1948.

The civil rights movement, which had largely been born in its modern form in Montgomery in 1955, had entered a relatively quiescent period on the eve of the 1960 presidential election. King and other leaders wondered whether demonstrations during the 1960 election campaign would be counterproductive. The dissension and confusion within the movement contributed to the insignificant position civil rights occupied on the nation's agenda.

THE CANDIDATES

John F. Kennedy

Compared to other leading Democratic candidates, John Fitzgerald Kennedy did not have a strong civil rights record. Indeed, one reporter observed that "as Kennedy entered the Democratic Convention in Los Angeles, he was the least popular among Negroes of all Democratic candidates; many Northern Negro politicians preferred even Lyndon Johnson to Kennedy." Adam Clayton Powell, prior to the convention, pointed out that Kennedy did not have a good record on civil rights "for a man from Massachusetts." Why was a northern Democrat the least favored option among black leaders?

Kennedy was mistrusted by blacks for the same reason he was not the candidate of labor or of liberals generally. He had begun his congressional career without a clear ideological label and on some issues, such as anticommunism, had been quite conservative. He was one of only two Democratic senators not to vote for the censuring of Joe McCarthy, a lapse that many liberals swore they could neither forgive nor forget. As a legislator, Kennedy was hardly a leader on liberal issues. Johnson observed privately that Kennedy "never said a word of importance in the Senate and never did a thing." This was a view shared by many on the Left, particularly when comparing Kennedy to liberal luminaries like Hubert Humphrey, or even moderates like Johnson. In the opinion of one Senate colleague, the career of John Kennedy in the Senate showed too much profile and not enough courage. Also, although Massachusetts was a liberal state, and comparatively supportive of civil rights, it did not have the large urban black population of such northeastern states as New York, Pennsylvania, or even Connecticut. According to a key black adviser, "Kennedy had no real Negro leadership in Boston."

The coolness and antipathy that blacks expressed toward Kennedy prior to his nomination had deeper roots than Kennedy's lack of activism on civil rights. Kennedy was a natural target of suspicion because in 1956 he had been the favorite vice presidential candidate of the segregationist South. Many questioned why a young, relatively unknown Yankee senator had received such extraordinary support from the Jim Crow South. The South was so important to Kennedy's ultimately unsuccessful nomination fight that at one point he turned to an aide and said with a smile, "I'm going to sing 'Dixie' for the rest of my life."

Although Kennedy immediately swung to the left on many issues after his loss in 1956, convinced that his party would nominate only a liberal in 1960, his record on civil rights remained mixed. The best example was Kennedy's vote on the 1957 Civil Rights Act, the first civil rights law since Reconstruction. At the height of the debate, a proposal emerged from the southern Democrats that local officials charged with impeding the right to vote be guaranteed a trial before a local jury. Kennedy was one of a handful of northeastern Democrats who joined with segregationist Democrats and conservative Republicans to narrowly pass this amendment, which eviscerated the bill's enforcement provision.

The vote did not go unnoticed by blacks. The NAACP rebuked Kennedy for his vote against a key element of the civil rights act and did so while praising Nixon. Two years later, Jackie Robinson, retired baseball star turned columnist and civil rights activist, attacked Kennedy's vote on the jury trial amendment, as well as the support he was receiving from southern governors. In 1959–60, Kennedy's major black adviser prior to his general election campaign, lawyer Marjorie Lawson, was still dealing with the aftermath of the vote in her efforts to promote Kennedy. Even two years later, the effects of Kennedy's anti–civil rights vote lingered.

Yet Kennedy's 1957 vote was strategically brilliant, if the goal was to win the Democratic nomination in 1960. After pleasing his southern supporters, Kennedy in the end voted for the entire bill, unlike most southern Democrats. Thus he could claim to be a strong supporter of civil rights, and only the more attentive portions of the black public would be aware of his earlier vote against their interests. Simultaneously, by removing a key element in the bill, he kept his political viability as a northerner who understood the South. There was even talk in 1957 of pairing JFK with a southerner as part of a Dixiecrat ticket in 1960. Kennedy was personally aware of the tactical effectiveness of his stance. When his brother Robert was heading to the South in 1959 to talk up his brother's chances, Kennedy encouraged him to remind white southerners that on the 1957 roll call votes, "the friends and the foes of the South split." Humphrey had voted for the North, while JFK had voted with Lyndon Johnson and the South.

Kennedy's talent for striking the right balance between segregationists and integrationists was also tested by the 1957 school desegregation crisis in Little Rock. As troops were sent in, emotions ran high in both North and South. Kennedy had long been scheduled to give a speech in Arkansas. Rather than cancel his talk, Kennedy went ahead and spoke. Contemporary press coverage and his own text reveals that his focus was entirely on labor issues. In letters that Kennedy received over the next three years, several supporters mention how much meeting Kennedy and talking to him after his speech convinced them that he understood the South's problems. Theodore Sorensen,

Kennedy's only companion on many of these journeys, emphatically denies that Kennedy watered down his opposition to segregation at such events. Yet the message that Kennedy was unusually friendly to the South clearly got through to many southerners. The comments of Osceola judge A. F. Barham in a letter to Kennedy, are typical: "I have met you . . . and my impression is that the Lord has already given you the capacity to understand us [white southerners]."

In a Mississippi speech in October of 1957, Kennedy did boldly state his views on civil rights. But he immediately followed his brief remarks on civil rights by saying, "I am not in Jackson to argue these questions, to attempt to persuade others of my views, or to be persuaded of theirs." Kennedy called for unity and attacked northern Democrats who sought to exclude southerners from the party. He stressed the need for "responsible, thoughtful leadership in the White House in 1960" and criticized Eisenhower's handling of the Little Rock crisis. Kennedy left it to his listeners to imagine exactly what a more responsible president would have done. Kennedy also won southern supporters on the basis of his willingness to speak to segregated audiences, which a number of his rivals, notably Missouri Senator Stuart Symington, refused to do. Kennedy's skill at symbolic politics carried over into nonpolitical settings. In his commencement address at the University of South Carolina in 1957, Kennedy went out of his way to praise perhaps the most famous defender of slavery in American history, John C. Calhoun. To many, this would appear to be little more than polite reverence for a local political hero and an unquestioned giant in American history. However, Calhoun's name was on the tongue of so many segregationists in this post-*Brown* moment that the reference could not help but aid Kennedy in his quest to seem palatable to white southerners.

While Kennedy was honing his image in the South, he still had problems with the black leadership of America. Most contemporary accounts of Kennedy's attitude toward civil rights in the 1950s highlight how little thought he gave to the issue. Kennedy was such a moderate on racial matters that the sacrificial lamb Republicans nominated to run against him in 1958 attacked Kennedy's alliance with the South on civil rights. Jackie Robinson noted with dismay how ignorant JFK appeared to be on civil rights and how uncomfortable he was with the subject when it came up during a meeting. In addition to what Robinson calls a "very bleak record on civil rights," Kennedy simply did not know the central concerns of the black community. Martin Luther King's assessment of Kennedy at the time was that he "was so concerned about being President of the United States that he would compromise basic principles to become President."

In 1959, Marjorie Lawson set about the difficult task of rallying black support for JFK, traveling to conventions of black professional groups across the country. Lawson tracked how prominent blacks in various locales viewed other likely Democratic contenders and warned that Kennedy's willingness to speak to segregated southern audiences was losing him support in the black community, particularly when compared to Symington's refusal to do so. Through Lawson, Kennedy became sensitized to how symbolic politics worked in the black community, but Kennedy still had no deep following among blacks, nor did he have a clear moral grasp of civil rights. As Lawson observed, "He thought of [civil rights] as something that had to be manipulated." Kennedy's adroit manipulation of racial symbols and issues helps explain how he became the Democratic nominee and contributed greatly to his eventual victory over Richard Nixon, a man who had been thinking about civil rights for much longer.

Richard Nixon

Nixon began 1960 with at least as strong a civil rights record as Kennedy and a much higher profile on the liberal side of the issue. Historian Stephen Ambrose claims that Nixon was "consistent in his denunciation of Jim Crow, as much so as any of his rivals for national leadership and much more so than most." Nixon, a Quaker from California, ended up as a liberal Republican on civil rights for reasons of personal history and regional background. In law school and college, he had been an opponent of segregation. However, Nixon's exposure to the politics of race began largely with his arrival on the national scene as Eisenhower's vice president.

Perhaps no comparison better brings out the difference between Nixon and Kennedy on race than how the South responded to their campaigns for the vice presidential nomination in 1956. Nixon, already serving as Eisenhower's vice president, had to launch a bizarre, nationwide campaign to maintain his spot on the ticket. Among the many reasons for dumping Nixon was the antipathy he stirred in the white South. An aide returning from a tour of the South reported to Eisenhower in early 1956 that "not one person was for Nixon" and that "Nixon is in some way connected in Southerners' minds with the Negro difficulty." What had Nixon done to antagonize the South? He had served Eisenhower by leading the Government Contracts Committee, which, while criticized by civil rights leaders as ineffective, had nonetheless given him a reputation as an integrationist.* Moreover, Nixon was a member of the NAACP, which was viewed by most southern whites as tantamount to treason against their way of life. Kennedy, by contrast, in the late 1950s made a financial donation to the NAACP but on the cagey advice of Marjorie Lawson did not join the organization. The contrast is stark; Kennedy, in his strong push for the vice presidency in 1956, benefited enormously from the support of rabid segregationists like Orval Faubus. Nixon, in the same year, was weakened by his connection with the civil rights movement.

The same pattern emerged in 1957, in the passage of the Civil Rights Act. Kennedy, as we have seen, straddled the fence on the most important civil rights legislation since Reconstruction. Nixon was the leading Republican proponent of the legislation and shepherded the bill to passage. At a crucial point in the debate, King wrote to Nixon to give him ammunition for the struggle against Jim Crow election laws. King promised that there would be two million new black voters on the southern rolls if the bill passed and that blacks would vote Republican if Republicans continued to support civil rights. Nixon immediately put King's information to good use.

---

* Even if the commission was just a PR move, as many liberals alleged, it did lead to headlines throughout the 1950s that emphasized Nixon's commitment to ending discrimination.

In a meeting with Republicans in Congress who were highly skeptical of the political wisdom of voting for a civil rights bill, given that most blacks voted Democratic, Nixon used King's name and his logic to sway them. He further told them that both King and his top aide had voted Republican in 1956. Nixon fought the jury trial amendment that Kennedy had supported and characterized it accurately as "a vote against the right to vote." In a letter in which King thanked Nixon for his "dauntless courage" in the Civil Rights Act battle, King again raised the issue of the growing black vote. These words seemed to have an influence on Nixon, and he became, according to political columnist Rowland Evans, "the spearhead of Republican efforts to capture a larger share of the Negro vote in 1958 and 1960." So prominent was Nixon on civil rights that when the black leadership needed to talk to a Republican about Little Rock, they turned to Nixon.

Nixon's civil rights advantage over Kennedy also had a personal component. Nixon, unlike Kennedy, had known Martin Luther King Jr. for several years by the time the 1960 election year began. King shocked many of his associates by privately endorsing Nixon in very strong language, saying he was the only presidential contender who really cared about civil rights, mentioning his "absolute sincerity"* on the question.

Nixon's record on civil rights as the 1960 race began was publicly very strong and, indeed, nationally progressive. While not without his blemishes early in his Senate career, Nixon was unquestionably a leading advocate of racial equality. During the general election of 1956, Nixon requested more material on civil rights from his speechwriter and was perhaps the only prominent national politician talking about close personal friends who were black. Nixon's appearances in the South also contrast sharply with Kennedy's at the same time period. During the 1956 campaign, Nixon was attacked by local Democrats for his membership in the NAACP. In the same year, Nixon spoke in Nashville on the topic of integration. Endorsing integration

---

* King did caution that if Nixon were not sincere, he was the most dangerous man in America.

as "morally right," he also offered his audience the sop that progress "would have to be slow" because of the complex nature of the problem. While Kennedy also endorsed civil rights in the South during this period, Nixon was in the South for the specific purpose of talking about integration. There is no record of Kennedy giving such a speech prior to the closing days of the 1960 campaign, and certainly not in the South. Nixon seemed to search out opportunities to be in the forefront on civil rights. In 1958, Nixon wrote a very sympathetic letter to a defeated Democratic congressman, Brooks Hays of Arkansas, a moderate on segregation who was defeated because of Little Rock. In his letter to Hays, Nixon praised his "statesmanship" and attacked the "demagoguery and prejudice" of his opponents. The letter, which received national coverage, conveyed to the white South that for Nixon, civil rights overrode partisanship.

On paper, the differences between Nixon and Kennedy on civil rights were far more symbolic than substantive. A single high-profile Senate vote on jury trials. A membership in the NAACP. A personal relationship with King. Outreach to a victim of prejudice. On the core issues of the day, such as integration of the schools, there was very little daylight between these two men. Both of them were, broadly speaking, in favor of racial equality, and both saw discrimination as a public relations problem for the United States in the ongoing cold war that they stridently supported. Yet politics, particularly racial politics, is often about symbols and context. Kennedy's vote on jury trials and his decision to speak to segregated audiences signaled to certain southerners that he was at least a racial moderate. Nixon's talk on integration as an issue in the South, his mention of personal friendships with Negroes, and his position within the White House as the strongest supporter of sending troops to Little Rock all sent the opposite signals to white southerners—here was a man committed to integration, perhaps soon. Nixon was even known to discuss how well integrated schooling was working for his two daughters; nothing short of intermarriage could have been more offensive to the white South.

Richard Nixon was, for most of the 1950s, the most prominent racial progressive in his party. The same could not even begin to be said of John Kennedy. Indeed, the most compelling evidence for Kennedy's weakness on civil rights is the glaring lacuna in Arthur Schlesinger's campaign broadside from the general election: *Kennedy or Nixon: Does It Make Any Difference?* In a book designed to harshly distinguish the two candidates for a highbrow, liberal audience, Schlesinger raised civil rights only faintly and toward the end. Even so partisan a defender of Kennedy as Schlesinger could not credibly argue his civil rights record was superior to Nixon's. Indeed, quite the opposite. In the spring of 1960, a quote was attributed to Schlesinger in which he correctly labeled Kennedy "slightly soft" on civil rights. That slight softness on black equality was an important asset to Kennedy in his fight to win the Democratic nomination for president.

ROWING WITH MUFFLED OARS: KENNEDY'S CIVIL RIGHTS STANCE AMONG DEMOCRATS

Long before the first primary ballot was cast, Kennedy's openness to the South was seen as quite influential on the strategic aspects of the Democratic nomination fight. Prominent columnist Carroll Kilpatrick argued that the conflagration in Little Rock, combined with the Republican nomination of Richard Nixon, a Republican with a strong civil rights record, would prevent the Democrats from running a moderate on race like Kennedy. Kennedy's outreach to the South, so carefully constructed since 1956, was seen as a potential barrier to his acceptance by the liberal wing of the Democratic Party. Kennedy's record on civil rights was so unacceptable to members of the party's liberal wing that their statements were later used by Republicans in the general election. One Republican pamphlet, entitled "Here's What They Say About Kennedy," quoted Eleanor Roosevelt saying Kennedy "has antagonized the mass of Negroes, and they will not vote for him at the head of the ticket."

The most serious challenge to Kennedy in the primaries came from Humphrey, an unapologetic proponent of civil rights. Humphrey had the strongest record on black issues of any national Democrat. His 1948 speech to the Democratic convention electrified northerners and led to the adoption of a civil rights plank so liberal that the Dixie-crats bolted the party. In the Senate, Humphrey had been the voice for progressive racial legislation. Humphrey remarked that he would "rather be right morally than achieve the presidency." Kennedy, by contrast, had a political style that avoided controversy, and he was portrayed often as a "high-minded moderate," a stance with particular appeal in the South.

The two primary states in which Humphrey would challenge Kennedy were Wisconsin and West Virginia, and racial politics played a role in both contests. In Wisconsin, Humphrey brought in Jackie Robinson to campaign with him in black areas. Kennedy made almost no effort to stir up support in the black community, perhaps assuming that it would go to Humphrey in any case. No leading figure in the black community came out to support Kennedy, nor could Marjorie Lawson get Kennedy to attend a single black event during the entire primary. While Humphrey was stumping through black neighborhoods and churches, Kennedy scheduled only one such black event, at a Jewish community center. At the last moment, Kennedy was unable to attend. As a substitute, he addressed the gathering over an amplified phone. Lawson found that Kennedy's staff in Wisconsin gave her almost no assistance or support in planning events, because "they really were interested in muffling the issue of race relations in Wisconsin" out of deference to white opinion and because blacks were supporting Humphrey. So unhappy was Lawson with this shabby treatment of her community that she initially refused to travel to West Virginia for the next primary. Humphrey also believed that a more sinister type of racial politics was practiced in the Wisconsin primary. "A last minute telephone drive passed the word to the Polish households of south Milwaukee that public housing—a code word for blacks—might spread from the north to the south if they failed to turn out for Kennedy."

During the West Virginia primary election, Kennedy did make time for black supporters. Lawson scheduled a talk at Bluefield State College, and her candidate demonstrated an ability to reach out to African Americans and connect with their concerns. Meanwhile, Humphrey, the candidate with the stronger record on civil rights, passion for the topic, and solid black support, made the mistake of staying at a segregated hotel. Picketers from the Congress of Racial Equality bedeviled Humphrey, who blamed the error on inadequate staff work. Humphrey was also hurt among the few blacks in West Virginia by the endorsement he received from former Ku Klux Klansman Senator Robert Byrd. Despite the support of most black leaders, Humphrey was defeated in both states and withdrew from the race.

After vanquishing Humphrey, Kennedy became the overwhelming favorite to take the nomination, and once again, the question of Kennedy's popularity in the South emerged. Kennedy had breakfast in his home with one of the leading segregationists in the country, Alabama governor John Patterson, as well as Sam Englehardt, head of the Alabama White Citizens Council, the genteel counterpart of the Klan. As Jackie Robinson opined in a widely read column, "Senator Kennedy . . . cannot expect any self-respecting Negro to support him with the image of Patterson, Englehardt and their ilk sitting across his breakfast table." Lawson was out on the West Coast, traveling on behalf of Kennedy, when word reached her of the Patterson breakfast. "I packed up and came home. The reaction was that violent." Governor G. Mennen Williams of Michigan, a leading advocate of civil rights, wrote to Kennedy warning him that such acts might give the black vote to Nixon.

At a reconciliation lunch with black leaders, Kennedy was asked if Patterson's breakfast represented some kind of secret deal on civil rights or segregation. Kennedy minimized the breakfast, denied any deal, and pointed out to the delegation that "some people will wonder what kind of deal I've made with you because we've had lunch." Kennedy's comment indicates an instinctive understanding of the racial tightrope he was walking, balancing breakfast with vociferous racists against lunch with a black delegation.

Despite such efforts at balancing, Kennedy still had more problems among blacks than among white southerners. Adam Clayton Powell made it clear that he found Humphrey, Symington, and Johnson acceptable, but he was uneasy with Kennedy because of his association with segregationists and the 1957 vote. As the Democratic convention opened in Los Angeles, Kennedy was still the least popular of all the major candidates among blacks. In a speech to the NAACP on the eve of the convention, Kennedy promised boldness on civil rights, as opposed to those who would "row to our object with muffled oars." Compared to Humphrey or many other liberals in his own party, Kennedy's oars on civil rights had been nearly silent, even when his voting wasn't weak.

Yet there was very little muffled about the platform that Democrats wrote for Kennedy days later; it was much stronger than the rhetoric Kennedy had been using on the campaign trail. Members of Kennedy's staff swore that the severity of the plank was accidental; they had intended to use it as a bargaining chip, but Kennedy's effective convention machine had rammed the proposed planks through untouched. It was the strongest platform on racial progress that any party had ever adopted and likely to cause trouble in the South. At least as important as the platform to the racial politics of 1960 was another convention decision made in Los Angeles: the choice of Kennedy's running mate.

The hectic and chaotic process by which Lyndon Baines Johnson ended up as the vice presidential nominee belies any grand plan, racial or otherwise. The record of that night at the convention is hopelessly confused, and the only clear fact that emerges is that the decision-making process was neither orderly nor calculated. Yet the inclusion of Johnson as a contender was always explicitly about returning the once solid South to the Democratic fold. Given the dualism of racial politics, his selection, therefore, predictably produced an outcry from black leaders, who felt that this was a "sellout" of their faction. This reaction was by no means universal; in fact, Johnson enjoyed surprisingly strong support from Congressman Powell, among others. Johnson was also a signal to white southerners. The selection of Johnson dovetailed nicely with a strong Democratic platform on civil rights. The South was given a familiar face and accent to go along with a northerner with a reputation for moderation; blacks were given a progressive platform and a northerner atop the ticket. With this mix of messages and messengers, the Democrats prepared to do battle with Richard Nixon and his as-yet-unnamed running mate.

RUNNING ON ROCKY'S PLATFORM: THE REPUBLICAN CONVENTION OF 1960

Richard Nixon would not face the type of brutal primary struggle that John F. Kennedy did. Although other Republicans probed for signs of weakness in Nixon's support, the nomination was his to lose, unless Eisenhower had more directly displayed the doubts that he harbored about his vice president. The racial politics on the Republican side would revolve around not the nominee but the platform.

Prior to the convention, Nixon and his staff realized that the only challenger likely to emerge was Nelson Rockefeller, the multimillionaire who had just entered politics by winning an upset victory for governor of New York in 1958, a bad year for Republicans nationally. Only Rockefeller had the money, public profile, and confidence to take on Nixon, who appeared to have the party machinery sewed up. Rockefeller had a progressive, but brief, record on civil rights. Generally speaking, Rockefeller was somewhat to the right of Nixon internationally and to the left domestically. Yet it was a sign of the deep and abiding distrust of southern whites for Richard Nixon that many southerners still preferred Rockefeller. Despite his weakness in the South, Nixon had the nomination in hand quite early; Rockefeller, realizing that he could not win, withdrew from contention. Once the threat from Rockefeller was dispatched, the only other possible candidate was Barry Goldwater, who had become an icon for the Republican Right. Goldwater championed the South's point of view on states' rights and argued that the federal government could not intervene in race relations. While Goldwater rose in the esteem of certain branches of the party because of his stance against civil rights, Nixon's record on race "doomed him with the right." Still, Goldwater and Rockefeller together helped Nixon appear to be a moderate, as indeed he was on most issues of concern to Republicans.

Nixon, as we have seen, had a strong record on civil rights. Still, the Republican machinery, guided by Nixon, forged a platform that was quite moderate on civil rights, particularly compared to the Democratic one. For example, it did not declare support for black sit-in demonstrations in the South, nor did it promise federal intervention to ensure employment equality, as the Democrats had in Los Angeles. The intent was clear: If the Republicans were only slightly to the right of the Democrats, they could stake a claim to many southern white votes. The platform written by the committee in Chicago was exactly tailored to this thinking. While it did pay lip service to civil rights, it was far more moderate and vague than the Democrats' civil rights plank.

Into the carefully scripted platform deliberations of the Republican Party, however, strode Rockefeller. Rockefeller threatened a floor fight over national security and domestic policy unless his demands were met. Nixon, worried that a contumacious debate over specific planks would damage his candidacy, met secretly with Rockefeller and hammered out a compromise. Among the planks that Nixon agreed to was a revised, and much stronger, civil rights section. The deputy attorney general, Lawrence Walsh, wrote the new plank, took the draft to Chicago, and showed it to several black leaders who had come to Chicago to urge the Republicans to match the Democratic platform on civil rights. They were impressed with the new language, which equaled the Democrats' in most respects. Now Nixon had to sell the compromise to the platform committee meeting in Chicago and to the convention at large.

The response among many delegates to Rockefeller's intervention was extremely negative. Barry Goldwater, leader of the Republican Right, went so far as to label it "the Munich of the Republican Party." Nixon's staff had a very tough task convincing the more conservative platform committee to go along with the compromise. Amid all the give-and-take on various issues, Nixon chose to fight most strenuously for the civil rights compromise plank. In the end, Nixon was able to preserve almost every substantive aspect of the plank; indeed, in some ways, it became even more aggressive. One journalist felt that the platform put Nixon firmly in favor of "sweeping antisegregation laws and decisions." Following the election, Goldwater blamed Nixon's loss upon the insertion of the radical pro–civil rights language and argued that the retention of the moderate plank would have guaranteed a Nixon win.

Nixon now had to confront the question that had caused such an uproar at the Democratic convention: the selection of a vice presidential nominee. According to Nixon's account, he narrowed it down to two choices, Thruston Morton of Kentucky and Henry Cabot Lodge of Massachusetts. Nixon argued in his retrospective on the 1960 campaign that he chose Lodge because he would help in the East, where Nixon needed help, whereas Morton was strong in the Midwest, where Nixon was already dominant. Nixon neglected to mention that choosing a border-state southerner like Morton would have greatly aided his southern campaign, in stark contrast with Lodge.

The southern delegates showed their mounting displeasure in subtle ways, as when delegates from Louisiana cast ten protest votes for Barry Goldwater. Yet the die for the election had seemingly been cast; Nixon would campaign for the presidency on a pro–civil rights platform that was the equal of the platform passed by the Democrats in Los Angeles. As segregationist Alabama governor John Patterson noted, the South could not see much, if any, difference between the two platforms on the issue of greatest concern to the region. Nixon would run with Lodge, a man with a strongly pro–civil rights stance bereft of regional connections with the South. Although both parties were talking tough on civil rights in their platforms, one ticket was led by a Californian, who had recently and repeatedly led a campaign against the South's most treasured defense against desegregation, the Senate filibuster, in the name of civil rights, and who had fought against the South on the 1957 Civil Rights Act. The other ticket was led by an easterner, who had cast a rare high-profile vote for the South during that same civil rights battle. Kennedy was near the middle of his party on this issue, while Nixon was one of the leading fighters for civil rights in his party. The contrast at the bottom half of the ticket was even sharper. Johnson, even though he had moderated his stance on civil rights and worked strenuously with Nixon and others to produce the 1957 CRA, was nevertheless perceived as a longtime segregationist politician. Johnson's presence on the ticket sent a message to the South that was clearly heard. Segregationist governors and senators across the South all knew and respected Johnson. More often than not, he had voted with them on civil rights, although increasingly less so as time went by. In a public letter to Johnson, distributed widely later in the campaign, Senator Richard Russell noted how Johnson had come to the South's aid whenever "extreme legislation" threatened it. No southerner could credibly make a similar claim about Henry Cabot Lodge or Richard Nixon.

KENNEDY IN THE GENERAL ELECTION: THE VIRTUE OF INSINCERITY

As the Republican convention came to a close, the first tactical confrontation between the campaigns came in Washington. Johnson had decided to embarrass the Republicans by scheduling a legislative session following the Republican convention, in which Republicans would be forced to vote against popular bills on housing and education. Yet one of the great legislative leaders of this century, Minority Leader Everett Dirksen of Illinois, thought he could turn the Democratic ploy against Kennedy and Johnson. The wily Republican simply wrote up as a bill the exact language of the Democratic civil rights platform and dared the Democratic majority to vote it into law. The Democrats now faced a dilemma. If Kennedy and Johnson voted for the civil rights bill, the South would be lost. Most major segregationists had not yet formally endorsed Kennedy-Johnson and could easily go with Harry Byrd, if not Nixon. On the other hand, voting no would risk losing support among blacks and raise questions about Kennedy's own sincerity on civil rights. How could the two Democratic nominees vote against their own platform, passed by such a wide margin only a few weeks before in Chicago?

Apparently, they could vote against their own platform with brazen ease, although the *New York Post* contended that "clearly, the Democratic masterminds had decided they could not risk the conflict with the South that even a modest fulfillment of their platform pledges would entail." The paper warned Kennedy that "the price of Southern comfort may prove to be prohibitive," because it showed Kennedy's cynicism on race. Kennedy tried to argue that the incident was merely "Republican political trickery" designed to block Democratic legislation on education and housing, which were, "in a real sense, civil rights bills." However, to the extent that this legislative shadowboxing attracted much attention, it redounded to Kennedy's benefit among southern whites. Both parties had adopted strong civil rights platforms, but Kennedy and Johnson were now on record voting against theirs, suggesting to southerners that a Kennedy victory would not mean tough new legislation on civil rights. Ironically, in attempting to expose the cynicism of the Democratic Party, Dirksen had merely given the white South evidence that it could trust Kennedy and Johnson on civil rights, no matter what their platform said. For the typical white southerner, cynicism on civil rights was preferable to sincerity, if sincerity meant federal intervention in their segregated way of life.

On the campaign trail, Kennedy's references to civil rights in his stump speeches were fairly consistent, vague, and brief. He frequently accused the Republicans of deception, in sending liberals like Hugh Scott of Pennsylvania to speak in the North on civil rights while sending Barry Goldwater south to talk of states' rights. Yet there is no doubt that Kennedy practiced the same tactics, albeit with a great deal more subtlety. His speeches in Michigan, Pennsylvania, and New York would feature his brief rhetoric on civil rights, but many speeches in the South did not mention it. In northern speeches in October, Kennedy attacked Eisenhower's foreign policy, in part for having only twenty-six blacks among over six thousand Foreign Service officers, even though African nations made up almost a quarter of the United Nations. One day later, in Miami, Kennedy made the same charges against Eisenhower, omitting only the reference to the number of blacks in the State Department.

The clearest example of the Kennedy campaign's political cunning on race is contained in the attack sourcebook for the campaign. Divided into subheadings, it contains Nixon quotes to use against the Republican and scripted responses to frequent attacks on Kennedy. To the charge that Kennedy is not strong enough on civil rights, the platform passed in Los Angeles is used as a defense. It also uses quotes from segregationists against Kennedy as proof of his fealty to the cause. Yet in the same book, under the heading "South," Nixon is attacked for being too pro–civil rights. His membership in the NAACP is used against him, as is a quote from David Susskind's TV program of May 1960, in which Nixon comes across as extremely sympathetic to civil rights and blacks in general. Nixon is further attacked for having had dinner with the president of Howard University. The attack book also includes the fact that Nixon frequently entertained African dignitaries in his Senate office. The nonpartisan Fair Campaign Practices Committee found that "some bigoted Democrats . . . peddled, never officially, but rather widely in white communities where the tactic would clearly pay off, a flier displaying three photographs of Nixon in various poses of affection and affinity with Negroes. Some were Americans in business suits and some Africans in tribal regalia. The caption presented the devastating fact: Nixon had been a member of, and a contributor to, the NAACP for ten years." The same attack book advocated a campaign to paint Nixon in the North as a bigot, which surrogates proceeded to do with aplomb.

Even when Kennedy spoke directly about civil rights in the South, it is important to note the emphasis that he placed on the executive branch. His most fervent endorsement of equality in the South came in a speech in South Carolina. Opening with an attack on Nixon's two-faced approach to civil rights, Kennedy is vague and easily misinterpreted in his own views:

> I think it is clear—that if we are to have progress in this area, and we must have progress to be true to our ideals and responsibilities, then presidential leadership is necessary so that every American can enjoy his full constitutional rights.

Importantly, Kennedy emphasized that his civil rights efforts (labeled "constitutional rights")* would focus on the executive branch. Throughout the campaign, Kennedy almost never endorsed new legislation to attack discrimination, arguing that the president could through moral and responsible leadership make the necessary changes.

---

* The phrase "constitutional rights" was itself a sop to white southern sensitivities, since it depended on one's view of the Constitution. Goldwater also advocated "constitutional rights."

By ironic chance, or by skillful scheduling, Kennedy's next major speech on civil rights was two days later in New York City. Earlier in the campaign, several aides, in particular Harris Wofford, had convinced Kennedy to endorse a "National Conference on Constitutional Rights and American Freedom." This brought together many of the leading figures in civil rights, including some Republicans. After attacking Nixon for giving one speech in the South and another in the North, Kennedy proceeded to demonstrate his mastery of the tactic. In one of his strongest statements on civil rights during the entire campaign, Kennedy mentioned legislative as well as executive action and made his famous pledge to eliminate discrimination in public housing with a stroke of the presidential pen. He also proposed ending discrimination in government contracts, protecting black voters, and desegregating schools, topics that were almost never on his tongue in other campaign speeches, certainly not in the South. Faced with an audience that included such major liberal figures as Hubert Humphrey and Eleanor Roosevelt, he changed his rhetoric. Yet even here, there was more talk than action; Kennedy called for a long series of conferences on civil rights after the election, while making no specific commitments to enact legislation.

Kennedy's personal involvement in the careful balancing his campaign practiced on race is incontrovertible. Kennedy was very concerned about the release of the final report of the constitutional rights conference. Wofford paraphrases Kennedy as saying: "I want to ask you now as a friend, honestly, do I need to release it now in order to win the election and get more black votes even at the price of some white votes? Do I need to do it or do you mainly want me to do it because it'll be a statement? Could I wait until the election is decided?" When Wofford conceded that the document could wait until after the election, and would have little effect on the black vote, Kennedy decided not to sign. Kennedy also canceled a meeting with King in Miami because he worried about white reaction. Kennedy's personal involvement came out as clearly when he made his speech in Harlem, on the same day as his constitutional rights conference. Kennedy's prepared text included such quotable phrases as calling the Democratic platform "the strongest civil rights platform in the history of American politics" and another criticizing Eisenhower for not appointing any blacks to the judiciary. Those sections were crossed out on Kennedy's copy and were not delivered. While we cannot be certain that it was Kennedy who struck out these potentially dangerous phrases, we do know that he had a penchant for such last-minute editing. The removal of those passages showed an adroit sense of the minefields in racial politics that existed in 1960, a sense that was entirely missing in Henry Cabot Lodge, speaking on that same day in Harlem. Nixon would long regret that his vice presidential nominee lacked the racial radar of the Kennedy camp.

NIXON YIELDS TO TEMPTATION: MIXED MESSAGES

When Richard Nixon campaigned in Atlanta shortly after the Republican convention, many blacks came out to cheer; it seemed that Nixon could do quite well among blacks nationwide. Yet it was during a trip to Georgia that Nixon was ultimately confronted with the tempting prospect of stealing the South away from Kennedy and Johnson. Nixon's campaign throughout Georgia was received so enthusiastically that Nixon now believed he had a chance of winning wide southern support, even with the civil rights platform he'd agreed to in Chicago.

Nixon included states' rights in his speeches in the South, a racist code word Kennedy studiously avoided. The response of southern audiences to Nixon's new rhetoric was quite strong. The trip south, which Nixon had planned as a tactical feint rather than a real attempt to win such Democratic strongholds as Georgia and North Carolina, became instead a turning point in Nixon's strategic thinking. After clearly opting for a pro–civil rights move designed to peel off northern Negroes in the key battleground states of the Northeast and Midwest, Nixon now chose to mingle his pro–civil rights record and platform with talk of local governmental authority and states' rights.

Lodge was designated to handle outreach to blacks, while Nixon handled most of the speaking in the South. Lodge spent the bulk of his time in the Northeast, while Nixon refused to campaign in Harlem.

Regardless, there was substantial black support for Nixon, because of his record. One black publisher in Detroit compared the tickets thusly: "The Nixon-Lodge ticket is a more attractive one on civil rights than the Republicans have ever put up and many Negroes feel that Lyndon Johnson is weak on civil rights." Yet the Republican straddle on civil rights lacked the deft skill that characterized the Kennedy-Johnson maneuvers, as Henry Cabot Lodge was about to demonstrate.

On the same evening that Kennedy spoke in New York City to several groups on topics foreign and domestic, including civil rights, Lodge also spoke to some of the same groups on a variety of topics. Kennedy's speech on foreign policy to Democratic officials made the front page of *The New York Times,* while his speech on civil rights was relegated to page 23. Lodge's speech on civil rights, however, was front-page news: NEGRO IN CABINET PLEDGED BY LODGE. Whether planned or not, Lodge's Harlem speech had surely overshadowed anything that Kennedy said in Harlem or to his liberal conference on constitutional rights.

Lodge's quixotic and sudden commitment to integrating the highest levels of national government was an uncoordinated and inept attempt to attract black support. Whoever edited Kennedy's Harlem speech would have known that pledging to integrate the cabinet would cause headlines from Maine to Mississippi. As Lodge met with southern Republicans in Winston-Salem, North Carolina, the next day, he faced public and private criticism of his pledge, which he hastily tried to reframe, if not retract. Nixon's fury at his running mate was immediate and intense, perceptible even to the press corps that he kept at a studied distance. What Nixon wanted from Lodge was the type of subtle racial electioneering Kennedy was practicing, using speeches that avoided inflammatory and provocative promises that could alienate white southerners.

So deep was the southern anger at Lodge that Nixon was forced to hold a public meeting with him to iron out differences, less than a month before the election. Yet Lodge's pledge was only the highest-profile example of his failure to grasp the delicate nature of civil rights issues in 1960. On the very day of the Nixon-Lodge meeting, Lodge appeared on NBC, advocating more blacks in the Foreign Service, the end of segregated schools and public facilities, and new legislation guaranteeing blacks the right to vote, again in the form of a pledge. With the possible exception of the legislation, Lodge said nothing that Kennedy had not advocated at one time or another in speeches in the North. Kennedy never offered these positions, however, on national television. Indeed, given the opportunity to do so during the televised debates, Kennedy did just the opposite, hewing to his vague emphasis on executive leadership. Lodge, a politician almost singularly lacking in understanding of the South, could not compete with Kennedy and Johnson in that respect. As historian Stephen Ambrose concluded, "Lodge could hardly have done more to help Kennedy and hurt Nixon.... Immediately after Lodge's pledge the polls showed a sharp decline in Nixon's Southern support." And when Nixon retracted his running mate's pledge about the cabinet, it alienated blacks and liberals.

Nixon and Lodge entered the final stage of the campaign in disarray on civil rights. Nixon's original strategy of seeking to take black votes away from the Democrats had become hopelessly muddled by his switch to pro-southern rhetoric. Then the campaign lurched back to strident advocacy of racial equality with the multiple pledges of Lodge. When these were almost immediately undercut by Nixon, the picture presented to both blacks and southern whites was one of confusion and political gamesmanship. Nixon and Lodge were running different campaigns, with Lodge still holding to the original game plan and Nixon trying to win parts of the South. By contrast, Johnson and Kennedy, while campaigning separately, were coordinated in their approach to civil rights and the South. It was at this moment that the travails of Martin Luther King Jr. entered the campaign and presented both campaigns with one last chance to make a moral statement on civil rights.

KING'S IMPRISONMENT AS THE SYMBOLIC MOMENT

The civil rights movement was in a quiescent period during much of 1959–60 because civil rights leaders were anxious that no demonstrations take place during the election season. However, that all began to change as a new tactic swept through the segregated South: sit-ins. These largely student-led demonstrations were the most direct challenges yet to the white hegemony of the South. The photos of calm, committed black students being abused by rabid white crowds were very effective at bringing civil rights back to the nation's attention. While the issue was by no means central to the political agenda of 1960, both parties felt obliged to mention sit-ins in their platforms.

Martin Luther King Jr. became involved in sit-ins in early October, and his arrest with a large group of demonstrators did not receive much national attention at first. Soon, however, King was singled out for special treatment. A local judge held that the arrest violated his parole on a traffic violation and immediately sentenced King to four months in a dangerous penitentiary far from the relatively progressive environs of Atlanta. King's imprisonment was now a matter of international focus. The threat to King's life was apparent to all of his close associates. While in prison, he could be killed in a staged escape or he could be put into an area with hostile white prisoners and come to an "accidental" end. Moreover, four months of hard time for a traffic violation seemed to be Jim Crow justice at its worst. Two weeks before an extraordinarily tight presidential election, the situation was instantly perceived by political observers to be electoral dynamite.

Immediately, conflicting pressures to act or remain aloof were put on both campaigns. Three southern governors informed Kennedy headquarters that any expression of support for King would cost the ticket the South. Wofford and Louis Martin, Kennedy's civil rights advisers, pushed for Kennedy to get involved. Wofford's idea was to have Kennedy call Coretta Scott King, the wife of the imprisoned leader, rather than release a statement critical of Georgia's judicial procedures. Wofford and Martin bypassed the normal chain of command and arranged for Sargent Shriver to present the idea directly to Kennedy. Kennedy's reaction was "impulsive, direct, and immediate." From his hotel room outside O'Hare, Kennedy dialed Mrs. King and spoke briefly with her.

When campaign manager Robert Kennedy heard what Wofford and Martin had done behind his back, he shouted at them, "You bombthrowers probably lost the election . . . you've probably lost three states and . . . the civil rights section isn't going to do another damn thing in this campaign!" Yet Bobby himself quickly got into the act and directly called the judge to plead for King's release. With these two phone calls, the Kennedy brothers symbolically put their sympathies with King and against the segregationist South. Shortly after the second phone call, King was released.

Nixon's campaign, however, had remained silent on the whole affair. Prior to King's release, Jackie Robinson, now a fervent Nixon supporter, made a personal plea to his candidate to top Kennedy and telephone King. Robinson's efforts failed to convince Nixon. Much later, Nixon blamed his press secretary, Herbert Klein, for not reporting Nixon's belief that King's sentence was unfair and then blamed the Eisenhower administration for not intervening as Nixon and the attorney general allegedly were seeking. Yet it was well within Nixon's power to express his feelings: in a symbolic gesture, to a reporter on background, or through an official statement. Indeed, a black White House aide, E. Frederic Morrow, attempted repeatedly to get Nixon's advisers or Nixon to send telegrams to Mrs. King or Georgia officials. Morrow was told by press secretary Klein that it would be poor election strategy to intervene. At the same time Morrow was trying frantically to get Nixon to take a stance, Deputy Attorney General Lawrence Walsh was also attempting to get Nixon or Eisenhower to speak out on the King imprisonment. Walsh tried numerous times to contact his boss, Attorney General William Rogers, or Nixon, both of whom were campaigning together. Walsh had written a statement that would have put the Eisenhower administration, or at least the Nixon campaign, squarely on the record against King's treatment. However, Eisenhower decided against involving himself in a local judicial matter, and Walsh was unable to contact either Rogers or Nixon until after Kennedy's dramatic intervention. Nixon's silence must be interpreted as a choice, certainly influenced by the backlash in the South against Lodge's statement only two weeks before. The burned fingers of the "Negro in the Cabinet" debacle taught Nixon to treat the red-hot King imprisonment gingerly.

Nixon's silence produced sizable political gains for Kennedy. The Kennedy campaign distributed over two million copies of a pamphlet entitled "No Comment Nixon Versus a Candidate with a Heart, Senator Kennedy." Handed out at black churches on the Sunday before the election, the pamphlet powerfully demonstrated Kennedy's moral commitment to black progress. If African Americans had been uncertain about which candidate to support between two men running on strong civil rights platforms but soft-pedaling aspects of their plans to soothe segregationists, this incident gave them a reason to vote Democratic.

Would Kennedy pay a price for his support of King, as he had been warned he would? There were some signs of southern anger; days after Kennedy's intervention, four honorary colonels on the staff of the governor of Georgia resigned in protest of Bobby's phone call to the judge. Yet the coverage in the mainstream media of Kennedy's involvement was surprisingly limited. In *Time,* King's release from prison appeared as the last item of the national news section. Kennedy's name did not appear until the final paragraph. As journalist Theodore White put it, "The entire episode received only casual notice from the generality of American citizens in the heat of the last three weeks of the Presidential campaign. But in the Negro community the Kennedy intervention rang like a carillon." Had Nixon made an issue of Kennedy's involvement, and given the press reason to highlight Kennedy's actions, Nixon might have benefited from a white backlash. Instead, Nixon was the victim of a surge in black support for Kennedy, without an accompanying Nixon boom among southern whites. Indeed, Nixon received the worst of both worlds. With King's father endorsing Kennedy, and King's top lieutenant telling blacks to "take off your Nixon buttons," whatever black support Nixon could have hoped to garner from his record and his platform evaporated.

This type of "narrowcasting" of a symbolic gesture was possible only because of the segregation in the regional and national media. The black press covered Kennedy's intervention extensively, but the white press made little of the story. Some articles did discuss Kennedy's phone call but noted that the reaction among southern whites was "milder than expected." Kennedy had found a way to convey to black Americans a moral commitment to their plight, while not greatly arousing the antipathy of segregationist whites.

Months before the arrest, in their second meeting, Kennedy had asked King what his campaign could do to reassure black voters of Kennedy's commitment to civil rights. King replied, "I don't know what it is, Senator, but you've got to do something dramatic." Owing to the unexpected actions of an obscure state judge in Georgia, King himself became the source of that dramatic gesture. As Kennedy himself said, in his only known comment on the affair: "The finest strategies are usually the result of accidents."

CONCLUSION: THE END OF REPUBLICAN RACIAL LIBERALISM AND THE SOURCE OF KENNEDY'S RACIAL BRILLIANCE

In a campaign decided by a paper-thin majority, any bloc of voters can claim credit for victory. Yet the return of blacks to the Democratic column was unquestionably a key component in Kennedy's victory. Kennedy improved on Stevenson's level of black support by at least 15 percent nationwide and, in some places, by far greater margins. Kennedy carried Illinois by only 9,000 votes and won the vast majority of the black vote, with some 250,000 ultimately voting Democratic. Kennedy received another 250,000 black votes in Michigan, a state he carried by only 67,000. Kennedy's black vote in either state was more than double his popular vote advantage over Nixon *nationwide*. Most significant, Kennedy managed to also do better in the South than Stevenson had. What alchemy of luck and strategy had allowed Kennedy to achieve this nearly impossible feat of improving vote totals among these bitterly antipodal factions?

First, Nixon's gaffes must be allocated their share of responsibility. Nixon's inability to adhere either to a moderate civil rights stance or to a pro–civil rights policy hurt him with both communities. Second, the role of Lyndon Johnson should not be underestimated. He had demonstrated the ability to work with civil rights leaders in 1957 and yet retained his strong support among whites in his own region. During the 1960 debates, Nixon unwisely attacked Johnson for his segregationist past. This probably served to rally southern support to the Democrats, rather than attracting blacks to the Republican banner. Johnson served as a human symbol of the Democratic Party's commitment to the white South. As segregationist senator James Eastland of Mississippi put it in a televised interview weeks before the election, Johnson "took everything relating to integration out of those civil rights bills. . . . He has always opposed Congress's implementing the segregation decisions of the Supreme Court." At the same time, Johnson did not hesitate to forthrightly endorse "constitutional" rights (typically undefined) in his speeches. If Kennedy was dancing a careful minuet on the politics of race, he could not have chosen a more agile dance partner.*

Kennedy also benefited from the relatively low priority given to civil rights by the nation at the time of the campaign. There were no major demonstrations or school desegregation crises inflaming the electorate on civil rights. Kennedy's ability to downplay his civil rights plank in the South was dependent on a lack of attention to the issue. Because the focus was on economics, foreign policy, and party loyalty, Kennedy won the South. Nixon's decision not to present a clear contrast on civil rights contributed to the issue's low salience to the electorate. Voters watching the debates saw no difference between the candidates on civil rights, while perceiving differences on other domestic issues. Finally, civil rights might have figured more prominently on the nation's agenda if Adam Clayton Powell had not maliciously sabotaged plans by King, Bayard Rustin, and A. Philip Randolph to have large pro–civil rights demonstrations at the two

---

* Johnson was crucial in preventing more southerners from rallying to the independent segregationist slate of Harry Byrd. Byrd actually won fifteen electoral votes (Mississippi, half of Alabama, and a faithless Nixon elector from Oklahoma) and would have won many more without the JFK-LBJ straddle on race. Even as it was, Byrd gave the popular vote plurality to Nixon; it is only through erroneously counting all Alabama Democratic votes as Kennedy's that Nixon can be denied his rightful place as one of five men to win the popular vote but lose the presidency.

political conventions. Kennedy's good fortune was that the only civil rights crisis that emerged during 1960 was one that his talents were almost uniquely designed to exploit.

Indeed, much of the credit for the success of Kennedy's straddle on race must be given to the candidate. If Kennedy demonstrated that a carefully crafted campaign could be successful, Nixon demonstrated how truly difficult was the crafting. Part of Kennedy's edge in 1960 came from his Irish background. Although Kennedy was largely ignorant of civil rights and African American issues generally, he was, by birthright, far more skilled in ethnic politics than Nixon. He grew up learning politics from such masters of ethnic gestures as his grandfather "Honey Fitz" Fitzgerald. As the Irish competed with the Yankee Brahmins, the Italians, and other ethnic groups in the cutthroat world of Boston politics, they learned the power of symbols and their ability to harness the resentment and hopes of oppressed groups. Kennedy also knew that white antipathy for blacks was not merely a southern phenomenon. One of the key rifts between Irish Democrats of Boston and out-of-state Democratic reformers was civil rights for blacks, an idea that struck the Irish as "strange and repugnant" because of their competition with blacks for low-wage jobs. During the campaign, Kennedy was influenced on civil rights by a "Boston Mafia" who worried about a northern backlash if Kennedy went too far on black equality. Parts of Kennedy's staff were "always really worried that anything he did pro–civil rights was going to lose white votes not only in the South but in South Boston." Understanding these two aspects of racial politics, the power of symbols to an oppressed group, and the sensitivity of whites to black progress gave Kennedy the tools with which to create his 1960 straddle on race. Like an anti-British speech on St. Patrick's Day, the phone call to King resonated with a minority group without angering the oppressors. Similarly, if Kennedy had been less sensitive to majority prejudice, he might have delivered his original speech that October night in Harlem, endorsing the appointment of black federal judges. If he had done so, the banner headlines might well have read KENNEDY AND LODGE PROMISE NEGRO JUDGES, CABINET. Kennedy also brought to the civil rights debate a coolness that characterized most of his political views. For Kennedy, "to be emotionally or ideo-logically committed is to be captive." When King came to the White House after the election, Wofford observed that there would always be a distance between them, because King approached issues morally and Kennedy politically. As Wofford put it, Kennedy "wanted to win the election and he also liked to do the right thing." These competing goals, victory and morality, did, as in the call to Mrs. King, occasion-ally demand the exact same action.*

If Kennedy's past helps us understand how he used racial politics to eke out his narrow victory over Richard Nixon, the shape of the next ten presidential elections can be seen in the contours of Nixon's defeat. Never again would a Republican attempt to equal the Demo-cratic Party's racial liberalism. Whether the black vote was moved by Kennedy's phone call, the Democratic platform, or some intangible trust in Kennedy, the message to Republicans was that black loyalties would be nearly impossible to shake. They had put their strongest civil rights ticket forward, along with a platform that was at least competitive with the Democrats, and lost significant ground among blacks. The Nixon campaign of 1960 was a high tide for racial liber-alism in the Republican Party, which they have never approached since.

---

* Kennedy's straddle on race affected even his inauguration. Entertainer Sammy Davis Jr. had endorsed JFK, and delayed his interracial marriage until after the election so as not to harm Kennedy in the South. The invitation for Davis to perform at the inauguration was abruptly withdrawn days before the event. With the election over, Kennedy's men now worried that southern senators would be offended by an interracial couple at inaugural proceedings.

★ ★ ★ ★ **3** ★ ★ ★ ★

LBJ WINS DESPITE CIVIL RIGHTS
The Blunt Racial Politics of 1964

If we have to get elected on civil rights, then we're already defeated.

LYNDON JOHNSON, JULY 24, 1964

The election of 1964 is considered by many to be the most racially polarized presidential contest in modern American history. As such, it has been seen as a watershed in the evolution of our two-party system in recent times. The treatment of racial issues by the presidential campaigns of 1964 was stimulated by the changing climate of the country in the matter of civil rights, but in turn, the strategies chosen by the campaigns also shaped that emerging climate. The attitude toward race adopted by both parties was radically different from those selected a mere four years before. In 1960, Nixon and Kennedy had both attempted to appeal to southern segregationists and to northern blacks. Kennedy succeeded in doing both, through immense skill and luck. In 1964, by contrast, the Republican candidate conceded the black vote to the Democrats years before the election, while Johnson knew that he would have a very tough time carrying the Deep South from the moment he made civil rights the focus of his formidable legislative skills. The first southern president since Reconstruction would be the catalyst for the final cracking of the solid South of white Democratic allegiance in presidential elections. The first major party candidate of Jewish descent*

---

* Goldwater was not Jewish, but his father's family was, leading humorist Art Buchwald to observe that he'd always known our first Jewish president would be an Episcopalian.

would lead the Republican Party into a near monochromatic whiteness from which it has yet to recover. These twin ironies accompany perhaps the greatest irony of 1964: what some consider the most racially charged modern election was not decided on the basis of race. Given that racial issues were at the top of the national agenda for much of the year and that the candidates presented the country with clearly different positions on them, this is a surprising outcome. Yet race as an issue was less decisive in the general election of 1964 than it had been in 1960. Although racial tensions did form the strategies of the two nominees, their campaign choices were ultimately decisive in reducing the role race played in the outcome.

1964 AS JOHNSON'S "GIVEN MOMENT": THE SETTING

As the 1964 election season opened, the contrast with the same period in 1960 could not have been more stark. Race was the dominant issue in domestic politics, as it had not been since Reconstruction. Moreover, at a time of relative peace and prosperity, neither security nor economic issues threatened to steal focus away from the burgeoning civil rights movement. That race could dominate the politics of 1964 was clear more than a year before any ballot was cast, with voters in one survey picking it as the most important issue, even over Cuban tensions and the economy. The prominence of civil rights in 1964 was produced by three key factors. First, the direct-action tactics of the newly invigorated civil rights movement had since 1960 focused the attention of the nation on the problems of Jim Crow. Led by new or previously ignored groups such as the Student Non-Violent Coordinating Committee (SNCC) and the Congress of Racial Equality (CORE), the civil rights movement entered its period of greatest success. Emblematic of the heightened attention to civil rights was the 1963 March on Washington, which brought together the entire civil rights leadership, along with key labor figures, and received the endorsement of Kennedy and a number of congressional leaders.

Another influence was Kennedy's own evolution on race. The straddler of 1960, who had been the favorite candidate of many segregationists going back as far as 1956, had gradually become the greatest presidential rhetorician on race since Lincoln. Kennedy's stirring speech to the nation, in the aftermath of his showdown with George Wallace over integrating the University of Alabama, adopted the symbols and words of King and put the moral authority of the presidency behind civil rights. For Kennedy and his followers, civil rights was no longer a topic on which people of good faith could disagree. After two years of delay and compromise on civil rights, 1963 finally saw the Kennedy administration moving forward; in effect, it took Kennedy two years to show which side he was on. The eventual delivery on his promise to integrate federal housing programs, as well as his dedicated effort to appoint blacks to high positions in all the departments of government, served to alienate the South and revive his standing in the civil rights community. So strong was the antipathy to Kennedy in the South by September 1963 that a movie marquee in Georgia advertising the Hollywood version of his PT-109 story read "See the Japs Almost Get Kennedy." In the patina of post-assassination hagiography, it is often forgotten how deeply much of the white South hated Kennedy at the time of his death.

Yet nothing was as important as the decisive role of Lyndon Johnson. In 1963, Kennedy had finally proposed a broad civil rights bill, attacking Jim Crow on a number of fronts. This revolutionary bill was assumed to have little chance of passage, unless it were so amended as to render it almost symbolic. In the aftermath of the tragedy in Dallas, it became clear within just a few days that Johnson would not let the bill die without a fight. Instead, he would make this bill the centerpiece of Kennedy's legacy. As one of his key African American supporters noted, Johnson had a knack for using the "given moments" to get legislation, particularly civil rights legislation, through Congress. Kennedy's sudden martyrdom was one such moment, and Johnson marshaled all of his formidable legislative skill in making the most of it. With its broad indictment of discriminatory practices in public accommodations, the Civil Rights Act threatened to alter the entire segregationist social system of the South. The immense press coverage of the battle, and the sloganeering on all sides, could not help but bring national attention to the issue of civil rights on the eve of the election.

It was also in the battle over the Civil Rights Act that the potential for polarization between the Republican and Democratic Parties became clear, in the persons of Goldwater and Johnson.

THE CANDIDATES

Lyndon Johnson

Today, Lyndon Johnson is recognized almost universally as the greatest proponent of racial equality to occupy the Oval Office. Yet his selection as vice president and his later ascension to the presidency were greeted with great apprehension by a number of leading figures in the civil rights movement, including Bayard Rustin, John Lewis, and James Farmer. The reasons for their misgivings are easy to fathom: Johnson had been, up until 1956, a supporter of segregation. As a white southern politician, Johnson faced a credibility problem with many blacks. For example, despite coaching, Johnson had difficulty pronouncing the then accepted term for African Americans, "Negro," without it sounding dangerously close to a poisonous homophone. Congressman Johnson's views on race were not out of step with the segregationist South, although there is evidence of a deep-seated egalitarianism in Johnson's family history and his own early years. One of the favorite tales of the Texas raconteur was his father's battle against the Klan in the legislature, when nationally and statewide they were at the zenith of their power. Later, as a New Deal Democrat, LBJ was a quiet integrationist as the head of a National Youth Administration program. And much later, LBJ was one of two southern senators who did not attend a southern strategy caucus to stop Truman's civil rights policy in 1949. Yet while he did not attend the caucus, he voted with the caucus on the bill, and as his closest legislative aide said later, "In twenty years he never strayed from southern orthodoxy." To adhere to southern congressional orthodoxy in the 1940s and 1950s meant opposing federal efforts to end such egregious examples of white supremacy as lynching and poll taxes.

Johnson's conservatism on civil rights early in his congressional career was crucial to his meteoric rise to majority leader. He established his credentials as a conservative with his opposition to civil rights at home and communism abroad, while his strong support for most spending programs made him acceptable to liberals. With a nearly even split between liberals and conservatives in 1950, Johnson became a surprise choice as the youngest Senate whip in history. Later, as majority leader, Johnson would shift on civil rights, from opposition to cautious support. In 1956, he was one of only two southerners in the Senate to refuse to sign the Southern Manifesto against desegregation. The next year, Johnson's leadership was essential to passage of the 1957 civil rights bill. Johnson understood southern senators as no northern Democrat could, and this understanding allowed him to work with, around, and through them. What motivated Johnson's strong move toward civil rights? Johnson felt that blacks would turn toward the Republican Party in 1960 unless the Democratic Party passed some sort of civil rights legislation. Johnson's strategic sense on race was not limited to the implications of civil rights legislation for black voting. He believed throughout his career that if he wished to become a national leader, he would have to move away from segregationism.

As vice president, Johnson continued to emphasize racial equality. In a speech in Detroit in January of 1963, he stated, "To strike the chains of a slave is noble. To leave him the captive of his color is hypocrisy." On Memorial Day at Gettysburg, LBJ firmly endorsed civil rights in blunt terms, saying, "Until justice is blind to color, until education is unaware of race, until opportunity is unconcerned with the color of men's skins, emancipation will be a proclamation but not a fact." One of the few areas in which Johnson exercised much power was civil rights, although some in the administration, particularly RFK, did not believe he was moving fast enough. Still, Johnson advocated putting Kennedy's own prestige behind the moral urgency of civil rights, even if it cost the ticket the South in 1964. Johnson suggested that the president travel to the South to confront southern racism "straight in the face." By 1963, when Kennedy was assassinated, Johnson had convinced a number of civil rights leaders in personal meetings that he was not the typical southern politician. In the first two weeks after the assassination, Johnson established a radically different tone from that of JFK's first cautious months in office by meeting individually with black leaders, including King, Farmer, A. Philip Randolph, and Roy Wilkins. He signaled to Congress and the nation that civil rights would be a top priority, and he never wavered in that commitment, even when he faced the rising white backlash of the summer of 1964.

Barry Goldwater

Growing up in Arizona, Barry Goldwater knew very few African Americans, and this may have prevented him from having an affinity for their concerns. It might have been expected that the mild exposure to anti-Semitism that Goldwater had as a person of Jewish descent would make him more sympathetic to black suffering, but this does not appear to have occurred. As one biographer concluded: "Throughout his life, he would accommodate the bigotry of others while personally distancing himself from it." Goldwater's record does, however, show some aspects of racial progressivism. As a business leader and National Guard pilot, Goldwater had a strong record of integrating those institutions. He worked for better race relations in Arizona and even joined the NAACP for four years. Goldwater believed that blacks and whites were equal before the law, and in his major book, *The Conscience of a Conservative,* he made clear his personal belief in racial equality. Yet his reluctance to force white southerners to give up public racism was largely responsible for his burgeoning popularity in the South. In particular, Goldwater had a narrow definition of what federal civil rights were and what actions the national government could take in their defense. Goldwater's distaste for government would almost always trump his belief in racial equality. As late as 1961, a very aggressive anti-Goldwater piece in *The New Republic* did not accuse him of racism or even of playing to prejudice.

By 1960, Goldwater was endorsing a Republican presidential strategy to peel off southern whites on the basis of racial politics. Goldwater was convinced that Nixon lost the 1960 race when he endorsed civil rights so strongly in the platform. In a speech to Georgia Republicans, Goldwater advocated the abandonment of the black vote. "We ought to forget the big cities. We can't out-promise the Democrats. . . . I would like to see our party back up on school integration. The Supreme Court decision is not the supreme law of the land." He also supported a segregationist amendment to give states complete control over education. Yet while he was serving up rhetoric that would greatly please southern audiences, Goldwater also criticized Robert Kennedy's Justice Department for not prosecuting voting rights violations in the South. At least up until the campaign season began, Goldwater "vehemently" supported the electoral rights of blacks, as well as the constitutional amendment to eliminate the poll tax. These views were consonant with his strict version of federalism: only certain rights were subject to national regulation, and many others were not.

Goldwater persistently accused the Democratic Party of being the party of racism or the party of hypocrisy on race. In a 1963 article, Goldwater wrote:

> When I spoke at a Republican rally in Jackson, Mississippi, I said that the time had come for all politicians to stop appealing for votes on the grounds of race, color or creed. It was the only mention of the race issue at the rally. When the democrats held their rally in Jackson, Mississippi, the incumbent senator, a Democrat, brought up the trouble at the University of Mississippi and blamed Republican President Eisenhower for his efforts on behalf of integration.

Goldwater claimed that the future success of the Republican Party in the South was contingent on the South's growing "moderation on the race question." It is difficult to square this national Goldwater with the Goldwater who famously claimed to a southern audience that it was time for the GOP to "go hunting where the ducks are" or, in clearer language, to go after southern whites and give up on black voters. Goldwater, like Kennedy and Nixon in 1960, would face a choice of rhetorical roads in 1964. Yet before Goldwater launched a general election campaign predicated on stealing the segregationist South from the Democrats, an uncomplicated and unabashed racist firebrand would demonstrate that fear, animosity, and resentment of blacks were not limited to the white South. In the surprisingly successful campaign of George Corley Wallace, the national extent of the white backlash first came into view.

THE DEMOCRATIC PRIMARIES AND THE CONVENTION: THE BIRTH OF THE BACKLASH

LBJ's fulsome support of civil rights left him open to a conservative challenger in the Democratic primaries. A segregationist Alabama governor, George Wallace, exploited Johnson's leftward tilt on civil rights and other domestic issues. Wallace claimed to have been an early supporter of John F. Kennedy and a participant in the Kennedy push for the vice presidency in 1956. Wallace sat at the head table during JFK's visit to Alabama in 1958 and drove the senator back to the airport. By 1963, Wallace was a strident opponent of Kennedy and had taken office as governor with a ringing endorsement of "segregation today, segregation tomorrow, segregation forever!" The speech, written by a Klan leader for the notoriously atextual Wallace, brought national attention to the young pugilistic governor. As a result of his prominence, he was much in demand as a speaker. It was during his successful speaking tour of northern universities that Wallace's cross-regional appeal became apparent. Although Wallace began hinting that he might run for president, the idea was dismissed by journalists because of Wallace's racism and LBJ's popularity. Wallace entered his first primary, Wisconsin, only because a former Joe McCarthy supporter showed up at Wallace's hotel suite in Madison to explain how easily he could get on the ballot.

There was never any chance that Wallace would knock off Johnson, since in this era primaries did not determine the allocation of the vast majority of delegates. At best, Wallace could wound Johnson so much that the president would alter his policies on race. Johnson did not formally enter the primaries against Wallace, allowing favorite son stand-ins to run in his place. Wallace was the only challenger, and few believed that a vociferous southern racist would attract northern votes, even from whites with doubts about civil rights. Yet in

Indiana and Wisconsin, Wallace scored extraordinary numbers, receiving 30 percent and 34 percent of the Democratic vote. With the Maryland primary coming up, Johnson worried that Wallace might hurt him greatly. As Johnson put it, "Alabama is coming into Maryland, Alabama is going into Indiana." The success of Wallace as a reverse carpetbagger, selling the white South's view of race to frightened northerners, would shape much of the 1964 campaign. Johnson avoided commenting much on Wallace, despite repeated queries from journalists during his press conferences. Even after Johnson's quiet efforts to rally his supporters, Wallace received 43 percent of the Maryland vote. Moreover, Johnson's narrow victory was made possible only by a doubling in black turnout and by what one historian called "creative vote totals" from Baltimore. Shortly after the Maryland primary, Wallace dropped out of the race, in part because of Goldwater's emergence as the Republican front-runner.

Clearly, given Wallace's stunning performance, Johnson could well have been expected to moderate his stance on the pending civil rights legislation. If a George Wallace could do well in Democratic primaries in northern states like Wisconsin and Indiana, or nearly win in a border state like Maryland, there would be plenty of political cover for a compromise with southerners on the bill. Yet even as Wallace was barnstorming against Johnson, LBJ spoke out in Maryland against prejudice and spoke in Georgia against southern racism. Far from moderating his liberalism in the face of the Wallace challenge, Johnson chose this time to announce his plans for a "Great Society" of equality and opportunity.

More important, Johnson continued to press Congress to pass the Civil Rights Act, refusing to make major changes to co-opt wavering conservatives and southerners. In nearly daily contact with Humphrey, the legislative leader on civil rights, Johnson stuck to his guns, believing all along that Senate Minority Leader Dirksen would get his Republicans to support the bill. In a seminal moment in congressional history, a coalition of northern Democrats and nearly all Republicans defeated a filibuster by southern Democrats in the Senate on June 10. A month later, Johnson signed the bill in a moving White House ceremony, before a number of civil rights leaders.

Two weeks after the greatest legislative victory for racial equality since Reconstruction, Harlem erupted in rioting. In the fires and deaths in Harlem, some saw the end of racial liberalism as a policy option. Johnson intimate John Connally asked LBJ, "New York, what the hell are they rioting for?" and listed the legislative protections that New York blacks enjoyed, including integrated schools and stronger legal safeguards than the Civil Rights Act just passed at the federal level. Johnson's fears of a white backlash, already primed by Wallace's near victories, reached a fever pitch at this point. "If they just keep on rioting in Harlem you are going to have unshirted Hell, and you're going to have it in New York, you're going to have the same type of rebellion there, and in Chicago and Iowa . . . this thing runs deep. You're going to see more cross-voting this year." It was not just political elites who immediately put urban unrest in the context of the upcoming presidential election. When hundreds of Italian Americans challenged blacks picketing police headquarters in New York City, many of the whites carried "Goldwater for President" signs. Johnson called in the top leadership of the civil rights organizations and begged them to take stands against the riots and to call a moratorium on demonstrations until after the election. With the exceptions of John Lewis and James Farmer, the civil rights leaders agreed to Johnson's request.

Just when LBJ had managed to dampen the fires of Harlem, he now had to deal with the potential for racial unrest at the 1964 Democratic convention in Atlantic City. Given its proximity to centers of black population such as New York, Philadelphia, and Washington, Johnson was worried about what might occur if the Democratic convention were picketed by angry black demonstrators. The spark that could set off the powder keg was the conflict over segregated southern delegations. "If they have a hundred thousand Negroes up there . . . and they picket this thing . . . and then the convention kicks them [segregationists] out, the impression throughout the country is going to be, well, they just got kicked out because the niggers wanted them kicked out," Connally told the president. Both Alabama and Mississippi had run segregated primaries, and SNCC activists had organized a counterparty in Mississippi, called the Mississippi Freedom

Democratic Party (MFDP). They held a primary and a convention and were publicly calling for seats at the convention, as well as the rejection of the white delegations.

Johnson had reports from Connally and others that the failure to seat the segregated delegations would have ramifications far beyond those two states. If Alabama and Mississippi were not seated, "all hell [would] break loose" in states like South Carolina, Virginia, Florida, and others. But Johnson also worried that some northern delegations would object to the seating of all-white slates.

> You got Wagner [mayor of New York City] and Daley [mayor of Chicago] . . . and Pat Brown [governor of California], you got about eight big states there, no none of them can go back home having embraced anything about Mississippi or Alabama because it's just fighting language with the people who make up their party . . . they can't go back home and say, by God . . . I seated these people that have been killing all these other people . . . [but] we can't go back home if they seat a bunch of niggers.

Johnson considered and rejected meeting with King to defuse the situation before the convention, because, as an adviser put it, meeting with King would be "an unnecessary affront to a large number of people at this particular time." As the convention opened, the conflict over segregated delegations festered. Johnson enlisted the FBI in a massive surveillance campaign, both to keep outside demonstrators from the convention site and to monitor the progress of the negotiations. Johnson had the FBI wiretap the phones of MFDP delegates King and Rustin and followed their strategies carefully. In their presentation to the credentials committee, the MFDP scored a public relations victory, with the riveting testimony of Fannie Lou Hamer. The blunt words of this Mississippi woman describing in vivid detail the murder of Medgar Evers as well as the brutality she had faced in her attempts to vote attracted the nation's attention. So damaging to party unity did Johnson consider Hamer's speech that the president chose to interrupt her nationally televised testimony by making "impromptu" remarks to the convention, thus cutting live network coverage of Hamer.

The deadlock over the seating remained unresolved and Johnson dispatched Humphrey to negotiate a compromise. Ultimately, the MFDP was offered two voting seats, while the Mississippi segregationists would be seated in full. The Democratic leadership also promised that 1968 delegations would be integrated. Johnson had bent over backward to accommodate conservative white Democrats, but he still had to work to sell the compromise to whites as well as to the MFDP's dispirited leadership. Johnson was mystified that some white delegates were not going to accept the compromise; he exclaimed to Senator James Eastland of Mississippi that "we won a victory and the poor folks [segregationists] don't understand it . . . they don't understand I'm the best friend they've got!" Johnson was furious that "his" convention was being portrayed on television as chaotic. With his three Oval Office television sets blaring in the background, Johnson demanded that his aide Walter Jenkins stop the black delegates from taking the seats of the Mississippi regulars. He told another aide to do something to get conservative white Democrats on the television, instead of complaining liberals like Edith Green and Joe Rauh. In the space of a month, LBJ had shifted from worrying about the response of liberal northerners to the seating of segregationists to worrying about the backlash among whites everywhere if angry blacks and their white supporters dominated the convention coverage. In paranoid hyperbole, Johnson expressed his fears that irreparable harm had been done to his reelection chances by the MFDP uproar at the convention.

> I think the Negroes are going back to Reconstruction period, they're going to set themselves back a hundred years . . . and I'm just trying to get a vice president for them . . . and here these folks go get everybody upset. . . . Hell, the Northerners are more upset . . . they wire me to tell me the Negroes are taking over the country, they're running the White House, they're running the Democratic Party . . . it's not Mississippi and Alabama anymore . . . you're catching hell from Michigan, Ohio, Philadelphia, New York, that nearly every white man in this country would be frightened if he thought the Negroes were going to take him over . . . we can't ever buy spots that'll equal this . . .

we've got five million budgeted but we can't undo what they've done these past few days.

Yet even as this event was taking place, Johnson was planning to choose Hubert Humphrey as his vice president. He knew from Connally and from many others that Humphrey remained anathema in the South, second in white southern antipathy only to Bobby Kennedy. The plea from South Carolina Democrats to LBJ was typical: "Please, please, anybody but Kennedy or Humphrey." Humphrey was still "Mr. Civil Rights" to many southerners. Johnson's selection of Humphrey despite his high profile on civil rights was an emphatically symbolic act. Johnson's awareness of this was clear; he dangled the carrot of Humphrey's nomination in front of the MFDP at the convention as a reward if they knuckled under to the compromise and, conversely, threatened them with a less pro–civil rights nominee if they did not agree. In the face of the brewing white backlash, Johnson chose one of the few men in the Democratic Party whose civil rights advocacy surpassed his own recently improved record. Even as Johnson's marvelous political instincts were becoming sensitized to the looming national white backlash, he would demonstrate during the general election an unwavering commitment to racial progress. The Republican Party, by contrast, would waver and eventually abandon its leadership role on civil rights during the 1964 primary and general campaigns.

IN YOUR HEART, YOU SUSPECT HE'S RACIST: GOLDWATER TAKES THE NOMINATION

At the onset of the 1964 primary season, the Republicans were gravely divided on matters of race. Before the Goldwater regulars took over the national party, the head of the Republican National Committee (RNC) commented in 1962 that whenever a Republican took 40 percent of the black vote, victory was at hand, suggesting that outreach to blacks remained on the agenda. The GOP still attacked the Democrats from the left on civil rights, pointing out that the 1957 and the 1960 civil rights bills were supported by far higher percentages of Republicans. The party also used old quotes from LBJ's segregationist days to vilify him for either racism or hypocrisy and excoriated Kennedy's delay in desegregating federal housing and in proposing his civil rights bill on accommodations. During the interim period between elections, the RNC had commissioned an analysis of voting in the forty-one largest cities. The report advocated a greater effort among minority voters in big cities. Yet at the same time, the RNC was looking at expanding its embryonic party networks in the South. Whatever the practicality of attempting both stratagems simultaneously, the emphasis on minority outreach does suggest that the national Republicans had not yet given up on black Republicans.

The Republicans in the early stages of the primary did not articulate a clear message on civil rights. The party initially announced plans to hold a formal meeting titled "Job Opportunities and Civil Rights" as part of their national "Party to the People" forums. Yet when the forum was actually convened in May of 1964, it was entitled "Automation, Unemployment, and the Paycheck." It did feature two pro–civil rights black Republicans, Frederic Morrow, former aide to Eisenhower, and William Robinson, an Illinois state representative, as well as Governor George Romney of Michigan, a white leader on civil rights. During the brief discussion of race, the panel unanimously supported the pending Civil Rights Act.

Yet while the Republicans still had pro–civil rights forces, the right wing of the party was increasingly unsympathetic to the cause. As Goldwater emerged as the consensus candidate of the Republican Right, the plausibility of his candidacy rested upon his popularity in the South and the West. The West would be won on the basis of a strident anti–federal government campaign, but the Goldwater strategy in the South was always reliant on a white backlash vote. Early supporters distributed maps showing how Goldwater could defeat Kennedy by winning the South. As a Goldwater adviser said in an interview given days before Kennedy's assassination, the hope for victory lay in a backlash against Kennedy's civil rights moves, even though "I hate to win on that basis."

Goldwater had to contend for the nomination with a number of other party figures, each more moderate on civil rights than he was.

Indeed, one of them, Nelson Rockefeller, remained one of the most prominent civil rights proponents in either party, even providing direct financial support to controversial figures like King. Goldwater's opposition to civil rights gave him the nomination, because he won an entire region, while his opponents split most other state delegations with each other and with Goldwater. Goldwater's victory brought about the twilight of black Republicanism. In the South the party of Lincoln had been the home of the few enfranchised blacks. In Georgia, the triumph of the Goldwater supporters at the state convention led to the virtual elimination of blacks from the party's leadership positions. In some states, the Goldwaterites were explicitly and unabashedly racist. Despite this, in his keynote address to the Georgia Republican State Convention, Goldwater argued that the Republican record on civil rights was strong and that the Democrats were guilty of hypocrisy on civil rights. Goldwater made the implausible claim that the increasing support among southern whites for the Republicans was simply a product of a nonracial revulsion at deceitful Democratic politicians.

Just as Johnson had to work for the Civil Rights Act while fighting off George Wallace in the Democratic primaries, Senator Goldwater was confronted with the bill as he battled his Republican rivals and prepared for the convention. In a moment of high symbolism, Goldwater opposed the bill against a majority of his own party and the advice of top Republican leaders. It was this vote, more than any other act by Goldwater, which ignited the most fervent opposition of the Republican establishment of Rockefeller, Lodge, and Pennsylvania governor William Scranton. Yet it came too late to provide an impetus for unity among Goldwater's competitors. Indeed, the tragedy for moderate Republicans in 1964 was that each of Goldwater's opponents won different primaries, and none was willing to put full support behind any of the others in time to make a difference against Goldwater's impassioned and unified following.

Goldwater made special appeals to southern Republicans on civil rights and law and order, statements that were designed to play to the white backlash. For example, his speech in May in Columbus, Georgia, reeked with obsequious deference to Jim Crow. In discussing the dangers of federal "centralization," Goldwater bemoaned the "distinct cultural loss" caused by federal intervention. "The structure of the federal system, with its fifty separate state units, has long permitted this nation to nourish local differences, even local cultures." Goldwater went on to praise Columbus for devising a local solution to the "grave problem" of racial discord and for creating "the outstanding race relations record of this city." The speech had a preface, written especially for a southern audience, which linked his theme attacking federal civil rights laws with violence in the streets. Goldwater did not limit his backlash themes to the South. In a speech at New York's Madison Square Garden in May, he made the link between civil rights legislation and the ongoing riots quite explicit.

> Where are the states which today are witnessing the most violence? I sadly remind you that they are the very states where there is the most talk about brotherhood and the very least opportunity for achieving it. I sadly remind you that we are seeing violence today in those very states which are proving that new laws alone are not the answer. There are too many of the old laws which aren't even working!

Goldwater's rhetoric on race helped him in several primaries. His strong showing in the crucial Ohio primary was interpreted by Governor John Rhodes as a sign that the backlash would sell outside the South, and the governor became a key and enthusiastic Goldwater supporter.

By a very narrow margin, and largely as a result of his sweep of southern delegates, Goldwater entered the 1964 convention as the likely nominee. However, the specter of an independent Wallace candidacy haunted the Goldwater forces. Given Wallace's cross-regional appeal to racial conservatives, he could take away any chance of a Goldwater victory. Goldwater even listened, on the eve of his convention, to Wallace emissaries who urged the Arizonan to pick Wallace as his running mate. Goldwater refused but continued his charm offensive in the press, praising Wallace as "a very able man." Ultimately, Wallace gave up all third-party aspirations, claiming that he had already succeeded at bringing states' rights to the attention of both parties. Since only the Republicans had made states' rights part of their agenda, they could naturally expect to inherit Wallace's followers.

The decision to put Goldwater atop the ticket did not automatically result in an anti–civil rights platform. A number of prominent figures, including Lodge, Rockefeller, and King, spoke to the platform committee advocating a strong civil rights plank. The opposing forces could not be as direct in their advocacy. White backlash was "the unspoken watchword of the 1964 convention . . . articulated only occasionally in soft whispers . . . but the presence of the white backlash tactic was felt all last week as the platform committee drafted the weakest Republican civil rights plank in memory." The platform drafts themselves indicate how sharply the issue of race was dividing the Republicans. Some call for the repeal of the 1964 CRA, others advocate going beyond it. One idea that made the final draft was a road map for future Republican campaigns against racial preferences:

> Finally, consistent with its historic opposition to racial discrimination, the Republican Party pledges its equal opposition to the rapidly evolving threats of inverse discrimination. A Republican Administration would oppose the shifting of jobs on the basis of arbitrary racial quotas, and also would oppose the abandonment of neighborhood schools, to meet racial quotas, or Federal pressure to force local authorities to bar children from attending the school nearest their home.

Even the strong section endorsing voting rights had some plums for conservatives and backlashers, since it discusses the dangers of fraud. As was seen first in the 1964 campaign, a national ballot security campaign could become a technique to depress black turnout. Overall, though the platform did not call for revocation of the Civil Rights Act and endorsed voting rights for blacks, the Republicans clearly hoped to benefit among whites on the basis of moderation and caution on civil rights. As the convention closed, Goldwater faced much criticism for the role that the white backlash had played in his victory and in his campaign's plans for November. An editorial in *Life* warned, "A truly national party cannot afford to be lily white, nor can a truly conservative cause. . . . Goldwater's grave danger, and his party's, is that he or his supporters may be tempted to bid for this ugly and silent vote." The truth was, Goldwater had been planning to bid for that ugly vote for at least four years. In the next few weeks, however, Goldwater would demonstrate that there were limits to his willingness to court the backlash.

THE GENERAL ELECTION CAMPAIGN: THE BACKLASH AND THE FRONTLASH

The riots of 1964 have been largely forgotten in the wake of the much greater riots that came after, such as Watts in 1965 or the nationwide turmoil following the assassination of Martin Luther King Jr. in 1968. Yet in their day, they received widespread attention. For much of July and August, riots were news across the country, particularly in the East. The potential of these upheavals to change the outcome of the presidential race was immediately apparent. Johnson was fearful that racial liberalism would be blamed if the rioting were not stopped. As he told press secretary George Reedy in late July, the nation was watching closely to see if the administration treated riots by blacks in the North as seriously as white racism in the South. At this moment of high tension, Goldwater offered to meet with the president to discuss the riot crisis. Johnson's initial response was one of grave suspicion. "Nothing good can come of that [the meeting]. He wants to use this forum, he wants to encourage the backlash, that's where his future is, it's not in peace and harmony." Johnson suspected that Goldwater and the people close to him were actually behind the riots and suggested that the FBI investigate the possibility. Johnson's logic was simple; the riots were helping Goldwater politically, so Goldwater or his supporters must have played some role in starting them. "It's not our friends, it's not our supporters, it's not our people that's going around stirring these things up, and let's leave the impression that he is, without saying so."

Yet despite Johnson's suspicions, Goldwater did not use the meeting to exploit the riots for political gain. The two men met briefly at the White House with little press notice and issued a joint statement removing the riots as an election issue. Even Johnson was forced to concede that Goldwater wasn't appealing to the white backlash:

He came in, just wanted to tell me how well I looked, and that he wanted to visit with me a little bit, that he was a half-Jew, and that he didn't want to do anything that would contribute to any riots or disorders or bring about any violence. Because of his ancestry he was aware of the problems that existed in that field and he didn't want to say anything that would make them any worse . . . thought he could have used it, I thought their intent was to use the White House as some kind of launching pad. . . .

In this and other discussions of his brief meeting with Goldwater, the surprise in Johnson's voice is evident, particularly when compared to the venom in his earlier discussions of Goldwater's putative motives.

As Johnson pondered why his opponent was not hitting hard on racial unrest, he also had the cheering news of an emerging "front-lash" against Goldwater. By the close of the Democratic convention, it was clear that Goldwater's stances on Social Security, the Tennessee Valley Authority (TVA), agricultural programs, and, most important, nuclear security were causing record high levels of defections by Republicans to the Democrats, according to most polls. The surveys were indicating that for every Democrat who was defecting to Goldwater, Johnson was winning three Republican votes. However, Johnson's claim that the Republicans were losing support because "they don't want to treat people alike and they don't want to treat all people as Americans" is untenable. Reports that crossed his desk at this time indicated that top leaders in his own party felt that civil rights was costing Democrats votes. The governor of Tennessee wrote to Johnson in August with this report on the backlash:

The so-called backlash that we read and hear so much about does actually exist. . . . People holding jobs with industry and government are afraid they are going to be forced out of jobs to make room for people who are not qualified either by training or experience . . . that white people will be discriminated against in future employment. . . . I find this exists in every state. . . . There is a feeling that law violators are not being apprehended and convicted while they continue to destroy life and property . . . any effort that can be made on the part of the Federal government to change a pattern of Negro thinking that accuses the police of "brutality" for the slightest enforcement of law should be made.

Throughout the early period of the general election campaign, Johnson maintained an extraordinarily large lead over Goldwater in every national survey. Johnson's only vulnerabilities revolved around racial unrest and white backlash. On nearly every other issue of concern, polls showed that Johnson was well ahead. Johnson's numbers never dipped far below 70 percent approval. As pollster Sam Lubell concluded, "The racial issue is the only one that can elect Goldwater."

Civil rights did have a positive influence on Johnson's support in one area; the response in the black community to Johnson's civil rights courage was immediate and overwhelming. This was apparent in the behavior of the leaders in the black community as well as in the masses. A. Philip Randolph, the dean of the civil rights leadership, endorsed a major party presidential candidate for the first time. Similarly, the highest-profile leader in the African American community, King, campaigned against Goldwater, if not for Johnson. And Johnson's reception in the black community was euphoric. On his way to Brown University for a speech, Johnson drove through a black section of Providence. Johnson's car was besieged, with onlookers pledging their support and even their love for the president. As the election neared, the percentage of blacks identifying as Republicans dropped precipitously, from 23 percent in 1960 to 12 percent in 1964. Nationwide surveys had trouble finding a single black Goldwater supporter.

Rather than writing off or catering to the backlash voters in the South, Johnson chose to confront his fellow southerners. Johnson calculated that an appeal to southern gentility would take the sting off opposition to black progress and sent his wife, Lady Bird, a native of Alabama, on a train tour of the South. Even so, Lady Bird faced counterdemonstrators and animosity during her tour, including signs demanding "Black Bird Go Home." The tour was to end in New

Orleans, after snaking through Virginia and down through the heart of the Deep South. Johnson flew out to meet his wife and to give a major address in New Orleans. In the planning for his appearance, his aides recommended caution. As a memo from one aide noted, the situation in Louisiana was so bad, the major thrust of the Louisiana Democrats' campaign was to accuse Goldwater of being a closet integrationist. Thus, "the less said about Civil Rights, the better." Similarly, Bill Moyers, in a wire to fellow aide Jack Valenti, advised the president to avoid "civil rights" but perhaps mention "constitutional rights" and praise the city for its progress on "settling their problems in the spirit of the golden rule." Yet Johnson threw all caution to the wind and gave perhaps the bluntest address on racial politics ever delivered by an American president. It was the speech of a white southern populist mourning the sad effects of racism on whites and blacks alike throughout southern history. Rather than listening to those who shouted, "Nigger, nigger, nigger!" to win elections, white southerners should recognize their common destiny with southern blacks.

> Now the people that would use us and destroy us first divide us . . . all these years, they have kept their foot on our necks by appealing to our animosities and dividing us. Whatever your views are, we have a Constitution, and we have a Bill of Rights, and we have the Law of the Land, and two-thirds of the Democrats in the Senate voted for it, and three-fourths of the Republicans. I signed it, and I am going to enforce it, and I am going to observe it, and I think any man that is worthy of the high office of the President is going to do the same thing. But I am not going to let them build up the hate and try to buy my people by appealing to their prejudice.

Far from soft-pedaling civil rights, Johnson had traveled to the Deep South to deliver the message that the days of Democratic racism were numbered. Would the flag of racial fears then be picked up by the opposing party?

GOLDWATER'S CHOICES: DESPERATION AND DECISION

Even prior to the Republican convention, Goldwater's chances were seen as dim. Johnson was far ahead in the polls, the nation was prosperous and largely at peace. Moreover, the post-assassination glow of Camelot still colored the White House. Nothing that occurred during the Republican convention or early general election season indicated a change in Goldwater's prospects.

Race had been key to Goldwater's winning the nomination, and in the general election, race was seen by the Goldwater camp as the only hope of a desperate campaign. Of all of Johnson's perceived vulnerabilities, an internal memo listed only one that could not be spun as a racial issue, the taint of corruption surrounding Johnson. The few other issues that were tilting toward Goldwater were all more or less amenable to a racial characterization in 1964 America: civil rights, juvenile delinquency, welfare fraud, crime and violence generally, and unnecessary government spending. As an unnamed analyst for the campaign noted, "There is considerable evidence to show that every time there is violence by Negroes, Goldwater gains supporters." One internal report advocated targeting voters who were torn between their traditional allegiance to the Democratic Party and "the pull of . . . prejudice."

Yet Goldwater's first move following the convention was to depoliticize the race riots. In contrast with his primary speeches blaming unrest on civil rights legislation, he met with the president to remove the riots from the political sphere. Goldwater's campaign missed numerous opportunities to play the race card. The general election campaign's anti-Humphrey pamphlet, for example, failed to attack "Mr. Civil Rights" on racial issues, instead focusing on foreign policy and his alleged involvement in advocating socialism in America. Another frequent target of Goldwater's ire was the Supreme Court. Since *Brown* v. *Board,* the Warren Court was anathema in much of the white South. Yet Goldwater during the general election campaign framed his attacks on the Court primarily around morality, federalism, separation of powers, and apportionment. In his speech in

St. Petersburg in September, he did attack the Warren Court, but for coddling criminals, without mentioning race. In a speech in October in Texas, Goldwater stayed focused on foreign policy and the dangers of communism, except for a brief screed against the Court and some mention of law and order. Certainly Goldwater's attacks on the Court were welcomed by those who saw the Court as going too far in protecting minorities. Moreover, crime and law and order were racial code words for many conservative whites. Yet in 1961 Goldwater had attacked the Court directly on integration. By the fall of 1964, he was retreating from some of the stridency of his appeals to backlashers.

Goldwater even endorsed the Civil Rights Act, which had been his highest-profile anti–civil rights stance; in a statement just after the Republican convention, Goldwater said, "I will not make civil rights an issue. Let's give this civil rights law a real chance to work. Let's use moral persuasion." There are two interpretations of Goldwater's new hesitancy to attack civil rights legislation and to link it to civil unrest in urban centers. One is that Goldwater had been sincere in his discussions with Johnson, and that, as he told the president, he did not want to be remembered by his grandchildren for whipping up racial fears. Alternatively, Goldwater was simply becoming subtler, attempting to attack the issue indirectly, knowing that an open assault on desegregation would alienate many moderate voters and attract very few new votes. Those who were antiblack were already likely to vote for him. Perhaps Goldwater had used race only when he needed to fight off Republican challengers and solidify his hold on the South and the backlash states in the North.

Goldwater on at least one occasion was repulsed by his campaign's attempt to exploit racial fears. His staff prepared a long-form film, *Choice*, which was intended to be a major part of the late campaign. In it, footage of northern riots is a constant theme. A moderate black trying to calm the looters in Harlem is shouted down. The central theme is not racial unrest, however, but an overall decline in morality, particularly sexual morality. Democrats who got wind of the upcoming national telecast focused on the racial aspects and called on Goldwater to call off the broadcast. Under mounting criticism, Goldwater deemed the whole film to be "racist" and canceled it.

Goldwater's reluctance to use racial fearmongering may have also stemmed from other sources. Since winning the nomination, Goldwater had come under increasing pressure on civil rights from some figures in the Republican Party. On the eve of Goldwater's formal selection, Scranton had penned an angry public letter attacking Goldwater for his "irresponsibility" on racial matters. A number of Republicans were also unhappy when Goldwater did not respond immediately to an endorsement from Robert Creel, the Grand Dragon of Alabama's KKK. At a unity conference convened by former President Eisenhower, Goldwater promised to uphold the existing civil rights laws if elected, although this did not satisfy liberals such as Rockefeller. By the start of the general election season, then, Goldwater had promised two presidents that he would moderate his rhetoric on race.

Still, much of Goldwater's campaign staff continued to believe that the white backlash was Goldwater's only chance for victory. It is therefore not surprising that his campaign zigzagged on this issue, as it did on so many others. Goldwater's running mate, conservative New York congressman William Miller, also shifted on race from week to week. On national television, Miller repeatedly refused to disavow the endorsement of the Klan leader.* "Senator Goldwater and I will accept the support of any American citizen who believes in our posture, who believes in our principles, who believes in our platform." Moreover, it was Miller who in an October speech in Philadelphia drew perhaps the crudest connection between civil rights and civil unrest:

> It's all right to send hundreds of FBI agents and U.S. Marshals into Philadelphia, Mississippi, to protect the civil rights of a few people there; but no White House effort is made to protect the property and civil rights of thousands of people in Philadelphia, Pennsylvania.

---

* Creel's statement certainly merited disavowal: "I like Barry Goldwater. I believe what he believes in. I think the same way he thinks." Creel added that he hated "Niggerism, Catholicism, Judaism."

The odious comparison of the murders of Chaney, Schwerner, and Goodman in Philadelphia, Mississippi, to civil unrest in Philadelphia, Pennsylvania, could have come straight from George Wallace's mouth. In the same speech, Miller attacked police review boards and denied the very existence of police brutality.

Yet scarcely a month before, Miller, in a speech in the neighboring state of Delaware, had attacked Johnson for hypocrisy on civil rights and used his old record of votes on lynching, poll taxes, and segregation against him. And it was Miller who wanted to hit LBJ hard about a racist covenant on his Texas property. John Grenier, the Goldwater staffer leading the southern campaign, opposed using the covenant issue, because he felt that the attack would backfire in the South. Finally, Miller went ahead without authorization and raised the covenant in a speech in Texas and then again repeatedly in the closing days of the campaign. Johnson's 1945 restricted deed was also the focus of a RNC press release on September 15. The confusion among Republicans on race was aptly demonstrated the very next day when, in another press release, the RNC welcomed Senator Strom Thurmond to the party. While attacking Johnson for signing a restricted deed almost twenty years before, the GOP welcomed the leading figure in the movement to preserve segregation.

If there was confusion about how to use racial issues at the highest levels of the Republican campaign, there was much less further down. In southern districts, brochures featuring the worst racial stereotypes and playing to white fears of black progress were endemic. If Goldwater was hesitant in some postconvention speeches to link peaceful demonstrators to violent looters, his campaign showed no such reluctance. And these tactics had their desired effect. The campaign's analysis of Goldwater's prospects in Georgia quotes an *Atlanta Constitution* columnist as saying, "The way things are going now, it's almost dangerous for Democratic candidates for Congress in Georgia not to be for Goldwater or to pronounce the word Negro correctly." Perhaps the most cynical exploitation of race was performed by one of the few remaining black Republicans, Clay Claiborne, assistant to the chairman of the RNC for Negro Affairs. Over 1.5 million leaflets were printed on election eve, urging blacks to write in Martin Luther King instead of voting for Johnson. The campaign, credited to the fictitious "Committee for Negroes in Government," was exposed by King and the media as a hoax before the election.

In the end, Goldwater's campaign, for all its confusion on race, did articulate a policy that was consistently more conservative and antiblack equality than Johnson's. As opposed to 1960, overwhelming majorities of voters saw the two parties as differing sharply on civil rights. Seventy-five percent of voters were aware of the Civil Rights Act, and of those, most were aware of which side Goldwater had supported. Did Goldwater's crushing defeat therefore represent a vindication of Johnson's policies on race? Did Johnson have a mandate to stay the course on civil rights?

CONCLUSION: THE MEANING OF THE LANDSLIDE

The victory of Lyndon Johnson was one of the great landslides of the century. Not only did he win a stunning majority in the electoral college, his popular vote margin of victory was nearly a postwar record. Moreover, Goldwater's name at the top of the ticket was poisonous for a number of congressional Republican incumbents and statewide officeholders. The devastation was nearly complete.

Nearly, but not entirely. The one region in which Republicans gained power was in the previously solid South. The five Deep South states that Goldwater won were the top states in terms of black population levels. Goldwater's message of racial conservatism carried the day with the white electorate of those states, sometimes by landslide numbers (87 percent in Mississippi). Of the 507 southern counties that Goldwater carried, 233 had never voted Republican. The Goldwater effect was present even in parts of the urban ethnic North, if more muted. While Goldwater was a disaster for most Republicans, of the twenty new Republican members of Congress, nine were from the South and five were from Alabama alone. Eisenhower and Nixon had won southern states like Virginia and Tennessee. Goldwater lost those states while winning the heart of Dixie.

There is no explanation for this pattern of success other than race. Goldwater was unpopular on any number of other issues and was a weak, undisciplined, and uncharismatic candidate as well. Wild accusations that Johnson was moving toward a one-world government and unilateral disarmament fit in only too well with Goldwater's inept handling of his supporters among the John Birch Society and the Klan. Goldwater's loose comments on nuclear weapons (such as expressing a desire to drop a warhead in the men's room of the Kremlin) were political dynamite and frightened much of the electorate. Even within the Goldwater campaign, there were those who saw their candidate's weaknesses clearly. A Goldwater trip to the South was met with "idolatry" and reactions "wilder than the Beatles would have gotten," but the internal campaign report also notes that Goldwater's oratory was low-key, listless, and sometimes stumbling. Goldwater's staff also realized that his plan to sell the Tennessee Valley Authority was causing even racist whites to vote for Johnson. An editorial in the *St. Petersburg Times* cautioned southern whites not to support Goldwater even if they agreed with his position on blacks, since so many of his other positions would have grave economic consequences for the region. Goldwater's opposition to most poverty programs, the TVA, aid to education, Social Security, the Rural Electrification Administration, and farm price supports surely cost him votes throughout the nation.

Outside the Deep South, race also had not mattered as much as it appeared it might in the summer of 1964. The cities calmed down from the brief riots of July. The brutal murders of the three civil rights workers, as well as other killings in the South, helped the civil rights movement retain the moral high ground. As journalist Theodore White concluded: "Backlash . . . was a midsummer political thunderhead—frightfully black and dangerous as it approached, but then over very quickly." Had rioting continued or worsened, there is little doubt that Goldwater would have done much better in the polls. In the end, Johnson's assessment, that the election had to be about something other than civil rights for him to achieve victory, was correct. One thing many Americans agreed with Goldwater about was civil rights. In a July Harris poll, 58 percent of whites feared that blacks might "take over" their jobs, while 43 percent and 38 percent of whites feared black inroads in their neighborhoods and schools, respectively. The temptation to make civil rights the dominant issue of the campaign, as it had earlier been in the public mind, must have been present for Goldwater, particularly because he was so out of step with America on most other issues. Civil rights was one issue that seemed to move Goldwater's crowds during the campaign. When his speeches touched on it, the response was immediate. But for the most part, Goldwater avoided the issue after the convention and instead attempted to convince his audiences to go back to the economic and regulatory system of 1931. Goldwater, like Johnson, devoted only one speech entirely to civil rights, and it was far more intellectual than visceral in its approach. Goldwater's decision to foreground economic and security policy, rather than his opposition to federal intervention on behalf of civil rights, contributed to Johnson's landslide.

The results of 1964 put the Republican Party at a crossroads. For some, the Johnson victory demonstrated that civil rights was not just another issue for the party of Lincoln, but the dominant moral issue that would splinter the party if there was "even a hint of appeasement of racists." For others, the choice revolved not around the conscience of Republicans, but around the fact of black electoral power:

> If the Republicans can do nothing to include the Negroes in their vision of America, they enter any future Presidential race with more than one-ninth of the nation locked against them. Their alternatives now are clear—either to try again to divide the Negro vote with the Democrats or accept the Negro vote as permanently hostile and make strategy accepting that hostility and appealing only to whites.

In the end, the elections of 1960 and 1964 represent extreme choices by Republican campaign strategists. The pendulum that had swung quite far toward civil rights in 1960 now had swung far closer to George Wallace, although it never reached his pure antiblack malice. Neither strategy was successful in the short term, but in the ashes of the Goldwater defeat, Richard Nixon and others saw hopes for a Republican renewal, based on peeling off white voters from their Democratic allegiance. The meaning of 1964 for Republican strategists was that the open racism practiced by Goldwater's southern supporters must be decried, denied, and denounced. Yet Goldwater's strong showing in the South and in parts of the North contained the broader import of the election for Republicans. If racial politics could draw white voters into the camp of a candidate as extreme and unelectable as Barry Goldwater, then it was indeed among the most powerful forces in American politics. What might it do in the hands of a more appealing messenger, capable of subtleties undreamt of by Barry Goldwater?

★ ★ ★ ★ **4** ★ ★ ★ ★

THE BULLETS, THE BALLOTS, AND THE BACKLASH

The Charged Racial Politics of 1968

People are terrified. . . . Sooner or later the white community is going to retaliate and all the patient work will be undone. And the majority of law-abiding Negroes are going to take the heat.

RICHARD NIXON, 1968

The 1968 presidential election was among the most fast-paced, violent, and confusing elections of the century. Among the issues that contributed to the extraordinarily rapid downfall of Lyndon Johnson, the collapse of the New Deal coalition, and the resurrection of Richard M. Nixon, race was the most crucial. The bitterness of much of the black poor that had long simmered in America's inner cities boiled over in 1965, and by 1968, it seemed that every summer would be marred by death, looting, and arson. When the election ended, the winner was the man who had promised to calm down the heated passions of white and black alike, by going slow on racial progress and by cracking down on violence and crime. Nixon, the self-styled spokesman for a silent majority, won a narrow plurality in a bizarre three-way contest. George Wallace, the most successful third-party candidate since Teddy Roosevelt in 1912, demonstrated the willingness of millions of angry whites to step outside established partisan norms and vote for an often vulgar racist whose policy proposals were scarcely more than slogans. Conversely, American racial liberalism suffered its worst repudiation as

Hubert Humphrey went down to a defeat far greater than the narrow margin would suggest. The election of 1968 signaled the end of the civil rights era and the beginning of Republican dominance in presidential elections, a dominance built in large part on the successful racial tactics of the Nixon campaign.

1968: THE SETTING

The political landscape of 1968 was the most troubled since 1932. A small overseas commitment in Vietnam threatened to become America's largest conflict since World War II, with no end in sight. The relatively minor riots of 1964 had become ghastly annual outbursts of bloodshed and arson. Violent crime rates soared. Johnson, the titan of 1964, was stuck in a credibility gap. In a number of nations across the developed world, a radicalized youth movement began to challenge established authority with aggressive new street tactics. Simultaneously, the civil rights movement became a far broader challenge to white America's values. In addition, many white Americans believed that Great Society programs either were ineffectual at addressing social problems or played a role in their gestation. Finally, many white Americans were also responding to the tremendous economic, social, and political progress of African Americans during the Johnson-Kennedy years. The backlash wave predicted for 1964 finally washed ashore in 1968.

Race was far from the only issue on the nation's agenda. Nearly every social institution, including the parties, was affected by the growing controversy over Vietnam. Yet Vietnam in the end could not figure as prominently as it should have in the election, because Nixon and Humphrey differed so little on the war itself. Both opposed immediate withdrawal yet suggested they would bring peace if elected. This made race easily the most important issue of the general election, implicated whenever the candidates talked about law and order, riots, or integration. Even Vietnam was in part a racial issue.

That race would be the major issue of the election was clear to a number of farsighted observers well before 1968. A Johnson aide analyzed the Democratic setbacks in the midterm elections of 1966 and looked to 1968 with trepidation:

> The single issue which appeared to be critical . . . was that of race rioting and the pace of Negro advances in our society. This is the only issue on which we seemed to have lost in the "blue-collar" Democratic precincts. . . . This is the one problem that will not go away, and which will cause even more difficult problems in the next two years unless some dramatic and successful efforts are made.

Riots had grown to dominate public discourse every summer. The first great upheaval was the 1965 Watts riots, in which thirty-four people were killed. In 1966, there were forty-three racial disorders and riots. In 1967, several cities experienced riots; in Detroit alone forty-three perished. The pictures on white America's television screens, of blacks throwing rocks at cops, carrying goods out of stores, dancing in front of burning buildings, could not help but make a powerful political impression. That most blacks were not participating, that riots had complex social roots, and that police brutality toward blacks was a pervasive practice in most American cities were facts television did a poor job of conveying.

The riots were even more inexplicable to most whites because of the great strides the black community was making thanks to civil rights legislation and the antipoverty programs of the Great Society. Black America, while still far poorer than white America, was gaining ground. The percentage of blacks at or above the national median income doubled outside the South, while the nationwide education gap between whites and blacks was cut by 75 percent. Black political participation shot upward, and black political influence grew accordingly.

Yet while black America could be described as embarking on a second Reconstruction in economics and politics, the civil rights movement was shifting to the violent and explicitly antiwhite rhetoric of "black power." When the slogan appeared some immediately labeled it the new racism. At the march where the slogan was first used, a favorite gospel song of the movement was recast by participants, in a cruel parody of King's theology: "I'm gonna bomb when the spirit says bomb . . . cut when the spirit says cut . . . shoot when the spirit says shoot." Leaders who had initially appeared dangerous and radical to some whites, such as King and the Student Non-Violent Coordinating Committee's John Lewis, now appeared moderate when compared to new figures such as Stokely Carmichael. Carmichael seemed to approve of the riots that plagued his own community. "If a white man tries to walk over you, kill him. One match and you can retaliate. Burn, baby, burn." Carmichael, who popularized the term "black power," defined it thus: "When you talk of Black Power, you talk of building a movement that will smash everything Western civilization has created."

Many of the new black leaders rejected integration; the riots were changing white attitudes as well. According to one observer, "From the day of the Watts riots on, the term 'integration' lost its force in politics . . . three nights of burning and bloodshed had stripped it of its luster." The riots and the new black power movement changed minds about the Great Society. Democratic mayors complained to LBJ that tax money was going to groups that harassed the police and worked against the party. Sargent Shriver, the head of the Great Society's flagship agency, had to defend himself before congressional committees investigating its role in the riots. As a White House memo argued, white Americans were sick of paying for new social programs and being asked to change; they were "tired of being improved." Many believed the vast increases in social spending had produced only crime and riots. Rational discussion of crime was impossible: ". . . a white, lower-middle-class citizen of Brooklyn or Chicago . . . doesn't give a damn about statistics—he is afraid, and more significantly, his womenfolk are afraid."

The change in white opinion was best captured by the response to the Kerner Commission report on the recent urban riots. The report argued forcefully that black riots originated in white racism. It also contradicted several conservative beliefs: there had been no nationwide conspiracy behind the disturbances, black America remained mired in poverty despite progress, and more aggressive government action against poverty and injustice was necessary. White Americans did not want to hear that the fires in the city were their fault, and the president who appointed the commission was not enthusiastic about the report. Even before the Detroit riots, 85 percent of white Americans felt that civil rights was moving too fast. As the election year opened, the president faced strong political pressure to endorse tough antiriot legislation.

The riots baffled Johnson, who had worked more closely with the civil rights leadership than any previous president. Johnson had understood the struggle against Jim Crow, but northern riots and black anger amid what he perceived to be extraordinary advances in black status dismayed him. After Watts, LBJ was reported to have said, "How is it possible after all we've accomplished? . . . Is the world topsy-turvy?" By 1967, Johnson's stupefied response had become virtual paranoia; a memorandum for the president outlined a plan of secret domestic surveillance led from the White House to combat the riots and "to investigate, coordinate, and provide political information leading to the full exposure of the subversive nature of the Peacenik–Black Power coalition." Johnson viewed the riots as examples of black ingratitude. "It simply wasn't fair for a few irresponsible agitators to spoil it for me and for all the rest of the Negroes . . . spoiling all the progress I've made in these last few years."

Johnson's resentment of the riots was understandable; domestically, the riots contributed to the collapse of his presidency, just as Vietnam decimated his credibility. Domestic unrest, as much as Vietnam itself, would also shake the two-party system and help defeat Johnson's putative heir, Hubert Humphrey.

THE CANDIDATES

Richard Nixon

To understand how and why Richard Nixon shifted on race in preparation for the election, it is necessary to return to the aftermath of the 1960 election. Nixon, Eisenhower, and RNC chair Thruston

Morton met at the White House in December 1960. Eisenhower rued the political capital he had spent on civil rights because blacks "just do not give a damn." Nixon lamented his running mate's promise to put a black in the cabinet, because it "just killed us in the South," while the black vote was essentially "bought" by the Democrats. Morton agreed with Nixon, saying that his attitude toward the blacks was "the hell with them." Nixon's belief that blacks would stay Democratic and that the white South would punish outreaches to them was central to his new strategy on race. After 1960, Nixon would never again be out in front on civil rights. Unlike many Republicans, Nixon in his halfhearted run at the nomination in 1964 had not emphasized his differences with Goldwater on civil rights. Instead, he attacked "the irresponsible tactics of some of the extreme civil rights leaders." While he endorsed the 1964 Civil Rights Act, he cautioned that demonstrations for civil rights only caused more hate. In short, Nixon "dropped his long-time advocacy of civil rights." After Goldwater took the nomination, Nixon campaigned furiously for the ticket, again unlike a number of Republicans who stayed home because of Goldwater's rejection of civil rights. It was Nixon's placing party above principle that put him in the lead for the 1968 nomination, over his rivals Rockefeller and Romney.

Nixon did help move the party back toward the center on civil rights following Goldwater's crushing defeat. However, his endorsement of civil rights was bland and far weaker than the rhetoric coming from the national Democrats and other Republicans. Following the Republicans' success in the 1966 midterm elections, Nixon became a very popular candidate in the South. In 1956 and 1960, Nixon had been the subject of deep southern suspicion because of his strong endorsement of desegregation, but now some, such as columnist Joe Alsop, accused Nixon of cutting a deal with the South on civil rights. Civil rights distinguished Nixon from other presidential contenders:

> Unlike Rockefeller, Romney and Percy, he has never particularly sought, received or bragged about support from either prominent Negro leaders or large numbers of Negro voters . . . but, most important of all, Nixon has not, like the others, contented

himself with lecturing the Southern Republicans from a distance; he has been down among them in good times and bad.

A southern Republican noted that the difference between Romney and Nixon was that Romney was sincere when he endorsed civil rights, but Nixon was only speaking the words "for the Northern press." In sum, Nixon's strategy from 1964 to 1968 emulated Kennedy's careful campaign to gain southern support in 1956–60 and was equally successful. Unlike Kennedy, however, Nixon did not attempt simultaneous outreach to blacks, which made the task far easier. By the time the primary season had opened, a "new" Nixon was ready to joust with his Republican rivals complete with a new attitude toward civil rights and blacks that could be summarized as "the hell with them."

George Wallace

The prospect of a third-party run by George Wallace was much discussed after 1966. Although few saw a realistic chance of victory, a Wallace candidacy would greatly alter the dynamics of the contest. Polls showed that Wallace attracted conservative whites who would otherwise vote Republican. In the view of an LBJ aide, Wallace would take four votes from a Republican for every one he took from Johnson. Moreover, a Wallace campaign "would act as a great spur to Negro voters to register and vote Democratic." A year before the election, a poll showed Nixon defeating LBJ in a two-person race, but losing if Wallace ran.

Wallace was not the same man who had proclaimed, "Segregation today, segregation tomorrow, segregation forever!" He now attempted to separate himself from racism, arguing that he was against the federal government, not against blacks. His announcement on a Sunday talk show produced an electrifying response, including spontaneous petition drives to get him on the ballot. Wallace had some success at forging a new image; at the start of the presidential season, only a minority of Americans thought Wallace was a racist. For some Americans, the new Wallace was attractive in the post-Watts era because he put the blame for unrest not on white society, but on the black perpetrators. Wallace used the riots and the increase in crime as indictments of the Great Society. The success of his attacks would lead him to do much better in November than many had anticipated; indeed, for a time, he would threaten to come in second.

Hubert Humphrey

Humphrey had also changed since he ran as "Mr. Civil Rights" in the 1960 presidential race. In part, Humphrey was affected by his long service as Johnson's vice president. Johnson's dominating personality seemed to sap Humphrey's independence and vision. Humphrey had lost standing in the black community, particularly among the younger and more radical leadership. For much of the black community, "it was very much a matter of what have you done for me lately . . . he seemed a tired and defeated man." Instead, Humphrey became the favorite candidate of the white South, at least among those white southerners who still considered themselves national Democrats. Humphrey, the firebrand of the 1948 convention, who almost single-handedly precipitated the Dixiecrat walkout, the "anathema" to white southern Democrats in 1960, and the congressional force behind the hated 1964 Civil Rights Act, now relied on southern delegates for the nomination. His southern support grew largely because of regional antipathy for Bobby Kennedy. Humphrey even sought out civil rights venues in which he could "offset . . . the bad image of Southern support the Vice President has." Humphrey was no longer the leading integrationist in the Democratic Party.

THE TORTURED ROAD TO CHICAGO: ALL HELL BREAKS LOOSE FOR THE DEMOCRATS

As 1968 opened, the smart money would have bet that Johnson would easily be the Democratic nominee. A number of antiwar liberals had nonetheless been looking for a challenger to run against Johnson in the Democratic primaries. Eventually, Minnesota senator Eugene McCarthy agreed to run, despite the odds. McCarthy then shocked the establishment by almost defeating Johnson in New Hampshire. Johnson's Pyrrhic victory against an underfunded challenger led Robert Kennedy, who had been pondering the move for months, to enter the race.

The Bobby Kennedy who announced his candidacy in March of 1968 was far more progressive on race than the man who had helped secure the South for his brother in the late 1950s. As attorney general, Kennedy initially believed that southern segregation would eventually wither away without much effort and considered black demonstrators to be nuisances who caused unnecessary problems for the administration. However, when the administration finally allied itself firmly with the civil rights movement, RFK became reviled in the white South. After 1964, as a senator, Kennedy was one of the leading spokesmen for black progress. Improbably, Kennedy was also one of the only liberal Democrats who had appeal among antiblack, blue-collar whites. Some surveys found many blue-collar Democrats who favored both Wallace and Kennedy.

Two weeks later, LBJ withdrew from the presidential race. In his memoirs, Johnson mentions the upheaval and riots in the cities as one of his primary reasons for leaving the race. Now the race came down to RFK, McCarthy, and Humphrey. Racial politics figured prominently in this three-way contest, because of the increasingly large role blacks played in the party. McCarthy had little support in the black community, although his voting record on race was quite strong. Humphrey had much of the black leadership behind him because of his long service to the cause. Kennedy, however, had the hearts of the black community. In most homes in Watts, there were no pictures of black radicals like Malcolm X or Ron Karenga, but there were pictures of Jack Kennedy. There were few pictures of McCarthy or Humphrey. So powerful was the connection between African Americans and Kennedy that many journalists were condescending in their coverage of the response a visit by Kennedy produced:

... he was the Liberator, come to free the oppressed.... The blacks knew it; and they clotted as they waited, old and young, Uncle Toms and Aunt Jemimas, Black Nationalists, cold-eyed extremists, solid black workingmen and their families. They would boil up like a volcanic cone about Kennedy's car, shouting,

"Bobby, Bobby, please! Oh Bobby, Bobby," in a sighing, near sexual orgy of exultation.

Even McCarthy conceded that 90 percent of blacks would vote for RFK.

The fulcrum around which the racial politics in the Democratic primaries would turn was Martin Luther King Jr. By 1968, King was the last link between mainline civil rights groups such as the NAACP and the Urban League and the young radicals. King had broken with Johnson over the war in August 1967, and rumors of a third-party candidacy by King on a peace and justice ticket had frightened Democrats for more than a year. If King and Wallace both ran, any Democrat would face the extraordinary challenge of running against two putative Democrats and one Republican. King claimed not to be interested in running but did pledge his support to a third-party candidate if no candidate opposed the war.

King's critique of American society was becoming increasingly radical and economic in focus. King launched a major initiative in 1967 involving a march on Washington by the impoverished. The idea disturbed Johnson greatly, as his keen political sense told him that now was not the time to push Congress in this fashion. Five days after Johnson withdrew from the race, King was assassinated in Memphis. As the news flashed across the country, the expectation was of massive unrest and rioting. Against the advice of many associates, who feared for his safety, Kennedy spoke in Indianapolis to an integrated crowd that had not yet heard about King's death.* He called on blacks not to pursue violence in their bitterness and despair. Kennedy was one of the few white politicians who could have spoken in the inner city at that moment of great tension.

In the aftermath of King's death, riots erupted in over a hundred cities. Kennedy contemplated a national address but rejected it because "[t]he rednecks would say, look at that damn nigger-lover, and the liberals would say, he'll exploit anything." At King's Atlanta funeral,

---

* Kennedy's personal courage in so speaking should not be forgotten. The police chief refused him an escort, so dangerous did he consider entering that neighborhood on the eve of King's death.

Bobby Kennedy was anointed the most popular political figure in the African American community. As a crowd of America's leading politicians and celebrities made the long march from church to grave, Kennedy was applauded more than anyone else by the largely black crowd. Yet much of white America was outraged at the greatest civil unrest since 1865. Troops had to be deployed in Washington, D.C., to protect the Capitol, the White House, and the monuments. The days of blood and fire in April would reverberate all the way to the November election, making law and order uppermost in many voters' minds.

Now the Indiana primary loomed as the first true contest between McCarthy and Kennedy. Indiana's political culture, particularly in the southern counties, was similar to that of a southern border state, and it had been a stronghold for the Klan in the twenties and thirties. Moreover, Gary, Indiana, was now the scene of bitter racial conflict. Some reporters traveling with Kennedy accused RFK of hedging his civil rights stances to assuage the white backlash. Still, it failed to change Kennedy's image as the black man's best friend; he was still heckled as a "coon-catcher" in several towns. Kennedy complained bitterly of the white attitude toward him and how it forced him to talk about law and order:

> So far in Indiana they seem to want to see me as a member of the black race—I don't think I can win if that happens. If it keeps up, I'm lost. . . . These people never ask me . . . "What can we do for the Negro?" They always ask: "What are you going to do about the violence?"

Kennedy won in Indiana, in part because of tremendous support among blacks. When he was subsequently defeated by McCarthy in Oregon's primary, he joked with an aide that they could have won if they had airlifted a black ghetto into Oregon, complete with soul food and rats.

During the brief contest with McCarthy prior to Kennedy's assassination, charges of antiblack activities were made against both candidates. Ads appeared in black newspapers, accusing McCarthy of voting against civil rights during his years in the Senate. These ludicrous ads were linked to the Kennedy campaign. McCarthy was also hit for wanting too much integration. During a debate in California, RFK accused McCarthy of planning to move thousands of blacks into Orange County, a conservative white district, in the name of integrated housing. The appeal to white racial animus was clear and effective. On the other side, McCarthy forces seized on charges that RFK had endorsed the FBI's bugging campaign against King, charges that Kennedy did not completely deny. McCarthy's forces even released a clumsy radio ad on black stations: "I used to be for Robert Kennedy, but then I learned about how he bugged my brother Martin Luther King's phone," said a black voice. These charges did not shake African American support for Kennedy, and the attacks on McCarthy's civil rights record were probably unnecessary overkill. The black vote was Kennedy's, and it was crucial to his success.

In the midst of the Democratic primary season, King's Poor People's Campaign (PPC) arrived in Washington. The campaign was a failure almost from its first moment. Even before King's death, such figures as Bayard Rustin had warned that the plan was vague, was unlikely to succeed, and could fuel a white backlash. The administration pondered whether to endorse, oppose, or be neutral toward the PPC. The initial response was to attempt to convince Ralph Abernathy, King's titular heir, that they were already working hard to meet the demands of the march leaders. Unconvinced by the administration's arguments, the campaigners settled into "Resurrection City," an encampment on the national Mall, and waited for Congress to deliver sweeping new legislation. At its peak, the PPC had about 2,600 participants living in huts, but the population fluctuated and control became difficult. Almost immediately, the leaders fought among themselves over issues large and small.* Rapes, robberies, and unhygienic conditions were reported. In the midst of the turmoil, Humphrey visited Resurrection City, with mixed results. He attempted to play the role of peacemaker, as he had in the MFDP seating dispute at the 1964 convention. Yet nothing could resolve the game of political chicken the administration was playing with Abernathy. To the extent that the campaign's

---

* Abernathy had particular trouble with a young Jesse Jackson, already viewed negatively by many King lieutenants for his opportunistic response to King's death.

demands were specific, they were politically impossible. Abernathy needed victory or violence, and the White House refused to send in troops until the campaign's own leaders had had enough of the anarchy of their Resurrection City. The PPC symbolized the impotence of liberalism in the face of black demands and also discredited the civil rights movement, which had moved from the triumph of 1963–65, to the tragedy of King's assassination, to the farce of Resurrection City, as poorly planned as it was politically inept. The hopes of a black-white coalition of goodwill and trust were further damaged by the shocking assassination of Bobby Kennedy, who had brought together blacks and blue-collar whites in his all-too-brief campaign. Weeks after the collapse of the PPC and Kennedy's killing, the Democrats limped into Chicago for their fateful convention, where Humphrey was expected to win easily.

The odds of a Humphrey nomination were strong even prior to RFK's assassination. Humphrey was the preferred candidate of many big-city bosses and southern party regulars. Humphrey, asked to explain his burgeoning popularity below the Mason-Dixon line, said, "We have all changed. I am a little older, and I hope not quite as intent as I have been. . . ." Despite his newfound southern popularity, Humphrey chose Ed Muskie of Maine as his running mate, the first time a Democratic ticket had been without a southerner or a border state native since 1940. Minnesota's Humphrey could not have tilted the ticket more to the North unless he had picked an Alaskan.

Yet Humphrey's choice of running mate, acceptance speech, and platform were all minor stories as the world's attention was riveted to street battles between protesters and Mayor Daley's hardened cops. The catastrophe of the 1968 Chicago convention for the Democratic Party has been told many times, and it certainly contributed greatly to Humphrey's defeat. For the most part, it was a nonracial confrontation between white youth and white police. The disaster in Chicago did, however, convey the message that the Democratic Party had no idea how to achieve domestic tranquillity and further highlighted the issue of law and order, which was indelibly stained with the politics of race. The bloodshed in Chicago could not help but raise the hopes of both Wallace and Nixon. In eight short months, the Democratic Party had almost destroyed itself, with the help of assassins, the Vietcong, and the simmering conflict over race in America.

THE REPUBLICANS: PARTISAN TRANQUILLITY

The greatest obstacle that Nixon had to conquer to gain the nomination was his "loser" image. Aided by the weakness of other candidates as well as state-of-the-art television ads, Nixon ably erased this image and won the nomination. Nixon also adroitly positioned himself on racial issues in the primaries. On his right, California governor Ronald Reagan was seen as the only Goldwaterite figure retaining popularity in the party. Reagan had taken a strong stance against civil disorder and most civil rights laws. According to a Nixon campaign memo:

> Reagan's strength derives from personal charisma, glamor, but primarily the ideological fervor of the Right and the emotional distress of those who fear or resent the Negro, and who expect Reagan somehow to keep him "in his place" or at least to echo their own anger and frustration.

Reagan's backlash appeal was so apparent that Reagan was seen as the only candidate "who could possibly neutralize Wallace." As early as 1967, Nixon was warned of the threat Reagan posed to his southern delegates, because Nixon's southern support was built on antipathy toward more liberal Republicans, whereas Reagan could command true passion from white southerners.

On Nixon's left on the racial issue were Rockefeller and Michigan governor George Romney. Romney had received over 30 percent of the Michigan black vote in 1966 and had split with Goldwater in 1964 largely over civil rights. Rockefeller, a longtime leader on civil rights, had an ease with blacks that was compared with that of Bobby Kennedy. But the black flight from the party made appeals to civil rights in the primaries a strategic dead end. Moreover, white southerners had become powerful in the GOP for the first time since the carpetbaggers and scalawags of Reconstruction.

In Oregon's primary, Nixon first hit hard on law and order, an issue that would become crucial to his general election campaign. Law and order had played a small part in Nixon's speeches up until that point, although it was one of his most reliable applause lines when working-class whites were present. Nixon, who wounded Reagan's chances severely by winning Oregon, immediately flew to Atlanta to meet with southern Republicans. Nixon promised to appoint conservatives to the federal judiciary, to oppose busing, and to reinterpret "all deliberate speed" in school integration. He also pledged to campaign heavily in the South and to include southerners in government. With the assistance of Senator Strom Thurmond, Nixon was able to hold the South against Reagan. Nixon had now all but secured the nomination.

As the Wallace candidacy became ever more certain, the strategic possibilities for Nixon in a general election became complex. He could tack left again, by adopting a conciliatory attitude toward civil rights, and compete for the votes of blacks and liberal whites. Living in John Lindsay's New York City, Nixon had seen firsthand that a Republican could succeed with blacks if he strongly endorsed civil rights. Some saw in Wallace the potential for cleansing the Republican Party of the segregationists and racial conservatives who had joined the party in 1964. Alternatively, Nixon could compete with Wallace for backlash votes in an attempt to "neutralize" the Wallace vote. Or, Nixon could seek to position himself in the middle on civil rights, between Wallace and the Democrats.

At the convention, Nixon's strategic choice became clear in his outreach to the South and his selection of a running mate. Nixon wooed the South in a closed caucus with delegates from six southern states, attacking busing, national intervention on open housing, and pressure on the South generally. Nixon's criticism of legislation targeted at the South was interpreted as opposition to the 1965 Voting Rights Act. When Nixon selected Maryland governor Spiro Agnew as his running mate, it was immediately seen as a gesture to the backlash. The GOP had not put a border stater or southerner on the ticket since Andrew Johnson in 1864. Agnew, who had a moderate record on most racial issues, such as school integration and open housing, had risen to national prominence with his forceful response to rioting in Maryland. In addition to hailing from south of the Mason-Dixon line, Agnew was the first Greek American nominated by a major party for national office. As such, Agnew was a backlash switch-hitter; he could be expected to attract the two main components of the movement, urban northern ethnics and white southerners. Jackie Robinson, among many others, charged that Agnew was an obvious deal with the South. Reagan praised Nixon's choice, saying: "That will be acceptable to the South. . . . [Agnew] has had a good record of dealing firmly with rioters." Agnew was also expected to appeal to Wallace voters. The contrast with 1960 is telling; in running with Agnew and not Lodge, Nixon moved the axis of his ticket six hundred miles to the South and many degrees more conservative on race. Also, when Agnew attracted the attention of the press, it was not a "Negro in the Cabinet" error as with Lodge, but rather racial jokes and slurs on slums. Such errors may have served Nixon's ends only too well.

Nixon's glide to the nomination was the exact opposite of Humphrey's torturous trek. Nixon outsmarted or co-opted all likely opponents and crafted a ticket well designed for the unusual three-way competition. The platform was also tactically effective, situated between Wallace's extremism and Humphrey's call for new legislative action. Most important, the partisan tranquillity of Nixon's victory conveyed the message that Nixon was a calming influence. Even when rioting erupted in Miami during the convention, it did more to emphasize the failure of Great Society programs than to discredit the Republicans. Every rock thrown, every building set ablaze, every riot and every street crime, helped Nixon—and Wallace.

THE GENERAL ELECTION: MANEUVERING AROUND WALLACE

Wallace's standing in the polls had not diminished as the year went on, as most had predicted it would. Instead, Wallace's support rose following RFK's assassination and then again following the Chicago debacle. In April, his support was 9 percent, rising to 14 percent in May, 16 percent following RFK's assassination, and hitting just over 20 percent after Chicago. The bloodshed and violence in Chicago only served to convince more white Americans that the time had come for a tough leader. When he spoke to a huge crowd in Illinois, signs were handed out by his campaign that read "Wallace, Daley, and the police." Wallace also used urban riots to recast his role in the fight against civil rights, by comparing the disorder caused by the marchers for freedom in Selma to the rioters of 1968, labeling both kinds of protesters "scum of the earth." He also likened civil rights demonstrators to common street criminals. For Wallace, a mugging in New York was similar to a march for voting rights in Alabama. "There has been more violence in one subway in New York City in one night than there has been in the entire state of Alabama or Mississippi in a year. But they don't talk about sending troops to the subways."

Much of the Wallace rhetoric on crime and disorder was nothing more than racist code words. Nonetheless, he did attempt to refine his image as a racist. Asked on camera to defend his 1962 pledge to uphold segregation forever, Wallace tried to hide behind states' rights, saying that he had advocated segregation as best only for Alabama. He also attacked the hypocrisy of those in Congress who advocated integration for others and sent their own children to private schools outside of D.C., an appeal designed to win over working-class whites who distrusted liberal elites. Wallace was masterful at appearing to be a simple Jacksonian figure, homespun and honest. Wallace also cleverly used the rhetoric of black radicals as a response to the charge that he was a racist: "Some militants have charged every white person in the country with discrimination. . . . Even President Johnson has been called a racist." If every white was a racist, the distinction between a Johnson and a Wallace could be obfuscated.

Wallace's followers were much less subtle in their appeals to race, which allowed Wallace to whip up fervor among his hard-core racist supporters without hurting his national image. A Wallace supporter attacked "race-mixing bureaucrats" and made blunt appeals to the white race to support Wallace. Another supporter, in a televised appeal, raised the specter of integrated hospital rooms for dying loved ones.

Still, the brutal rhetoric of divisive violence appeared in Wallace's own speeches with regularity. "We don't have riots in Alabama. . . . They start a riot down there, first one of 'em to pick up a brick gets a bullet in the brain, that's all. And then you walk over to the next one and say, 'All right, pick up a brick. We just want to see you pick up one of them bricks, now!' " Even Wallace's odious record on civil rights helped him woo votes in the North. The repression visited upon peaceful demonstrators by Alabama's police had shocked most of the nation, but some northern whites saw it as appealing. As early as 1965, an antiblack crowd in Chicago had gleefully sung, "I wish I was an Alabama trooper . . . so I could shoot the niggers legally." Wallace's reputation as a racist helped him with a number of voters, and it was so solidly fixed that the "new" Wallace did not need to be as explicitly racist to get those votes. He could thus more easily reach out to less extreme whites who were merely disturbed by the ongoing unrest.

The expanding Wallace appeal was to those whites who felt that civil rights had moved too fast. In almost every speech, Wallace said that the message of the riots was that civil rights legislation didn't work:

> We have tried every other solution. The previous administrations have passed every civil rights bill known to man . . . and the more bills they passed . . . the more activity we had in the streets. So we have spent billions of dollars in the poverty program to give people money and you still have street mobs.

So successful was Wallace's message that in September, he would claim to have replaced Humphrey as Nixon's major opponent.

RUNNING FOR NATIONAL SHERIFF

Wallace's rhetoric was gasoline on the fires in America's cities and forced candidates to address civil unrest. Even in his absence, however, it would have been near the top of the agenda. LBJ's pollster believed it would be the dominant issue of the election as early as 1967. By 1968, the candidates competed to be more pro-police. Of course, Wallace set the bar high: "American policemen are the thin line between anarchy and the people on the street." Comments like "There's nothing wrong with this country that we couldn't cure by turning it over to the police for a couple of years" help explain Wallace's thunderous response when he was invited to keynote a national police convention.

Humphrey attempted to address crime and riots, but saddled with Chicago, he had a difficult time of it. Over and over, he would refer to his experience fighting the Mob as mayor of Minneapolis in the forties, an unpersuasive analogy since few could confuse organized crime rackets with street riots. Humphrey also made a terrible strategic error in calling for more police training, because it suggested that the police bore some responsibility for the rioting. In speeches, he referred to police officers with "an eighth-grade education, many times little or no knowledge at all of constitutional law, statutory law, little or no training or experience in modern police methods. . . ." Humphrey argued that more police training would help prevent riots, perhaps believing that police would be touched by his promise to increase their funding while ignoring his condescension. However accurate a diagnosis of the origin of race riots, this was not a message that helped Humphrey win votes among whites concerned about law and order.

Humphrey gave the opposition plenty of ammunition. Commenting on the summers of rioting, Humphrey said:

> People will not live like animals. I'd hate to be stuck on a fourth floor of a tenement with rats nibbling on the kids' toes—and they do—with garbage uncollected—and it is—with the streets filthy, with no swimming pools, with little or no recreation. If I were living in the slums I think you'd have had a little more trouble than you've had already because I've got enough spark left in me to lead a mighty good revolt under those conditions. . . . I don't want to be misunderstood. I believe in law observance. I not only deplore violence, I say it cannot be condoned.

Agnew gleefully exploited this statement, after slicing off the introduction and the conclusion, leaving only Humphrey's apparent endorsement of rioting as justified and his personal pledge to lead a riot. Even taken in context, it was not a politically deft statement, since those who were prone to search for deeper causes of ghetto riots were probably already with Humphrey. Humphrey tried to use the recently passed "Safe Streets Act of 1968" to show he was tough on law and order, but compared to the red-meat slogans of Agnew and Wallace, his response was tepid and often backfired. Humphrey's lectures on federalism and how crime was not really a presidential responsibility were similarly ineffective. Humphrey protested that he was running for president, not sheriff, but it seemed that the country was looking for both.

By contrast, Nixon's use of law and order was technically brilliant. His running mate, Agnew, was dispatched around the country to out-Wallace Wallace. "You've seen one slum, you've seen them all," was Agnew's laconic dismissal of the need to campaign in ghettos. Widely criticized in the press, the statement aided the effort to woo white backlashers. Nixon himself relied on television, crafting an ad campaign that raised the issue of crime and riots and seemed to offer soothing hope that Nixon would solve the crisis. The most memorable Nixon ad featured a middle-aged white woman walking alone down a dark urban street, while the announcer recited bleak statistics on the frequency of violent crime. This ad, like others with a law-and-order theme, was targeted at areas that had suffered riots. None were explicitly racial, but they were designed to appeal to white fears. While in the studio, Nixon praised one of his law-and-order ads, because "this hits it right on the nose . . . it's all about law and order and the damn Negro–Puerto Rican groups out there." Nixon adviser Roger Ailes expressed his desire to have a "good, mean, Wallaceite cab driver" in a staged appearance with Nixon. "Wouldn't that be great? Some guy to sit there and say, 'Awright, mac, what about these niggers?'"

The strategic environment of the Wallace candidacy gave Nixon a tremendous advantage on law and order, the dominant domestic issue. With Wallace on his right, Nixon would automatically look moderate. Humphrey was constrained on law and order, because for many blacks and white liberals, even the phrase "law and order" was anathema. Thus, in a year in which the two surest applause lines before almost every audience were calling for peace in Vietnam and law and order at home, Humphrey had to speak carefully and complexly on both. A voter concerned about law and order had three choices: a candidate who sympathized with rioters because there weren't enough swimming pools in the inner city, an extremist candidate who wanted to put a bullet in the brain of every rioter, and a soothing candidate who promised tough but measured action. The role law and order played in Nixon's victory cannot be underestimated.

APPEALING TO THE NEWLY ENFRANCHISED

As in 1960 and 1964, the flip side to appealing to racially conservative whites was the effect that such campaigning would have on the black vote. Thanks to the Voting Rights Act, more blacks were registered than at any time in history. Yet Nixon, who in 1957 had been captivated by King's promise of two million black votes, would not even begin to compete for the much larger black vote of 1968. Nixon adviser Pat Buchanan did at one time suggest outreach to blacks. "These people are not locked in to LBJ; they are not particularly hostile." But by the summer of 1968, Nixon's camp had decided that the black community, while a "tempting target," was not where they would focus their efforts. Nixon's outreach to the white backlash ended any chance of black support. The black community suspected Nixon because of his closeness to Strom Thurmond, his opposition to more urban spending, and the fear that he had made a secret commitment against integration. One of the largest black newspapers did endorse Nixon, but the event was so unusual, it was treated as a "man bites dog" feature. The numerous black endorsements of Nixon in 1960 had become scarce, and even his former supporter Jackie Robinson now proclaimed that he would support any Democrat over Nixon, whom he now accused of racism. Nixon and his running mate almost never appeared in black areas or before black groups. The decision to avoid black audiences was probably wise. Nixon's welfare policy, influenced by Daniel Moynihan's controversial study of the pathology of the black family, would have received a poor reception from most black audiences. All Nixon could offer a black audience was his advo-cacy of black capitalism, law and order, and cutting back on social programs. Nixon was also unlikely to win black votes when he implied that it would be damaging to white children to be in the same class-room with black students who were several grades behind them. The negative response of the black community to Nixon was broad and if not monolithic, certainly overwhelming. A camera crew sent to Harlem to get footage of "good Negroes" for a Nixon ad titled "Black Capitalism" was advised to leave for their own safety. There were more blacks for Nixon than there were for Wallace, but not by much.

Surprisingly, it was Humphrey who suffered the most abuse from black audiences. In Watts, demonstrators shouted, "Honky go home!" and interrupted Humphrey several times, an incident covered widely by the media. When Humphrey met with a number of black leaders in Detroit, Congressman John Conyers told Humphrey bluntly, "You're behind the times." Humphrey, who had been too far ahead of Jack Kennedy on civil rights in 1960, had lost his radical position to Bobby Kennedy and others. Humphrey also faced Wallace heck-lers when he appeared in the South and radical student protesters when he appeared in the North. Rather than positioning Humphrey in the sane center, being viciously attacked by all sides simply con-vinced many that Humphrey could not handle law and order. In Boston, Humphrey was even spit on.

Humphrey was in part responsible for his treatment. In refusing to compete in the primaries directly, he allied himself with the party bosses and made his nomination partially dependent on southern dele-gations previously pledged to Johnson. Also, Humphrey had put his arm around Georgia's ax-wielding racist governor, Lester Maddox, in pursuit of party unity, which certainly did not do much for his image in the black community. It is difficult to imagine Bobby Kennedy's arm around a racial demagogue like Maddox, or even Maddox allow-ing his shoulder to be so used. Such appearances also made Hum-phrey's criticism of Nixon's closeness to Strom Thurmond ring hollow, although there surely was a huge difference between a photo oppor-tunity with Maddox and the close coordination that the Nixon cam-paign had with Thurmond on policy and strategy. In the end, most blacks were firmly in the Humphrey camp, and many had a great deal of affection for Humphrey's record and his almost instinctual urge for a more just society. However, the passion that Kennedy had evoked was not present, and Humphrey's image as a unifier was surely hurt by the negative reaction in Watts and elsewhere.

ENDGAME: HUMPHREY'S SURGE, WALLACE'S FREE FALL, AND NIXON'S TIMING

In the closing month of the campaign, Humphrey rose rapidly in the polls, cutting Nixon's lead significantly. A partial break with Johnson on Vietnam was a key factor in Humphrey's rise, but a strategic decision to attack Wallace also played a part. Wallace had hurt the Democratic coalition deeply in the North by pulling many union members away from the party. This was apparent early in the campaign, when Humphrey had to skip the traditional Labor Day parade in Detroit because of doubts he would draw a respectable crowd. In a later visit to Michigan, Humphrey saw many workers wearing Wallace hats. Humphrey's staff initially felt that Wallace hurt Nixon and argued that any attempt to decrease Wallace strength would only aid Nixon. Humphrey was advised, therefore, not to attack Wallace, but to treat him as "beneath contempt." Yet as the campaign wore on, a different strategy was chosen, because, as an internal memo put it, "those 1.1 million new union votes are reason enough to begin using the bare knuckles now." Humphrey's decision to go after Wallace in the closing weeks may also have been influenced by an extraordinary article that Muriel Humphrey brought to her husband's attention. Wallace's burgeoning popularity had even reached Manhattan, where Wallace spoke to a massive crowd:

> It is as if . . . George Wallace had been awakened by a white, blinding vision: they all hate black people. . . . They're all afraid. . . . They're all Southern! The whole United States is Southern!

In his speech, Wallace shouted:

> People are always talking about George Wallace, he just appeals to the rednecks . . . and the peckerwoods, and the crackers, and

the woolhats . . . well, there are a lot of us rednecks in this country, and they don't all live in the South!

Humphrey began to chip away at Wallace's northern redneck support. The unions launched a massive voter outreach campaign, conveying the message that Wallace was antiunion and a vote for Wallace would help elect Nixon. Humphrey may have had no choice but to go on the attack; in early October, *The New York Times* suggested that Wallace could get twice as many electoral votes as Humphrey and take more than fifteen million votes.

Just as Humphrey was taking the gloves off, Nixon also launched an attack on Wallace. His forbearance up until this point was based on the belief that Wallace support would surely fade as election day neared. Also, the Nixon campaign's understanding of Wallace's effect on the race was quite sophisticated. The Republicans knew that in the North, Humphrey was, by narrow margins, the second choice of Wallace voters, whereas in the South, 80 percent of Wallace voters preferred Nixon to Humphrey. In October, Nixon launched a coordinated southern assault on Wallace. Nixon endorsed "freedom of choice," an "integration" policy favored by white southerners because it preserved segregated schools. Humphrey then attacked freedom of choice, and within days, Republican ads appeared on southern radio stations, pointing out the difference. The most important player in Nixon's assault on Wallace in the South was Thurmond. In the closing weeks of the campaign, he aggressively sought to prove that Nixon was as good a candidate as the South could get. Thurmond, along with Wallace perhaps the most famous segregationist in the nation, was uniquely qualified to vouch for Nixon. Ads arguing that a vote for Wallace would elect Humphrey, the true integrationist, appeared in the South in the last two weeks.

Speaking in the North, Nixon also attacked Wallace by name. Yet there was a crucial difference: Humphrey attacked Wallace's racism, Nixon attacked his style. Wallace had memorably promised to run over any protesters who tried to lie down in front of the president's car, and it was this hotheaded comment that Nixon attacked. Later, given the explicit opportunity to comment on Humphrey's "apostle of hate and racism" judgment of Wallace, Nixon returned fire at the idea that someone might find racism in Wallace. "I'm not going to engage in questioning the motive, the intentions of Governor Wallace. . . ." For Nixon, apparently, Wallace was not a racist, but just uncouth, unpresidential, and most important, unlikely to deliver domestic tranquillity. In his attacks on Wallace north and south, Nixon never disavowed integration as a goal, nor did he forswear his commitment to racial equality. He was not, however, above carefully calibrating his stance on racial issues and his rhetoric on law and order to appeal to racially conservative whites. He focused his southern challenge to Wallace in the peripheral South (Florida, North Carolina, Tennessee, Virginia) and border states, working to convince whites that a vote for Wallace was in fact a vote for integration in the person of Humphrey. Wallace's support began to drop in September and October. Both Humphrey's assault on Wallace as a racist and Nixon's attack on him as a disruptive force seemed to have an effect. The percentage of Americans who felt that Wallace was a racist went from 40 percent to 67 percent, and the percentage who believed that Wallace would bring law and order went from 53 percent to 21 percent by October.

Nixon's reluctance to attack Wallace as a racist, as well as his clever use of code words, provoked a response from Humphrey. Two weeks before the election, Humphrey lashed out at Nixon on race: "I think that Mr. Nixon has failed to show the courage that he ought to on the race issue. . . . I believe that Mr. Nixon wants to slow down the pace, tread water on this delicate issue." Considering that most white Americans felt that civil rights was moving too fast, accusing Nixon of wanting to "slow down the pace" or "tread water" on race was practically campaigning for him. Accusing Nixon of insincerity on race may also have backfired; white southerners in particular hoped he was being insincere when he blandly endorsed integration. When the candidates entered the final stretch, the clearest distinction to be drawn between them was on the race issue.

CONCLUSION: NIXON'S MANDATE FOR STASIS ON RACE

On election day, Nixon defeated a surging Humphrey, while Wallace took five states of the Deep South. The narrow plurality victory of Richard Nixon masked a striking mandate on race. The contest had been about race; with none of the candidates offering America a clear choice on Vietnam, the major issues the election revolved around were race and law and order. In voting for Nixon, white America expressed a belief that too much change had happened too fast. They voted for the candidate whom they judged best able to bring back a more tranquil America. The presence of Wallace served to disguise the depth of the divide between blacks and whites in the ballot box. If Richard Nixon did, as Humphrey accused, pander to the worst racism in the white American soul, then almost 60 percent of the electorate (and an even greater majority of whites) had voted for either a racial panderer or a racist. The Kerner Commission had written that America was becoming two nations, one black, one white, and the meaning of the election of 1968 was that this had important electoral consequences. For example, in 1960, if Nixon had been able to win just 40 percent of the black vote, instead of 32 percent, he would have beaten Kennedy decisively. Eight years later, Nixon was able to write off all but the smallest fraction of black support (he received at best 12 percent) and win the White House. That a candidate could, in a three-way race, and in the face of extraordinary expansion in black suffrage, surrender the black vote and win, validated the Republican strategy of "the hell with them." For the rest of the century, Republicans would not reach out to blacks and would never lose the white vote to the Democrats. Another disturbing pattern emerges when the three elections of the 1960s are looked at together. For a variety of reasons, the elections of 1960 and 1964 were not ones in which race was the dominant issue. The Republicans' sole victory came when race was at the top of the nation's agenda, in one of the most racially charged and polarized elections in modern U.S. history.

The bloodshed in the cities for the four summers prior to the election and the rioting at the Democratic convention convinced many voters that liberalism was bankrupt. The Great Society, while unquestionably contributing to black economic and social progress, had coincided with the worst domestic unrest in a hundred years. The deaths of King and Kennedy contributed to Nixon's victory, not merely in the removal of the competition of Kennedy and the leadership of King, but also in the destabilizing effect their assassinations had on the average American. If a Nobel Peace Prize winner and the heir apparent to a political dynasty could both be murdered within weeks of each other, perhaps the time had come for a law-and-order president to put the nation to rights again. Had Kennedy chosen not to walk through that California hotel kitchen and thus avoided Sirhan Sirhan, or if James Earl Ray had missed King, an entirely different election would have taken place. Yet with both King and Kennedy dead, Nixon won an electoral mandate to slow down civil rights and crack down on violence.

The election of 1968 also showed how race and the war had destroyed the Democratic coalition. Wallace, a former Democrat, had been much closer to the Republican rhetoric on race, federalism, crime, and the war. While his campaign did still contain elements of economic populism, the Wallace movement, funded in part by far right conservatives, was an example of what journalist William Grieder calls "rancid populism." It was a populism that had attracted support among whites in the North and the South. Of Wallace's nearly ten million votes, more than 40 percent were cast by nonsoutherners. In his acceptance speech, Nixon spoke of his desire to reunify the country. His political priority, however, over the next four years would be to unify his plurality support with the Wallace voters. If the Republican Party could bring the Wallace voters into their coalition, they would have a virtual lock on the White House. Moreover, such a coalition would have no need of black support.

★ ★ ★ ★ **5** ★ ★ ★ ★

NIXON BUSES TO VICTORY
The Unnecessary Racial Politics of 1972

> . . . we must realize that old political loyalties have been dissolved by the racial sit-
> uation and that we have an unprecedented opportunity to garner votes in large
> blocks. To capitalize on this opportunity we need a carefully conceived "master
> plan" for the Administration to implement.
>
> HARRY DENT TO PRESIDENT NIXON, OCTOBER 13, 1969

Richard Nixon, elected by a marginal plurality in 1968, would four years later receive an electoral mandate greater than that of any previous Republican president. He could not have done so without the implementation of Dent's "master plan" to exploit the racial tensions that continued to simmer during Nixon's first term. In 1968, Nixon had promised the nation that he would bring domestic order and slow down the march of civil rights. In large part he delivered on those promises, consolidating previous civil rights gains while forestalling new initiatives. The key domestic issue of 1972, busing, was one of those new initiatives. The brief period in which busing dominated American politics coincided almost exactly with Nixon's reelection drive. Busing would further stress the Democratic coalition and further alienate blue-collar whites from their ancestral partisan ties. While Nixon's busing position continued his policy of "stasis" on race, for the Democrats, change was in the air. The Democratic Party for the first time unequivocally associated itself with the idea of a color-conscious reordering of society, of which busing was only the earliest example. The Republican attacks on busing and quotas in 1972 provided the archetype for the next thirty years of partisan conflict on race. In 1972, the Republicans became the color-blind party, while the Democrats were forced to defend busing, affirmative action, set-asides, and hiring quotas. Busing was portrayed as the leading edge of a wave of color-conscious policies in which whites would perpetually lose. The Democratic Party would struggle with the legacy of 1972 for decades to come.

1972: THE SETTING

The America of 1972 was far more peaceful than it had been four years before. The annual inner-city upheavals that characterized the summers of 1964–68 had subsided. Nixon, who had promised to bring law and order to America, would consistently claim credit for the sudden downturn in rioting. In foreign affairs, the Nixon record by 1972 was impressive. The election may have been decided when Nixon broke with twenty years of China policy and shook hands with Mao in February of 1972. While the Vietnam War still went on, the number of U.S. casualties had dropped precipitously. The economy, while not booming, was reasonably healthy.

Desegregation was proceeding, if fitfully, in the South. Nixon would later take credit for the advances in integration achieved under his administration, and the facts are impressive. In 1968, 68 percent of black children in the South attended all-black schools; six years later, only 8 percent did. The Nixon record in other civil rights fields, such as contracting and voting rights prosecutions, was less impressive, but still substantial. Even critics of Nixon acknowledge that his administration's record on race was, in hindsight, fairly progressive. Yet early on in his administration, Nixon made a conscious decision to convince America that he was not pressing hard on civil rights. Nixon directed his aide with the greatest knowledge of the South, Harry Dent, to circulate to southerners a *New York Times* article critical of the administration's civil rights policy. Nixon publicized the opposition of black groups like the NAACP in order to shore up his image with racially conservative whites. Ruling as a racial moderate, he often advertised himself as a racial conservative.

Black political and economic power was growing in the sixties and early seventies. Young black family income approached that of comparable whites, and the number of blacks in college had doubled while black illiteracy had been cut in half. In the North and the South, blacks were voting in record numbers, and blacks were winning elections in every region. In 1968, twenty-nine mayors were blacks; in 1972, there were eighty-six. By 1972, twelve blacks sat in Congress, far fewer than their proportion of the population, but a significant improvement over the pre–Voting Rights Act years. The black vote was typically Democratic, although there were still important black Republicans, such as Senator Ed Brooke of Massachusetts.

The big question mark was George Wallace. If he made another third-party run in 1972, the election could be very close. In late 1971, polls suggested that Wallace might have an issue on which to run. When asked what the nation's problems were, most Americans chose the Vietnam War, the national budget, or crime in the streets. But when asked what problem affected them most, more Americans chose busing than any other issue. The issue of busing lurked in the background of American politics until January of 1972, when it became central to the campaign discourse, much to the benefit of George Wallace and Richard Nixon.

THE CANDIDATES

Richard Nixon

Richard Nixon in 1972 had more experience running for national office than any candidate in U.S. history with the exception of Roosevelt in 1944. In three of his previous four national campaigns, he had run as a proponent of civil rights. However, in his most recent campaign, 1968, he had moved significantly to the right on civil rights. The 1972 campaign would continue Nixon's retreat on racial issues. Still, early in his administration, some black leaders saw Nixon as better than LBJ on certain issues. Columnist Carl Rowan commented:

> It just may be that the Nixon administration is not too bad in the field of civil rights, but you can get hooted out of any Negro

audience in America by saying so. Yet it is Nixon's team that has given the Chicago school system two weeks in which to end racially discriminatory practices in assigning and transferring teachers. Lyndon B. Johnson is rated a great civil rights president, but he would never let the Justice Department do anything in Chicago that might upset Mayor Richard Daley.

The cautious enthusiasm for Nixon shown by Rowan and others disappeared by 1972. Perhaps they accurately perceived Nixon's true feelings. Nixon was careful in public to couch his opinions on racial issues in a way that avoided any explicit appeal to racism, but in private Nixon stated that federal programs to aid blacks were of marginal use because of the genetic inferiority of blacks. The chief policy adviser on urban affairs, and Nixon's most prominent liberal appointee, Daniel Moynihan, was the author of a memo that called for benign neglect of black problems by the administration. The memo caused a firestorm of criticism, and Moynihan unconvincingly claimed that he had only been suggesting neglect for black militants, not blacks generally.* Nixon's private comments on racial matters indicate his own endorsement of benign neglect as a tactic: "You are not going to solve this race problem for a hundred years. Intermarriage and all that, assimilation, it will happen, but not in our time."

Nixon did move forward on integrating construction unions, with his revolutionary "Philadelphia Plan." However, Nixon would eventually undercut his attempt to integrate the unions and was accused by many lawyers in his own Justice Department of political vacillation on school integration. Nixon was also criticized for his attempt to reward his southern supporters by weakening the 1965 Voting Rights Act. Overall, the Nixon that appeared before America in 1972 was at best a racial moderate who had done little to improve his

---

* Moynihan allegedly brought up controversial research on the genetic inferiority of blacks in a meeting with Nixon's top black appointee, James Farmer. According to Farmer, Moynihan said, "Well, Jim, what your people need are some of our genes," greatly offending Farmer. Moynihan today denies that any such conversation took place. Whatever the truth of this incident, it is illustrative that the leading liberal of the Nixon administration was famously unpopular in the black community, and had been so since the mid-1960s.

image in the black community that had rejected him so decisively in 1968. Success in school integration was a notable accomplishment, but victory twenty years after *Brown* seemed at best justice delayed and not much to cheer about.

Moreover, throughout his first term, racial issues appeared to offer Nixon a way to enhance his governing coalition. Facing a Democratic majority in Congress, Nixon was forced to look for issues on which he could peel off key Democrats. Moves to slow down civil rights would attract racial conservatives such as Democratic senator Robert Byrd, who penned an angry screed to Agnew in 1969 demanding that the federal government stop "meddling in racial matters." In an effort to please racial conservatives, Nixon would consistently play politics with civil rights. Despite some impressive civil rights achievements, the conclusion of historian Stephen Ambrose is well supported: "Nixon had to be hauled kicking and screaming into desegregation on a meaningful scale, and he did what he did not because it was right but because he had no choice."

George McGovern

South Dakotan George McGovern grew up without any significant exposure to African Americans or their concerns. As a senator, McGovern had a solid voting record on civil rights, but no great support in the national black community. Like McCarthy in 1968, McGovern in 1972 focused on the Vietnam War. On civil rights, as with almost every issue on the agenda in 1972, McGovern was to the left of his party, but civil rights was hardly a dominant concern. McGovern's tiny support in the party at the start of the primary season was drawn almost entirely from groups least affected by white backlash or racial issues: white college students, white upper-class liberals, and antiwar activists. White ethnics, southerners, working-class voters, and union members were assumed to be behind other candidates, such as Muskie and Wallace, while blacks had not yet coalesced around any candidate. They certainly were not flocking to McGovern. A staffer would later comment that McGovern never learned how to connect with blacks.

The boldest stand McGovern took on race prior to his run for the presidency would come back to haunt him during the general election. In the aftermath of Humphrey's defeat, McGovern was named head of a commission charged with reforming the presidential selection process, including making the party more racially inclusive. Attention to race was merited; in 1968, though blacks made up well over 10 percent of the nation's population and more than 20 percent of the Democratic Party in the electorate, blacks received only 5 percent of the delegate slots. After much debate, the commission required that state delegations be proportionally representative by age, sex, and race. While McGovern in his memoirs goes to great lengths to show that the committee had not endorsed quotas, the changes were immediately portrayed as such by the media and in fact often ended up working in just that fashion. It would be months before McGovern would realize how damaging quotas were to the Democratic coalition.

RACE IN THE DEMOCRATIC NOMINATION FIGHT: MUSKIE'S FALL, WALLACE'S RISE, AND MCGOVERN'S SURVIVAL

The story of McGovern's extraordinary dark horse victory in the 1972 nomination fight is one of the great epics in American politics. Much of McGovern's appeal and his success had little to do with race; his main issues were the war and Nixon's assumed dishonesty. Yet at several points, racial issues would prove decisive in the primaries. Racial issues would twice play a role in the downfall of the presumptive front-runner, Ed Muskie of Maine.

Muskie, Humphrey's running mate in 1968, had long been seen as the Democratic front-runner. A handsome and intelligent liberal-centrist, he loomed as a formidable challenger to Nixon and, along with Senator Henry "Scoop" Jackson of Washington, was the Democrat most feared by the White House. Muskie's first major gaffe occurred when he ruled out a black running mate in a talk at a black church. Muskie appeared to be endorsing a ceiling to black political aspirations and received a great deal of hostile coverage in the press. A prominent black Democrat warned that blacks might now rally against Muskie, while Nixon jumped at the opportunity to portray his leading opponent as a racist. White Americans would certainly

vote for a Negro as vice president, said Nixon, and to suggest otherwise was "a libel on the American people." Republicans suggested
Edward Brooke, the black Republican senator, would make a fine
vice presidential nominee. The RNC's internal summary of the
Democratic race found Muskie was now fourth among blacks, well
behind Edward Kennedy and Humphrey. In an analysis leaked to the
press, the RNC accurately predicted that Muskie was facing serious
problems, because he had "slurred" blacks with his vice presidential
remark, favored busing, and had no concrete national program.

While Muskie's failure to win decisively in New Hampshire had
little to do with racial issues, his collapse in the Florida primary that
followed can be attributed to busing. Schools throughout the South
had finally begun to give up on segregating schools by law, but many
now sought to keep schools largely segregated through other means.
School district lines were drawn so that little, if any, integration
would take place. Aided by existing residential segregation and
increasing white flight, school districts could claim to be integrated,
while maintaining schools that were largely racially pure. On the eve
of the primaries, a frustrated federal judge in Richmond ordered
cross-county busing, so that suburban whites would be bused into
city schools and urban blacks bused to suburban schools. Busing
within districts had attracted much opposition but cross-district busing thrust the issue into the presidential contest with a ferocity that
caught Muskie and others by surprise.

By February 1972, the number of Democratic candidates was
astonishing: Wallace, Muskie, McGovern, Humphrey, Scoop Jackson, New York mayor John Lindsay, New York congresswoman
Shirley Chisholm, Eugene McCarthy, and Senator Vance Hartke.
Each now had to take a stand on busing. Chisholm, Lindsay,
McGovern, Hartke, and McCarthy supported busing. Wallace and
Jackson opposed it. Humphrey and Muskie attempted to finesse the
issue, with Humphrey opposing busing children to schools inferior to
the ones they currently attended. Without directly saying so, Humphrey was against busing white children and in favor of busing black
children. Muskie saw busing as the worst possible remedy to segregation, but one that he was prepared to accept. Earlier, Muskie had

confessed to a reporter, "That busing problem, now, there's a son-of-a-bitch. I don't know what the answer is." McGovern had also expressed doubts about busing to a few reporters, but then immediately retracted those statements and endorsed busing. It would not win him many votes in Florida, a state in an uproar over busing. Humphrey, Chisholm, Lindsay, and McGovern all attempted to appeal to Florida's blacks and succeeded in splitting the vote badly. Wallace, however, had only Scoop Jackson competing for conservative whites, and emerged from Florida with an overwhelming plurality of 41 percent.

The resurgence of George Wallace was a source of great joy in the White House, because he highlighted the divisions within the Democratic Party. Nixon's campaign kept close tabs on Wallace and provided Wallace with poll results and advice on how to attack Democratic rivals. Pat Buchanan, a Nixon speechwriter and political operative, encouraged mischievous Republicans to vote for either McGovern or Wallace, the unelectable left and right candidates. Wallace's secret alliance with Nixon was surprising because of the documented role Nixon had played in illegally funneling cash to Wallace's more moderate opponent in the 1970 gubernatorial race in Alabama. Following Wallace's 1970 victory, the White House concentrated on keeping Wallace in the Democratic primaries and out of the general election.

Every liberal Democrat now not only had to stake out a position on busing, they also had to address the sudden rise of Wallace. Muskie again misplayed the politics of race, complaining bitterly to reporters that Wallace's victory in Florida "shows that some of the worst instincts of which human beings are capable are all too prevalent in our elections." Muskie had been maimed by McGovern in New Hampshire and wounded by Wallace in Florida, but perhaps equally damaging was this bile-filled attack on Democratic voters. McGovern, who just a week previous had launched an attack on Wallace for demagoguery on busing, took an entirely different tack in the aftermath of the Florida primary. Rather than criticizing the white voters of Florida, McGovern said attention must be paid to their legitimate concerns. McGovern edited out from his remarks a lengthy assault on Wallace and instead criticized Muskie and others who saw Wallace supporters as racist. The Wallace voters were actually angry about the war, inflation, and even, incredibly, poor-quality appliances. McGovern hoped to reach out to Wallace supporters without compromising his views on busing.

While it is unquestionably true that Wallace's appeal was broader than racism, race and white fears were the motivating force behind his resurrection as a candidate. Even when he was ostensibly addressing foreign and welfare policy, Wallace's words were loaded with racial references, as when he attacked his Democratic opponents who had "voted to give away millions of dollars to welfare loafers and to Hottentots 10,000 miles away who spit in our faces. . . ." Surely the welfare loafers were as African as Hottentot tribesmen in the minds of Wallace's listeners. The near-universal white antipathy to busing gave Wallace's unapologetic racial conservatism credibility. Other candidates did not have the luxury of opposing busing with full-throated venom, either because they had hopes of winning black support or because their consciences prevented them from appealing to racial animus. Wallace, observing the tortured, ambivalent statements that Humphrey, Muskie, and others made about busing, brought laughter to his audiences when he shouted, "They're a-hemming and a-hawing and they're about to break into the St. Vitus Dance!" Wallace had no compunction about playing the demagogue on busing, falsely alleging that busing students sixty or more miles a day was common. The same month that busing thrust Wallace back to the nation's attention, the National Black Convention in Gary, Indiana, voted narrowly against busing, thus giving Wallace and other opponents cover. Liberal Democrats in the House also began to moderate their positions on busing, in response to the public outcry against it. In Wisconsin, Wallace did not campaign and still managed to come in second to McGovern. Looming ahead was the Michigan primary. Michigan, recently the home of racial liberals like Governors Williams and Romney, was now roiled over the issue of busing, perhaps even more so than Florida. Cross-district busing was to begin in September in Detroit, and Wallace looked so formidable that Humphrey was pressed to respond. Conservative columnists Evans and Novak gloated over Humphrey's delicate dilemma:

Humphrey's Michigan managers are pleading with his national
headquarters to send radio-television commercials showing that
Humphrey, contrasted with McGovern, opposed suburb into
ghetto busing. Fearful of backlash from Humphrey's vital black
constituency in the city, national headquarters has so far refused.

The battle lines were clear. Wallace was for "taking the batteries out
of the buses" immediately. McGovern endorsed busing, even in cases
where white children might be bused to inferior schools. Humphrey
tried to position himself between Wallace and McGovern, without
alienating his black base. But now even McGovern hedged on busing,
expressing his hope that cross-district busing would be held unnecessary by judges. His oft spoke wish was that busing would retreat as
an issue entirely, since for him, it ranked ninety-second on the
nation's agenda. Unfortunately for McGovern, busing had become
the most important issue for many whites in Michigan. In April,
when Michigan party leaders invited McGovern, Humphrey, and
Muskie to a fund-raising dinner, but snubbed Wallace, Wallace held a
counterrally, which attracted many more people than the official
event, humiliating the other candidates. Labor leaders predicted that
Wallace would take 45 percent of the union vote in Michigan.

Shortly before the Michigan and Maryland primaries, Wallace
was shot by a deranged loner. Wallace still won both primaries, taking
51 percent of the Michigan vote, a stunning rebuke to mainstream
Democrats. Wallace's departure left racial conservatives in the Democratic Party without an effective voice for their concerns. Humphrey
now had a clear strategic opening to McGovern's right, and busing
was a potent wedge issue. Although Humphrey continued to attack
busing in debates in California, the grassroots McGovern campaign
won a narrow victory and McGovern became the apparent nominee.
The winner of the primaries had been one of the strongest proponents of busing, even though a majority of Democrats opposed the
practice.

THE "QUOTA" CONVENTION: MCGOVERN'S TATTERED VICTORY

After California, McGovern had enough delegates to take the Democratic nomination. However, the other candidates refused to endorse him or release their delegates. Organized labor indicated its displeasure with McGovern in a booklet attacking his record, including, implausibly, his civil rights votes. The desperation of the stop McGovern movement is best symbolized by the unlikely alliance between Humphrey and Wallace. Wallace still controlled a large bloc of delegates, and any stop McGovern movement would have to involve him. Humphrey, who had during the primaries contemplated reaching out to Wallace by giving him veto power on a vice presidential nominee, now considered offering him the vice presidency. It was at the convention that Humphrey completed his evolution from the civil rights crusader of 1948 to a centrist Democrat on race, by aggressively wooing Wallace delegates.

Humphrey masterminded an attempt to take California's crucial delegation away from McGovern. In retaliation, McGovern forces upheld a challenge, from a group led by Jesse Jackson, to Daley's Chicago slate of delegates. Using McGovern's rules on racial and sexual representation, the challengers argued that they were the more representative delegation and should be seated. When the anti-Daley faction was seated, many felt that McGovern had just given away Illinois's votes in the name of racial quotas. Chicago columnist Mike Royko ridiculed the outcome:

> There's only one Italian there. Are you saying that only one out of every 59 Democratic votes cast in a Chicago election is cast by an Italian? . . . Your reforms have disenfranchised Chicago's white ethnic Democrats, which is a strange reform. . . . Anybody who would reform Chicago's Democratic Party by dropping the white ethnic would probably begin a diet by shooting themselves in the stomach.

The legacy of McGovern's reform commission now dealt a serious blow to the image of the Democratic Party among many white Americans.

Yet these same reforms produced a remarkably more inclusive convention. While elected white Democrats stayed away from Miami in droves, blacks and Latinos were represented in greater numbers than at any convention in U.S. history. Their influence had grown as well. The Congressional Black Caucus (CBC) had issued in early June "non-negotiable demands," including full employment, a guaranteed annual income of $6,500, an urban homestead act, national health insurance, 15 percent racial set-asides in federal contracting, a proportional share of cabinet posts by race, and home rule for D.C. The National Black Political Convention requested statehood for majority black cities, community control of courts in black areas, a 50 percent cut in defense spending, and ending aid to Israel. Black leaders prodded McGovern for a written response to their demands as the convention neared. The threat to McGovern's razor-thin majority was obvious; McGovern could not afford to lose his black delegates en masse. McGovern had earlier endorsed a guaranteed national income in a speech to social workers and even reparations for slavery. Now, faced with new and politically suicidal demands from credible black organizations, McGovern chose to fully endorse busing and "providing federal appointments and jobs at all levels to Blacks proportionate to their percentage of the population as a general formula." Of the black demands presented to McGovern, these were quite moderate, but for much of white America, busing and racial quotas were anathema. Busing also reappeared directly at the convention, in Wallace's fiery speech and in a platform fight. McGovern forces voted down Wallace's strong antibusing plank as well as a more moderate one that opposed cross-district busing. By now, McGovern was so far left of the center that the prospect of balancing the ticket with a southerner was quickly discarded, once Florida governor Reuben Askew had rejected McGovern's offer. In any case, a southerner with enough stature to make a difference would be so incompatible as to be a subject of ridicule. As *Newsweek* put it, "McGovern couldn't win the South if he had Robert E. Lee on his ticket."

NIXON'S CONVENTIONAL CHOICES

Nixon faced no strong challengers for the nomination of his party, and most of his moves during the primary season were intended to position him effectively for the November election. Nixon was briefly flanked on his right by Representative John Ashbrook, who sent mailings to Florida Republicans emphasizing Nixon's alleged support of busing. At the same time, Representative Pete McCloskey ran to Nixon's left, attacking Nixon's southern strategy and calling for moral leadership on racial issues. Nixon, at the zenith of his popularity, brushed aside both challengers with ease. The White House and RNC then focused on the general election. Nixon's first move was to highlight his opposition to busing in an address to the nation in March of 1972.

As early as 1970, Nixon speechwriter Pat Buchanan had advocated the abandonment of racial progress by the administration:

> Let me say candidly that for the foreseeable future, it is all over for compulsory social integration in the USA; because that body of public approval which must be present for a social change of this magnitude is not there . . . in every school in which it has been tried racial violence is becoming the rule. . . . The second era of Re-Construction is over; the ship of Integration is going down; it is not our ship; it belongs to national liberalism—and we cannot salvage it; and we ought not to be aboard.

Buchanan argued that if the administration did not adamantly oppose integration, it would be outflanked by Wallace. Within the White House, speechwriter Ray Price and Nixon adviser Leonard Garment launched a counterattack against Buchanan's extremism, and until 1972, they succeeded in moderating Nixon's racial stances. Yet in an election year, Nixon felt compelled to address busing in a nationally televised speech. Buchanan pushed hard for an outright ban on busing, while moderates pointed out that if 75 percent of America opposed busing, 75 percent also favored integration. Consequently, Nixon came out strongly against busing, but for integration. The speech effectively conveyed what Nixon privately believed: busing was "poisonous" and must be opposed.

Nixon's dramatic televised speech to the nation on busing demanded a response from the Democrats. Wallace questioned the sincerity of Nixon's antibusing stance but claimed credit for Nixon's move to the right. Humphrey felt that Nixon was following his moderated busing stance and praised the speech. After a liberal uproar, Humphrey backtracked and accused the president of manipulating race. McGovern, however, responded with a clear and articulate denunciation of Nixon's speech. As the only leading Democratic candidate to consistently attack Nixon's busing stance, McGovern gained credibility among liberals. However, Nixon's speech reflected the broad national consensus against busing, as an avalanche of letters to the White House in the days after the speech showed.

Some staffers now advised Nixon to tone down his opposition to busing, as it would only help George Wallace and alienate the many Americans in favor of integration. There was also concern that the press would make Nixon pay a price for exploiting busing. Moreover, Republican operatives believed the Democratic nominee would surely defuse the issue by taking a moderate position on busing. Still, the White House strategists consistently advocated forcing Democratic candidates to go on the record on busing, for example by planting busing questions with reporters. Whichever side Democrats chose, they would lose votes.

The Nixon reelection campaign did not hesitate to use racial dirty tricks in effort to divide the Democrats and prevent the nomination of Ed Muskie. Buchanan suggested running ads on black radio stations trumpeting Muskie's statement against an African American vice president and advocating a vote for Chisholm in the primaries. Republicans also forged a statement on Muskie's stationery in a clumsy attempt to make him look like a bigot. It is impossible to know whether these activities affected Muskie's sudden downfall, but they do demonstrate an extraordinary willingness to play the race card.

Nixon also had to decide whether to keep Agnew on his ticket, a decision with obvious racial implications. Agnew had built upon his

1968 image as a spokesman for white ethnics and the racial backlash. When the prospect of Agnew being dropped for Brooke, the black senator from Massachusetts, was raised, the idea was dismissed as improbable because it didn't agree with the racial strategy of the White House. As one contemporary analyst observed: "Political operatives have encouraged the President to use the racial issue obliquely to heighten tensions that split the Democrats. A Brooke nomination . . . raises the issue by settling it." In keeping Agnew, Nixon symbolically appealed to the backlash vote.

Quotas were also a subject of discussion in the Nixon camp. Buchanan argued that if the Republicans adopted quotas at their convention, "we will automatically surrender a strong suit—our opposition to 'quota democracy' . . . our political interests in 1972 dictate that we juxtapose our Party with the McGovernized quota-ridden Democratic Party—not that we emulate them. . . ." Rather than adopting quotas, the Republicans would attack the Democrats for disenfranchising Italian Americans, farmers, elderly Americans, and others through quotas. In Nixon's two convention films, non-whites appeared very little, with a short feature on minority enterprise in one and a long interview with his Hispanic valet being the only minority presence in the other. Despite a much publicized hug from entertainer Sammy Davis Jr. at the podium, Nixon's avoidance of blacks set the stage for his general election, in which Nixon would not make any attempt to woo the black community. He would, however, find that racial issues were quite effective at wooing other Democratic constituencies.

BLACK OUTREACH: MALIGN NEGLECT AND FEAR

As the conventions ended, McGovern was behind with almost every conceivable social group except African Americans. Harry Dent, Nixon's southern backlash expert, did ponder outreach to southern blacks on a number of occasions, even suggesting using black insurance salesmen as Republican recruiters. Yet the administration failed to mount any sincere effort to attract blacks to their banner. As a group of black White House staffers concluded, Nixon was "basically a stranger to blacks." If benign neglect is a fair characterization of at least some aspects of Nixon's domestic policy, malign neglect is an apt sobriquet for the tactics some in the White House successfully advocated. Buchanan, for one, did not just oppose affirmative action for blacks, he advocated replacing it with affirmative action for Catholics:

> [I]nstead of sending the orders out to all our agencies—hire blacks and women—the order should go out—hire ethnic Catholics, preferable [*sic*] women, for visible posts . . . give those fellows the "Jewish seat" or the "black seat" on the Court. . . .

The same juxtaposition of blacks and Jews with white Catholics would come up when Buchanan made the case for aiding parochial schools:

> There is a legitimate grievance in my view of white working class people that every time, on every issue, that the black militants loud-mouth it, we come up with more money, whether for their colleges, for civil rights enforcement, for ghetto schools, for new appointments. The time has come to say—we have done enough for the poor blacks; right now we want to give some relief for working class ethnics and Catholics—and make an unabashed appeal to these patient working people, who always get the short end of the stick. If we can give fifty Phantoms [jets] to the Jews, and a multibillion-dollar welfare program for the blacks—neither of whom is ever going to thank this President— why not help the Catholics save their collapsing school system?

Buchanan represented the hyperbolic fringe of racial conservatism within the Nixon White House, and many of his policy suggestions and speech additions were never adopted. Still, Nixon assigned substantial campaign resources to wooing white ethnics and endorsed aid to parochial schools. A Nixon campaign ad showed a white construction worker placidly eating a sandwich while the voice-over alleged that voters like him would pay the bill when one out of every two Americans were put on welfare, as McGovern planned. As pollster Sam Lubell saw it, welfare was the 1972 code word for race, just as law and order had been in 1968. Nixon's campaign would not win black support while running ads implying that blacks were simply out for more cash from poor white construction workers.

When Nixon did attempt outreach to the black community, as when he invited the leaders of the African Methodist Episcopal Church to breakfast, he was occasionally humiliated. The bishops publicly snubbed Nixon's invitation, a rejection that was immediately trumpeted in a Democratic National Committee (DNC) press release. The few prominent black Nixon supporters (Jim Brown, Sammy Davis Jr., and James Brown) faced boycotts and bitter opprobrium from their community. Nixon staffers did make a feeble attempt to peel off black voters from McGovern by attacking the slaveholding ancestry of his new running mate, Maryland's Sargent Shriver, who had been trumpeting his Confederate roots in southern speeches. The White House prepared a press release that highlighted the "darker" side of Shriver's border state heritage, including the fact that he still displayed an 1809 runaway slave handbill in his mansion. The campaign also tried to gather a group of black Republicans for a picnic at Shriver's plantation to bring further attention to his slaveholding roots. Local Republicans in Washington, D.C., prepared a brief pamphlet attacking McGovern's civil rights record, mostly on missing various votes on civil rights or procedural matters.

The sum total of Nixon's outreach to blacks during the campaign of 1972 is meager. Sammy Davis Jr.'s endorsement, a feeble attack on McGovern's strong voting record, and a press release about Shriver's southern heritage were not likely to move black votes. Consequently, McGovern never worried that blacks might defect to Nixon. What concerned the McGovern campaign was turnout. Among blacks, McGovern was not igniting the enthusiasm that had been seen for LBJ and RFK. As civil rights leader John Lewis observed, "The black community is very anti-Nixon, but . . . I don't see any great outpouring of support for McGovern." Internal memos of the campaign indicate county-by-county attention to black population levels and turnouts. If McGovern had a prayer of beating Nixon, he would need every black vote. In the last month, the campaign made a strong push to its black base, hoping to score a record turnout and fight the apathy in the black community. McGovern's rhetoric on race became inflammatory as he accused the president of mounting efforts to deceive minorities:

> You can stand against the men in business suits who are trying to trick black people out of polling places just as men in sheets and hoods once barred them with violence. . . . I want America to come home from the exile of racist politics, so that never again will a president attempt to win White votes by denying Black rights. . . . Lyndon Johnson told us: "We shall overcome." But Richard Nixon tells us: "I don't care."

McGovern also accused the Republicans of secretly supporting militant black and Hispanic organizations that opposed voting.* Turnout was also a concern; McGovern frequently told black audiences that if blacks in 1968 had turned out at the same rate as in 1960, Humphrey would have won.

The part of McGovern's new rhetoric that received the most media attention was his linkage of Nixon to the KKK. Instead of accusing Nixon of cynically exploiting racial issues, as McGovern had in the spring, he now simply labeled Nixon's administration racist. Instead of giving Nixon partial credit for progress in civil rights, as he had earlier, he told blacks that "the Nixon Administration has put down black people every chance it has had." As McGovern fell further behind in the opinion polls, and as blacks continued to lack enthusiasm for him, the exigencies of the campaign seemed to demand a change in tactics. The traditional issues of the civil rights movement were vanishing; voting rights and public accommodations access were approaching near unanimous support within the public sphere. The symbols that McGovern had to use to fight black apathy were

---

* The Republicans were, in fact, contemplating secretly funding a militant black candidate, to draw off black votes.

the vanishing villains of a successful movement. The new issues of busing and affirmative action were relevant to blacks and whites, but it became apparent that if McGovern stressed these issues, he would lose in a landslide.

THE SOUTHERN STRATEGY: DIXIE GOES REPUBLICAN

The most important electoral battle in the general election of 1972 was begun before the last ballot was counted in 1968: the struggle to inherit the Wallace vote. Books such as *The Emerging Republican Majority* argued that the political party that spoke to the concerns of Wallace's white, racially conservative constituency would become the dominant political party of the era. As the majority of Wallace's vote came in the South, Nixon focused a great deal of domestic political capital on wooing those voters, with appeals on race, defense, patriotism, and traditional values. Yet the South was also courted with lax civil rights enforcement. Six Justice Department attorneys resigned and endorsed McGovern because of Nixon's politicization of civil rights enforcement. Nixon also sought southern support through judicial appointments. When the Senate, led by Democrats, rejected two southerners for the Supreme Court, Nixon claimed the opposition was motivated by antisouthern bias. When Nixon visited Atlanta in late October, the fruits of the southern strategy were apparent, as the second largest crowd in Atlanta history greeted him with extraordinary enthusiasm.

McGovern continued to be unpopular throughout the South and had written off the region as unwinnable by May. When the general election began, many top southern Democrats simply endorsed Nixon. Other Democratic officeholders made it clear that they would not appear with McGovern or vote for him. In the South, McGovern was the weakest candidate the Democrats had ever run. Additionally, the contrast between Nixon, who had wooed southerners for four years, and McGovern, who barely campaigned in the South, was stark. In the end, Nixon won huge majorities among southern whites, taking 75 percent of the vote in the periphery states of the old

Confederacy and an astonishing 86 percent of the white vote in the Deep South.

BUSING: INHERITING THE WALLACE NORTH

Opposition to busing was an integral part of Nixon's southern strategy, but busing was also crucial in converting northern Wallace supporters into Nixon voters. No other issue had as much impact. In the working-class neighborhoods of Michigan, hundreds of signs proclaiming "This Family Shall Not Be Bused" hung in windows. Six mayors of suburban Detroit cities crossed party lines to endorse Nixon because of busing. In a national ad run by Democrats for Nixon, busing was the most prominent domestic issue cited. The White House coordinated the antibusing statements of surrogates, arranging for Bob Dole to fly to Michigan to attack McGovern's stance on busing, and paid for billboards of pro-busing McGovern quotes in northern cities. A foreign policy speech by Agnew in Detroit was altered to include an attack on busing, and the attorney general was directed to focus his speech entirely on the antibusing actions of the administration.

The strategic dilemma of busing was twofold for McGovern. First, it was the greatest wedge issue separating him from vital constituencies: southerners, white ethnics, union members, and suburbanites. But almost as important, busing did not produce much fervor even among its supporters. There was no March on Washington for busing, as there had been for civil rights in the sixties. Proponents of busing defended it "with increasingly little heart, and only because they are against the kind of people who oppose it—the word has become simply an identification tag among whites denoting sympathy with black demands for equality." Busing was a two-sided code word; to racial conservatives, opposition to busing meant sympathy with their worldview, while for racial progressives, support of busing would separate the true civil rights advocates from the Johnny-come-latelies. With even Wallace paying lip service to equality, busing served as an effective litmus test for both sides of the racial divide. Yet the passion was almost entirely on one side of the debate. While the NAACP released a powerful report in defense of busing entitled "It's Not the Distance, 'It's the Niggers,'" even the black community was divided on the wisdom of busing. Although McGovern, Chisholm, and the NAACP would angrily point out that busing was more frequently used to enforce segregation than to relieve it, the antibusing passion seemed immune to facts. Supporters of busing were always on the defensive, rather than leading a popular social movement. Yet, faced with the unwavering opposition of the vast majority of whites, McGovern, unlike Humphrey and Muskie, did not alter his fundamental support of busing, although he did express sympathy for white parents facing busing to inferior schools. No one could mistake McGovern's position, particularly when McGovern endorsed a key tenet of the busing movement, that busing white kids to inferior schools would quickly lead to better schools. McGovern never regretted his fulsome support of busing, but it had substantial political costs in 1972.

THE QUOTA CONUNDRUM

The idea of quotas, the concept of which McGovern supported, was to be one of the major factors in the wrecking of his campaign and the triumph of Richard Nixon.

THEODORE WHITE

The 1972 presidential race was the first in which quotas and affirmative action were important issues. While never achieving the salience of busing, quotas were a vital part of Nixon's campaign to define McGovern as a radical. McGovern was vulnerable to attacks, because during the primaries he had broadly endorsed proportional representation of racial minorities in government hiring. The backlash against quotas was perhaps strongest among one of the Democrats' core constituencies, Jewish Americans. For many Jews, quotas were anathema, because quotas had historically been used to exclude Jews from elite universities and occupations. At the convention, black delegate

Walter Fauntroy was reported to have received a promise from McGovern that blacks would now receive 10 percent of federal jobs. Although both Fauntroy and McGovern denied the statement, it aroused serious concerns among Jewish leaders. Hyman Bookbinder, of the American Jewish Committee (AJC), saw a link between racial quotas for convention delegates and job quotas and was also upset about the increasing use of quotas in education and employment in New York. The AJC sent a letter to both Nixon and McGovern, asking them to state their positions on quotas and proportional representation. In his reply, Nixon came out firmly against quotas and proportional representation, while endorsing the vague concept of affirmative action. McGovern's response was far more equivocal. While rejecting rigid quotas, McGovern was silent on proportional representation, perhaps because that exact phrase had been part of his campaign speeches for months. Following the uproar over quotas, McGovern did change his rhetoric on affirmative action. In the California primaries, he had promised Latinos proportional representation. Returning to California in September, McGovern retreated from proportional representation under heavy pressure, particularly from Jews, to reject racial quotas in employment. McGovern, however, still advocated proportional representation in front of black audiences. As he had done with busing, McGovern labeled quotas a "phony" issue, used to "justify retrenchment in our already inadequate efforts to realize equality of opportunity for Americans of every racial, religious, or ethnic strain and sex." Nixon's policy on quotas was described in the press as a "ban," while McGovern's stance was seen as an endorsement of some type of proportional representation, forcing McGovern to attempt the difficult task of distinguishing between that concept and quotas. In the end, Nixon, long perceived negatively by the vast majority of Jews, doubled his support among Jews, from an anemic 18 percent in 1968 to a respectable 37 percent in 1972.

In addition to aiding Nixon's outreach among Jews, quotas helped win labor votes. Labor had publicly supported civil rights for decades, but some unions were all white, or nearly so, and very resistant to integration. Some union members feared affirmative action because

of their veneration of the seniority system; others were surely motivated by racism. Union leaders felt that the quotas at the convention
had cost them influence in the party; if women, blacks, and the young
had guaranteed representation, why not labor? Labor leader George
Meany spoke for many of his socially conservative members when he
complained that because of quotas, there were two times as many
"open fags" as AFL-CIO members in New York's delegation. For the
first time in decades, the AFL-CIO did not endorse the Democratic
nominee, a crucial blow to McGovern's prospects. The seeds of
labor's revolt had been planted years earlier, perhaps most significantly by the "Philadelphia Plan." Launched by Nixon in an attempt
to integrate the nearly all-white construction unions, the plan required
federal contractors to make and meet targeted goals for black employment. The plan had opposition in Congress almost from its start, with
one Republican calling it "as popular as a crab in a whorehouse."
Before the project could be expanded to other cities, officials leaked
that they might let it die. By raising the issue of integrating unions,
Nixon might win civil rights plaudits. More certainly, however, he
could, by killing the expansion, position himself as the defender of
union seniority against racial quotas. The debate set two of the
Democrats' core constituencies at each other's throats. Former attorney
general Ramsey Clark accused Nixon of cunning manipulation in
first constructing and then gutting the Philadelphia Plan: "Now that
they have made 'quota' a racist word, the Plan has been denounced
by the planners." While blue-collar workers were drawn to Nixon
for a variety of reasons, including Vietnam, abortion, welfare, and
McGovern's perceived elitism, quotas greatly helped Nixon to win a
majority of union votes in November.

NEIGHBORHOODS AND ETHNICS: THE MELTING POT BOILS OVER

Public housing and integration were also on the nation's agenda in
1972. Nixon had succeeded in finessing the issue in 1968, but by
1972 he was urged to stop the federal integration action in the public
housing project in Forest Hills, New York, because of the political

bounty it would bring among Jews and white ethnics. Forest Hills was the highest-profile example of a white neighborhood rising up in anger over integrated public housing, but many whites across the country were opposed to housing integration. Often the reasons given were nonracial, such as property values, safety, and overcrowding, but the ethnic character of the neighborhoods was central. The Nixon campaign was even blunter, directly linking integrated housing to busing.

McGovern attempted to respond to white concerns about integrated housing, lamenting both the destruction of neighborhood character and the creation of residential "apartheid" in the cities, laying the blame on blockbusting real estate shysters and the Nixon administration. Later, McGovern would explicitly endorse the preservation of neighborhood identity as a principal goal of federal housing policy. This sounded similar to the rhetoric that Nixon and Agnew were serving up to ethnic audiences across the country. However, McGovern had also called for the government to "break the tight ring which keeps millions of blacks penned up in our city slums, by providing low-cost and mixed income integrated housing in the outer city and the countryside." On the eve of the election, McGovern came out against Forest Hills–type projects, saying that communities must be fully consulted before public housing is put in their midst. Since communities like Forest Hills would never approve, this was an obvious retreat from his support for integrated public housing. The sudden shift made McGovern appear as opportunistic as Nixon on racial matters.

Integrated public housing was symbolic of the distance between McGovern and white ethnics, traditionally strong Democratic supporters. White ethnic coolness to the Democratic ticket stemmed in part from a perception that McGovern represented an elitist stratum that saw white ethnics as ignorant bigots. The White House had carefully studied what were labeled "peripheral urban ethnics" and found that their resentment of integrated housing, busing, and other racial matters divided them from McGovern. Nixon's campaign focused much more time and attention on white ethnics than did the Democrats. As one Democratic ward leader in New Jersey put it,

"George McGovern talks about blacks all the time. He talks about Chicanos all the time. He talks about poor whites. But I still haven't heard McGovern use the word 'Italian.'" Outreach to blacks, whether through affirmative action or housing, or simple rhetoric, obviously irritated some white ethnics.

In the last week of the campaign, both Shriver and McGovern made appeals to white ethnics, with McGovern calling for an "Ethnic Heritage Studies Program." Shriver, speaking two days later, articulated a complex vision of an "American symphony" of ethnic groups, which he juxtaposed against the failed metaphor of the melting pot. Criticizing the schools for "implanting Anglo-Saxon conceptions of righteousness, law, order, and popular government," Shriver argued that different groups experience different realities and give words like "quota" different meanings. Although Shriver was at pains to eliminate quotas from his "New American symphony" of diversity, the message was far more complex than the simple ban that Nixon was advocating. Shriver's rarefied imagery and almost postmodern discussion of perceived realities also could scarcely help defend against the charge of liberal elitism that the White House was using against McGovern. As Republican campaign surrogates were encouraged to point out:

> McGovern, who supports racial quotas in every public school, who has endorsed forced bussing as essential—spent $1400 to send his daughter to an almost lily-white public school in Bethesda—and so keep her out of the integrated neighborhood public school in the City of Washington—where she should have gone. McGovern thus favors forced bussing—for other people's children, not his own. McGovern favors racial quotas in the public schools—for other people's children, not his own.

This rhetoric appealed directly to the resentment among working-class and middle-class white ethnics, who felt that upper-class liberals were forcing them to pay the costs of integration. The Nixon campaign used housing, busing, affirmative action, and welfare, as well as nonracial cultural issues, to steal a crucial component of the New Deal coalition from McGovern.

CONCLUSION: NIXON'S UNNECESSARY COURTSHIP OF THE BACKLASH VOTE

Richard Nixon received the electoral votes of the entire United States, save only Massachusetts and the District of Columbia. McGovern failed to carry even his home state in one of the great landslides in U.S. history. Race was unquestionably a vital part of both McGovern's and Nixon's campaigns, as both in different ways tried to increase the nation's focus on race. In particular, Nixon methodically exploited racial tensions to aid in the construction of his spectacular majority. McGovern, desperately behind, used his own racial tactics to whip up black fervor. McGovern also tried to convince voters that busing and quotas were false or at least insignificant issues, but despite McGovern's best efforts, most Americans felt that these were important issues and ones that positioned them with Nixon and against McGovern. Nixon, who highlighted both issues in the closing days of the campaign, won a tactical victory in making sure his racial issues were high on the nation's agenda.

Of course, Nixon's victory was also the product of numerous nonracial issues and strategies. Nixon's extraordinary boldness in foreign affairs, as well as the drastic decline in urban unrest that occurred on his watch, helped build his majority. Nixon's chances were aided as well by the removal of Wallace as a third-party threat. Additionally, Nixon benefited from the folly of his opposition, which seemed to have a knack for "political suicide," in the words of John Lindsay. The confusion and left-wing extremism of the Democratic convention in 1972 was a gift to the incumbent Nixon. Yet Nixon's victory was also a product of the ugly politics of race. From the southern strategy, to the dirty tricks against Muskie, to the appeals to white resentment on busing and quotas, Nixon's campaign relished using race in an underhanded way. In late October, when Nixon was almost thirty points ahead of McGovern, the campaign was still pushing hard on busing, fighting for every angry white vote. The true tragedy of Nixon's racial campaigning in 1972 was not only that it happened, but also that it was so unnecessary. Had Nixon run as a strong proponent of civil rights in 1972, with a heavy outreach to the black community, he would have still been elected by a solid majority, so long as Wallace stayed out of the general election race. Obviously, many of the moves on school desegregation and busing took place when Nixon was less popular and his reelection much less certain. But in his memoirs, Nixon admits what most political observers knew: Once McGovern was nominated, particularly after the Eagleton fiasco, Nixon was assured of reelection. There was no need to play the race card so heavily in the closing months.

Nixon argued repeatedly, of course, that opposition to quotas and busing had nothing to do with bigotry. The shift that 1972 represented, from color-blind equality to race-conscious remedies, certainly opened up the possibility that one could oppose these remedies and remain committed to racial equality. Yet in the name of future racial harmony, in the name of Nixon's own stated goal for his second term "to quiet the angry voices," a wiser candidate and a less venomous campaign staff might have seen the merit in downplaying the divisive issues of race. Nixon could have opposed busing and quotas without making those stances central to the election. Running against McGovern in 1972, Nixon had a host of issues to exploit; he and his staff repeatedly chose racial ones. To use a Nixonian football metaphor, the Republicans were playing hardball on race when they were thirty points ahead with a minute to play. Among the many political sins that Richard Nixon committed in his long career, his decision to further inflame the racial divide during the campaign of 1972 must rank high.

The meaning of the 1972 landslide for the Democratic Party was also quite clear. The votes of Middle America, the crux of the New Deal coalition, had to be recaptured. As a young ambitious Georgia governor watched Wallace give his valedictory convention address in Miami, he commented to a reporter that a Democrat who campaigned hard and avoided alienating the Wallace constituency could win the White House. James Earl Carter had just the candidate in mind to pull the Democratic coalition back together again.

FORD GIVES UP ON BLACKS
The Absent Racial Politics of 1976

The importance of race to the presidential election of 1976 is not immediately apparent. Racial issues almost never appeared in the campaign discourse, and both candidates sought to avoid racial politics at different times during the contest. Gerald Ford was a different man and a different Republican from his predecessor, Nixon, who had exploited racial division with an almost instinctual fervor. Ford, for reasons of either strategy or conscience, let sleeping racial issues lie and did not reach out to blacks or racially conservative whites. On the other side, Jimmy Carter achieved Bobby Kennedy's dream of bringing together blacks and blue-collar whites in a reconciling coalition. He did this, however, not by forthrightly addressing busing and affirmative action, but by adroit vagueness on racial issues. Carter constructed the most integrated campaign in American history and ably rallied the support of the most antiblack members of the New Deal coalition, white southerners. It was only in the aftermath of the election that the centrality of race became clear. To a degree greater than that of any president before or since, James Earl Carter of Georgia owed his victory to black voters. Moreover, from 1964 to 1992, the election of 1976 was the only victory for Democrats. Carter's ability to parse the politics of race was crucial to his singular achievement, but so too was the strategic failure of Ford to grasp the importance of the black vote in a close election.

1976: THE SETTING

The political landscape heading into the election season of 1976 was dominated by a single issue: Watergate. Although Ford had promised that "our long national nightmare" was over, the effects of Watergate could not be ignored. Watergate put character ahead of issues for many voters. Four years before, Nixon had defeated George McGovern, a man of far greater rectitude, largely because Nixon had been closer to the public on almost every issue. Foreign policy was also smaller in the public mind; the onward progress of détente and the end of America's longest war helped focus the attention of the nation not on policies but on the personalities of the men who wished to be president. Domestically, America was still reeling from the inflationary shock of the oil shortage and the recession of 1974–75. Yet heading into the election year, the economy marginally improved. With two moderates running atop their parties, there were few stark differences in economic policy, once again reinforcing character's central role.

Explicitly racial issues were also less pressing by 1976 than they had been in any election since 1960. Of course, the Boston busing crisis of 1974–75 had captured the nation's attention. As the conflicts between blacks and whites became more violent, Ford put the 82nd Airborne on alert, and the city teetered on the brink of anarchy. The opposition to busing in Boston was bitter, and explicitly racist, as demonstrators waved bananas and screamed at the black children to go back to Africa. A later court decision reduced the scope of the busing order, the city calmed down, and the issue of busing receded. White fears of urban upheavals were also less pressing. Pollster Louis Harris found that the percentage of whites who felt threatened by black demonstrators had dropped by more than half to 30 percent. The issue of quotas, which Nixon had used so effectively in 1972, was no longer as salient, perhaps because Richard Nixon was not inflaming the white public about it.

By contrast, policy toward Africa was increasingly seen as symbolically important to the black community. The Congressional Black

Caucus demanded a meeting with the secretary of state to discuss African concerns. Politicians had to be careful about issues such as Angola, South Africa, and Rhodesia, which now had greater domestic implications. Still, the major issues of the 1976 election were character and the economy, and racial issues would seldom capture headlines from the primaries to the final tally in November.

THE CANDIDATES

Gerald Ford

Gerald Ford, who had represented western Michigan in Congress for a quarter century before rising to the vice presidency, had a typical northern Republican voting record on civil rights. He had supported the civil rights movement in the 1950s and 1960s, voting against the segregationists on the jury trial amendment of the 1957 civil rights bill. By the late 1960s, however, he began to waver in his support for integrated public housing, and when busing became a dominant issue in Michigan, Ford led the opposition. Still, as a prominent black Democrat concluded, Ford's civil rights record in Congress was "no worse than Truman's, Johnson's, or Kennedy's." Four days after taking office, Ford signed bills mandating that busing be used only as a last resort. When Boston erupted, Ford registered his disapproval of the busing order but allowed his attorney general to enforce the law. Ford never wavered in his opposition to busing as a policy, but he seldom played it for political gain.

While Ford's position on busing was similar to Nixon's, the differences between the two men in matters of race were substantial. Ford's first official meeting as vice president had been with black administration officials. In his first few weeks as president, Ford met with black Republicans, civil rights leaders, and the CBC. Ford's "open door" policy toward black leaders contrasted sharply with Nixon's reluctance to have such meetings. Ford immediately increased spending on enforcement of civil rights laws, and some of his black supporters boldly predicted great gains in black electoral support in 1976. Yet while Ford gave black leaders access to the White House that they had not had under Nixon, he refused to make special appeals for their support. When he spoke to the NAACP conference in 1975, his appearance alone set him apart from Nixon's policy of ignoring the annual meeting, but he left the delegates feeling "empty-handed" by his avowed policy of not presenting a special agenda of issues to black audiences. Still, Ford had reason to hope for more black support than the anemic 12 percent Nixon had received in 1972.

Jimmy Carter

Jimmy Carter had a number of handicaps facing him as he contemplated a run for the presidency. In addition to being a one-term governor of a medium-size state, with little name recognition and little access to funds, Carter was from the Deep South. No one from that region had been nominated for the presidency by a major party since Zachary Taylor in 1848. The ban on "Deep Southerners" in the White House was inextricably linked to the politics of race. Controversies over slavery, Reconstruction, and Jim Crow made most southerners unacceptable to the national electorate.

Carter was raised in Plains, Georgia, amid the most explicitly racist setting for any president's upbringing since Woodrow Wilson's boyhood in Virginia. The son of a comparatively wealthy landowner, Carter grew up surrounded by blacks of far lower social status. Many called him "massuh," and the rigid social code was omnipresent. While Carter's mother was racially progressive for the times, Carter's father was a committed segregationist, who refused to allow blacks in the house except as servants. Carter stood up to his father on segregation when he was a young man and later became the sole white male in his community to refuse to join the White Citizens Council, the genteel version of the Ku Klux Klan. Carter also unsuccessfully attempted to integrate his church. At the same time, Carter was immersed in an irredeemably racist social structure. As a member of the local school board, he never objected to the segregated school system or to the inherently unequal funding of black and white schools. He voted for a shortened school year for blacks, who were expected to pick cotton while white children were in school. As late as the spring of 1976, Carter's peanut farm paid black workers less than white ones. Members of his family, such as his brother, Billy, remained "out-and-out racists" in the opinion of many black neighbors, because they refused to allow blacks into their homes.

In his early political career, Carter did not stand out as a progressive on racial matters. In his quixotic campaign for the governorship in 1966, Carter failed to make the runoff, losing to more conservative Democrats. Ultimately the election was won by a rabid race baiter, Lester Maddox. When Carter launched his next campaign in 1970, his primary opposition was former Governor Carl Sanders, a well-known liberal with strong ties to Georgia's black community. Carter chose not to compete with Sanders for that vote and instead ran a campaign that "aimed at the instincts of white people who feared integration." Carter campaigned at an all-white segregationist academy in defense of private education, cozied up to Lester Maddox and George Wallace, and generally made it clear he was on the side of the rednecks in Georgia's culture wars. Julian Bond, a prominent black politician in Georgia, alleged that Carter funneled money to a fringe black candidate to steal votes from Sanders. Carter supporters circulated a picture of Sanders in a champagne shower with two towering black basketball players for his Atlanta Hawks team, an image designed to appeal to the small-town prejudices of Carter's supporters. In the end, Carter swept into office on the strength of the redneck vote, with almost no black support at all.

A contemporary anecdote had Carter saying to a black supporter, "You'll hate the way I campaign, but you'll love the way I govern." Though Carter denied the statement, it is an accurate description of both his campaign and his tenure as governor. The change was immediate. Though he had celebrated his election victory with Maddox, Carter proclaimed in his inaugural address that the era of racial discrimination was over. Carter's less progressive supporters were shocked; this was not the Carter they had suppported. As one reporter put it, "The sound of Lester Maddox's jaw dropping still echoes in the Statehouse." Carter's governorship saw the greatest advance for black Georgians since Reconstruction. The number of blacks employed by the state climbed rapidly; black appointments to governing boards and state agencies went from three to fifty-three during Carter's four years in office. Carter also honored Martin Luther King with a holiday and hung his portrait in the statehouse, a very unusual act for a southern governor in the early 1970s. Carter, who had been elected without any significant black support, quickly became a very popular figure in Georgia's black community.

A WALLACE WITHOUT RACISM: CARTER IN THE PRIMARIES

Jimmy Carter decided to run for president earlier than any of his rivals, making his intentions public two years before the general election. Carter, a former southern governor without national stature or an experienced staff, was initially seen as the darkest of dark horses. In his marathon uphill race to the nomination, racial politics proved crucial, in a peculiar way. Carter's campaign would, throughout the long march to the White House, emphasize blacks but not black issues. One of Carter's key advisers, Gerald Rafshoon, noted in the margins of a 1973 memo for Carter that "mistakes of the past caused too much emphasis on black issue + foreign affairs . . . previous emphasis on black [sic] needs rethinking."* Rafshoon, a creative non-political thinker, called for a campaign that would be a dialogue between television sitcom characters Fred Sanford and Archie Bunker or, in other words, blacks and racially conservative whites. The strategy of deemphasizing race appeared early in Carter's campaign. In his announcement letter to supporters in late 1974, Carter did not mention racial issues at all. While his formal announcement a week later did passionately endorse racial equality, it was far more specific on Carter's opposition to welfare spending. Carter's opposition to forced busing was subtly suggested but was conflated with a call for an analysis of the impact of government programs such as public housing, prisons, and welfare on real Americans. Carter's attacks on welfare fraud and waste and on public housing and his calls for the

---

* Tellingly, Rafshoon also had to ask his boss, "Where do you stand now?" on desegregation.

federal government to listen to "the people" sounded like the white boy populism of George Wallace. Unlike Wallace or Nixon, Carter seldom raised his opposition to busing, the hottest racial issue of the period. Carter studiously avoided contentious racial topics such as quotas, affirmative action, and, when possible, busing, although he was eager to address civil rights broadly and vaguely.

Carter knew that certain racial issues had the potential to shred the Democrats' delicate electoral coalition. At a 1974 gathering of Democrats attended by Carter, a debate over quotas divided delegates, although leaders had tried to keep social issues off the agenda. Labor leaders argued that quotas had been disastrous for the Democrats in 1972 and must be abandoned entirely. Blacks and feminists argued for a continuation of the 1972 policies. Ultimately, the convention decided to finesse the issue by endorsing affirmative action and opposing quotas, without clarification. When the likely presidential candidates gathered for an issues convention in Louisville in late 1975, the hall was picketed by antibusing activists angry over a local busing plan. Almost all the candidates dodged the issue, including Carter. Carter's position was complex; he opposed forced busing but advocated busing at public expense for any student who wished it. He also opposed a constitutional amendment to stop mandatory busing and promised to carry out any court order that demanded busing, all the while advocating nonbusing solutions.

Carter, who throughout the campaign would be accused of vagueness on the issues, had taken a similar position on the other divisive social issue of the early primaries, abortion. He condemned abortion as morally evil but was against a constitutional amendment to overturn *Roe* v. *Wade*. He could speak to pro-life and pro-choice groups and leave both with the impression that he was on their side. Similarly, Carter could trumpet his opposition to mandatory busing before a white audience and not mention it a few hours later before an integrated audience. Carter also would include Martin Luther King in his stump speech list of great Americans if blacks were present, but not for many all-white audiences, a practice for which he was criticized during a nationally televised interview and that he pledged to stop. Throughout the campaign, Carter was aided by his indefinite posture on many issues, and race was no exception. Carter's own polling told him that many voters assumed he was conservative on racial issues just because he was a white southerner. When they were told that he had the support of many prominent black Americans, they simply became confused. Critics charged that Carter cynically took vague positions on busing and other racial issues to keep support from blacks and conservative whites. Carter argued that the diversity of his support showed he was a healer who brought opposing factions together. But most impressive was Carter's ability to submerge all issues, including racial ones, beneath the selling force of his personal integrity and character.

Throughout 1975, the white southerner who received the most attention was not Carter, but Wallace. As the roiler of the Democratic primaries of 1964 and 1972, and the spoiler of Democratic hopes in 1968, Wallace was seen as a far more formidable force than the little-known Carter. As late as January 1976, Wallace was so symbolically potent that other candidates were asked by the media whether they would run on the same ticket with Wallace. Wallace had continued to evolve on the question of black equality, and his campaign literature now emphasized God far more than busing. Issues such as abortion, school prayer, and general law and order were the focus, although busing was still attacked. The new Wallace even flew young blacks to Montgomery to persuade them to join his campaign and had a public reconciliation with "Daddy" King, Martin Luther King Jr.'s father.

When the preprimary positioning finally ended, and voters made their initial choices, Carter shocked the political establishment by winning Iowa and New Hampshire in an extraordinarily crowded field. Carter failed, however, to win the next big contest, Massachusetts. The Massachusetts primary demonstrated that busing was still a potent issue. Wallace, who ran hard on the issue, won many precincts in Boston. But the overall winner was Scoop Jackson, who had also trumpeted his opposition to busing. Carter came in fourth, behind Wallace and Morris Udall, the only liberal to do well. Carter blamed his defeat on Jackson's exploitation of the busing issue, which Carter piously pledged to avoid. Carter recovered his momentum with a strong victory in Florida, buoyed by an overwhelming vote in the black community. Some, including civil rights leader Julian Bond, felt that blacks were voting less for Carter than against Wallace. In any case, with the white electorate divided, Carter's black support made the difference, and Carter's victory signaled the end of Wallace's stranglehold on southern primaries.

Carter's campaign, the most integrated in U.S. history, organized in the black community as early as October 1975, often working through black churches. Other campaigns did not emphasize the black vote, because they either didn't expect black support or didn't have the resources. For the first time, according to Carter's deputy campaign manager, Ben Brown (the highest-ranking black in Democratic campaign history), blacks were participating in large-scale grassroots activism, rather than just passively receiving "walk-around" money funneled through their leadership to encourage turnout.

Carter's moment of greatest danger in the primaries came when he spoke with a reporter about public housing. Here, the vague candidate who appealed equally to blacks and Wallace whites suddenly got off message with a disturbingly specific choice of words. Carter endorsed the right of neighborhoods to maintain their "ethnic purity" and criticized government attempts to alter their character. Very quickly, a media frenzy developed, and Carter had to clarify what he meant by "ethnic purity," a phrase that even a Carter supporter, Congressman Andrew Young, felt contained disturbing echoes of Nazism. Carter now spoke of "black intrusions" into all-white areas and the bad effects of "injecting" a "diametrically opposite kind of family" or a "different kind of person" or even "alien groups" into ethnically pure neighborhoods. Carter's comments merely added to the controversy, which became a full-fledged firestorm. Carter, who had resisted pleas from his staff to apologize or retract the statement, finally backed down when both his wife and Young made emphatic requests that he do so. Carter hastily scheduled an event in Atlanta, in which his standing as a racial progressive could be vouched for by Daddy King and other local blacks. While Hosea Williams, a former Martin Luther King associate and longtime Carter foe, led thirty protesters angry at Carter's ethnic purity comment, King accepted Carter's apologies. Weeks later, the Carter staff was still using King in advertising and brochures to convince the black community that it had all been a misstatement.

Carter's comments came under attack from Republicans. Arthur Fletcher, deputy assistant to Ford for urban affairs and one of the few blacks in the White House, called Carter's comment "race baiting": "The votes in Indiana and Michigan are so important that Carter felt he had to say to middle-class blue collar voters that 'I won't let the blacks break your neighborhood up.'" Ford himself attacked the comment and said he would never use that kind of language. It was not only Republicans who felt that Carter had intentionally used "ethnic purity" to reassure racially conservative whites. The timing of the statement, coming just as Wallace had been effectively eliminated as a candidate, and right before the Texas, Indiana, Michigan, Pennsylvania, and Missouri primaries, led some, including Udall, to accuse Carter of carefully planning his statement to appeal to conservative white southerners and ethnics. Some reporters believed that the entire statement had been planned at Carter headquarters. A Republican pollster reported to the Ford campaign that the comment, intentional or not, had been effective, because for every black vote he lost, Carter picked up four white ones.

The Michigan primary was a key test of Carter's appeal in a northern industrial state, given the antipathy that unions and white ethnics seemed to have for his campaign. Following the "ethnic purity" comment, it also became a test of his support in the black community. Carter rallied black voters assiduously in Michigan, while a prominent supporter used a low blow against Carter's major rival in Michigan, Udall. Coleman Young, the fiery black mayor of Detroit, called on blacks to vote against Udall because he was a Mormon, a faith that did not admit blacks to its priesthood. Young contrasted this with Carter's famous attempt to integrate his Baptist church in Plains. The irony was that Udall had not practiced his faith for almost twenty-five years because he disagreed so strongly with the Mormon Church's treatment of blacks, whereas Carter, after failing to integrate his church, had continued his membership in a segregated congregation. Carter, given the opportunity to disavow Young's disingenuous slur on Udall's religion, never did so. Thanks to strong black support, Carter won an extremely narrow victory over Udall in Michigan, thus effectively removing the last viable contender from the race.

After eliminating late-entering rivals Jerry Brown and Frank Church, Carter secured enough delegates to guarantee the nomination. The improbable nominee from a region whose obsession with race had prevented its politicians from competing for the presidency had adroitly used race to win.

FORD VERSUS REAGAN: SO CLOSE THAT BLACK REPUBLICANS MATTERED

Gerald Ford in 1976 faced the toughest intraparty challenge of any incumbent president in this century. An unelected vice president who rose to office in the greatest scandal in the nation's history, Ford was saddled with a poorly performing economy, a resurgent opposition, and a notable lack of charisma. Ronald Reagan, a hero to conservative Republicans throughout the nation, spent much of 1975 contemplating a campaign against Ford. Reagan's issues were the economy, taxes, and foreign policy, particularly anticommunism. However, Reagan, unlike Ford, would raise busing in stump speeches and took the strongest position against it, advocating a constitutional amendment to stop busing, a step that Ford initially opposed. In defeating the Reagan challenge, Ford was forced to adopt a number of conservative positions, including hardening his opposition to busing. The first casualty of Reagan's challenge was the last great fighter for civil rights in the Republican Party, Nelson Rockefeller. Selected by Ford to be his vice president in 1974, Rockefeller remained a thorn in the side of conservatives, particularly southern conservatives. In a gesture to conservatives, Ford announced that Rockefeller would not be his running mate.

Ford's initial campaign plans did not include outreach to black Americans or much attention to racial issues. In a twenty-nine-page campaign plan in early 1975, the black community is not even mentioned. In a state-by-state analysis of key primary battlegrounds with

Reagan, race is almost never addressed, not even in Massachusetts, which was still convulsed over busing. Ford's failure to reach out directly to blacks did not prevent the remaining black Republicans from registering a strong preference for Ford over Reagan. In the Illinois showdown with Reagan, Ford received 78 percent of the black vote. Black Republicans were particularly strong in the South, and in Florida and North Carolina, their leadership endorsed Ford. Black turnout in the hard-fought Republican primaries in Tennessee and Kentucky, though small, may have been enough to win those states for Ford. Ford even ran ads on black radio stations during the Michigan primary. Even if few blacks responded, each was almost a sure vote for Ford, because of Reagan's anemic support among blacks. Reagan could not even retain the loyalty of his closest black associate, Robert Keyes, who endorsed Ford.

The preference for Ford over Reagan among black Republicans was a product of the two men's contrasting history, style, and rhetoric. Reagan had opposed every major civil rights act, while Ford had supported them. During the campaign, Reagan even questioned the value of the civil rights movement of the 1960s and then retreated into stale platitudes and anecdotes when reporters pressed him on it. Reagan came from the Goldwater wing of the party, while Ford was a northern Republican with ties to Rockefeller. Finally, Reagan's rhetoric and issues often mirrored George Wallace's (albeit in a much sunnier style), and he attracted many of the same supporters. Ford's pollster found that Wallace and Reagan supporters were almost indistinguishable in attitudes. As Wallace's candidacy was throttled by the Carter juggernaut, Reagan relied on former Wallace backers in Republican primaries in states like Michigan and Texas. Reagan's campaign sent out one hundred thousand brochures to Wallace supporters in Georgia, anticipating that they would want to vote for Reagan instead.

Why was Reagan the choice of many former Wallace voters and racially conservative whites? Certainly Ford was more moderate than Reagan on many domestic and foreign issues, but Ford was also more moderate on race. Even after eighty-eight members of Congress asked Ford to endorse a constitutional amendment to ban busing,

Ford remained ambivalent. Ford's opposition to busing was expressed in moderate tones; he even discussed how his own children had been bused without problems. In many ways, Ford's position on busing was similar to Carter's, except that Governor Carter had once supported an antibusing amendment, although candidate Carter now denied that.

By contrast, Reagan's rhetoric against busing was unrestrained, and he fulsomely endorsed a constitutional amendment. A conservative group ran independent ads touting Reagan's fervor against busing and contrasting it with Ford's failure to endorse a constitutional amendment. Reagan linked declines in educational achievement to compulsory busing. In a nationwide telecast in the midst of the primaries, Reagan highlighted his opposition to busing and alleged that busing was causing racial bitterness and animosity.

Reagan was also the only major candidate in 1976 to echo Nixon's 1972 diatribes against quotas. In another national telecast Reagan claimed white people were being victimized:

> ... we have adopted legislation to guarantee civil rights and eliminate discrimination of all kinds. Certainly no one of us would challenge government's right and responsibility to eliminate discrimination in hiring or education.* But in its zeal to accomplish this worthy purpose, government orders what is in effect a quota system both in hiring and in education. They don't call it a quota system. It is an affirmative action program . . . if you happen to belong to an ethnic group not recognized by the federal government as entitled to special treatment, you are a victim of reverse discrimination . . . if your ancestry . . . is Czechoslovakian, Polish, Italian, or if you are of the Jewish faith, you may find yourself the victim of discrimination. . . .

Quotas and busing had been two issues that had pulled Wallace voters to the GOP in 1972, and Reagan utilized both in his desperate

---

* Ironically, Reagan himself had challenged government's right and responsibility to eliminate discrimination in hiring and education in speeches throughout the 1960s.

struggle with Ford. His campaign did not hesitate to put even blunter racial symbols into play. Reagan supporters in North Carolina distributed a racist flyer that alleged that Ford was going to name black Republican senator Edward Brooke as his running mate. Even Ford's advocacy of black rule in South Africa and Rhodesia hurt him among some conservative whites, who approved of Reagan's more sympathetic attitude toward the white racist governments.

In June, it became clear that the Ford-Reagan contest might go all the way to the convention and be decided on the floor, for the first time since 1948. In this pressurized situation, Ford now proposed new legislation against busing and met with congressional leaders to convey his dismay at the behavior of federal courts in busing cases. Although short of a ban, the bill would have made busing much harder for judges to impose. Speaking in Indiana, Ford unleashed a rare public attack on federal courts that were "practically running our school boards." The audience of Indiana Jaycees erupted with applause for Ford's new populist rhetoric. Even with Ford's adoption of more conservative positions on a number of issues, including busing, the primaries were ultimately inconclusive; the nomination would be decided at the convention. Still, the significance of the 1976 Republican primaries for the evolution of American racial politics was obvious; it was the last Republican contest in which black voters mattered and the first in which former Wallace voters were crucial.

THE DEMOCRATIC CONVENTION: CARTER'S RACIAL UNITY PLATFORM

At the Democratic convention in New York, Carter had to negotiate several difficult racial matters. First, there was the tension between his forces and the traditional black leadership. The Caucus of Black Democrats did not endorse Carter until the last minute. Many of the members had been delegate nominees for other candidates in the primaries and were defeated by Carter forces. Carter's campaign had succeeded in going around the leaders and reaping a harvest of black votes, particularly in the North. Other blacks had sometimes called Carter's supporters "cracker lovers" in the primaries, perhaps because Carter's success in the black community represented a challenge to established black leaders. As one Carter staffer put it, "The Carter train has gone and it is filled with black voters, which proves certain leaders have lost control of their constituencies. What they do may not really matter." In particular, Jesse Jackson was singled out for exclusion, with a Carter aide asking sarcastically, "Jesse who?" in response to a reporter's inquiry. Jackson had been given money in 1972 to register black voters and campaign for McGovern, but he was promised no such benefits in 1976. "We can't grease wheels that squeak but don't produce votes," said another Carter aide. Unlike McGovern in 1972, Carter's margin of victory was so substantial that he did not have to negotiate on matters of substance with black leaders or even make much room for black leaders who had supported other candidates in the primaries.

Jackson tried to influence the running mate selection process by demanding that Carter consider Los Angeles mayor Tom Bradley for the slot, but the Carter staff had already circulated Bradley's name, as well as that of Barbara Jordan of Texas, as possible black running mates. Although Carter never seriously considered either politician, including them was seen as a gesture to an important constituency. Carter's choice, Walter Mondale, was surely one that pleased most black Democrats. Mondale's record on racial equality extended back to the 1950s, when he had worked closely with the leadership of the NAACP. Mondale had been so pro-busing that he had been known as "Mr. Busing," although he now amended his position quickly to mesh with Carter's.

The platform also had to address busing. Busing was more than just the most important racial issue of 1976; "it symbolized for blacks whether the federal government would support genuine integration or would remain content with the mere appearance of equality." The party could not cavalierly abandon busing, despite its widespread unpopularity, without offending one of its core constituencies. The platform committee had locked horns on busing since April, when the chair had been forced to resign largely because he opposed busing. In the end, the Democrats adopted a platform endorsing "mandatory transportation" as a euphemism for busing. Hamilton Jordan, Carter's campaign manager, carefully noted that the only difference Carter had with the platform was that he strongly opposed busing. Carter's blur on busing was now complete; he opposed busing, but also a constitutional amendment to ban it. He felt it was a terrible solution but ran on a platform supporting it, which he disavowed, with a running mate with a long pro-busing history, which Mondale now denied. A voter concerned about busing had a tough time figuring out whether to vote for Carter.

The Democratic platform also euphemistically advocated "compensatory opportunity" as opposed to affirmative action or quotas, thus papering over another potential divide in the party. The delegate quotas that had led to the highest rates of black representation in convention history in 1972 were still present, in muted form, in 1976. DNC chair Robert Strauss had offended the Black Caucus in late 1975 when he suggested that having affirmative action for party committees would result in "mediocrity." Strauss ultimately compromised and endorsed "diversity," which he set at 20–25 percent of all committee slots being given to minorities. As the convention neared, black activists complained that they were receiving fewer delegate slots than they had in 1972. When the rules committee debated "goals and timetables" for black representation, the Carter delegates suddenly went neutral. After a great outcry from black leaders, Carter quietly yielded the point. Blacks did not have as large a portion of the overall delegate total as they had in 1972, but their influence was greater, particularly those who had been with Carter all along. The message of inclusion was clear, from the rousing speech of Texas's Barbara Jordan, to the ringing benediction by Daddy King, to the singing of the anthem of the civil rights movement, "We Shall Overcome," in Madison Square Garden. A white southern Democrat, from the wing of the party that had split off from FDR's coalition over the status of blacks with alarming regularity since 1948, now pledged his commitment to racial equality. Carter left the convention with an extraordinary lead over Gerald Ford, who was still battling Reagan for the nomination.

FORD'S INEPT NEGLECT OF THE BLACK VOTE

Ford ultimately defeated Reagan at the Republican convention in Kansas City, but Reagan's disappointment at his narrow loss was obvious, as was his failure to wholly endorse his victorious rival. Reagan also tightly restricted Ford's choice of running mates, leading Ford to pick conservative senator Robert Dole. Wounded by Watergate, the economy, and the bruising battle with Reagan, Ford entered the general election twenty points behind the new face in American politics, Jimmy Carter.

Blacks had played almost no role in the final showdown with Reagan, perhaps because their percentage of the convention delegates dropped from 4.2 percent in 1972 to 3.4 percent. Although Ford's black aides had been trumpeting their man's openness to blacks and the growing bipartisan nature of the black vote, Ford's campaign made little to no effort in the black community in the general election. The black vote had been crucial in a few close states in defeating Reagan, but now the Ford campaign simply assumed that blacks would vote for Carter no matter what outreach was adopted. The Presidential Campaign Task Force saw Catholics as a voting group that could be wooed from the Democratic coalition but paid little attention to black voters. The best that could be done with blacks was to "find issues that will make Democratic militancy less successful and increase interest in the Republican party. . . ." The memo also cynically suggested that the recent uptick in black unemployment could result in lower turnout, a benefit to Ford's chances. Additionally, since press coverage had suggested that Carter was buying the black vote through payoffs to ministers, the task force suggested identifying some uncommitted black clergy "and work[ing] out a plan to neutralize the Democratic effort . . ." implicitly by buying up some ministers. Ford's chief of staff was told to give up on the black vote because of Carter's popularity with blacks. The strategy was to push aid to Africa, emphasize the black business community, and hope for the best.

Given the campaign's attitude toward black voters, it is not surprising that Ford's effort in the black community was poorly funded, woefully late in getting off the ground, and ultimately ineffectual. Although a coordinated campaign was suggested as early as November 1975, no such plan was successfully implemented. By the time James Baker, campaign chair, asked in September 1976 for more outreach to the black community, it was far too late. The "Black Desk" at People for Ford began operating only a month before the election. As late as October, the grandly titled "State Coordinators for Black Voter Mobilization" had coordinators in only nineteen states. The conversion of individual blacks to Ford was cause for celebration at the Black Desk. When the Black Desk held a press conference, only one local reporter came, although all the major media outlets were invited.

The sheer ineptness of Ford's outreach to blacks was stunning. In the closing weeks of the contest, Ford's campaign distributed a brochure entitled "Black Voters for a Republican Congress." It boasted of 286 high-level black federal officials, but most of them had achieved their positions through the civil service system rather than presidential appointment. This pathetic attempt to elide over the paucity of black faces in the Ford administration did not go unnoticed by Democrats. At about the same time, the only Ford print ads directed at the black community appeared, picturing Vernon Jordan and Jesse Jackson, who had not endorsed Ford at all. The deceptive ads were withdrawn when these leaders made public their displeasure with such tactics. In the last week of October, an "Independent Clergy Campaign Committee" was organized to rally black churches behind Ford, but its sole press release alleging that Carter was a deceptive "Shimmy Jimmy" received little coverage.

The campaign failed to target any television ads at the black community, although they did purchase a few token ads on black radio stations, solely so the media could not report that they had entirely surrendered the black vote to Carter. Ford's top media consultant believed that targeting ads at blacks was hopeless, since they were all in Carter's camp. The media staff was also told two months before the election that the black vote had never affected the outcome of any presidential election and could safely be ignored. Some in the Ford campaign did hope that Carter's status as a white southerner would lower Carter's support in the black community, but they made no effort to make an appeal to blacks.

Ford continued in his strategy of offering no special policies for blacks and even made that the major comment he made on race during the campaign.

> I would like as many supporters in the black community as possible. I have always had it in my own Congressional races. . . . I intend to do what I can in presenting the broad programs I have recommended and I believe they will help and assist all minorities. But to go out and offer a particular piece of legislation for any segment of our society in order to get them to vote for me, I think it is the wrong approach for a Presidential candidate. I want help and assistance from the black community, but I don't intend to sacrifice my overall approach.

The Ford message to blacks was particularly sanctimonious given the policy pirouettes the president was dancing for any number of other constituencies, with stances designed to win their votes. Ford piously refused to play the grand game of American politics with blacks, when they knew he was playing it with everyone else.

In early October, any hope that Ford would win substantial black support disappeared when his secretary of agriculture, Earl Butz, made an outrageous racist comment. When asked by a reporter in an informal setting why the Republicans didn't win more black support, Butz replied that all "coloreds" cared about was having "tight pussy, loose shoes, and a warm place to shit." Ford, torn between his anger at the remark and his loyalty to Butz, waited four days to demand his resignation, a delay that made the president appear tolerant of such behavior. The Black Desk at the Ford campaign officially had no comment, although they tried to link Butz's remarks to Carter's "ethnic purity" comment of the spring. Arthur Fletcher, a black Ford adviser, went on TV to argue that blacks found Butz's comments funny. The Butz affair received a great deal of coverage on network news and throughout the media and was perhaps the last thing black voters heard about Ford before they entered the voting booth. The Ford campaign had "given up on the black vote before Mr. Butz's remark," but Ford missed an opportunity to speak strongly against prejudice by firing Butz immediately. Also, unlike

Carter when his ethnic purity comment had become a scandal, Ford had no ongoing outreach to the black community to fall back on.

Indisputably, the Ford campaign made no sincere effort at the black vote. The Ford record on civil rights was substantial, in terms of enforcing the laws and increasing aid to black colleges, but Ford never put that record before the black electorate, instead almost keeping it a "secret" according to his most prominent black appointee. Ford's final image in the black community was of a man who blandly endorsed racial equality, but strictly avoided appealing to black voters, and who was ambivalent about prejudice in high places. This was an improvement over Richard Nixon, but the man Ford had to compete with for black votes had a special connection to the black community, which Ford could not equal.

CARTER'S BLACK APPEAL: MAGNETISM WITHOUT SUBSTANCE

> The cadences with which he speaks are much more familiar to us. He gives us a sense of intimacy—we grew up with him.
>
> ELEANOR HOLMES NORTON, ON JIMMY CARTER

Surprisingly, Jimmy Carter, like Ford, was not making many special policy appeals to black Americans, although he was not politically tone-deaf enough to trumpet that to the world. When his staff met to discuss issues for the general election, they created a list of twelve issues, not only avoiding the topic of civil rights, but actively pushing code words that would appeal to racial conservatives.

> The current welfare system is demeaning to the recipients, overly burdensome to the taxpayers, and overly bureaucratized. It is wasteful, duplicative, inefficient, discouraging to work, and encouraging to family break-up. We need a streamlined, simplified welfare system with strong work incentives.

This was rhetoric that Democrats had been calling racist for a decade when Republicans used it, but it positioned Carter well to continue to win the votes of Wallace whites. Only Jesse Jackson questioned whether Carter's anti-Washington and antiwelfare rhetoric represented an attack on social programs vital to blacks. In the Democratic attack/response book, distributed to campaign staff, civil rights and minorities are scarcely mentioned. Compared to the policy positions designed to appeal to women voters, black issues were given short shrift. When Vernon Jordan, president of the Urban League, had given his "State of Black America" speech in January, he had listed a number of issues that black America favored, such as vastly increased aid to cities, a full employment plan, a guaranteed minimum income, tax increases on the wealthy, one million new public-sector jobs, new integrated public housing, strong enforcement of court-ordered desegregation, more social spending generally, and tough gun control. Unlike McGovern, who had explicitly endorsed racial set-asides, busing, and many other demands of black groups, Carter made only a few broad promises to his black audiences, such as national health care, an increase in aid to cities, and advocacy of majority black rule in Africa. Carter also could point to his record of appointing blacks in Georgia's government, which contrasted sharply with Ford's very white administration.

Despite Carter's vague stances on issues of concern to black Americans, he won enthusiastic responses from black audiences across the country. Part of the explanation was the common religious experience Carter shared with most blacks. As a Southern Baptist, Carter understood the language of the black church in a way that no northern white could. For one black Republican, Carter's status as a born-again fundamentalist Christian was "the secret of his success with blacks. Whites do not understand this. . . . There are more evangelicals in the black church than any other." Many candidates spoke at black churches, but when Carter did it, he had an instant ease, a "soul thing," because of his grasp of evangelical doctrine. The black church remained the most influential institution in the black community, and ministers felt more comfortable exhorting their followers to vote for a fellow Baptist, who spoke of redemption and sin with casual frequency.*

---

* Carter's outreach to black churches led to a minor uproar when it was revealed that his campaign was paying black ministers for their support.

Carter also shared a regional heritage with most blacks. The vast majority of blacks either lived in the South or were first- or second-generation migrants from it. Given that no region had treated blacks with greater cruelty, Carter's unquestioned passion for racial equality made a deep impression. "To watch Jimmy Carter speaking to a black audience is to watch the myth of redemption acted out in reality. He speaks intimately, softly, respectfully, even lovingly." Although both Ford and Carter attacked racism, an endorsement of racial equality from a southern politician seemed to mean more than the same words from a northerner. Even Carter's childhood upbringing among the offspring of his family's servants, which could have been used against him to devastating effect, worked in his favor. As Andrew Young put it: "Jimmy Carter grew up with black people. He didn't have to study about race and poverty at Harvard. And we have a kind of radar about white people. We know the ones who are in our corner and we know that Jimmy Carter is comfortable among us." For southern blacks, Carter could also play to regional pride, a powerful force among both races in the region.

The Carter campaign was clearly counting on black support in the election. In addition to the early organizing that Carter had already conducted prior to the primaries, the DNC now committed a record amount of money to voter registration in the black community. The issue differences with Gerald Ford were subtle, as both men were downplaying racial issues, but Carter was committing vast resources of time and money to the black vote, while Ford was ignoring it.

THE FORD RESTRAINT ON RACE

Ford had given up on the black vote before the race began. This made an outreach to racially conservative whites an obvious strategic option, since there were practically no black votes to be lost. Would Ford attempt to steal the Wallace vote from Carter, who sometimes appeared to be Wallace without the racism? If Ford was going to do so, the issues to hit were busing and quotas.

Ford was never able to make much of an issue of busing, in part because Carter's own antibusing stance made it difficult. Indeed,

Carter had attacked "Ford's busing" in a primary speech in Michigan in May. Ford's advisers were confused about how to play busing— should they attack Carter for failing to desegregate the Atlanta schools, an appeal to blacks and liberals? Or should they attack Mondale, who favored busing but sent his own children to private schools, an appeal to conservative whites? Ford finally did reluctantly endorse a constitutional amendment forbidding the assignment of students to schools on the basis of race, which Carter now opposed. Yet Ford at a number of points in the campaign avoided making busing the central thrust of a speech or an appeal. Similarly, his running mate seldom emphasized that he was a longtime opponent of busing, while Mondale had the strongest pro-busing record in Congress.

Unlike Nixon in 1972, Ford never made an issue of the quotas that the Democrats were using within their own party. Ford's own administration continued using racial set-asides in construction and other areas, which may have explained his reluctance. Additionally, Carter did not openly advocate proportional representation in employment, as McGovern had done. But the greatest difference between 1972 and 1976 may have been the character of the Republican nominees. Nixon, thirty points ahead, continued to pound hard on divisive racial issues, while Ford, a few points down in the closing weeks, refused to use race to win votes. The contrast was most stark in their efforts to woo Jewish voters, the voting group that cared most about racial quotas. Nixon had written a public letter to the American Jewish Committee attacking racial quotas; when Ford spoke to the AJC, he did not even broach the subject. A Jewish weekly, reviewing the issues of concern to Jewish voters, argued that the positions of the two candidates on racial quotas were similar; both were opposed. Another Jewish magazine had Carter favoring quotas, with Ford firmly against. Carter had succeeded in blurring his position on the two hot racial issues of the day, busing and affirmative action. Regardless, quotas were simply not salient, and Ford made no effort to change that or even to force Carter to take a clear stance on the issue. Had Carter taken a firm position for or against racial set-asides, Carter's ability to attract racial conservatives and blacks would have been attenuated. As it was, Carter almost never mentioned affirmative action, quotas, set-asides, or proportional representation of any kind, although he frequently promised to make high-profile appointments of blacks.

Ford's restraint on busing prevailed even as the race tightened to a statistical dead heat in the last week. During a visit to Buffalo on the eve of the election, Ford was advised by Congressman Jack Kemp and by the editor of the local newspaper that Ford could win huge political gains by merely mentioning busing, and if he promised Justice Department intervention, Republican turnout would skyrocket. In his remarks, Ford avoided the topic; Ford narrowly lost New York, a state that would have given him the White House. That same week, Ford's solicitor general, Robert Bork, endorsed busing as a limited remedy in some cases, while opposing it in others. A Ronald Reagan or a George Wallace would never have let his Justice Department take such a mixed stand a week before an election. Unlike Nixon, Ford believed in a depoliticized Justice Department. His attorney general, Edward Levi, was a strong proponent of racial equality, and when Levi told Ford to stay out of the busing issue, Ford did. Ford's message on busing was in many ways as ambivalent and confused as Carter's, making it impossible for Ford to exploit the issue.

Why did Ford refuse to make special appeals to black voters yet also refuse to use race as a wedge issue? The answer to the first question may have been that by 1976, the Democratic advantage among blacks had been so engrained that it was accepted as a political law. Ford's refusal to cater to the concerns of whites who opposed busing is harder to explain. Some in the campaign saw busing as a key social issue that could attract Democratic votes. Another strategic campaign memo, however, argued that

> . . . the problems in running a major busing issue are difficult. It is not at all clear that traditional bread and butter issues would be set aside by antibusing Democrats in order to vote Republican. The best thing would be to catch Jimmy Carter on busing, since he stands to lose more by a position than the Republicans. This could probably be organized so as to get a real debate going among Democrats.

Whether it was this pragmatic advice or Ford's conscience, a review of the media coverage, speeches, and internal documents of the Ford campaign indicates that divisive racial issues such as busing and quotas were never central to Ford's campaign, as they had been in Nixon's 1972 effort. Had Ford been less circumspect on racial issues such as busing, he could have won key states like Louisiana and New York.

The Ford restraint on race won him few plaudits in the black community. Jesse Jackson argued that "the code word for racism in this campaign has been the bus . . . and the President himself no less is willing to play with our basic and fundamental piece of legal legislation that has ramifications for our other rights." A top NAACP official alleged that Ford had "staked his political fortunes on the degree to which he can inflame the nation over an issue that concerns only a tiny fraction of all the children who ride buses." An NAACP spokesman alleged that Ford was "using the busing issue to send a message to bigots everywhere." Given that Ford and Carter had almost indistinguishable positions on busing, these comments are inexplicable. A Carter supporter, Barbara Jordan, would say of Carter's opposition to busing only that it "does not quite suit my needs." Ford's quiet opposition to busing was portrayed as rank bigotry; Carter's was ignored.

CONCLUSION: FORD'S MISSED CHANCE

Jimmy Carter barely defeated Gerald Ford to win the White House, and in that victory, the black vote was universally recognized as crucial. Most whites had voted Republican, and it was only Carter's extraordinary 90 percent margin among blacks, as well as a surprise uptick in black turnout, that gave the Georgian the presidency. Black voters made the difference in Alabama, Florida, Louisiana, Maryland, Mississippi, Missouri, New York, North Carolina, Ohio, Pennsylvania, South Carolina, Texas, and Wisconsin. Without the black vote, Carter would not have carried any region of the country.

The blunt truth remains that Ford refused to compete for the black vote, and had he done so, he would have been elected to the White House. As Ford's media consultant put it, "We utterly failed to communicate with the black voters of America. . . . I have to conclude this was the biggest single factor in our defeat." Could Ford have launched a credible campaign for the black vote? Certainly Carter would have been vulnerable. The Ford campaign considered attacking Carter for his antiblack behavior in the 1960s, when he voted raises for white teachers but not for blacks, kept black students picking cotton while white students were in school, and allied with redneck voters and Lester Maddox to win the governorship in 1970. Carter's continuing membership in the whites-only Order of Moose was also contemplated as a target. A bold foray into the black ghetto was also fervently advocated by a Ford staffer, who noted Carter's reluctance to personally speak in black areas for fear of being too closely allied in the white mind with the black cause. At the very least, the visit would help "neutralize" anti-Ford feeling among blacks. In the end, neither Ford nor Carter would venture far into the ghetto, the perfect symbol of how both campaigns did not want to highlight issues of race. If Ford had wanted the black vote, he could have attacked Carter's record on race, made targeted appeals to blacks as he had to other groups, and made sincere, coordinated campaign efforts, including appearances in black neighborhoods. Ford did none of these things and gave away the black vote without a fight. Had Ford received a fifth of the black vote, he would have won enough states to defeat Carter handsomely.

Ford chose neither to emulate the Richard Nixon of 1960 and highlight civil rights to appeal to blacks nor to emulate the Nixon of 1972 and use race as a wedge issue to fray the Democratic coalition. This strategic choice allowed Carter to win an extraordinary majority among blacks and be competitive among more conservative whites. The question for the Republican Party was, what now? With the Democrats dominating the White House, both houses of Congress, and a majority of governorships and statehouses, the immediate future for the GOP was almost as bleak as it had been following the post-Goldwater collapse of 1964. Political historian Wilson Carey McWilliams wrote that Carter's victory might foretell the end of the Republican Party and the beginning of a new Era of Good Feeling, in which one party dominated all regions of the country.

Some felt that the Republicans simply had to compete for the black vote if they were going to be a viable party. Dole, Ford's running mate, complained that he had been scheduled to speak to Jews, Hispanics, and many other groups, but not blacks, and that had been a major mistake. If the black vote gave Carter the White House, and if one of Ford's biggest errors was to fail to make more than an inept, token appeal for black support, then the message of the 1976 election for Republicans should have been to reach out to the black electorate.

Carter's pollster, however, was sanguine about the stability of black support for the Democrats. In a postelection analysis, Pat Caddell told Carter that blacks would stay with the Democrats as long as the party "fulfills the easy task of being more sensitive to their concerns than the Republicans." Would the Republicans ever make winning the black vote a difficult task for the Democrats?

CARTER AND THE POLITICS OF FEAR
The Forced Racial Politics of 1980

It's going to be all right to kill niggers when he's president!

AMBASSADOR ANDREW YOUNG, OF RONALD REAGAN, 1980

After you get through booing, who the hell are you going to vote for?

MAYOR COLEMAN YOUNG TO A BLACK AUDIENCE, ENDORSING CARTER

Racial issues were far from the minds of most voters in 1980. Two issues dominated the public discourse: the wretched state of the economy and the decline in American stature in the world. Beyond economic and foreign concerns, the election revolved around widespread disdain for Carter, balanced against fears of Reagan's allegedly extreme views on domestic policy and military matters. Racial issues seldom surfaced. In one sense, this reflected an emerging consensus on many racial matters. Not even Ronald Reagan, Goldwater's ideological heir, could openly challenge the core civil rights victories of the 1960s. Not even Jimmy Carter, a man who owed much of his political success to African Americans, would propose a program for blacks that might upset white opinion. The presidential campaigns of 1980 reflected a weary centrism on racial matters. In the midst of that weariness, Carter attempted to inject a primal fear of Ronald Reagan's racial beliefs into the political discourse, without much success. In Gallup polling, racial issues almost failed to register as a national concern.

Yet amid the noise of the 1980 election, racial politics can be discerned at key points. Truly, racial politics was so embedded in our national elections that not even high unemployment, rising inflation, and an ongoing foreign policy crisis could eliminate it from the campaign. Ronald Reagan benefited from his historic position atop the white backlash, while Carter would make a calculated attempt to frighten blacks to the voting booth.

1980: THE SETTING

As the 1980 election season began, Americans were uncertain about their national leadership and about America's role in the world. Carter made a nationally televised speech about moral malaise in the national psyche. American spirits were further dampened when radical Iranian students captured American embassy workers. Throughout the marathon of the 1980 campaign, the hostages would be a constant sideshow, a lingering accusation against America's current leadership.

The economy was deeply troubled, with little growth amid high inflation, rising unemployment, and skyrocketing interest rates. As with every previous downturn in the economy, the burden fell harder on black than on white. Yet the rise in unemployment did not seem to bring greater national attention to the most economic of racial issues, affirmative action. The Supreme Court had spoken in 1978 to the legality of affirmative action in admissions programs, when in the memorable 4–1–4 *Bakke* decision, it upheld some efforts at diversity but ruled quotas illegal. The cautious moderation of that split decision seemed to echo the nation's own mood about many racial matters. By 1980, busing had fallen almost entirely off the national radar. Fewer intercounty busing plans were implemented, and when they were, little uproar ensued. Major busing plans went into effect in 1980 in St. Louis, Indianapolis, and Dallas, without significant conflict.

The economic distress of America's inner city did erupt in riots in Chattanooga, Orlando, and Miami's ghettos, but these events failed to put racial issues on the nation's agenda. By the start of the general election campaign, when *Time* put a graphic of the typical U.S. voter's brain on its cover, the issues pictured in this fictional cranium ranged from nuclear power to the Equal Rights Amendment, but none related to race.

THE CANDIDATES

Ronald Reagan

In the presidential debate of 1980, Ronald Reagan would make a revealing gaffe, speaking of a time "when this country didn't even know it had a racial problem." As Carter quickly pointed out, for the victims of racial oppression, there was no such halcyon era. But Reagan's statement revealed a fundamental truth about his upbringing in small-town Middle America. Reagan grew up in a world in which African Americans were occasionally seen and almost never heard, although his parents raised him to be without racial prejudice. Throughout his public life, Reagan would resort to one or two time-worn anecdotes involving his personal opposition to segregation during the era in which it was widely practiced. Reagan relentlessly used his private opposition to racial discrimination to mask his consistent failure to endorse public efforts to fight it.

Reagan's debut on the national scene was his electrifying 1964 televised speech in favor of Barry Goldwater. Reagan would always be perceived as part of Goldwater's movement, a movement that, while ostensibly nonracist, opposed the key civil rights acts of the 1960s with unapologetic fervor. Reagan's speech, like most of Goldwater's, avoided any explicit appeal to the racially conservative whites abandoning Johnson over the issue of civil rights. Still, like his mentor, Reagan disliked federal legislation to enforce even the most basic rights of access. His stock phrase was "You can't guarantee someone's freedom by imposing on someone else's."

Reagan's first run for public office quickly taught him that racial politics could not always be avoided. During the 1966 primary for the gubernatorial nomination, Reagan faced two moderate Republicans. At a black Republican convention, the other two insinuated that Reagan was racist. Reagan, in a rare public display of fury, shouted an obscenity, crumpled up his speech, tossed it into the audience, and stalked out of the event, muttering curses. The press coverage was brutal. Throughout his career, Reagan would react with visceral anger to any suggestion that he was racially insensitive or prejudiced. There would be many such charges. During the same campaign, as white fears of urban riots and crime reached their apex, Reagan ran ads warning that the cities were becoming "jungles. . . . In the backlash context of 1966, it touched a nerve especially among low-income whites who lived near the ghettoes."

As governor, Reagan would appoint blacks to several positions and set up a minorities office to guide outreach to blacks and Hispanics. However, issues kept putting barriers between Reagan and the black community. Reagan, who had opposed federal housing bills because he argued nondiscrimination in housing was a state matter, now sought to repeal California's open housing law. Reagan was unable to explain the contradiction, simply stating that even bigots and racists had a constitutional right to dispose of their property as they saw fit.

Reagan was an icon of resistance to the whole array of social movements sweeping California and the nation from 1966 to 1974. Reagan was a hardliner about campus disturbances and urban riots. Reagan observed, "The greatest proof of how far we've advanced in race relations is that the white community today hasn't lifted a finger against the Negroes." Praising whites for not killing blacks en masse was not exactly winning Reagan many black supporters. Nor was it accurate; far more blacks were killed by whites than the reverse during the riots of the 1960s. Reagan's comment on the death of King was similarly misguided; the death was "a great tragedy that began when we began compromising with law and order and people started choosing which laws they'd break." King's southern opponents since 1955 had long argued that nonviolent civil disobedience would only lead whites to respond with violence; Reagan echoed that sick canard, even as King was mourned by a shocked nation. Reagan also campaigned for reelection in 1970 on a platform that aggressively attacked welfare fraud, which for many voters was implicitly a racial issue. The contrast of Reagan's racial stances with the contemporaneous acts and rhetoric of men like Nelson Rockefeller and Robert F. Kennedy could not be starker. The earliest perception of Reagan by many critics was of a "heartless know-nothing foe of the poor, higher education, and racial minorities." While his overall record as governor does not support that image, it remained indelibly associated with him for many Americans.

From his first political speech, Reagan had been extremely popular in the white South. Reagan refused to criticize George Wallace, which some suspected was a political calculation to win the South's support for the nomination in 1968. Nixon's pollster found that Reagan was associated in many white minds with the backlash against black progress. As late as 1980, Reagan blamed the Voting Rights Act of 1965 for the humiliation it brought to the South. Some might have seen decades of electoral racism as humiliating, but for Reagan, the federal cure was the problem. Reagan traveled extensively throughout the South, giving speeches to largely white audiences, "learning how to gain political support and backing . . . by discovering firsthand which code words for race would work." Much of his popularity had nothing to do with race, deriving instead from his stances on taxes, foreign policy, abortion, and school prayer, but Reagan's reputation since 1966 as the smooth spokesman for the white backlash surely didn't hurt.

In 1976, Reagan used his southern popularity effectively against Gerald Ford in the primaries, while at the same time, Reagan's record contributed to Ford's overwhelming victory among black Republicans. During the competition with Ford, Reagan mentioned a "young buck" standing in a grocery line buying luxuries with state aid. Reagan, alerted that the phrase was an offensive reference to black males, never used it again, though he defended it as a nonracial term common in his Illinois hometown. It was also in the 1976 campaign that Reagan repeatedly told his audiences about a "welfare queen" who fraudulently bilked the system for hundreds of thousands of dollars. While he never referred to the woman by race, the original case did involve a black woman (as was known to many in his audiences). Even after reporters pointed out the many errors and exaggerations in his welfare queen story, Reagan continued to tell his erroneous version, which was quite a crowd pleaser.

In the heat of the campaign, Reagan felt betrayed when one of his earliest black appointees, Robert Keyes, endorsed Ford and charged his former boss with racism. So hurt was Reagan by Keyes's allegation that when Keyes later called Reagan from his deathbed to make peace with his old boss, Reagan refused to take the call. That Reagan, a master of the sympathetic gesture, would refuse to talk to a dying man who had once been his friend demonstrates how personally Reagan took any allegation of racism.

Was Ronald Reagan a racist? There is very little credible evidence to suggest that he was personally afflicted with prejudice. An "insensitive" joke in 1965 to a black politician about cannibalism in Africa is a rare exception. Such jokes were common in Reagan's Hollywood and were even told by black comics. Many of his closest associates, who do not hesitate to raise criticisms about flaws in his management style, do not attribute any prejudice to Reagan. Reagan did not "think in terms of race; it was no big deal to him." Yet this attitude itself was an irritant to many minorities. Not to think about race was to suggest that race was not a problem. Although Reagan said in 1967 that "bigotry and prejudice is [sic] probably the worst of all men's ills," Reagan opposed federal efforts to ensure racial equality. Thus, Reagan was perceived by many blacks as more dangerous than a blatantly racist politician. He was an amiable white man who could never be tarred with the charge of racism, but who did not see racism in others as a problem and opposed most public efforts to fight it. Reagan, who lacked racial animus himself, became the first prophet of color-blind politics. Yet he was also a man blind to the pain that ignorance and racial insensitivity could cause minorities and to the damage that it could do to his party.

Jimmy Carter

By late 1979, it was clear that Carter's presidency had not been a successful one. He would have to struggle mightily to win his own party's nomination. One bright area, seemingly, in Carter's administration was his record of assistance and outreach to African Americans. Carter trumpeted his appointments of blacks to high office throughout government. The number of black federal judges rose from sixteen to forty, and the number in the South went from zero to sixteen. Carter appointed more black judges than all previous presidents combined. From its earliest moments, the Carter administration carefully monitored the number of black appointees. Racial balance in key departments such as Education was watched carefully. Even the prominence of white officials in the national media was examined to make sure that minority appointees were not perceived as "figureheads."

Carter's accomplishments also included fighting discrimination in banking and applying economic pressure to the white minority governments in Africa. On affirmative action, the most contentious racial issue of the period, Carter had quietly expanded the scope of federal affirmative action plans and set far more precise goals for various localities in contracting. As one Carter supporter put it, he had "moved the government out of the shadow of 'benign neglect' into the sunshine of 'affirmative action.'" In Carter's boldest attack on racial conservatism, he moved against segregated southern academies, some of which had been quietly receiving tax exemptions. When news of this leaked, over 115,000 protest letters flooded into the White House and a nationwide ad campaign was mounted to defend these "private Christian schools."

Nothing that Carter did on these issues could change the simple fact that his economic and fiscal policies were far more conservative than black political leaders wanted. As Carter cut his domestic budget deeper each year to fight inflation, black supporters began to waver. A memo from Carter's top domestic adviser warned that Vernon Jordan of the Urban League and Benjamin Hooks, the head of the NAACP, were talking openly of moving to the Republicans, and even Coretta Scott King said she was tired of defending Carter's conservative policies.

The worst strain was yet to come: the 1979 ouster of UN ambassador Andrew Young. Young, who had been the most important black supporter of Carter in 1976, had secretly met with Palestine Liberation Organization officials in violation of U.S. policy and then been less than forthcoming about his actions. The outcry among American Jews and other supporters of Israel was immediate and intense. Carter demanded Young's resignation in a highly embarrassing moment politically and diplomatically. The civil rights leadership launched a spirited defense of Young, including a statement signed by Jordan, King, and Hooks. Jesse Jackson was even less temperate, saying that Carter had "decided to sacrifice Africa, the third world, and black Americans" in the name of Israel. The growing divide between

Jews and blacks, fundamental components of the New Deal coalition, had again been exposed. Young, however, immediately acted to reduce the damage to Carter. In his resignation letter, Young pledged to support Carter's reelection, and he made a conference call to black politicians asking them to support the president. Still, having axed his highest-profile black supporter, Carter could not be sanguine about his support among blacks, particularly if a liberal challenger emerged. One black leader predicted that the Young debacle "is going to assure a Republican takeover in 1980 unless Teddy Kennedy is convinced to seek the Democratic nomination. Carter sealed the coffin on the black vote—his only hope for reelection."

A REPUBLICAN BLACKOUT: REAGAN'S NONRACIAL ROAD TO DETROIT

From the opening of the Republican contest for president, Reagan was the front-runner. As such, he had a tremendous ability to control the agenda of the primary and choose the issues he wished to run on. What is extraordinary is the absence of racial issues in Reagan's campaign. In 1976, he had made a televised address in which he emotionally attacked affirmative action as damaging to whites. Reagan had also tried to distinguish himself from Ford with the stridency of opposition to busing. Four years later, neither issue was prominent in his campaign literature or speeches. Reagan had not altered his positions on these issues; what had changed was his position within the party. Running against an incumbent president in an uphill battle in 1976, Reagan had to hit hot-button issues like quotas and busing to reach the Republican base. By the time he became the front-runner for an open nomination, Reagan's staff was more worried about keeping Reagan's image moderate.

Civil rights was also not raised by any of the other Republican contestants, save Illinois's John Anderson, whose quixotic campaign for the nomination was doomed from the beginning. George Bush of Texas, who emerged as Reagan's major opponent after the Iowa caucuses, could have made civil rights an issue. Bush, who had run against the 1964 Civil Rights Act in his first campaign for U.S. Senate, assiduously wooed Houston's black voters in his 1966 race for the

House. Unlike Reagan, Bush endorsed antidiscrimination legislation to ensure equal housing rights, even though this was unpopular in his own district. Bush, however, never sought to highlight his differences with Reagan on civil rights. Similarly, when Reagan attacked Bush for insufficient conservatism on social issues, he slammed Bush for his stances on abortion, the Equal Rights Amendment, and gun control, but he never mentioned civil rights. When Bush and Reagan met to debate in Texas in April, black issues were not raised.

Thus, the minuscule black vote, which had been crucial in a few Republican primaries in 1976, went essentially unwooed, as did the white backlash. Anderson, Bush, and Reagan split the black vote in most primaries. Still, the irrelevance of the black vote was obvious to all; had Bush won 100 percent of the black vote throughout the primaries and caucuses of 1980, Reagan's margin of victory would have scarcely been altered.

Although Reagan met with members of the Black Republican Council immediately before the convention, the absence of blacks at the gathering of Lincoln's party was obvious. Only 55 of 1,993 delegates were black, the lowest percentage since 1968. This was even more glaring as the convention was held in Detroit, a majority black city. In choosing a running mate and in the platform fight between moderates and conservatives, there was almost no discussion of racial issues or outreach to black voters. The Republican convention and platform purposefully avoided many divisive social and racial issues to foreground economic and foreign policy. Republicans did notice belatedly that there was no separate plank addressing blacks and added a bland one. One sign that blacks might not be entirely ignored in the fall was that Ronald Reagan personally intervened to ensure that the NAACP's Benjamin Hooks be given prime speaking time at the convention.

THE BLACK VOTE SAVES CARTER AGAIN: THE DEMOCRATIC PRIMARIES

Carter, the incumbent, would face a much tougher road to the nomination than Reagan; he would have to beat a legend. Edward Kennedy, scion of a political dynasty, seemed initially to be everything that Carter was not: charismatic, decisive, firm in his liberalism, and touched by grandeur. As the brother of JFK and RFK, Kennedy was also expected to inherit their heroic status within the black community. The black vote would be "one of the bloodiest fronts in the looming Democratic war" because both men had strong claims to it. Carter, however, outhustled Kennedy in his pursuit of black leaders. As with so many other aspects of the 1980 primary campaign, Kennedy lost the game before it began, because of Carter's superior organization. Using the clout of the presidency, Carter lined up endorsements from key black figures, including the mayors of Washington, Los Angeles, Detroit, Atlanta, Newark, Oakland, and Richmond. Kennedy had no important mayors in his camp. In desperation, Kennedy's campaign recruited Ron Brown, a young black activist at the Urban League, to help woo black voters and leaders. The Carter forces carefully monitored Kennedy's efforts among blacks; when Kennedy met with a group of black intellectuals at a private luncheon, Carter was urged to do the same.

Carter's personal involvement in the effort to lock up the black primary vote was extensive. He made repeated calls to black leaders as the primaries drew close. On the phone log of his call to D.C. delegate Walter Fauntroy, Carter noted, "He is really sweating—undecided. I put on heavy persuasion." When Jesse Jackson said critical things about Kennedy, Carter was urged to call and thank him. Jackson criticized both candidates, but he seemed to come down particularly hard on Kennedy. Jackson attacked Kennedy for seeking "an accommodation" with George Wallace, sponsoring crime legislation with Thurmond, and ending the political career of Massachusetts senator Edward Brooke, previously the highest elected black official in America. Carter also received Coretta King's endorsement, despite her earlier wavering.

In choosing between Carter and Kennedy, black voters were not presented with many policy differences. Both men were supporters of affirmative action, the racial issue of highest profile in 1980. Certainly, if black voters felt that greater social spending was a priority, the Kennedy proposals were the more generous, but it was uncertain if a President Kennedy could get such a program through an increasingly conservative Congress at a time of economic upheaval. One clear difference was that Kennedy had always been a strong proponent of busing and continued to support it, although it was the "least desirable" way to achieve desegregation. Busing, however, was not a burning national issue by 1980, and neither candidate made an effort to change that.

Carter's efforts to shore up black support paid off in the primaries. In Florida and Alabama, Carter crushed Kennedy among blacks, getting more than double his vote, while in New York and Pennsylvania the black vote was split. Only in Illinois did Kennedy dominate Carter among black voters. Carter seemed to retain his connection with southern blacks, while Kennedy did better in the North. But the black leadership by and large remained with Carter or opted for neutrality.

Kennedy refused to concede and continued his fight up until the convention. Carter's campaign worried that a black caucus endorsement of Kennedy would be the spark that would cause a revolt among Carter's disaffected delegates. But Carter's black support remained firm, and he was resoundingly renominated, with a seconding speech by King flaying the Republicans for failing to support a holiday for her assassinated husband.

There are many reasons Kennedy failed to beat Carter in 1980, including the hostage crisis, Kennedy's private life, and a generally unimpressive campaign. But had Kennedy played smart for the black vote, his chances would have improved immensely. The key may have been that Kennedy's staff was far less integrated than Carter's, a strategic disadvantage that Carter exploited. Carter's top black aide, Louis Martin, a veteran of JFK's 1960 run, cunningly figured out where Carter needed to apply himself to prevent a revolt among black Democrats. Carter's campaign went out and nailed down support from black leaders long before Kennedy realized black support would not automatically be his.

The importance of Andrew Young and Jesse Jackson also cannot be underestimated. Young, effectively fired by Carter, could have refused to support the president or endorsed Kennedy. Had he done so, black voters might well have rallied to him, a black man struck down for speaking truth to power. Similarly, an endorsement of

Kennedy by Jackson would have made a huge difference. Jackson, a minor figure in King's movement, had risen in prominence in every successive year, largely acting outside the closed circles of the established civil rights leadership. Jackson's fiery rhetoric and street credibility could have given Kennedy much greater turnout and support among blacks. Kennedy, who failed to attract either man to his banner, became the first in his family to demonstrate an ignorance of the vital role of black voters in modern Democratic politics.

TAKING BLACKS FOR GRANTED: CARTER'S INITIAL SILENCE ON RACE

When Carter pollster and strategist Pat Caddell wrote his first cut at a general election strategy, the black vote was almost a nonpresence. Although the fourth point in the memo is turnout among blacks, blacks are not mentioned again in a fifty-page analysis. Much more attention was paid to combating Reagan's outreach to blue-collar whites. When Carter's political brain trust had met earlier to choose themes for Carter's reelection campaign, racial issues were ignored. Following the Kennedy defeat, a memo to Carter from his top domestic policy adviser, Stu Eizenstat, laid out the top nineteen issues to be dealt with at the convention. Not one dealt with blacks or civil rights. In a postconvention Caddell memo, blacks and civil rights are mentioned only in passing as part of special interest outreach. Caddell's reticence on race had early roots: in 1976 following Carter's narrow victory, Caddell had advocated moderation on civil rights, out of fear that "our 'affirmative' actions may provoke a backlash among either the Southern base or among Northern Catholic ethnics . . . we must guard against becoming prejudiced in reverse."

While Carter had been strong on a number of low-profile civil rights issues, many blacks argued that he was not addressing substantive issues of concern to their community.* They reminded him that he

---

* Of course, Carter's campaign may have been devoid of substance in many areas, not just civil rights. One of his top advisers advocated shorter talks with no "issues, policy, or substance" because these were not appropriate during a campaign.

was elected by blacks and angrily charged that Carter had failed to keep his promises to blacks. A black congressman pointedly noted that if judges were left out of the count, Carter's appointment record was no better than that of Nixon, a man elected with nary a black vote. What, then, had blacks gotten for their overwhelming support for Carter in 1976? Before Carter met with the Congressional Black Caucus in June, he was warned that the CBC had threatened to tell blacks to stay home in November if Carter did not address their concerns.

What was the black agenda for 1980? The top issues were expanded business and employment opportunities for blacks, continued enforcement of civil rights laws, expansion of the Voting Rights Act, more appointments to high office, sanctions against the racist regime of South Africa, and increased aid to black Africa and the Caribbean. Yet there was no single issue to arouse the fervor of partisans on either side of the racial divide. As an official of the Urban League said in September, "Many blacks view the campaign as more of the same old rhetoric, and after November it will be more of the same old life." Carter could not ignite the enthusiasm among blacks that had given him the election in 1976. Particularly in the South, where white evangelicals were flocking to Reagan, Carter needed to have at least the support levels he had gotten in 1976. Nationwide "[b]lack dissatisfaction with Carter's first term record is one problem the President faces. But a bigger obstacle is rampant apathy among voting age blacks."

Long after the nomination had been decided, a desperate Edward Kennedy, appearing before the NAACP, uncorked the most strident racial rhetoric of his campaign, accusing Carter of cynical moderation on race:

> There are even those who say that we can win regardless of our policies, that we can in effect take black votes for granted . . . there surely is a right-wing threat, but I am convinced that we will not defeat it by tilting towards it. Rosa Parks did not win her victory for justice by moving to the middle of the bus.

Carter's campaign, which had brilliantly outfoxed Kennedy on race in the primaries, was tacking to the middle on racial issues as the general election loomed. Still, Carter confidently told a group of black Democrats that "I have a secret weapon, and that is the black people of this country, who know they have a friend in Jimmy Carter."

JOHN ANDERSON AND BLACK VOTERS: THE LAST GASP FOR REPUBLICAN RACIAL LIBERALISM

There was in 1980 a brief moment when it seemed possible that the black vote might not be overwhelmingly Democratic come November. In the Republican primaries, John Anderson had done well among the few black voters left in the GOP. When he bolted the party to make an independent run at the White House, Anderson threatened to make Carter work hard to retain black loyalty. Anderson's record on race was strong. In addition to supporting the historic 1960s era civil rights legislation that Reagan had opposed and Carter had not aggressively endorsed, Anderson was the only one of the three to support busing in the era when busing had been a litmus test of commitment to the black cause. So ably and eloquently did Congressman Anderson argue against a constitutional amendment to ban busing that black leaders effusively praised him in the early 1970s. Earlier, on the day King was buried, Anderson had led the fight to pass open housing legislation. By some accounts, it was the issue of civil rights that had started Anderson on his journey from moderate conservative to liberal icon.

Carter's campaign feared Anderson's potential to split the liberal vote. An internal memo by black staffers highlighted the threat he posed to black unity: "There is a very strong possibility that John Anderson will capture more Black votes than any independent candidate in recent times . . . unless and until we succeed in convincing Black voters that Anderson is not worthy of their support he will probably get more black votes than Reagan." Carter's campaign attacked Anderson for not voting for the strongest versions of the 1964 and 1965 civil rights bills, but there was really very little about Anderson's record to impugn.

Indeed, Anderson's campaign manager hoped to take many black votes from Carter. The Anderson-Lucey platform aggressively endorsed affirmative action and threatened to terminate federal funding to all noncompliant institutions. Anderson spoke to national black groups, with some positive reactions. When Anderson and Reagan met for a debate without Carter, Anderson made much of his racial liberalism. As opposed to Reagan, who stated that federal aid was damaging the cities, Anderson advocated an urban investment fund, a community trust fund, and a jobs program for the inner cities. He accused Reagan of consigning urban black youth to high unemployment and societal neglect. In the end, however, like Kennedy, Anderson failed to dislodge blacks from their Carter allegiance. Anderson's failure had less to do with campaign stratagems and more to do with black antipathy toward Ronald Reagan. In an election between Carter, a strong proponent of civil rights, and Reagan, an avatar of states' rights, most black Americans did not want to risk voting for a well-meaning liberal Republican, who by election day had the distinct odor of gadfly about him. Anderson got fewer black votes than Reagan, a failure by any measure.

REAGAN'S UNEXPECTED OUTREACH TO THE BLACK VOTE

Reagan entered the election with very little expectation of black support. The goal of the campaign was to break up the Democratic coalition through appealing to white southerners, blue-collar whites, urban ethnic whites, and white rural voters in the Northeast. Despite this, the Reagan campaign made a surprisingly sustained effort at the black vote, perhaps influenced by the lesson of Ford's neglect. Observed a black Reagan staffer: "A speech by Jerry Ford to blacks could have turned around Ohio and Mississippi and won the 1976 election." Another one of Reagan's few black aides pushed Reagan to visit a decaying South Bronx neighborhood that Carter had promised to improve in 1977 and then ignored. The visit was almost a disaster. Reagan was jeered by local residents, who challenged him to speak directly to them and not to a crowd of national reporters. When Reagan tried to do so, he was interrupted by hecklers. Showing a flash of deep anger, Reagan shouted at a screaming black woman, "I can't do a damn thing for you if I don't get elected!" The powerful image of

Reagan confronting angry urban residents "turned the event into a major campaign plus." Ironically, the most dramatic black outreach of the Reagan campaign probably gained Reagan votes from racially conservative whites.*

Still, the South Bronx speech was part of a series of notable attempts to broaden the Republican Party early in the general election. Reagan spoke to the National Urban League, aptly comparing his visit to JFK's speech to Protestant ministers in 1960. Reagan argued that conservatives were not "anti-poor, anti-black, and anti-disadvantaged" and that the greatest threat to blacks was the Carter recession. He promised strict civil rights enforcement and a social safety net for the "truly needy" and claimed that he had appointed more blacks in California than all previous governors combined. Reagan also met with Jesse Jackson in Chicago, although the meeting was seen as a fiasco by his campaign, since they believed Jackson was only using them for publicity and ambushed the candidate with a harassing crowd of supporters as Reagan left. Jackson, who had publicly toyed with the idea of endorsing Reagan, now resoundingly rejected his positions on states' rights and South Africa. Still, Reagan was emphatic that the various outreach efforts would pay off: "I think we have opened communications and made them realize that I for one . . . really intend to solicit the black vote."

Perhaps the biggest surprise came when the Reverend Ralph Abernathy, King's top aide, Hosea Williams, a key King lieutenant, and the black mayor of Fayette, Mississippi, Charles Evers, endorsed Reagan. While almost every other black political figure was behind Carter, Reagan could claim to have greater support from prominent black leaders than any Republican since Adam Clayton Powell

---

* There is the faint trace of a disturbing pattern contained in this anecdote. In addition to this shouted outburst at a black woman, there was his vitriolic reaction before a black Republican crowd in 1966 mentioned above, and his angry refusal to speak to the dying Keyes. Reagan also had a public shouting match with a black woman in Miami in 1968; the woman angered Reagan by pointing out the paucity of blacks in the Republican Party and at the expensive fund-raiser Reagan was attending. Perhaps part of Reagan's appeal to the white backlash was that he was the rare white politician who would show public anger at blacks without apology or hesitation. It was particularly noteworthy in such an otherwise sunny personality.

endorsed Eisenhower in 1956. However, Abernathy was at the nadir of his authority within the civil rights movement. Shunted aside by more eloquent and effective leaders such as Jackson, Young, and even King's widow, Abernathy had felt slighted by Carter in 1976. Former associates spoke of his current situation and his Reagan endorsement with as much pity for "poor Ralph" as anger. Similarly, Williams's endorsement was a product of his antipathy for Carter rather than any outpouring of enthusiasm for Reagan.

Ronald Reagan had the worst civil rights record of any Republican nominee since Goldwater, and he did not make a single policy concession to the black vote during the general election. Yet unlike Ford, a man with a much better record on civil rights, Reagan made an effort to win the black vote. Even Jackson praised Reagan's outreach and found areas of agreement with him. Unlike Nixon, Reagan avoided divisive racial issues. However, Reagan's past and two campaign decisions would eventually give Carter an opening to paint Reagan as a racist.

REAGAN'S SILENCE ON RACE

Reagan's central focus in the 1980 campaign was on the economy and foreign policy, and his advertising and speeches downplayed most social issues. Even when Reagan did address social issues, he seldom included any with racial implications. In speeches directed at housing and education, two of the most racially charged issue areas in American politics, Reagan did not mention race even in code. Reagan did not bring up affirmative action in his speeches, and his major mention of it came in response to a reporter's question. The inflammatory rhetoric of Reagan's 1976 campaign and Nixon's 1972 speeches is almost entirely absent.

> I recognize the need to offer opportunity to those people to whom opportunity has been denied for a long time. But I also lived in a time when we had quota systems that denied people equal opportunity. They were used to prevent people from get-

ting jobs in the places they wanted to work. I see affirmative action becoming a kind of quota system . . . we have turned affirmative action into a kind of reverse discrimination. But, short of that, I think we must do everything in our power to make sure that we never return to bigotry and prejudice and the denial of people's rights.

Reagan's position was, in this framing, almost indistinguishable from that of Carter, who also opposed quotas.

The most prominent mention of race by Reagan was in a national broadcast in October, in which he tried to use urban poverty against Carter.

I stood . . . in the South Bronx in New York. You'd have to see it to believe it . . . it's like bombed-out London. Empty hulks of buildings, blocks that are bulldozed flat, covered with rubble, no jobs. . . . I stood there on that spot because that's where—in 1977—the President said that he would have a program to revitalize that area. . . . Well, none of that's taken place. And while I was there, a man stood in front of me—middle-aged, black, not antagonistic at all, and with no bitterness—but just with a longing in his voice, said to me, "Can you tell me that I can have hope? That I can look forward to, once again, taking care of my family, providing for my children?" Well, how do you answer that? You can have hope, though. I still have faith in the people of this country.

The eyewitness accounts of the visit to the South Bronx are entirely lacking this poignant encounter between Reagan and a "good" black man. Moreover, Reagan's audience for this speech is presumed to have never seen a ghetto and to be ignorant of urban devastation. Still, Reagan could not be accused of appealing directly to racial conservatism with this rhetoric.

Reagan's avoidance of racial issues can have several interpretations. Perhaps Carter's vulnerabilities on economic and foreign policy matters were so glaring that any time spent on other issues was seen as a distraction. Richard Wirthlin, Reagan's chief pollster, argues that there was no need to use affirmative action when other issues were working so well against Carter. While majorities of Americans opposed affirmative action, a candidate who made opposition to it central to his campaign ran the risk of being painted as a bigot. Reagan had no need to take that gamble.

Alternatively, as with Wallace in 1968, perhaps Reagan's image as a racial conservative was so firmly fixed in the minds of many white Americans that he did not need to make any reference to it. And Reagan did make at least one large symbolic gesture to white racial conservatism. Immediately before his major efforts at black outreach, Reagan opened his general election campaign by speaking in Neshoba, Mississippi, the site of the brutal murder of three civil rights workers by local police and vigilantes. Wirthlin and others begged Reagan to cancel his appearance there, precisely because of the message it would send. Incensed at Wirthlin's refusal to let the matter drop, Reagan threw his speech at his pollster during an argument in Reagan's bedroom. At the fair, Reagan endorsed a revamped policy of "states' rights," perhaps the hoariest of all southern code words. To promote states' rights in a county where men were murdered for advocating federal intervention carried a powerful message. Reagan's blindness to racial sensitivities undercut his outreach to blacks, as he flew from Neshoba to the bedside of ailing black leader Vernon Jordan. It also gave the Carter campaign hope that they could recover their momentum among black voters.

"ALL RIGHT TO KILL NIGGERS": CARTER'S CAMPAIGN OF FEAR

> Carter hoped to increase turnout by scaring blacks with the prospect of a Reagan presidency.
>
> POLITICAL ANALYST AL HUNT

Carter's campaign never took seriously the idea that they would lose a significant portion of the black vote to Ronald Reagan. However, an internal campaign memo warned of "an erroneous but widespread belief among Blacks that all of the current presidential candidates are unworthy of strong Black voter support. Senator Kennedy and several Black leaders have done a great deal to promote the spread of this attitude among Blacks through their unfair but vociferous criticism of this Administration's economic policies and civil rights record." The memo warned that disillusionment and frustration with electoral politics were at an all-time high in the black community. What should Carter do? In addition to the typical outreach maneuvers of a registration drive and an integrated campaign, Carter was advised to attack the Klan in a major speech. Reagan's record should also be attacked, not to dissuade blacks from voting for him, but to give them reasons to turn out for Carter.

Reagan was a difficult target for the Carter camp. Democrats hoped to use the "strapping young buck" comment and Reagan's labeling welfare programs "demeaning" and "insulting" to blacks. Carter's camp also looked for a chance to point out that Reagan had in 1976 stated, "Isn't it time we laid off South Africa for a while . . . [let] South Africans work at solving their problems while we solve our own." But there was no "smoking gun," no comment approaching the Earl Butz slur on blacks that hurt Ford. Reagan's antipathy to civil rights legislation was not accompanied by any evidence of deep-seated animosity to black Americans. By the start of the general election, it was also clear that Reagan would at least make a token effort at the black vote, unlike Ford. The danger for Carter was that this effort, while unlikely to take votes away, would at least soothe black fears of a Reagan victory. Carter needed that fear and set out to create it.

While Reagan's appearance in Neshoba was heavily criticized, it was his bizarre introduction of the KKK into the campaign that gave Carter the opportunity he had waited for. Reagan, perhaps stung by criticism of his Neshoba speech, attacked Carter in early September for opening his campaign in Tuscumbia, Alabama, the town that gave birth to the Ku Klux Klan. The parallel was obvious—if Reagan was wrong to start his campaign in Neshoba with its dark civil rights past, why was it not wrong for Carter to launch his in Tuscumbia? Reagan again demonstrated his blindness to racial sensitivities; he hadn't understood that what angered his critics about Neshoba was not that he had spoken there, but that he had endorsed states' rights on ground indelibly stained with the blood of martyrs in the fight against states' rights racism. Additionally, Reagan had his facts wrong, as Tuscumbia was not where the Klan began.

However, now that Reagan had brought the Klan into the campaign discourse, Patricia Harris, a black cabinet secretary, tried to link Reagan to the Klan because a branch of the group had endorsed the Republican platform. Days later, Carter spoke at Ebenezer Baptist Church in Atlanta, perhaps the most famous civil rights pulpit in the country. Carter brought together Reagan's backfired attempt to tie Carter to the Klan as well as the Neshoba Fair speech:

> You've seen in this campaign the stirrings of hate and the rebirth of code words like "states' rights" in a speech in Mississippi, in a campaign reference to the KKK, relating to the South. . . . Hatred has no place in this country. Racism has no place in this country.

In another September speech, Carter alleged that the election of Ronald Reagan would divide the races.*

The worst fearmongering, however, was left to Carter surrogates. Andrew Young claimed that if Reagan were elected, "it's going to be all right to kill niggers," based on Reagan's endorsement of states' rights. Carter forces ran ads in black newspapers claiming that Republicans wanted to stop Carter because he had appointed too many blacks to high office. However, the Carter campaign's clumsy effort to depict Reagan as a racist backfired because the majority of Americans simply did not think the nice man from California was a hater. At a press conference after his Atlanta speech, reporters pressed Carter on whether he had meant to call Reagan a racist, and

---

* Carter also followed the advice of his black staffers and attacked the Klan itself. In August, Carter's administration seized on a dubious church burning in New York to portray Carter as a brave fighter against a rising tide of Klan violence. The only problem was that there was little evidence of any Klan involvement.

Carter retreated. Similarly, the campaign disavowed Young's "kill niggers" comment and the newspaper ad, but the damage had been done. Carter's managers later argued that the effort to paint Reagan as racially divisive was both accidental and beneficial, but they were in error on both counts. The effort was intentional and ultimately made Carter appear desperate and opportunistic.

CONCLUSION: THE TRIUMPH OF COLOR-BLIND POLITICS?

When the managers of the various campaigns of 1980 met to rehash the election, racial issues and politics were almost entirely absent from their discussions. The politics of race were by one measure irrelevant to the 1980 election. Had Ronald Reagan suddenly adopted the racial liberalism of John Anderson, or if Carter had not attempted to scare blacks into voting Democratic, the outcome would have been relatively unchanged. Carter did succeed at winning the vast majority of the black vote, taking 82 percent versus 14 percent for Reagan and 3 percent for Anderson. Turnout among blacks was heavy, but white voters preferred Reagan to Carter by a great enough margin for him to handily defeat Carter.

Reagan had attempted to keep race and racial issues out of the election, except for his surprising outreach to black voters and his appearance in Neshoba. Given that the most important issues were trending his way, Reagan never had to highlight his opposition to affirmative action. Carter, who tried to boost black turnout by fear-mongering, demonstrated that the days when messages could be easily limited to one racial group were over. Inflammatory ads in black newspapers and a speech in a black church accusing Reagan of racism were covered in the general media and damaged Carter's image. Why did Carter try to clumsily link Reagan to racism and raise the issue of the Klan? Perhaps it was the closeness of the 1980 election throughout the summer and fall that made Carter resort to tactics he had abjured in 1976, or perhaps it was Reagan's image as a racial conservative. Another possibility does suggest itself: Perhaps the difference was that Reagan had reached out to blacks, and Carter used fear to keep them in the Democratic camp. Some summer polls had Carter with less than 75 percent of the black vote, a number that would have been a stunning rejection of a Democrat.

For some Republicans, the 1980 election confirmed that the black vote was out of reach. Reagan had given prime convention time to the head of the NAACP, spoken in the South Bronx, and even received the endorsement of the putative heir of Martin Luther King and still failed to get more than a minuscule fraction of the black vote. But that was never the aim of Reagan's black outreach. A Reagan staffer conceded that the campaign "just wanted to show moderates and liberals that Reagan wasn't anti-black." The intended audience for Reagan's black outreach was white voters.

The overwhelming rejection of President Carter left unanswered questions about where America was on racial matters. Did Carter's loss signal a shift in the nation's mood on racial equality? Did Reagan have a mandate to end affirmative action even though he had not campaigned on it? Would Reagan, who had at least tried for black support, make an attempt to broaden his party's base by continuing the effort once in office? Would black Americans continue to vote for white Democrats as the lesser of two evils? Jesse Louis Jackson, the rising star of black politics, had begun to advocate a "third" political option for black America. As the nation continued to move to the right on social issues, the logic of a black political movement would grow in force. Blacks had voted overwhelmingly for white Democrats in four elections since 1968, and their candidate had won only once, barely, after the greatest scandal in our nation's history. Could they do any worse voting for a black candidate?

★ ★ ★ ★ **8** ★ ★ ★ ★

THE AGE OF JACKSON
The New Racial Politics of 1984

Run! When you run, your enemies can't write you off and your friends can't take
you for granted!

JESSE JACKSON, 1983

It's not so much white drift so much as it is white flight . . . when they say in the
South that the national Democratic Party is too liberal what they really mean is that
Jesse Jackson is too powerful in the Democratic Party.

COMMENTATOR BILL MOYERS

The presidential election of 1984 would reveal an electorate
more segregated than at any time in modern history. Reagan won a historic victory as he defeated the hapless Walter
Mondale in forty-nine states. Yet his landslide was almost entirely
white, as it had to be to overcome Mondale's advantage among
minorities. Mondale, the Democrat with the strongest record on civil
rights since Humphrey, won an even greater landslide among black
voters to no avail. Reagan was a racial inkblot test read entirely differently by whites and blacks. But the racial politics of the 1984 campaign was almost exclusively an intramural affair among Democrats.
The first credible black candidate for president posed an excruciating
dilemma for many Democrats. The Reverend Jesse Jackson's hopeless quest for the Democratic nomination would arouse a white backlash that contributed significantly to Reagan's victory. Jackson's
campaign reflected the deep anger of the black masses, who accurately perceived that white Democrats had strategically turned away
from them in order to court centrist white voters.

1984: THE SETTING

In 1982, it had seemed that America was prepared to reject Reagan-omics and Reagan. The sharp bite of the 1981–82 recession convinced many Americans, black and white, that the president's economic poli-cies were detrimental to the common man. Democrats had defeated a number of Republican incumbents in the midterm elections, and the president's advisers were not sanguine about his reelection hopes. By January of 1984, however, the Reagan recovery was under way, and his popularity with the American public was restored. Compared to the economic and geopolitical situation that had confronted Carter in January of 1980, Reagan was very well off indeed, and his staff looked forward to the contrast between 1980 and 1984.

Blacks, who had given Reagan anemic support in 1980, continued in their disdain. Reagan's first term was a period of great uncertainty for mainstream civil rights groups. The victory against de jure segre-gation left them without clear goals or opponents. Swiftly, however, the enemy became the Reagan administration. Unlike Nixon and Ford, the Reagan administration refused even to pay lip service to many civil rights shibboleths and almost courted a contentious rela-tionship with the established black leadership. The great majority of blacks disapproved of Reagan's civil rights policies, while only 29 percent of whites did. Yet the mood of the country on civil rights was not clear. While Americans continued to loathe racial quotas, a majority supported affirmative action without quotas. Busing, the least popular civil rights initiative for over a decade, now attracted some support, even as it declined in practice. Still, as many as seven-teen antibusing bills were proposed in Congress, showing that the issue had not entirely lost its salience.

Prior to the campaign, very little attention was paid to issues such as affirmative action, busing, or civil rights enforcement. Even fol-lowing the campaign of Jackson, which ostensibly put race on the agenda, no racial issues were on the minds of Americans in press cov-erage or polls. An internal Republican poll found the economy and foreign affairs atop the agenda, with social issues ranking very low in the public mind. Ironically, it was only on a few social issues such as women's rights, health care, and civil rights that a Democrat was favored over Reagan. Yet at the core of the election of 1984 would be the leadership qualities and personal attributes of Ronald Wilson Reagan. Before the campaign began, it was obvious that blacks and whites would disagree sharply in their judgment of Reagan.

THE CANDIDATES

Ronald Reagan

Candidate Reagan in 1980 had reached out to blacks in a calculated appeal to white moderates. Once in office, Reagan quickly moved to supplant the established civil rights leadership that had largely opposed him. The administration sponsored a conference of conservative black academics and activists and placed many of them in administrative posts. Reagan and his supporters made no secret of their belief that the existing black leadership was composed of whiners and complainers who exacerbated the poverty and dependence of African Americans. Within the administration, however, civil rights was treated as just another social issue, far less important than Reagan's three vital goals, cutting taxes, increasing military spending, and reducing domestic government expenditures. This angered many true believers within the administration, who wanted Reagan to take a far firmer stance against busing and affirmative action. Reagan also faced pressure from supporters such as Jerry Falwell to intensify his opposition to busing.

Racial conservatives and modern defenders of segregation like Representative Trent Lott won a momentary victory when the administration seemed willing to grant formal tax-exempt status to segregated schools. These all-white academies operated throughout the South, providing white families with an alternative to integrated schools. A little-noticed clause in the 1980 Republican platform had promised that "independent schools" would be protected from the "unconstitutional vendetta" of the IRS. A firestorm of criticism erupted, and Reagan eventually changed sides, implausibly arguing that he had merely wanted to clarify that such schools were not eligible for exemptions. The imbroglio hurt Reagan with racial conservatives and blacks, since one group felt that a promise had been broken and the other that a huge step backward had been narrowly avoided.

Reagan's image also suffered when the issue of a national holiday for Martin Luther King Jr. arose. Senator Jesse Helms, a longtime opponent of desegregation, busing, and civil rights, spoke for many unreconstructed racists when he labeled King a lawbreaking, Communist womanizer who did not deserve such an honor. Reagan angered some on the Right when he refused to open secret files on King and ultimately endorsed the holiday, support that was essential to the bill's passage. Reagan, however, when asked about Helms's charges, insensitively said that the truth would be known in thirty-five years when the files were released, a response that infuriated King's widow and others who revered the civil rights leader. As one Republican insider put it, "In one sentence, he blew away all the gains he might have made by signing the bill." A similar dynamic occurred when Interior Secretary James Watt mocked diversity by claiming to have appointed "a black, a woman, two Jews, and a cripple" to a commission. Watt, a New Right icon, was fired only after his support in Congress evaporated. Instead of taking the opportunity to act swiftly against racial insensitivity, Reagan looked indecisive to all concerned.

When Reagan was about to meet with black clergy, a staffer thoughtfully outlined why the meeting might go badly. The clergy could be expected to be angry about Reagan's moves to aid segregated academies, loosen the Voting Rights Act, weaken affirmative action, and cut back on domestic spending.

> While no single category of acusation [*sic*] might in and of itself present a cause for alarm, the cumulative effect of all of them together has created distrust and bitterness within the minority community . . . there is a widespread sentiment that the Administration is "anti-black" or engaged in a systematic effort to roll back civil rights achievements of the past. Although the charge is not true in fact, we have not helped ourselves. We have not put our best foot forward rhetorically, and a series of mishaps in timing and tactical judgment have strengthened the impression of insensitivity.

Reagan's domestic spending cuts, the extraordinary jump in black unemployment in the 1982 recession, and his overall attitude of malign neglect of civil rights also helped produce an angry black response. Benjamin Hooks, who had spoken at the 1980 Republican convention, echoed many black leaders when he called for "the elimination of Reaganism from the face of the earth." Reagan also had no high-ranking blacks capable of defending his record. Sam Pierce, the only black in the cabinet, had very weak relations with the civil rights community. An anonymous White House official admitted that his "biggest contribution is staying in place as a black face in the administration. No one can say we don't have a black Cabinet officer."

If Reagan reinforced his negative image in the black community, he also failed to deliver concrete results to racial conservatives. Busing, affirmative action, and voting rights law and enforcement were largely unchanged. Of course, much of the inaction came from the steadfast defense of these policies by members of Congress, federal judges, and activists, but the preservation of the status quo also came from Reagan's consistent failure to put racial policy anywhere on his core agenda. It simply was not a priority for the Reaganauts. Edwin Meese, the leading voice for social conservatism within the Reagan White House, admitted in his memoirs that the main vehicle for change on social policy issues was always intended to be the judiciary. Through appointing advocates of color-blind policies such as Antonin Scalia and Sandra Day O'Connor to the judiciary, and Clarence Pendleton and Clarence Thomas to civil rights regulatory agencies and commissions, Reagan was in effect laying the groundwork for a gradual (and more deniable) assault on racially preferential policies. While these appointees did occasionally draw attention to racial conservatism, without the White House bully pulpit, racial issues seldom rose to national prominence.*

Still, although racial policy was given a surprisingly low priority

---

* In 1983, Reagan tried to fire the outspoken vice chair of the Civil Rights Commission, Mary Frances Berry, and two other liberal appointees. A court battle ensued, ultimately resolved by Congressional intervention, which led to Berry's reinstatement. The entire incident did much to damage Reagan's already poor image in the civil rights community.

in the Reagan White House, the statements and actions of the administration did little to change the impression that Reagan was at best conflicted on civil rights. On numerous occasions, Reagan spoke with sorrow and pain about the "totally false image" of him as an insensitive bigot. However, a man who led an administration that took months to figure out a position on tax exemptions for whites-only schools could not have expected any other image. In a remarkable understatement, White House spokesman David Gergen conceded that Reagan was not "a crusader for civil rights."

Walter Mondale

Few white men in American public life have advocated racial equality with greater consistency than Walter Mondale. Civil rights was one of the key issues that drew Mondale into politics and into a close association with Hubert Humphrey. As a young attorney general, Mondale made civil rights one of his top two focuses. Of course, in Minnesota, with its minuscule black population, such a stance was "morally correct and politically shrewd . . . there was limited political risk in supporting civil rights." Mondale's first step toward national prominence also stemmed from his interest in civil rights. Working directly for LBJ, Mondale had been a crucial player in resolving the fight over segregated southern delegations at the 1964 Democratic convention. In 1965, when LBJ gave his ringing endorsement of voting rights for blacks by promising that "we shall overcome," Mondale described it as the "five most dramatic seconds in my public life."

In the Senate, Mondale's greatest legislative victory was his successful shepherding of open housing legislation in 1968, against steep odds. Over the opposition of racial conservatives like Senator Robert Byrd ("Decent housing does not necessarily have to be integrated housing"), Mondale slowly gathered the votes. Later, Mondale led the fight to protect busing from angry congressional majorities. So strident was Mondale in his defense of busing that one reporter labeled him "Mr. Busing," a label that stuck well into the 1980s. For a brief period in the late 1960s and early 1970s, Mondale moved away from a lifetime of incrementalist, positive rhetoric and spoke in bitter terms about the need for radical reform. He told the NAACP in

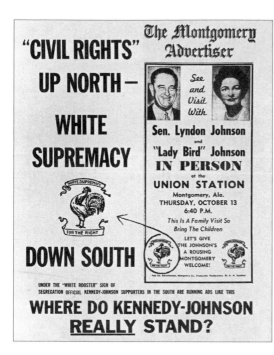

★ "CIVIL RIGHTS" UP NORTH—WHITE SUPREMACY DOWN SOUTH, 1960: Republicans attempted to link the Kennedy-Johnson ticket to Southern racism with this ad in the North. By exposing LBJ's alliance with white supremacists, Republicans hoped to get the votes of racial liberals in the North. *Fair Campaign Practices Committee Archives, Lauinger Library Special Collections, Georgetown University*

★ WASHINGTON...HARLEM...AFRICA, 1960: This unofficial anti-Nixon brochure was distributed in Virginia, and linked Nixon to Martin Luther King Jr., Harlem, and Africa. Note that Nixon is shown in very close proximity to young black women. The caption also notes that Nixon was a member of the NAACP. While the brochure was not sanctioned by the Kennedy campaign, the attacks followed the suggested avenues outlined in the campaign's "Assault Book." *Fair Campaign Practices Committee Archives, Lauinger Library Special Collections, Georgetown University*

LAWRENCE E.

RECEIVED JAN 9 1961 CENTRAL FILES

Suggested Statement Dictated by Judge Walsh -- 10/31/60

Dr. Martin Luther King, a clergyman, was ordered imprisoned for four months on a charge of operating an automobile in Georgia without a Georgia driver's license. Originally, Dr. King had been fined and placed on probation with respect to this charge, but this probation was revoked and he was committed after he had participated in a demonstration for the purpose of eliminating racial discrimination in the dining room of Rich's Department Store in Atlanta, Georgia. He is now on bail pending appeal.

It seems to me fundamentally unjust that a man who has peacefully attempted to establish his right to equal treatment free from racial discrimination be imprisoned on an old, unrelated and relatively insignificant charge, driving without a license. Further, it is important that the nations of the free world understand that this is not the action of the U. S. government. Accordingly, I have asked the Attorney General to take all proper steps to join with Dr. King in an apprppriate application to vacate this sentence.

★ **SUGGESTED STATEMENT DICTATED BY JUDGE WALSH, 1960:** This statement opposing the sentence of Dr. King in Georgia was rejected by President Eisenhower. Nixon also rejected several pleas to come out against the treatment of King, thus providing a strategic opportunity to Kennedy. The Republican silence was deafening. *Dwight Eisenhower Presidential Library, Abilene, KS*

- 5 -

South. Let's talk plainly about why he has made so many trips down there. Why are so many Republicans expecting more Southern States than ever to vote for their ticket? It is not because their party organization is stronger there. It is principally for two reasons:

First, because I am a member of a minority group--and all the forces of bigotry and prejudice, led by the Ku Klux Klan, are condemning me with lies and hate; and secondly, because my Party Platform is the strongest civil rights platform in the history of American politics.

What is Mr. Nixon's platform--not his Northern platform or his Southern platform--but his platform? He has been on two nation-wide debates. On the first, in his list of domestic problems, he didn't even mention civil rights. On the second, when pressed for an answer, he favored only two token bills: statutory authority for his do-nothing Government Contracts Committee, which his party voted down in the spring--

★ **LET'S TALK PLAINLY, 1960:** This excerpt from the text of Kennedy's October 1960 Harlem speech shows the removal of the most inflammatory passages, including a reference to the Ku Klux Klan. *John F. Kennedy Presidential Library, Boston, MA*

★ **LBJ'S CIVIL RIGHTS BILL AND YOU, 1964:** The Goldwater campaign was explicitly racist throughout much of the South. This Texas advertisement tried to exploit white fears about the Civil Rights Act of 1964. *Fair Campaign Practices Committee Archives, Lauinger Library Special Collections, Georgetown University*

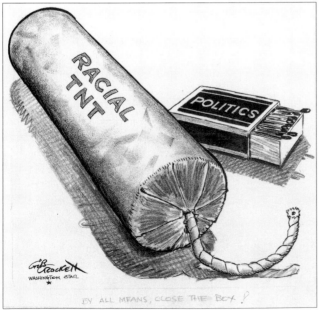

★ **BY ALL MEANS, CLOSE THE BOX!, 1964:** The urban riots in the summer of 1964 were widely perceived as potential threats to Johnson's election hopes. Two days after this cartoon was printed, Goldwater met with LBJ at the White House and pledged to not make the riots an issue in the fall campaign. *Permission of Mrs. Florence Crockett*

The world of Spiro Agnew

★ **THE WORLD OF SPIRO AGNEW, 1968:** In the backlash year of 1968, Agnew's blunt insensitivity aided Nixon's outreach to the silent majority. *Oliphant © Universal Press Syndicate. Reprinted with permission. All rights reserved.*

★ **"WHERE DO YOU THINK YOU'RE GOING?," 1972:** As part of his Southern strategy, Nixon encouraged the impression that he was slowing down efforts at desegregation. *Minneapolis Star Tribune*

★ **DEMOCRATIC NATIONAL CONVENTION, 1976:** Martin Luther King Sr.'s moving benediction at the close of the 1976 Democratic National Convention demonstrated how Carter sold himself as a racial healer. A shared sense of deep religious faith was part of Carter's appeal to blacks, and caused many to overlook his position(s) on busing and his avoidance of most racial issues. *Library of Congress, Prints and Photographs Division, U.S. News & World Report Magazine Collection*

★ **"I AM DISAPPOINTED IN MY OPPONENT," 1980:** President Carter attempted to frighten blacks into remaining loyal, as the fervor and loyalty of black voters were tested by economic troubles. Carter ultimately looked mean and desperate in trying to paint Reagan as a racist. © *Tribune Media Services, Inc. All rights reserved. Reprinted with permission.*

★ "WE'RE VOTING FOR THE MAN," 1984: Like many Republicans before and since, Ronald Reagan tried to rally black support by highlighting the endorsements he received from a few black celebrities. In 1984, this was the extent of his outreach to black voters, and it memorably failed.

★ BLACKS FOR FRITZ, 1984: Jesse Jackson's strong showing in the 1984 Democratic primaries prevented Mondale, a true warrior for civil rights, from receiving many black votes, thus enabling Gary Hart to launch a sustained and debilitating challenge. Jackson also diminished Mondale's stature throughout the primaries and well into the general election. © *Tribune Media Services, Inc. All rights reserved. Reprinted with permission.*

★ **DUKAKIS-JACKSON SUMMIT, 1988:** This July Fourth meeting between Jackson and Dukakis did not lead to any lessening of the breach between them. The ironic impact of Jackson's presence in the 1988 Democratic primaries was the selection of Dukakis, a candidate without credibility or support in the black community. Dukakis, like Mondale, never figured out a way to handle the challenge Jackson represented. *Steve Liss/TimePix*

★ **BAND AIDS, 1992:** The 1992 Los Angeles riots seemed to puzzle the Bush administration, which released eight statements in 48 hours, and only belatedly called for further investigation of the Rodney King beating. Bush finally paid some attention to urban policy, after three years of stagnation and neglect. © *Tribune Media Services, Inc. All rights reserved. Reprinted with permission.*

★ **HELL RAISER, 1996:** Pat Buchanan became the spokesperson for the angry white males of 1992 and 1996, as his hero, George Wallace, had been in 1964, 1968, and 1972. Following Buchanan's victory in New Hampshire in 1996, the media made further disclosures about his anti-Semitism, white supremacist ties, and inflammatory comments. The Republican establishment rallied behind a fading Bob Dole, in the face of the Buchanan onslaught. Buchanan ended the century by vanishing into irrelevance as a gadfly third-party candidate, becoming the true loser of the 2000 presidential race. *TimePix*

PEPCID vs. TAGAMET vs. ZANTAC: THE HEARTBURN WARS

TIME

HELL RAISER

A Huey Long for the '90s,
PAT BUCHANAN
wields the most lethal
weapon in Campaign '96:
Scapegoat Politics

★ **RENEE MULLINS, 2000:** The daughter of James Byrd, Mullins is seen here at the sentencing of one of her father's killers. Mullins traveled around the country to speak to black audiences, appeared at the Democratic convention and in NAACP brochures, and did the voice-over for TV and radio ads paid for by an anonymous donor to the NAACP's National Voter Fund. Mullins consistently accused George W. Bush of indifference toward the vicious lynching of her father. The NAACP's effort was crucial in rallying blacks to Al Gore. *Andrees Latif/Reuters/TimePix*

1971 that "the sickening truth is that this country is rapidly coming to resemble South Africa." It was also during this period that Mondale and his wife went on a welfare diet, eating only what those at the poverty line could afford, and marched with Cesar Chavez. He also angered the South by personally visiting the segregated academies that operated quietly in a semipublic fashion, while the woefully underfunded black public schools languished.

Eventually, the white backlash tide rolled into Minnesota, and it changed Mondale's rhetoric and politics. In 1972, facing reelection, he was warned that white anger at busing was surging, and his profile was far too high on the issue. Unfortunately, the select committee that he chaired was scheduled to release an explosive pro-busing report weeks before the election. Several aides suggested that Mondale kill the report, while others urged that Mondale remain courageous. Mondale chose a middle path, issuing a strong report in favor of busing in January of 1973, after his reelection. Mondale's rhetoric on busing gradually cooled as the backlash grew and Mondale's mentor, Humphrey, also shifted right on civil rights. Mondale, like many wealthy white liberals, also reluctantly removed his own children from public schools and sent them to elite private schools.

Mondale's selection as vice president was seen as a sop to true liberals unhappy with Carter's vague moderation. During the period of uncertainty prior to the selection, Humphrey appeared before a black group and asked them to give Mondale "favored son" treatment in light of Mondale's strong civil rights record. On the campaign trail, Mondale gave vague answers to questions about desegregated housing and schools in the North. When pressed, he responded sarcastically that all the reporters wanted to know was "how many blacks I want to move into Polish neighborhoods."

In the Carter White House, Mondale was the liaison to many liberal groups, including African Americans. Mondale privately believed that Carter was offending the core constituencies of the party, including blacks. For example, Carter's Justice Department initially wanted to side against affirmative action in university admissions. Mondale intervened aggressively, telling Carter that the move would be "a political signal of the worst kind. . . . Why turn away from our campaign promise to support affirmative action?" Carter also gave Mondale an expanded role in African policy. In a meeting with the prime minister of South Africa, Mondale could not resist calling for one man one vote, a sudden change in U.S. policy that diplomats had to struggle with for months.

As Mondale prepared for his expected run for the nomination, it was assumed that he would inherit the majority of black votes. Unless Ted Kennedy entered the race, no politician had a record on civil rights as strong as Mondale's. No white politician, that is.

THE RISE OF JACKSON

No one anointed him. Jesse just reached out there and grabbed it for himself.

RON BROWN, 1983

Throughout 1983, rumors flew that the Reverend Jesse Jackson was contemplating a run for the White House. Among the factors pushing Jackson to make the run was the deep anger in the black community against the policies of the Reagan administration. Jackson was also personally offended by the behavior of white Democrats in the Chicago mayoral election of 1983. Harold Washington, a Jackson ally, faced Mayor Jane Byrne and Richard Daley in a bitter Democratic primary. Mondale had promised to support Byrne years before, and other top Democrats came to support Daley. Even after Washington's primary victory, the wound to black pride was painful; it seemed that blacks were expected to vote for white Democrats but get nothing in return. The general election saw extraordinary levels of defection among white Democrats, who turned out in record numbers for the Republican, who ran on the ugly slogan "Before It's Too Late." In a polarized election pitting whites against blacks, Washington narrowly won, a victory noticed by blacks nationwide. Jackson, who claimed to have registered over three hundred thousand new voters in Chicago, argued that the Washington victory could be a model for national success.

While Jackson had been growing in stature since 1968, his relations with top black leaders were often strained. Jackson initially came to national prominence over the corpse of Martin Luther King Jr. At the time of the assassination, Jackson had not been at King's side but would later falsely claim to have cradled the dying pacifist in his arms. Against the explicit instructions of King's associates, Jackson appeared before the Chicago City Council, wearing what he claimed was a shirt stained with King's blood. From that moment on, Jackson, with his extraordinary oratorical talents and passion for justice, was a national figure. Many of King's aides could not forgive Jackson for the method of his rise. To some traditional civil rights leaders, Jackson seemed "a flashy trespasser" who had not paid his dues and had leapfrogged ahead of his betters through media savvy, boldness, and brazen chicanery. Still, by 1983, Jackson's popularity with the black masses and his success with the media made him the leading figure in the black community. When rumblings of a possible black presidential candidate emerged, Jackson was on every list.

In early 1983, black leaders, disturbed by the actions of national Democrats in Chicago, met to discuss increasing the influence of the black vote in 1984. To many, it seemed that black America was caught between an actively hostile Reagan administration and a Democratic Party inattentive to their needs. The idea of a black candidate was much discussed. While the tactic was widely supported, Jackson was not. Names of black politicians who had electoral experience were floated, but none of them volunteered to take the plunge. As Jackson traveled the country and spoke to black audiences, the chant inevitably arose: "Run, Jesse, Run!" The black leadership was still deeply split, with Jackson's candidacy actively opposed by the heads of the three leading civil rights organizations, the leader of the largest black labor coalition, and the mayors of Detroit, Los Angeles, Atlanta, Philadelphia, and Birmingham. The criticism of Jackson was blunt and personal. "You can't teach Jesse anything. He never has been disciplined," said Willie Brown, the black Speaker of the California State Assembly. The head of the Congressional Black Caucus echoed a constant charge against Jackson when he alleged that he lacked follow-through and was far more talk than action. Jackson's chances were also derided by white Democrats, who felt that he couldn't win and would only divide Democrats.

Despite these critics, Jackson made himself the candidate of black

America, because he was the only one with the courage to make the run. Jackson's motivation was simple: Increase the influence of black America (and his own). Jackson complained that white Democrats had supported Republicans when blacks won primaries and that the Democratic Party was simply moving too far to the right in response to Reaganism. By running, Jackson could challenge moderate Democrats in the primaries and then fight against conservative Republicans in the general election. As he put it, blacks were tired of "being the party concubines . . . they have fun with us, then they marry other people. We want to be full partners." Unlike a typical candidate, Jackson was motivated by pride, not victory. Jackson's campaign, by normal standards, appeared doomed. Not only had he been the last to enter the race, but he hadn't assembled a staff, raised money, or opened offices in key states at the time of his announcement. He didn't even have a campaign manager. The rules of the Democratic contests also seemed stacked against Jackson. Some states still had winner-take-all rules at the congressional district level, and most had threshold levels of support for a candidate to win any delegates at all. A record number of states were selecting delegates through caucuses, which typically favored the best-organized candidates with establishment support. Unless Jackson could appeal beyond the black community or greatly enhance black registration and turnout, he would not win many delegates.

The strategic implications of a Jackson run significantly altered the Democratic primaries. Of the other announced candidates (Gary Hart, Reuben Askew, Fritz Hollings, George McGovern, Alan Cranston, and John Glenn), Mondale was the only one who could expect substantial black support. With Jackson in the race, Mondale's lead over the rest of the field was severely lessened.

JACKSON STUMBLES OVER HYMIETOWN

Before a single primary vote was cast, Jackson demonstrated his ability to shake up the established rules of a nomination fight. A black navy pilot had been shot down over Syria, and Jackson believed that the Reagan administration was not working hard enough to secure his release. Over the objections of the State Department, and in violation of the informal code of "politics stops at the water's edge," Jackson flew to Damascus to personally negotiate for the pilot's release. When he succeeded, his high-risk gamble paid off with a White House press conference and greater news coverage than even a primary victory would have given him. Jackson, who had already been receiving more press than the rest of the field (save Mondale) combined, once again was the top of the news. Yet Jackson's moment of triumph contained within it signs of the anti-Semitism that would dog the rest of his campaign.

In winning the pilot's release, Jackson had been greeted with great enthusiasm by Syria's Hafez Assad, a dictator who still proudly harbored one of Hitler's top killers and also sponsored some of the most extreme anti-Jewish terrorist cells. Jackson told Assad that if the mission failed, Jackson would be "beat up on" by Zionists in the upcoming Democratic debate. Louis Farrakhan, the outspoken leader of a Black Muslim group, accompanied Jackson, and he already had a growing reputation for anti-Jewish statements. But it was the comment Jackson made two weeks after his Syrian triumph that would forever change his role in Democratic politics.

Speaking to two black reporters in a cafeteria at National Airport, Jackson, after saying, "Let's talk black talk," called Jews "Hymies" and referred to New York as "Hymietown." As anti-Semitic slurs go, Hymie was fairly mild, certainly no worse than the penchant of many Jews to refer to blacks as *schwartzes* (Yiddish for black). A few weeks later, the remark appeared toward the end of a lengthy *Washington Post* article on Jackson's relationship with Jews; it slowly ignited a firestorm of criticism. Jackson's initial response was neither credible nor uplifting. He wavered between pleading amnesia and issuing partial denials. Jackson and his followers also darkly alluded to a Jewish plot to wreck Jackson's campaign. Jackson's wife accused Jews of organizing a "conspiracy" that resulted in a media "crucifixion" of her husband. Charging that Jews in the media were secretly colluding to crucify Christians was hardly likely to end allegations of anti-Semitism. As the matter simmered, Jackson's public appearances were picketed by the extremist Jewish Defense League. The Anti-Defamation League, another watchdog against anti-Semitism, issued a nineteen-page memorandum outlining all the comments Jackson had ever made that were anti-Jewish.

Unfortunately for Jackson, he had from his earliest days been prone to statements that seemed anti-Semitic. In 1972, he had taken potshots at Jewish slumlords and fight promoters, alleging that they were particularly guilty of exploiting blacks. He also offended a Jewish ally by constantly referring to him as "the little Jew" even after complaints. In 1979, he had echoed one of the oldest anti-Semitic charges, that Jews controlled banks and the media. He had even compared Jewish critics of Andrew Young to the Ku Klux Klan. Jackson's controversial hugging of Yassir Arafat and his advocacy of a Palestinian homeland were also seen through the prism of his alleged anti-Semitism. Even Jackson's facial expression during a visit to the Holocaust memorial in Israel was debated, as was a quote attributed to him during the tour: "I am sick and tired of hearing about Holocaust." The Hymietown controversy metastasized as Jackson's campaign team debated the appropriate response. Many of Jackson's advisers had an attitude succinctly characterized by one as "fuck the Jews," although others pleaded for Jackson to apologize.

Finally, instead of lying or pleading a failure in memory, Jackson confessed in a speech at a synagogue that he had said "Hymie" but denied that it reflected any deep-seated animosity toward Jews. The tardy speech failed to end the furor. The picketing by Jewish activists continued. The first question aimed at Jackson during the New Hampshire debate focused on alleged anti-Semitic comments. The "Hymietown" imbroglio changed the Jackson candidacy in fundamental ways. First, it caused the media to remove the kid gloves in their coverage of the first major black presidential candidate. Up until this point, the press had not dwelled on Jackson's flimsy qualifications for the presidency, his lies at the time of King's assassination, the serial allegations of mismanagement at his charities, his $100,000 salary running those charities, and their funding by Arab governments. Odd statements Jackson had made, such as labeling the Founding Fathers "militarists," became fair game. Second, and more important, the effort by many Jewish groups to scuttle Jackson's candidacy through public denunciations put tremendous strain on black-Jewish relations. Many blacks now rallied to Jackson's defense, as Jews and other whites retreated. The "Hymie" incident confirmed for many whites the picture of Jackson as an unpresidential loose cannon who, in the later words of Marion Barry, "never run nothin' but his mouth." Yet for many blacks, Jackson now appeared a black man under siege by the white establishment for a minor peccadillo of language. Mondale, who had worried from the beginning whether he could attract centrist whites without offending blacks, now had to worry that any gesture of conciliation to Jackson would offend the Jewish community.

THE WINNOWING: JACKSON, HART, AND MONDALE
STRUGGLE FOR THE SOUL OF THE PARTY

Jackson, whose campaign was almost paralyzed by the anti-Semitic allegations in February, now faced a test of strength on Super Tuesday. With multiple southern primaries taking place on the same day, Jackson would be exposed as an egotistical pretender to the leadership of black America if he did not receive enough votes to continue to receive federal funding. Jackson's showing in New Hampshire (fourth place, with 5.3 percent of the vote) had been relatively strong in a very white state, but unless Jackson could win delegates where blacks were present in large numbers, his candidacy and his reputation would be fatally damaged. When Super Tuesday ended, Jackson had won a partial victory. Although he failed to win a single state, he did win enough support to maintain his federal funding and won majorities in four largely black southern districts. Super Tuesday also reduced the field to three candidates, Hart, Jackson, and Mondale.

The three represented very different Democratic Parties. Jackson, although he preached the politics of the rainbow, in which all skin colors and ethnicities would be represented, by and large received support only from blacks. Mondale represented the traditional New

Deal voters, minus the blacks. Hart was labeled the candidate of the yuppies and seemed to speak for white, upwardly mobile young people. Jackson's role in the contest was crucial. Although he trailed both candidates in almost every contest, he made it possible for Hart to stay viable. Indeed, Hart even encouraged Jackson to get into the race, knowing how much it would hurt Mondale. There was never much chance that Hart would receive significant black support running against Mondale. Not only were his main interests military and industrial policy, but he had spoken out against public housing and busing in his first campaign for the Senate. Hart's record and style made it impossible for him to compete with Jackson. As Hart's pollster told him, he was locked in a "white primary" with Mondale.

In the "black primary," Mondale attempted to exploit the existing divide between Jackson and much of the black establishment. Many of them felt eclipsed by Jackson's growing prominence and were very willing to reap the rewards of being early ticket buyers on the Mondale train. Jackson reacted with bitter anger at black Mondale supporters, labeling them participants in plantation politics, in which the white master reaped black votes. With such inflammatory statements and his strong grassroots support, Jackson made his candidacy a litmus test of blackness. In primary after primary, Mondale's endorsements from the top of the black establishment could not prevent Jackson from getting the majority of the black vote. In Philadelphia, Mondale's campaign resorted to deception, papering black wards with sample ballots marked with an X for Jackson at the top, but misleadingly urging votes for Mondale delegates further down the ballot. Jackson got 75 percent of the popular vote in Philadelphia despite the opposition of the black mayor, but thanks to racial pettifoggery, Mondale reaped the delegates.

Mondale and Hart both struggled with how to handle Jackson. They ended up treating him with great respect throughout the entire campaign, far better than they treated each other. Hart's campaign contemplated hitting Jackson with a tough question on arms control during one of the debates, in an attempt to expose Jackson's lack of experience and preparation, but rejected it as too risky. For Mondale, Jackson was a bull in a publicity china shop; every disagreement ended up in the media. Diplomacy consequently became difficult. Yet Mondale and Hart had not only the mercurial Jackson and his black supporters to deal with; they had to be wary of the white backlash against the reverend.

Jackson emphasized his race and simultaneously complained that he was pigeonholed as the black candidate by the media. He was introduced to black audiences as "the sun of thunder: six feet four inches of intellectual power, a bad black dude!" Jackson's speeches pointed right at the fears of many whites: "We picked their cotton. We cooked their food. We nursed their babies. Now we can run their cities. We can run their states. We will run the country!" A poll among Democrats found Jackson the least acceptable candidate, but his popularity soared among blacks. Jackson now personified and inflamed the problem that had merely been abstract for Mondale in 1982: how to retain black support while reaching out to Reagan Democrats. As a senior Mondale aide said in May: "If any candidate looks like he's sold out to get Jackson's support, he's lost 58% of the vote right there." Jackson's prominence played right into Republican plans to demonize the Democrats as captives of special interests.

By late spring, Mondale had won the nomination in a particularly unimpressive fashion, by lobbying party officials for their uncommitted votes, rather than winning a splashy victory in a primary. Mondale won only eleven of twenty-nine primaries, with solid victories in just five states. In only three states did he win even a plurality among white voters. And Mondale's margin of victory came almost entirely out of the primary rules, which awarded extra delegates by complex formulas. Mondale, with 39 percent of the vote, took 49 percent of the delegates, while Jackson received 10 percent of the delegates for 18 percent of the votes. For Jackson, this was tantamount to racism, and he complained bitterly about it for many months. Mondale, for his part, resented Jackson, believing correctly that had Jackson not run, the nomination would have been sewn up by February, providing Mondale with the time to build his strength for the general election.

JACKSON HOLLOWS MONDALE'S VICTORY: THE PRECONVENTION MANEUVERS

Jackson was a continuing source of frustration to Mondale, a traditional politician who could not understand Jackson's motivation or
his behavior. It had long since become mathematically impossible for
Jackson to win. But neither Jackson nor Hart made any gestures of
withdrawal. By the standards of traditional politics, Jackson should
have stopped his campaign after Super Tuesday or after his defeat in
New York. Yet Jackson's crusade continued, much to the chagrin of
the Mondale camp. Jackson's potential to bring black voters to the
polls was emphatically displayed in the primaries. Black turnout was
up 19 percent in Illinois, 28 percent in Pennsylvania, 43 percent in
Florida, 82 percent in Alabama, and 103 percent in New York. Black
registration went up 1.2 million in eleven southern states alone, and
Jackson had received 77 percent of the expanded black vote nationwide. Mondale would need that kind of fervor in November, but he
could not grasp what Jackson was after.

Jackson, hoping to re-create the excitement of his daring trip to
Syria in January, visited Castro's Cuba just before the Democratic
convention. In Cuba, Jackson gave a fiery speech emphatically laud-
ing Castro and the Cuban revolution. Any other American politician
would have been ostracized for such behavior, and it made it more
difficult for Mondale to make peace with Jackson. At the same time,
Louis Farrakhan made headlines by calling Judaism a "dirty religion"
and claiming that the state of Israel had been illegal since its found-
ing. Mondale quickly attacked the statement, but Jackson delayed,
unwilling to disavow one of his key supporters. Farrakhan had been
a continuing problem for Jackson. In March, Farrakhan had called
Hitler a great man. In April, he reignited the Hymietown affair by
issuing a public death threat against the black reporter who had
reported the comment. The threat was taken seriously by police,
since Farrakhan had threatened Malcolm X days before his assassination by the Nation of Islam. Now, with the attack on Judaism in
June, the pressure on Jackson to repudiate Farrakhan became extreme.
Still he resisted, saying, "Jesus repudiated the politics of assassination

but he did not repudiate Judas." He also bitterly complained that white politicians were not asked to denounce or disassociate from the Klan. However, Jackson missed the point: no white politicians were campaigning with Klan leaders or had Klansmen providing their personal security. Jackson did try to get Farrakhan to apologize for his more extreme statements, but Farrakhan simply stated, "Prophets don't apologize." Jackson could not afford to attack Farrakhan directly, because his campaign believed that it would hurt him with his black base, where Farrakhan had stature.

Just as Farrakhan was a problem for Jackson, Jackson by extension became a problem for Mondale. Mondale's campaign had long been urging a public attack on selected entrenched interests. After the nomination was wrapped up, several advisers proposed publicly breaking with Jackson at the NAACP convention that summer, by launching a reluctant assault on his refusal to repudiate Louis Farrakhan and on several of his more radical positions. Although a speech was drafted, Mondale refused to attack Jackson, because he feared it would create "World War III." Said one of Mondale's advisers, William Galston, "That was the last opportunity to draw a line that middle-America could discern as being significant. In the Jewish community and beyond Mondale did not have the guts to stand up. That perception would be fatal in the fall."

Jackson refused even traditional gestures at unity during the pre-convention period. He angrily rejected appearing with Mondale at a unity dinner to retire McGovern's campaign debt. Whenever Mondale and Jackson met, Jackson would harangue Mondale at length, complaining about the rules of the nomination fight that had just finished, as well as the runoff primary system in the South. He publicly jeered at Mondale by calling Humphrey "the last significant politician" to come from Minnesota. Jackson complained that he had been "ghettoized" and pleaded for a summit with Mondale before he would withdraw. When Jackson, shortly after a private conciliation meeting with Mondale, again attacked Mondale and threatened a black boycott, Mondale finally blew up. In a TV interview, Mondale outlined bluntly why Jackson would not be considered as his running mate. Mondale later shouted at Jackson in a phone call that if he didn't make peace with the Jews and stop bitching to the press, the gloves might really come off. Jackson told Mondale contritely, "This is the best conversation we've ever had." Had Mondale finally brought Jackson on board?

THE DEMOCRATIC CONVENTION: A TEMPORARY RECONCILIATION

While Mondale was at last expressing his anger at Jackson, he was also in the midst of selecting his running mate and planning his convention. Mondale needed to fight his image as the captive of special interest groups, as well as unite his fractured party. He would fail memorably at both tasks.

Mondale, like Carter before him, had a very public selection process for his running mate. Mondale hoped to create excitement by making a "nontraditional" pick such as a woman, a black, or a Hispanic. His campaign believed it would ignite fervor among the Democratic base and remake Mondale's staid image into that of a risk taker and trailblazer. However, the response to his eight finalists was underwhelming. While the list did have three women, two blacks, a Hispanic, and one white male, it was clear that by any traditional standard, only the white male (Senator Lloyd Bentsen of Texas) was qualified for the presidency. Of the remaining seven, four had no experience above the municipal level, and two others had been in office less than a year. Geraldine Ferraro, the eventual nominee, was a House member lacking seniority, influence, or even name recognition. No one of similar stature had been elected vice president or president in modern memory. Her central qualification was her sex. The parade of unqualified politicians arriving at Mondale's home was a caricature of affirmative action. Hart accused Mondale of "pandering" to party constituencies with his process, alleging that some were for display only.

Ferraro's selection was seen by many as an act of weakness and capitulation rather than bold leadership. The National Organization for Women had threatened to nominate a woman from the floor if Mondale picked a man. Because Hart and Jackson still retained delegates and many of Mondale's female supporters might bolt to support a woman, Mondale could have faced the unprecedented insult of seeing the convention reject his selection if he had chosen a male. Many Jackson delegates also took credit for the selection by wearing buttons saying, "Ferraro, thank Jesse!" since Jackson had called for the nomination of a woman or a black. Forces within Mondale's own party gravely damaged his stature by emphasizing their ability to push him around.

Both Hart and Jackson made platform demands in return for their endorsement of Mondale. Jackson's primary demands were a stronger stance against apartheid, racial quotas, massive defense cuts, an end to runoff elections in the South, and a revision of the primary rules that had denied him so many delegates. The quota issue deeply divided the delegates, as a solid majority of Jackson delegates favored them, while most Hart and Mondale delegates favored affirmative action without quotas. Mondale's original plank explicitly rejected quotas, but Jackson's forces demanded an endorsement of them. Eventually language advocating "verifiable measurements" in affirmative action programs was included, and this effectively papered over the disagreement. Jackson forces won their most important substantive victories on Africa policy and an agreement to form a commission to study primary rules. Mondale refused to budge on runoff elections, which were popular among white southerners.

At the convention itself, the tension between Mondale's and Jackson's black supporters erupted at a meeting of black Democrats. Coretta Scott King upbraided those blacks who had booed Andrew Young the day before for speaking against Jackson. King's speech, which contrasted Young's years of service to civil rights with the "lesser" credentials of Jackson supporters, offended many, and she herself was booed from the podium. The widow of Martin Luther King Jr. was reduced to tears by the treatment, and Young bitterly referred to Jackson delegates as "a bit unwashed." The Jackson camp's effort to portray "Mondale blacks" as racial traitors had now exposed a bitter divide along age and class lines in the black community. Jackson's closest aide was impolitic enough to say that Mondale was hunting for "black eunuchs." As the victor of two primaries

(D.C. and Louisiana), the winner of the popular vote in two others (South Carolina and Virginia), and the leader of 384 delegates, Jackson believed that he, and not King and Young, had the national organization and resources that Mondale needed.

In return for Jackson's endorsement, Mondale had also agreed to give the reverend an hour of prime time. The unease among Mondale supporters prior to the speech was palpable. Would Jackson reprise his Middle East statements that had angered so many Jewish voters? Would he diminish Mondale or build him up? Some had feared all along that Jackson would walk out of the convention or emulate George Wallace and actually launch a third-party effort, which would doom Mondale's already shaky campaign. Jackson had toyed openly with both ideas and had told black voters to "wait for his signal" in his speech before they rallied behind Mondale. As veteran political reporter David Broder put it, Jackson "can disrupt the convention and trigger a bigger national backlash." Instead, Jackson's speech was, along with Mario Cuomo's, the highlight of the convention and the most watched by the TV audience at home. Jackson demonstrated his extraordinary charisma while also seeking conciliation with those who had opposed him. He effectively apologized again for his ventures into anti-Semitism and rallied his followers behind Mondale. After a spring and summer of tension and misguided diplomacy between Mondale and Jackson, it seemed that Mondale's delicate treatment of Jackson had been rewarded.

THE REPUBLICAN GENERAL ELECTION STRATEGY

When Reagan's men met to plot their leader's reelection, they well understood that one of their chief assets was the extraordinary connection between Ronald Reagan and the American public. Many voters who disagreed with fundamental aspects of Reagan's policy goals still professed affection for the man. Most core components of the New Deal coalition had been penetrated by Reagan's appeal, including Hispanics, Jews, and working-class whites. Yet one group was immune to Reagan's magic: African Americans. Moreover, the weakness among blacks had a broader overtone. The architect of Reagan's strategy, Richard Wirthlin, knew that Reagan was very vulnerable on the "fairness" issue, the perception that Reagan lacked sympathy for the less fortunate, which had "racial overtones."

> Of course, civil rights is a component of fairness but rather than attempting to outdo Mondale on the fairness issue by more aggressively going after the black vote we took the tax issue and turned it into a fairness issue . . . we might have gone to the civil rights issue even more aggressively than we did but we thought it would have much broader resonance by casting our defense of unfair/uncaring in the context of the unfairness of Mondale's stated intention of increasing taxes.

Instead of combating Reagan's image on civil rights, the Republican strategy was to change the definition of fairness. Reagan's campaign knew well before the election that 90 percent of blacks would vote against them, but instead of attempting to reduce that number, they sought to get 58 percent of the white vote to counterbalance the Democrats' strength among blacks. Reagan made almost no effort to woo the black vote, as he had in 1980. Of course, the level of hostility to Reagan in the black community was far greater than it had been in 1980, so there were fewer options. Although Reagan had spoken to the NAACP during the 1980 campaign, he did not do so in 1984, probably because of the negative reception Vice President Bush had received in 1982. No prominent civil rights leaders came out to support Reagan in 1984, and the black outreach focused on a few endorsements from black sports figures. Billboards of Muhammad Ali with Reagan appeared in a few black neighborhoods, but it was a far cry from 1980.

Although Reagan never aimed to win black votes, he did construct a relatively diverse convention. Reagan's acceptance speech memorialized a Vietnamese immigrant at the Olympics who cheered a black man pushing a white woman in a wheelchair. The speaker's list at the Dallas meeting "looked like a GOP Rainbow Coalition," with as many minorities as could plausibly be placed at the podium.

One of the most captivating speakers was a black minister from Los Angeles, who gave reasons why blacks should support Reagan. Yet away from the podium, the convention hall was overwhelmingly white, with blacks making up only 4 percent of the delegates. The platform, like Mondale's first draft, attacked racial quotas directly.

The most significant strategic decision the Republicans made on race came in their effort to harness the white backlash against Jackson. Particularly in the South, the response to Jackson's prominence was thunderous. The North Carolina Republican Party sent out thousands of fund-raising letters warning that "your vote may already be canceled because radical Jesse Jackson has already registered enough liberal Democrat voters in North Carolina to cancel out your vote for President Reagan. . . ." North Carolina Republicans conducted a massive voter registration drive in response to Jackson's efforts. Similar actions were taken across the South. In Selma, a famed voting rights battleground in the 1960s, whites created the Selma Area Voting Encouragement (SAVE) group, which registered whites in record numbers. The incumbent white mayor of Selma attributed the success to Jackson: "Jackson helped me with the turnout because he inflamed whites . . . he helped me raise funds, and he got whites registered. . . . Jesse Jackson made people so mad . . . for every black vote he got, the Republicans and independents registered two whites." The head of the Texas Republicans admitted that the massive upsurge in black registration "scares the bejeebers out of me." The results were astounding. The 1,342,000 new southern black voters were overwhelmed by 3,078,000 new southern white voters. The calculated effort to register whites in response to Jackson's black outreach had been planned as early as the fall of 1983. Reagan's campaign was so concerned about Jackson's efforts to register southern blacks by then that it advocated not targeting southern states until "we can assess more clearly the impact of the massive drive to register blacks."

The Reagan effort to ride the Jackson backlash was not limited to registration. Bush was sent to speak to a Jewish group at the height of the Farrakhan controversy and angrily attacked Democrats for softness on anti-Semitism in not repudiating Jackson and Farrakhan. For one Reagan aide, this was "a beautiful stroke. . . . Hart and Mondale don't dare attack Jesse because they are afraid of him, but they are also feeling the heat from the Jewish community." Even inviting Jackson to the White House following his success in Syria was a brilliant move. While it was unlikely to change Reagan's image in the black community, it did boost Jackson's stature. The longer Jackson stayed in the Democratic primaries, and the more trouble he gave Mondale, the better Reagan's chances. Just as Richard Nixon privately cheered the success of George Wallace in the Democratic primaries of 1972, a Reaganaut must have been pleased by Jackson's surprisingly strong challenge to Mondale.

Overall, the Republican strategy on race was to ignore blacks, except as a scarecrow to spur white registration. There was no plan to inflame the racial divide by raising affirmative action. The Reagan strategists intended to use social issues as a wedge to divide Democrats from their loyalty to Mondale, but the issues they focused on were school prayer and, to a lesser extent, abortion. The one exception was an ill-planned attack on busing in Charlotte, North Carolina. While Charlotte had been antibusing in the 1970s, the community was relatively proud of their record on busing by 1984, so Reagan's sally was met with silence and then criticism from the local community. Reagan had no need to take a risky stance on any racial issue. Safely ahead of Mondale's on the most important issues of the day, his campaign contented itself with quietly combating Jackson's registration efforts.

JACKSON'S POSTCONVENTION PETULANCE

> It was very embarrassing. I didn't know what he was going to do and I tried to put the best face on it.
>
> WALTER MONDALE, ON JACKSON

Following the convention, Mondale's staff believed that Jackson had been mollified and would work for Mondale wholeheartedly. Almost immediately, however, Jackson resumed his public attacks on Mondale and even refused to explicitly endorse him. Rather than taking his grievances privately to Mondale, Jackson complained to reporters that Mondale had no themes that would attract black voters. The tensions between Jackson and Mondale simmered well into the general election season. Finally, a unity meeting was scheduled for St. Paul, and fifty black leaders flew in to meet with Mondale. The mood was ugly, and Mondale was bitterly attacked for his alleged failures on policy and style. Mondale refused their request for a multibillion-dollar jobs program as the price of their endorsement. In the end, though, the black leaders decided to stick with Mondale. From that point on, Jesse Jackson became an active surrogate for the Mondale campaign, although this was kept quiet in Jewish neighborhoods and the white South.

Yet the very fact that a meeting was necessary reflected Mondale's failure to unite his party. In the classic model of presidential politics, the general election is the period when a candidate should reach beyond his party's constituencies to independents and to the other party's voters. Mondale appeared to have the worst of both worlds: many white Americans believed he had gone too far in winning Jackson's support, yet Jackson continued to snipe at him, refusing to make peace. The press covered their strained relations well into September. Even Mondale's campaign chair admitted that the St. Paul meeting was "the last day of the primary campaign between Mondale and Jackson." Long after the convention, and Jackson's conciliatory speech, the Mondale campaign had to devote considerable efforts to placating the mercurial Jackson. The ongoing tension and confusion was also felt by Ferraro, who commented in 1985:

> "Jesse's got to have his self-respect, his self-respect." That's what his people kept telling us over and over . . . and it used to drive us nuts, really nuts, because we could never be sure what that meant.

Mondale, fighting an immensely popular incumbent in a time of peace and prosperity, probably never had a chance to win. But the continuing dissension with one of his party's key constituencies was the nail in his electoral coffin.

CONCLUSION: MONDALE FAILS THE JACKSON TEST

Long before election day, the Democrats were prepared for a memorable, Goldwateresque shellacking. Their fears were prescient, as Reagan swept to victory in every state in the Union save Minnesota. Mondale, despite his lengthy battles with Jackson, did win the overwhelming majority of black votes. More than a quarter of his vote came from blacks, and in the South, blacks made up almost half of his support. This says as much about Mondale's weakness with whites as it does about his strength with blacks. While black turnout was significantly higher than in 1980, it was simply not enough to overcome the white antipathy for Mondale. In some southern states, Mondale's share of the white vote fell below 20 percent.

Mondale's advisers as early as 1982 had concluded that the big question for the 1984 election would be "What message would attract white middle-class voters without alienating traditional constituencies?" The flip side of that challenge was equally perplexing: "How would Democrats convince blacks that the party had not abandoned them without antagonizing whites?" Certainly, the form in which that conundrum presented itself was unexpected; few Democratic insiders could have predicted that Jackson would run, or run as well as he did. Moreover, Jackson, obviously unqualified for the presidency and yet desperate for legitimacy, presented special problems. If the black candidate had been a more traditional politician, Mondale would not have had such difficulty in negotiating quiet compromises away from the media spotlight. If Jackson had not been so deeply flawed by anti-Semitism or so closely associated with a rabid race baiter like Farrakhan, unity would have come much easier. The tension with Jackson was never entirely resolved, and Mondale remained bitter about Jackson's role in his defeat. "He inspires and he scares but he never neutralizes," said Mondale much later of Jackson.

Mondale had limitations in his confrontation with Jackson. Jackson's style and motivation were difficult for Mondale to grasp. While Mondale had a great civil rights record, the man from Minnesota lacked an understanding of modern black political culture, in contrast with Jimmy Carter. Mondale also could not compete with Jackson in oratory or charisma. Even as Jackson was losing primary after primary to Mondale, it was Jackson who attracted the media attention and mass acclaim or disdain. Jackson made Mondale seem even more dull and less telegenic than he actually was. He diminished Mondale intentionally and unintentionally.

Did race contribute to the Republican victory directly? Although Reagan almost never injected race into the campaign, his image as a racial conservative was seen by many as a vital component of his white landslide, particularly in the South. A longtime observer of Mississippi's politics argued that Reagan's southern dominance had its roots in "a great deal of underlying racism. . . . Reagan is a polarizing figure whether he wants to be or not, in a race-conscious state as ours." Democratic analyst Bill Moyers was even blunter.

> George Bush was in Mobile, Alabama . . . and made to an all-white group a speech saying the party of Mondale and Ferraro . . . is not the Democratic Party that the people of Alabama remember. Well, the party that the people of Alabama remember is the party of the old George Wallace and Bull Connor.

Mondale's racial liberalism hurt him greatly in the South, and Jackson's candidacy served to make race much more salient.

The elections of 1984 ended with blacks more politically isolated than at any time since 1960. The nation, except for the House of Representatives, seemed to be in the grip of Reaganism. In many ways, the isolation of blacks was symbolized by the differing reactions in the public mind to two men: Jackson and Reagan. For most blacks, Jackson was a heroic figure, demanding justice and equal treatment. For many whites, Jackson was the epitome of an "uppity" black, refusing to pay his dues by running for lesser offices as white candidates did. The backlash against Jackson was deep and played a significant role in Reagan's victory. It did not get spoken of openly often, but it resided deep in the psyche of many whites. As one Jewish leader put it:

Nobody wanted to admit that when Jesse Jackson gets up there on network television and there are ninety million people out there watching, and he says "Our time has come . . ." nobody wants to say "Fuck you, Jackson, your time has not come." But that's what they're thinking. Because if your time has come, then what has happened to my time?

The fiery rhetoric that separated Jackson from many established black politicians, and gave his campaign the appearance of a crusade to black Americans, ignited a backlash among many whites. Similarly, whites saw Reagan's sunny side and blacks only its shadow. Most whites thought Reagan was fair, unprejudiced, and a moral man. Overwhelming majorities of blacks disagreed on every point. For blacks, Reagan was indelibly stained with prejudice, and it made it worse that he was so successful at hiding this from other Americans.

Walter Mondale had the unenviable task of running against a man whose extraordinary personality gave him a Teflon insulation against most standard attacks. At the same time, Mondale had to circle ever closer to Jackson, to avoid an open breach with one of his party's vital constituencies. The closer he drew to Jackson, the more he inherited Jackson's negatives with many whites. Could Mondale have played hardball with Jackson and dared him, and by extension African Americans, to compromise or take another four years of Reagan? Would Jackson have actually launched a third-party campaign or led a black boycott on election day? The answer remained unknown, because Mondale rejected the advice of his campaign to directly attack Jackson in the summer of 1984.

Mondale did succeed in convincing voters that he was a candidate who could protect the civil rights of blacks, but very few voters saw this as an important issue in 1984. That image may have even hurt Mondale, who made "fairness" part of his final assault on Reagan. Following the election, a Democratic study found that many white voters saw "fairness" as a code word for handouts to undeserving blacks. The report was so damning of Democratic prospects to regain white Reagan Democrats that the head of the DNC ordered all copies destroyed.

Amid the wreckage of the Mondale-Ferraro debacle, Democrats knew the challenge they had identified in 1982 continued unabated. How could they convince white voters that fairness meant not unearned black privilege, but racial equality and societal concern for the unfortunate? For Republicans, the challenge was far more subtle. Could they find another candidate who managed to effortlessly benefit from the white backlash? Reagan had given the Republicans "plausible deniability" on race. As long as Reagan led the party, they could quietly and incrementally attack selected civil rights gains, without seeming racist to most whites. If they could not find another candidate with Reagan's unique gifts, would Republicans then compete with Democrats for the black vote, or would they seek to openly stoke the racial resentments of whites for electoral gain?

FURLOUGH FROM THE TRUTH
The Cynical Racial Politics of 1988

You can't find a stronger metaphor for racial hatred in this country than a black man raping a white woman. . . . And that's what the Willie Horton story was.

SUSAN ESTRICH, DUKAKIS CAMPAIGN MANAGER

There was nothing racial about Willie Horton . . . we had a concerted effort in our campaign to make sure that race was not used in any way, shape or form in the development of this issue.

LEE ATWATER, BUSH CAMPAIGN MANAGER

The 1988 presidential campaign was the most racially charged contest since 1968. Unlike in the elections of the sixties, however, there was no nationally prominent issue dividing the races. Instead, the campaign of George Bush deliberately racialized the election to hold the white Reagan electoral majority together in the absence of Reagan's personal charm and manly image. The Republicans cunningly used prison furloughs and the death penalty to reignite white fears of black crime and to remind white voters of the alleged leniency of liberal Democrats toward black miscreants. Michael Dukakis, a bland northeastern governor, failed to significantly integrate his campaign or to understand the nature of racial politics in America. Perhaps because of Dukakis's ignorance of black political power, he also could not figure out how to solve the problem of Jesse Jackson. As in 1984, the pride and petulance of Jackson would prove damaging to a liberal white nominee. Yet Jackson, in the end, was not the central focus of the racial politics of 1988. That position would be occupied by a vicious black criminal,

William Horton, whose arresting visage became as familiar to the American populace as that of the vice presidential candidates. Lee Atwater, the cutthroat genius of Bush's surge in the polls during the summer of 1988, succeeded in his avowed goal of making Horton a household name. In so doing, he made George Bush president.

1988: THE SETTING

The nation was at peace and relatively prosperous. A popular incumbent, with solid approval ratings, had done what no incumbent since Eisenhower had done—completed two terms in office. In his last two years, Reagan's approval ratings recovered from the damaging revelations of Iran-Contra and the costly attempt to put Robert Bork on the Supreme Court. Yet Reagan's appeal remained a white phenomenon. Black Americans by overwhelming margins continued to perceive Reagan as a heartless defender of the rich and powerful, who was at best racially insensitive and quite possibly a racist. His administration in its second term certainly made no effort to reach out to blacks. Shortly after his landslide victory, Reagan's Justice Department contemplated a frontal assault on affirmative action. Although outrage among civil rights groups and their allies in Congress, as well as the opposition of more moderate Republicans in and out of the administration, ultimately scuttled the plan, the suggestion certainly did nothing to enhance Reagan's appeal among blacks. Even in the last year of his presidency, Reagan showed no hesitancy in becoming the first president in modern history to veto a civil rights bill. Also, Reagan had not made diversity a focus; his cabinet featured only one token black in a minor position.* Reagan had abjectly failed to convince blacks that he was an advocate of equal opportunity and civil rights. Yet in white America, Reagan remained "the Gipper," an immensely popular political figure.

---

* Reagan simultaneously fed doubts about his competency and about the importance of blacks in his administration when he failed to recognize the one black in his cabinet during a meeting with urban leaders, referring to his cabinet secretary as "Mr. Mayor."

There were reasons for optimism on the Democratic side. With strong black support, the Democrats had surprised many observers by taking back the Senate in 1986, giving them a confidence boost as they looked ahead to the presidential election. Locked out of the White House since 1980, Democrats hoped that the country had forgotten the economic and geopolitical mess of the Carter years. Most important, they would not have to run against Ronald Reagan, whose near mystical connection with the American public had decimated Carter and Mondale.

Among African Americans, however, there was a growing dissatisfaction with the Democratic Party. During the Reagan presidency, the number of blacks who considered themselves independent of either political party rose from 9 percent to 22 percent, as the percentage of blacks who identified as Democrats dropped substantially. Even as this defection went on, much of the white Democratic establishment remained convinced that the key to electoral success was to appeal to conservative and moderate whites, the Reagan Democrats. This was particularly so in the South, where, excepting the 1976 Carter victory, the Democratic Party had won a total of two states in the four elections since 1964. In hopes of nominating a moderate or conservative southern Democrat, Democrats made the southern primaries even more influential in the road to the nomination.

Two questions would govern the strategic choices of the campaigns of 1988. Would the Republican nominee inherit Reagan's popularity and receive credit for the economic growth during his years in office? By contrast, would the Democratic nominee be able to reconstruct the New Deal coalition that had dominated the presidency from 1932 to 1964, by bringing back northern ethnics and white southerners?

THE CANDIDATES

George H. W. Bush

George Bush on paper had a better civil rights record than did the man he sought to succeed. Unlike Reagan, who had opposed almost every civil rights bill ever proposed, Bush had a mixed record and, indeed, came from the moderate wing of the Republican Party by birth. His father, a senator from Connecticut, had been a strong proponent of civil rights, similar to Henry Cabot Lodge and other northern Republicans. Bush, raised in a tradition that viewed civil rights almost as a patrician obligation, had been involved with philanthropic efforts to aid blacks at Yale. Yet in his first try for political office, the pattern of his opportunistic involvement in racial politics was indelibly set. Running for the Senate in his adopted home state of Texas in 1964, Bush faced opposition from Republican conservatives, who saw him as a weak moderate Yankee, with a high-pitched voice and ties to the eastern establishment. In that campaign, Bush ran as a Goldwater Republican, endorsing states' rights and the poll tax and attacking those who donated money to that "militant" Martin Luther King Jr.:

> He told his crowds anything that would attract them. One line that grabbed them, and was used over and over again to predictable hollers and whoops, was that Congress had passed "the new civil rights act to protect fourteen percent of the people" but that he was as much concerned about "the other 86%."

Bush said that what was in a person's heart was more important than where he stood on specific legislation, a slogan adopted by his son decades later.

Following his defeat, Bush launched a bid for Congress in 1966. Running against a segregationist Democrat in a district where blacks made up a sizable percentage of the electorate, Bush moderated his civil rights stance and received 35 percent of the black vote, ten times what he had won in 1964. He quickly established a reputation on race more suiting the son of Prescott Bush. Bush met with black leaders and made a very courageous stance in favor of housing integration in 1968, for which he received death threats from outraged whites. After 1970, Bush's service as RNC chair, ambassador to China, and director of the CIA seldom gave him an opportunity to address racial issues. In the 1980 Republican primaries, he had had some black support but never attempted to differentiate himself from Reagan on civil rights, although he did quietly apologize for opposing the Civil Rights Act in 1964. During his time as vice president, he had never been explicitly allied with those like Attorney General Meese, who wanted an aggressive, anti–affirmative action push, or with those who defended the civil rights status quo within the Reagan administration.

Bush, who had had three positions on abortion during his career in politics, demonstrated a similar principled consistency on racial matters. In 1964, Bush had played the race card with abandon to establish his toughness with suspicious Texas conservatives, who saw him as an effete eastern Republican. In 1966–68, Bush had moved back toward the civil rights liberalism of his father. Since then, he had scarcely addressed racial matters at all, making it an open question as to which George Bush would run for president in 1988, the Texas race baiter or the courageous moderate who had challenged Houston's whites on housing integration.

Michael Dukakis

Michael Dukakis ran for president with the blankest slate on the question of civil rights of any Democrat since Kennedy; he had no record on national civil rights issues. As governor of Massachusetts, a state with a very small black population, he also lacked the deep friendships and political connections with black leaders that Jimmy Carter had had in 1976. Dukakis did, of course, have a solid record of nominating blacks to office during his years as governor, and he had received black support in all of his elections. Yet one could not say of Dukakis that civil rights or the struggle for black equality was central to his political life, as one could have of LBJ, Humphrey, Carter, Mondale, Bill Clinton, or Bobby Kennedy.

The issues that excited Dukakis (to the extent that he ever got excited) were almost designed to leave black audiences unenthused. Dukakis enjoyed the minutiae and complexity of public policy. He preached the politics of dry competency long before he ran on that "platform" in 1988. Although it might be supposed that Dukakis's personal history as the son of Greek immigrants would give him greater sensitivity to the interplay of ethnicity and politics, he instead appeared as the apotheosis of WASP-ish dourness. His rhetoric and his speaking style were alien to most black audiences (and many white ones as well). Even Mondale had given passionate speeches in favor of black equality. Dukakis had the unique talent of making many Democrats long for the oratory of Walter Mondale. The irony of the 1988 Democratic primaries was that the strongest run by a black man for the nomination in history produced a nominee singularly unappetizing to black Democrats. The irony of the general election was that Dukakis, for whom civil rights was not a priority and for whom the black struggle had no visible emotional resonance, would become tarred by a vicious assault against racial liberalism.

JACKSON'S NEW STYLE: A REAL RAINBOW

Jackson remained a dominant figure in Democratic politics even before he announced that he would again seek the presidency. After Hart's candidacy was derailed by a sex scandal, Jesse Jackson briefly led in the informal preprimary campaign for the Democratic nomination. Jackson received more support from the national black leadership than in 1984, as well as triple the support from the white masses. Jackson's new white support was a product of four years of sustained outreach. Jackson had appeared at plant closings, farmers' rallies, and any other place where he could make his case against Reaganomics. The response of economically depressed whites to his rhetoric was emphatic. Jackson used his economic populism to explicitly address white anxieties about his race. As he told white workers at a plant closing: "When they close down the plant and lock the gates, the lights go out. And when the lights go out, we all look amazingly similar in the dark." Jackson spoke in the white flight Chicago suburb of Cicero, where Jackson and other civil rights marchers had been stoned and black families firebombed in the recent past. Even there, white workers cheered and chanted, "Run, Jesse, Run!" Jackson even visited the ailing George Wallace in Alabama and prayed with the repentant demagogue.

Jackson's new campaign staff was far more integrated. Whites with long résumés in Democratic politics replaced blacks in key positions. His campaign manager, Gerald Austin, was a New York Jew, a powerful symbol of Jackson's effort to mend fences even with his most vociferous critics. Some blacks complained that Jackson had forgotten his roots, and a former top aide, Donna Brazile, complained that Jackson was "whitening his message." The most prominent black supporter of Jackson was no longer the anti-Semitic and bigoted Louis Farrakhan but the popular and "safe" Bill Cosby. Jackson's new style was even reflected in his clothing, which seldom featured African dashikis and other untraditional sartorial choices. Jackson was also talking very different policies. The 1988 campaign focused less on black pride and radical third world globalism and more on economic populism and drugs. Jackson proclaimed he was "the five star general in the drug war," angry at the way drugs were tearing apart the inner city, even if his policy proposals were vague and unformed. Perhaps the best symbol of the change was Jackson's careful distance from the Tawana Brawley rape hoax, an ugly circus run by a little-known black cleric, the Reverend Al Sharpton. Sharpton and his associates turned black anger at the criminal justice system into a daily media assault of wild claims and offensive rhetoric. The 1984 Jackson might well have been drawn into the patently false allegations of gang rape by white prosecutors and police officers, but the 1988 Jackson wisely left the slander and defamation to Sharpton.

The change in the Jackson campaign was real and broad. Said Ann Lewis, one of Jackson's key new white advisers: "'84 was a crusade. This is a real campaign." Yet while Jackson was far more professional and popular with whites than in 1984, he still presented the same dilemma to white Democrats. Said one high-ranking party official: "If it's seen that the nominee won because he was the guy Jesse Jackson wanted—that's the kiss of death." Before the first vote was cast, Jackson was seen as the kingmaker, the man barred from the nomination who could still pick the winner. The idea that Jackson could actually take the prize seemed not to have occurred to anyone, except perhaps Jesse Louis Jackson.

LAST WHITE MAN STANDING: DUKAKIS WINS BY DEFAULT

Along with Jackson, a crowded field of white men vied for the Democratic nomination. None of them made any serious effort to woo black voters; all conceded that the black vote was Jackson's. Consequently, racial issues seldom arose in campaign literature or the early debates. The expectation was that neither Iowa nor New Hampshire would be decisive, because each had quasi–favorite son candidates. Jackson's much stronger showing in the early primaries, where he drew about 10 percent, was little noted. Even when Jackson won between 20 percent and 30 percent in the very white states of Minnesota, Maine, and Vermont, it was seen as relatively unimportant. The first true test for Jackson was considered to be Super Tuesday, on March 8. Every southern and border south state except two held primaries, plus contests in Massachusetts, Rhode Island, Hawaii, Nevada, Idaho, and American Samoa.

Three men survived the massive contest: Tennessee senator Al Gore, Dukakis, and Jackson. Gore built his campaign around appealing to Reagan Democrats, particularly in the South. He even echoed Reagan's 1984 criticism of the Democrats, attacking those who supinely catered to special interests. Gore won just enough primaries on Super Tuesday to justify continuing his campaign. Dukakis had put together credible showings in a few southern areas with wins outside the South. But the real winner was Jackson, who doubled his support among whites and won first or second in sixteen of twenty-one contests. He also took 27 percent of the popular vote in the fourteen southern states, more than any other candidate, and won nearly a third of the southern delegates. Still, the press perception remained consistent: Jackson was not a real threat to take the nomination. The question was which white candidate, Gore or Dukakis, would defeat the other?

Three weeks later, Jackson shocked the nation by winning a massive victory in Michigan, beating Dukakis 54 percent to 29 percent. Even though Dukakis had the support of Mayor Coleman Young and much of the party establishment, Jackson's forces utilized a strong get-out-the-vote drive to overwhelm Dukakis. Now Jackson had won more votes in primaries and caucuses than any other candidate and even pulled within a few votes of Dukakis's lead among the delegates. Instead of a power broker, Jackson now appeared to have a legitimate chance at the nomination. *Time* put him on the cover with the single banner headline JESSE!?, suggesting the electrifying surprise and confusion that reigned among many Democrats. His supporters shouted, "Win, Jesse, Win!" at his rallies, and Jackson started contemplating cabinet appointments. Three days after Michigan, Jackson was invited to a Washington breakfast with the elite of the Democratic establishment, a symbol of his newly enhanced status. The rebel of 1984 was now being brought into the inner circle.

Jackson campaigned aggressively in Wisconsin, the next major primary, drawing huge crowds and mass excitement unlike any seen in Democratic politics since the passing of Bobby Kennedy. Yet Wisconsin was the first sign that Jackson's reign as front-runner would be brief. In part, this was because of Jackson's own undisciplined behavior. Unable to stay on the message that had won Michigan, he unwisely wrote a public letter to Panamanian strongman Manuel Noriega, grandiosely calling on the dictator to step down. The ineffective grandstanding reminded many of Jackson's reputation as a showboat. Even though Wisconsin's Republican governor encouraged Republicans to enter the Democratic primary and vote for Jackson, Dukakis managed to beat back the Jackson tide. Dukakis also defeated Jackson in Connecticut, but when the two candidates appeared the next day on the *Today* show, Jackson seized control of the interview and left Dukakis appearing weak and unable to handle the voluble and charismatic Jackson.

The Democratic nomination would be decided in New York. If Dukakis could defeat Jackson decisively here, the nomination would be his. If Jackson managed another victory, he would either win the nomination or be denied by the entry of a "white knight" candidate like New York governor Mario Cuomo or Delaware senator Joseph Biden. The unfathomable costs to the party of a brokered convention, a blatant maneuver to deny Jackson the nod, was a prospect that frightened many Democrats. The New York primary electorate was approximately one-quarter Jewish and one-quarter black, posing a challenge and opportunity for Jackson. Would Jackson's fence-mending with the Jewish electorate erase the memories of the anti-Semitism of 1984?

Surprisingly, the candidate who first played ethnic politics in New York was the now desperate Gore, who decided that the most effective way to win white and Jewish votes in New York's primary was to deride Dukakis for being soft on Jackson. Consequently, he won the endorsement of New York's Jewish mayor, Ed Koch, already gaining prominence as a critic of Jackson and a bête noire of local blacks. Koch alleged that Jackson had a bad record of telling "lies under stress" and that any Jew would be "crazy" to vote for the black preacher. There was an audience for that message; buttons appeared proclaiming "I'm a Tough Hymie—Jews Against Jackson." For the five days leading up to the New York primary, Koch was glued to Gore's side and made Gore's campaign look racist, according to Gore's press secretary. Gore became the first Democratic rival since Jackson's entry into presidential politics in 1984 to attack his obvious lack of qualifications, pointedly stating that "we're not choosing a preacher, we're choosing a president." Gore's advisers worried that the comment would be seen as prejudiced, and the reaction from Jackson's campaign manager was obscene and immediate. Gore's message to white voters, especially Jews, was that they could vote against Jackson and anti-Semitism only by voting for Gore.* Simultaneously, Dukakis sympathizers quietly circulated the message that a vote for Gore was in effect a vote for Jackson, because the longer the race remained three-way, the longer Jackson remained relevant.

Gore's desperate moves against Jackson, and Koch's embarrassing attacks, probably hurt Gore. Dukakis won a strong victory on April 19, taking 57 percent versus 37 percent for Jackson and a meager 10 percent for Gore. Jackson won 97 percent of the black vote, which is not surprising since Dukakis did not campaign in black areas, except

---

* Convincing white voters that they should send a message to Jackson with their vote was nothing new in the 1988 primaries. Second-tier candidate Senator Paul Simon had run a desperate television ad on the eve of the Illinois primary, in effect warning white voters that a vote for Dukakis was a vote for Jesse.

for one symbolic trip to a black precinct in Harlem. Gore was now eliminated from the race, and it was clear that Dukakis would be the nominee. Most of Jackson's victories, outside of Michigan, had been possible only because of the split in the white vote among two or more candidates. Dukakis had won the race to be the last white man standing. Yet the role that Jackson played in the 1988 primaries was very different from the one he had played in 1984. Then, he had merely delayed the nomination of Mondale and prolonged the race. In 1988, however, Jackson denied the black vote to any prospective white challenger to Dukakis. Given Dukakis's issue focus, his lack of connections to black leaders, and his singularly unappealing political style, it is inconceivable that he would have won even a plurality of the black vote against, for example, New Jersey senator Bill Bradley, Arkansas governor Bill Clinton, New York governor Mario Cuomo, or even Missouri representative Richard Gephardt. The presence of Jackson in the primaries led directly to the nomination of a man who lacked credibility in the black community and lacked understanding of the exigencies of black political life.

Although he no longer had any chance of victory following New York, Jackson made no move to withdraw. As the late Dukakis victories continued, some argued that this was actually giving the diminutive Massachusetts governor stature with the electorate and keeping his name in the papers. By this way of thinking, the comparatively tranquil Republican primaries were denying George Bush the opportunity to show he was a fighter and a strong candidate. Unfortunately for Dukakis, the early lock that Bush got on his party's nomination actually gave Bush time to devise a devastating general election strategy, a strategy that would demonstrate the continuing puissance of race in presidential elections.

BUSH SEIZES ON HORTON

George Bush was far from the natural heir of the Reagan mantle. However, Bush had much of the Republican Party establishment solidly behind him. On the issue of civil rights, he faced little challenge. While Bob Dole, Bush's principal rival, had voted for the 1964

Civil Rights Act that Bush had opposed, Dole never attempted to brandish his relatively strong record on racial issues. By contrast, Representative Jack Kemp, a true Reaganite Republican, paid more attention to black voters and issues than any other Republican did. Kemp, a former NFL star, talked of black outreach in almost every speech and had a record of working with African Americans in Congress. As Republican representative Newt Gingrich said, in reference to Kemp's NFL past, "Jack has showered with guys most Republicans will never meet." Kemp's outreach to blacks did not depend entirely on a history of shared bathing; he talked of revitalizing the urban core by aggressively promoting entrepreneurial zones. Yet Kemp failed to organize his campaign effectively and was quickly eliminated from the contest.

Bush's campaign used victories in New Hampshire, South Carolina, and on Super Tuesday to effectively capture the nomination. Still, the Bush campaign was greatly troubled. As he won primary after primary and became the acknowledged nominee, polls consistently showed him trailing Dukakis by as much as twenty points. The polling also confirmed that the American people had little positive knowledge about Bush. What they knew of Bush suggested that he was a weak leader. The caricature of Bush as a follower who lacked independent vision seemed even stronger than the image that most vice presidents had faced when they reached for the presidential nomination. The media went so far as to sexualize Bush's weakness, making it a manhood question. As early as 1987, *Newsweek* asked on its cover whether Bush could fight off his image as a "wimp."

The good news that Bush's campaign staff found in the polls was that while the voters didn't like Bush much and didn't have much knowledge about him, they knew even less of Dukakis. Two Bush staffers, Andrew Card and James Pinkerton, discovered a story that they believed would convince voters that Dukakis was unfit for the presidency: the story of Willie Horton's furlough. Horton, a murderer serving a life sentence, had been released on weekend furlough, in a program started by Dukakis's Republican predecessor. On his tenth furlough, Horton had fled the state. In Maryland, Horton had viciously beaten a man and repeatedly raped his fiancée over a four-hour period. Both were white. The story seemed tailor-made for a critique of liberal attitudes toward crime. The facts were somewhat different. The penalty for murder in Massachusetts, life without parole, was stronger than in many other states. Nationwide, the average length of time served for first-degree murder was eleven years, while in Massachusetts it was over nineteen. Thus, in many states, Horton would have already been on permanent furlough for his original 1974 murder. Moreover, many other states had furlough programs, as did the federal government. Dukakis, characteristically, resisted emotional calls for an end to the furlough program, resting his decision on academic studies showing that furloughs were effective in maintaining order in prisons and rehabilitating prisoners to life back in society.

Yet his campaign had long anticipated that Horton would be a source of trouble. As Dukakis campaign manager Susan Estrich put it:

> Here's [Bush's] first ad. There's this big black dude in his prison cell with street clothes on, whistling softly as he packs his toothbrush and a few incidentals before setting out on a weekend of pillaging.

The first to attack Dukakis for the Horton furlough was Al Gore, again demonstrating Gore's willingness to play the race card in his outreach to moderate whites. New York, scene of Gore's attack on Jackson, was also where he unveiled the Horton issue. Although Gore never mentioned Horton's name or race, that was unnecessary. The message was immediately apparent in the materials that the Gore staffers handed out to reporters: Dukakis was weak on black crime. Bush campaign officials would later disingenuously claim that it was Gore's use of Horton that brought the issue to their attention, but the story had already appeared in the mass media. Still, the Gore attack made clear that Dukakis had no scripted answer ready for his most glaring vulnerability, another indication to the Republicans that Dukakis was not ready for national prime time. When Bush staffers Card and Pinkerton brought the Horton story to Lee Atwater, Bush's campaign manager, Dukakis's inability to play defense must have been as obvious as the appeal of the Horton story.

Lee Atwater was the perfect architect of the Horton campaign, by background and by belief. Schooled in the crucible of South Carolina's politics, Atwater knew how powerful race was in moving the white electorate.* At a young age, Atwater had distinguished himself as a master of the low blow and the cheap shot, a win-at-all-costs political consultant with a burgeoning reputation as a fighter. Moreover, Atwater was very open about his low opinion of the American voter. Since they could absorb only small amounts of information at a time, a campaign needed to be based on emotions and symbols, not facts. Atwater thus was already looking for "the easy-to-digest tale that made listeners feel—usually, repulsion—rather than think . . . and so he began the search for wedge issues for George Bush—simple, impressionistic issues that appealed to attitudes, created a reaction, not a thought." The furlough of William Horton was the ideal issue for such a campaign.

In May, the Bush campaign assembled focus groups of Reagan Democrats in New Jersey who were leaning toward Dukakis. Along with Dukakis's opposition to the death penalty, and his veto of putting the pledge of allegiance back in the schools, the Horton story effectively pulled these swing voters back to the Republican Party. In another focus group in Alabama, a group of Dukakis leaners became Bush supporters when one of the focus group participants related the Horton story. The results of the focus groups were taken to Kennebunkport, Maine, where Bush was relaxing after locking up the Republican nomination. Although Bush hesitated in choosing such an ugly strategy, it was made clear to him that "it was the only way to win." While Dukakis was still struggling with how to handle Jackson, the most powerful black man in America, Bush was scheming how to exploit the misdeeds of a criminal member of the black underclass.

JACKSON AND DUKAKIS: THE POLITICS OF PIQUE

Meanwhile, the Dukakis campaign was in a quandary. While they wanted Jackson to endorse the governor and get out of the race as

---

* Atwater was also the Bush staffer most attuned to black culture, at least musically. It was Atwater who convinced the GOP to pay Ray Charles $25,000 to appear at the convention.

soon as possible, they also did not want to appear to be publicly begging Jackson. Even after Dukakis secured an absolute lock on the nomination following the California and New Jersey primaries in June, Jackson refused to concede, and Dukakis refused to woo him. As a key Dukakis staffer said after the election, the Dukakis camp was very aware that "voters seem to judge the strength and skill and character of the Democratic candidate on how effectively he gets along or copes with Jackson." Although Dukakis went out of his way to praise Jackson in speeches prior to the convention, Jackson's staffers still complained that Dukakis did not understand Jackson or his needs. There was also a profound lack of trust between the two men. Dukakis refused to meet with Jackson one-on-one during the primaries, despite repeated entreaties for a "summit" from the Jackson camp. Dukakis was afraid that without witnesses, Jackson would twist his words in the media.

Even before his loss became certain, Jackson began to campaign for the second spot on the ticket with Dukakis. He told his audiences to "keep hope alive" with regards to the vice presidency and even fed the press warnings that he would tie the convention in knots if he weren't the running mate. Aware that Jackson had been offended by Mondale's early rejection of his candidacy in 1984, Dukakis staffers made it clear that Jackson was in the competition for the job. Thus began an odd and pointless ballet between the two camps. Jackson, told by many in his own campaign and outside it that he should stop dreaming of the vice presidency and remove himself from consideration to avoid embarrassment, relied on the assurances from the Dukakis campaign that he was a contender. Dukakis headquarters was in fact telling Jackson that, but only out of concern for Jackson's pride; he was never, in fact, a serious candidate for the nomination. Jackson continually diminished Dukakis, particularly when he bragged, "I'm going to push him until I get a response," or when he claimed that he had earned a "right of first refusal" to the vice presidential slot. Jackson even enjoyed mocking Dukakis's height. In a joint appearance before the Congressional Black Caucus, Jackson stepped onto Dukakis's discreetly placed riser. Now elevated far above his normal towering height, Jackson joked that he had been waiting years for "equal standing." When a meeting was finally arranged at

Dukakis's home during the July Fourth weekend, Dukakis inquired whether Jackson would accept the job, if offered. Jackson's immediate answer was yes. Yet Jackson left the Dukakis home furious, feeling that "he'd been treated like a nigger," according to one Jackson associate, because Dukakis had never engaged him on matters of policy or strategy. Dukakis, who had wanted an endorsement, was also disappointed, and the tension over the vice presidency persisted. Jackson continued to jet around the country, "campaigning" and attracting twice the press coverage of Dukakis, the nominee.

Aware of how badly Mondale had been hurt by the prolonged fight with Jackson in 1984, Estrich and other top Dukakis aides had been working to resolve all platform conflicts with the Jackson forces before the nomination. The Jackson campaign threatened multiple floor flights, which finally caused the Dukakis side to suggest that if that happened, Jackson might find himself addressing the nation after midnight. Jackson's negotiators shot back that a speech outside the convention hall would suit their man just fine. Dukakis staffers pressured Jackson to withdraw and endorse Dukakis, to no avail. Dukakis resisted entreaties from Cuomo, Gephardt, and other party officials to call Jackson personally. Dukakis seemed to think that all Jackson was after was money for the fall to run his get-out-the-vote effort.

In the midst of the negotiations, Dukakis chose Texas senator Lloyd Bentsen as his running mate, a conservative southern Democrat* with a surprisingly strong record on civil rights. However, Dukakis's campaign, running on the theme of competence, displayed a remarkable inability to handle the logistics of the selection process. The one promise that Jackson had extracted from Dukakis was that Jackson be notified before the media. But Jackson found out about the nomination from a reporter nonetheless, owing to an embarrassing chain of snafus. His pride wounded, Jackson aired his anger publicly and resorted to the powerful imagery of slavery:

---

* Dukakis eliminated Gore from consideration in part because of the outrage among blacks at the way he had treated Jackson in New York; Jackson had also made it clear that Gore was unacceptable.

It is too much to expect that I will go out and be the champion vote picker and bale them up and bring them back to the big house and get a reward of thanks, while people who do not pick nearly as many voters, who don't carry the same amount of weight among the people, sit in the big house and make the decisions.

Jackson and Dukakis had long been scheduled to speak to the NAACP immediately prior to the convention. Rather than enthusiastically endorsing the Dukakis-Bentsen ticket, Jackson in his NAACP speech lashed out in anger, still stinging from the way the vice presidential nomination had been handled. "I will never surrender! . . . I may not be on the ticket, but I'm qualified! That's what I know! Qualified!" Dukakis's speech later that week was received unenthusiastically, in part because of his treatment of Jackson. Moreover, Dukakis offered little to the NAACP other than a recitation of his hiring record in Massachusetts. Some in the press speculated that Dukakis had slighted Jackson over the nomination in order to impress those in the white electorate who disliked the black preacher. Whatever the motivation, the continuing tension between Jackson and Dukakis moved much of the excitement over the Bentsen selection off the front page. Jackson launched a flashy bus caravan from Chicago to Atlanta, ending in a tumultuous rally that Democratic insider Bert Lance compared to Christ's arrival in Jerusalem. The mood of the crowd was angry, but Jackson gave a moderate speech, reminding the crowd there was no need to demonstrate outside the convention because his supporters had secured representation inside.

Following the rally, Jackson made direct contact with Dukakis, claiming that his supporters would be difficult to control unless Dukakis met with him immediately. Thus, on the eve of the convention, Dukakis and Jackson met for the first time since the unsuccessful July Fourth meeting. Ultimately, Jackson traded peace for a prime-time speech, jobs in the Dukakis campaign for several staffers, a small jet for Jackson's campaigning in the fall, and the agreement to once again change the delegate selection rules for the next presidential contest. The headlines were very positive for Dukakis, such as DUKAKIS

GIVES JACKSON NOTHING or another suggesting that Dukakis had "faced down" Jackson. Jackson seemed suddenly aware of how damaging he was to the Democrats' chances, telling Dukakis not to make concessions or "the press will burn you." Dukakis's love-in with Jackson was ultimately very successful, with Dukakis including praise for Jackson's children in his acceptance speech and Jackson appearing with Dukakis and Bentsen at a press conference to demonstrate the unity between the party's left wing and right wing. Jackson's convention speech reminded Democrats that he was the party's most electrifying speaker, although his praise for Dukakis was less than overwhelming. Still, it seemed Jackson had been mollified and was on board for a unified assault on Bush in the fall.

THE MUGGING OF MICHAEL DUKAKIS: HORTON IN THE GENERAL ELECTION

Bush's campaign was also avoiding the black community, if for very different reasons. Because of the hostility among most blacks to Republican politicians, Bush didn't make "any measurably overt moves" toward the NAACP or other black groups. Bush's staff saw the black vote as ungettable and never targeted it. Yet racial politics was a potent divider of the electorate, as had been clear since the conventions. In a poll of convention delegates and the general public, almost two-thirds of Democratic delegates had agreed that the government paid too little attention to blacks, while only 14 percent of the Republicans had felt that way. The general public (34 percent) was closer to the Republican position, and the white public was much more so. The Republican platform attacked preferential treatment of racial minorities, while the Democrats had endorsed, once again, affirmative action without quotas. Had Dukakis not been the nominee, it is easy to imagine Lee Atwater convincing Bush to highlight his opposition to affirmative action. However, Dukakis's record provided much more attractive targets than racial quotas.

As they had planned since May, the Bush campaign began a concerted effort to inject Horton's furlough into the campaign. The campaign made no secret of its intent. Bush media guru Roger Ailes bluntly told a reporter: "The only question is whether we depict Willie Horton with a knife in his hand or without it." There were three components to the assault on Dukakis. First, Bush began including attacks on Horton's furlough in most of his campaign speeches. For Bush, the Horton case had "come to symbolize . . . the misguided outlook of my opponent." Bush's stump speech contrasted his endorsement of the death penalty for first-degree murder with Dukakis's alleged endorsement of weekend vacations for murderers. The official Bush campaign also shot a devastatingly effective ad of convicts walking through a revolving door. The ad was highly deceptive and led many to believe that the furlough program was unique to Massachusetts, and also that Horton's case was typical rather than an extreme exception. Yet neither in Bush's speeches nor in this ad was Horton identified by race. Atwater, Ailes, and other Bush supporters used this to defend their later claims that the furlough issue was about crime, not race.*

But Bush didn't have to mention that Horton was black, because the other components of the Horton campaign were doing such a marvelous job of appealing to white fears. An allegedly independent political action committee released an ad featuring Horton's mug shot, which represented, according to one of the ad's creators, "every suburban mother's greatest fear." Another PAC spent $2 million to send Horton's victims on a speaking tour. Independent ads were made featuring close-ups of Horton's victims blaming Dukakis for their pain and loss. Cliff Barnes, the fiancé of the woman raped by Horton, appeared on Oprah, Geraldo, and other television shows. Some state Republican organizations distributed flyers superimposing Horton's image next to Dukakis's, with accompanying descriptions of Horton's horrific crimes and statements by his white victims. While the Bush campaign issued late and faint condemnations of some of the more lurid race baiting promulgated by their fellow partisans,

---

* The Bush team shot the "revolving door" ad twice, because the first time, they felt that black actors were too prominently featured. However, even the whitened version appealed to ambient racism in the white electorate; a study showed that white viewers severely overestimated the ratio of black to white convicts in the ad. Given that other Republicans were doing everything they could to bring public attention to Horton's specific case and his race, this level of misperception is not surprising.

these had "the faintly hollow ring of Casanova lamenting the decline of chastity in the world."

At least as important as these activities by Republicans was the continuing attention to the Horton matter by the national media. This was emphatically encouraged by Bush's campaign; Mark Goodin, Bush's Washington spokesman, kept Horton's mug shot taped above his desk to remind him to bring up Horton to every reporter who called. More significant, one of Ailes's associates passed a copy of the independent Horton ad to *The McLaughlin Group,* a prominent television talk show. Once it aired the riveting ad, the rest of the news media used outtakes repeatedly. Every time Bush mentioned Horton in a speech, many local and national news broadcasts would include the Horton mug shot; thus, viewers learned that Horton was a black man. The visual quality of the Horton story, its odor of scandal, and its lurid mix of sex, violence, and race made it almost irresistible to news organizations. For the typical news director, the choice between blandly recapping a speech by George Bush or including a short reference to a black murderer who kidnapped and raped white women was an easy one. So frequent were the references in the news to Horton that it has been seen as the quintessential example of a campaign maximizing the use of unpaid media. But more than money was saved by the campaign; it also temporarily preserved Bush's reputation as a kinder, gentler Republican. Once the Horton mug shot was widely known, George Bush could make apparently nonracial references to the Horton story, which immunized him from the charge of racism during the campaign. The media bought the claim that the furlough ad merely highlighted the two candidates' differing attitudes toward crime; even a *Washington Post* editorial endorsed this view.

The nature of the Horton campaign has come under repeated examination since the 1988 election, and Bush supporters have tried to rewrite history on several key points. In addition to claiming that Gore's use of the story was pivotal to bringing the matter to Republican eyes, they have tried to prove that the issue was all crime and no race. The idea that the Horton campaign had nothing to do with race is laughable. Atwater himself demonstrated the racial character of the issue when he brought up Horton after seeing Jesse Jackson on

Dukakis's doorstep during the vice presidential selection period. "So . . . maybe he [Dukakis] will put this Willie Horton on the ticket after all is said and done." Apparently, one black man applying for a spot on the ticket reminded Atwater of his favorite black criminal. Even the refusal of the Bush campaign to refer to Horton with any other sobriquet than the diminutive "Willie" must have struck many southerners as a throwback to the era when grown black men were treated as children.

The other claim by Bush supporters was that the truly odious Horton ad was merely the product of overzealous Republicans acting independently. This contention also strains credulity to the breaking point. The creators of the "independent" ad (Floyd Brown, Larry McCarthy, and Jesse Raiford) had previously worked for Roger Ailes, Bush's main media adviser. In a postelection investigation by the Federal Election Commission, the head of the political action committee stated that Bush campaign manager James Baker had full veto power over every ad. While Baker had eventually requested that the ad be withdrawn, he did so twenty-five days into a twenty-eight-day ad buy. By then, Horton was well on his way to becoming a household name, just as Atwater had intended.

Whether it was Bush's ads and speeches, the bluntly racist activities of independent Republicans, or the lurid and shallow coverage by much of the media, the Horton issue cannot be underestimated as a factor in Dukakis's swift plummet in the polls. The "revolving door" ad prepared by Ailes was almost universally seen as the "single most effective" of the campaign. By the time of the election, Horton was as well known to the American electorate as the vice presidential candidates. And those who had seen the Horton ad were more than twice as likely to feel that crime and law and order were the most important problems facing the nation, an effect that was even stronger among white women. In one poll, the most common reason given for opposing Dukakis was his "leniency to criminals." Yet in assessing the effectiveness of the Horton campaign at scaring whites and painting Dukakis as an effete racial liberal, one must also account for the extraordinary passivity of Dukakis's response to the injection of race into the politics of 1988.

DUKAKIS'S UNILATERAL DISARMAMENT ON RACE

In an early June campaign memo prepared just as Dukakis locked up the nomination, it was argued that the Democrats should not go after groups such as blacks, Hispanics, or urbanites, but rather target the ten million Reagan Democrats. The clearest example of Dukakis's willingness to go along with this strategy came when he visited the Neshoba County Fair, where Reagan had endorsed states' rights in 1980. Dukakis's speech was scheduled on the anniversary of the unearthing of the bodies of the three civil rights martyrs, a date of great symbolic importance to many blacks and racial liberals. Donna Brazile, the highest-ranking black woman in Dukakis's campaign, argued strenuously that Dukakis must mention the anniversary, but pressure from local conservative Democrats at the last minute convinced him to remain silent. Dukakis seldom campaigned in black areas, and his emphasis on white Reagan Democrats until the very end of the election was perceived as a slight by many blacks. Just as Dukakis had avoiding getting too close to Jackson in the primaries, he treated the black electorate gingerly in the general election.

Dukakis was also still having problems with Jackson. Jackson discovered a new set of slights in the way Dukakis treated him following their peace summit in Atlanta and retreated into the background. Prominent black Democrat Barbara Jordan, a member of Dukakis's steering committee, accused Jackson of supporting Dukakis "grudgingly and reluctantly." Jackson's lengthy speeches did not even mention Dukakis until near the end, and Jackson was cautious and halfhearted in praise of the Massachusetts governor. Jackson once again complained that he needed to meet with Dukakis one-on-one, while Dukakis continued to complain that he had not been fully endorsed by Jackson. Yet Jackson had reason for displeasure. Dukakis's staff had designed a schedule for Jackson that kept him at arm's length and out of states where he might offend Reagan Democrats, particularly the South. Jackson also complained directly to Dukakis's top aide John Sasso that he was not receiving enough money for his campaign work and that Dukakis was focusing too much on white voters. Only in the last two weeks of the campaign, when it was clear that Reagan Democrats were unreachable, did Dukakis reach out to Jackson and make a rare appearance in a black neighborhood.

Dukakis's decision to woo racially conservative whites also limited his ability to respond to the Horton attacks. As journalist Jack White concluded:

> Dukakis of course might have spiked the Horton offensive early on by pointing to its racial implications. But the Massachusetts Governor was pursuing his own racially callous strategy, ignoring black supporters in an attempt to reach out to fickle Reagan Democrats, who abandoned their traditional political home at least in part because it is seen as the party of minorities.

The Dukakis campaign has long since become legendary for its incompetence, indecisiveness, and lack of strategic vision. However, among its myriad mistakes, none was more glaring than the failure to respond to the Horton attacks in a timely or effective manner. Although members of his staff had been warning Dukakis for months that Bush would use the issue against him, Dukakis remained serenely confident that it could not become a campaign issue. After all, Dukakis reasoned, the federal government had a program at least as permissive, and the Republican hero, Reagan, had overseen a furlough program in California with even greater problems. As the devastating Horton campaign gathered momentum, staffers begged Dukakis to respond. He finally agreed and made one major speech accusing Bush of "exploiting human tragedy" but then demonstrated his utter ignorance of modern campaign procedures by refusing to make the statement part of his stump speech, because he had already made the case once. Dukakis apparently believed that the truth was so powerful that its simple appearance in one speech could defeat a deceptive tale repeated nationwide in speeches, leaflets, and television ads. Although the campaign also enlisted Jackson to attack the Horton ads, the effort was poorly planned.

Finally, the Dukakis campaign did make a TV spot that tried to link Bush to an even worse tragedy that had occurred in the federal furlough progam. The ad, entitled "Furlough from the Truth," told the story of Angel Medrano, a federal convict who escaped from a halfway house and murdered a young pregnant woman. Far more graphic than the official "revolving door" spot of the Bush campaign, the ad showed a mug shot of the Hispanic killer and a murder victim in a body bag. The ad tried to avoid the charge of racism by not using Medrano's name, but the charge of racism, and of hypocrisy, was made anyway. Dukakis, who had failed to effectively respond for months to the Horton campaign, except to attack it as exploitative in one late speech, now demonstrated that Democrats could exploit human tragedy just as luridly. However, they failed to do it as effectively, because their campaign could not link Bush as directly to the Medrano furlough. Moreover, the Democratic message was muddled and halfhearted compared to the coordinated and carefully planned Republican exploitation of Horton. The Medrano ad was symbolic of the frustration, bitterness, and tactical incompetence that characterized the last months of the Dukakis campaign.

Throughout the campaign, Dukakis failed to address the heart of the Horton issue by attacking the undercurrent of racism in Bush's use of it. Given numerous opportunities to speak out, Dukakis seemed simply depressed and disappointed that the media was buying the Republican take on Horton. Late in the campaign, when reporter Sam Donaldson confronted Dukakis with the story, promulgated by Atwater,* that Horton actually supported Dukakis, Dukakis responded wearily, "He can't vote, Sam." Dukakis could not even bring himself to label as "lies" Republican leaflets alleging that because of Horton, all the murderers and child molesters were voting for Dukakis. Until the very end, Dukakis never showed his deep anger to the American public at Bush's utterly cynical use of race and crime. The nadir of Dukakis's ineffectual response to the Horton campaign came in the final debate. Dukakis's staff prepared him with a moving statement about how his own family had been hurt by vio-

---

* Atwater told reporters, "I assume the reason he [Horton] endorsed him is that he thinks he'll have a better chance of getting out of jail if Dukakis is elected. I don't know if Dukakis would let him out, but I think there'd be a better chance."

lent crime and with pointed attacks on Bush for ignoring the federal and California furlough programs. The very first question of the debate, however, ruined any hope of a Dukakis comeback. CNN's Bernard Shaw made the Horton case personal, asking what Dukakis would want done to a criminal who raped and murdered his wife, Kitty. The question, unlike any ever asked before or since in a presidential debate, was Dukakis's great opportunity to show America that he was outraged both by crime and by the racism of the Horton campaign. However, Dukakis's factual and chilly response to the prospect of his wife's brutalization convinced many Americans that Dukakis was the out-of-touch softy on crime portrayed by Lee Atwater. Dukakis had blown his last chance to address the crime fears so effectively whipped up by the Republican juggernaut.

CONCLUSION: PLAYING THE RACE CARD REAGAN DIDN'T NEED

> While race has been a perennial issue in presidential campaigns . . . no campaign in recent memory stands out in this regard as much as the 1988 presidential campaign.
>
> POLITICAL SCIENTISTS JAMES GLASER AND EWA GOLEBIOWSKA, 1996

The debate over the appropriateness of the Horton ads, leaflets, and speeches continued long after Bush's forty-state victory over Dukakis. Certainly, the case of Horton conflated issues of race and crime. Just as Nixon's law-and-order slogans of 1968 appealed to legitimate concerns about expansions in the rights of the accused and the spiraling rate of crime, Bush's rhetoric on Horton and the death penalty did highlight a partisan difference in attitude toward crime. Lee Atwater even made a populist defense of his Horton campaign, arguing that its very effectiveness proved its legitimacy as an issue. The case could be made that in voting for Bush on the basis of the Horton furlough, many citizens were choosing a Justice Department and federal judiciary who would be "tough on crime." Yet Bush's use of Horton remains a classic example of "coded racism," intended to activate white hostilities to blacks. In the end, Bush and his associates must be held culpable for the nature of the white response. Even if some voters were merely responding to the crime element in the Horton story, the postelection surveys suggested that the final two months of relentless emphasis on black crime pushed racism among white voters to a twenty-year high.

George Bush would have probably preferred not to win the presidency by waving the bloody shirt of Horton's victims, particularly knowing as he must have that blaming Dukakis for the furlough program had a number of logical fallacies. In later years, Bush reacted with anger to the suggestion that he had run a racist campaign. Yet Bush's reputation is indelibly tainted with the inescapably racial nature of the Horton onslaught. Perhaps Bush had little choice. Reagan had been able to pull white Democrats away from their partisan identity with his strong leadership style and his reputation as a genial spokesman for the white backlash. Bush had no such stature; the milquetoast wimp with the fractured syntax and blurry ideological positions had to find another way to attract Reagan Democrats. In effect, Bush established his manhood, his toughness, by emphasizing how harshly he would treat black criminals, symbolized by Horton. The awkward patrician even began to paraphrase macho film star Clint Eastwood in contrasting his attitude toward crime with Dukakis's. Implicitly portraying himself as the defender of white womanhood against rapacious black male sexuality, Bush addressed the lingering doubts of many Americans about his leadership abilities.

The message of 1988 for the Democratic Party was that race remained a powerful force in the American electorate, even when the great debates over racial policy of the past were either resolved (voting and public accommodations) or quiescent (busing and affirmative action). Dukakis had hoped to campaign on his record of competent management of the Massachusetts economy and on nonideological issues such as job training and environmental protection. Bush effectively used social issues to hammer home the message that Dukakis was yet another in a long line of liberal Democrats out of touch with white America, particularly on the question of race. The campaign would not have been as effective against any other nominee. Dukakis's strategy of political pacifism provided Bush with an immense tactical advantage, which Atwater and others exploited with lusty glee. One of the causes of Dukakis's failure to respond effectively to the Horton campaign may well have been the white nature of his campaign's inner circle. As the election moved out of Dukakis's reach, a campaign adviser cracked with gallows humor at a strategy session that "all of the white men in America that are for Dukakis are probably in this room." The Dukakis campaign had, in fact, far too white a staff for the task at hand: finding a way to respond to Bush's cynical use of racial fears that did not dismiss white anxieties about black crime or exacerbate them.* Dukakis's campaign failed to listen to black concerns, failed to campaign in black areas, and failed to understand the nature of the Horton challenge. The campaign's paucity of blacks in top positions also affected the ham-handed manner in which Jackson was treated. As the top-ranking black in the Dukakis campaign observed:

> . . . the attitude among the white folks in the Dukakis campaign with respect to anything to do with Jesse was fear and trepidation, if not loathing, because of the simple calculation that Jackson had the ability to destroy Dukakis' chances in November.

For the Democrats looking ahead to 1992, the picture was bleak. Since FDR, more Americans considered themselves Democratic than Republican; regardless, the Republicans had won five of the last six presidential contests, some by extraordinary margins. To win, a Democrat would have to insulate himself against charges of racial liberalism, of being weak toward black crime, and of favoring unearned black privilege. A Democratic nominee would also have to come up with a way of handling Jesse Jackson that did not alienate blacks, as Al Gore had in New York, or diminish the nominee's own standing, as with Mondale and Dukakis. As Dukakis adviser Sasso

---

* Dukakis's campaign became even whiter following the departure of Donna Brazile, the highest-ranking black woman on his staff. Brazile had mentioned Bush's alleged marital infidelity to a reporter and was fired immediately. The contrast with Bush was stark: no one was fired for alleging that Horton was endorsing Dukakis, and no one criticized Republicans who printed pamphlets stating that child molesters and murderers were rallying to Dukakis.

concluded, Jackson had clearly hurt Dukakis: "I watched him . . . with Walter Mondale and Mike Dukakis, two men who . . . were deeply committed to civil rights, to inclusiveness, and I thought that he, at times, went out of his way to make them appear weak."

For the Republicans, they had once again demonstrated both the power of the race card in American politics and their ability to win national elections while ignoring the black electorate. Newly appointed GOP chair Lee Atwater talked about targeting the burgeoning black middle class, with the goal of getting 15 percent in 1992. Seldom have a man and a mission been so ineptly paired. One thing seemed certain amid the crushing defeat of Dukakis in 1988: After Horton, Democrats truly did not have to worry about the Republicans taking the black vote away anytime soon, particularly with Atwater leading the effort.

FORGETTING ABOUT RACE
The Squelched Racial Politics of 1992

Let's forget about race and be one nation again.

BILL CLINTON, MARCH 1992

The day he told off that fucking Jackson is the day he got my vote.

WHITE ELECTRICIAN TO TWO REPORTERS ON THE 1992 CAMPAIGN TRAIL

The 1992 presidential election represented a tidal shift in American racial politics, a shift imperceptible to most voters because it caused an extraordinary decline in the salience of race. After losing five of six presidential races, the Democratic Party now chose a nominee who demonstrated an ability to appeal simultaneously to racial conservatives and African Americans. As the Republicans forswore both sincere outreach to blacks and the ugly race baiting of 1988, Clinton was able to downplay racial issues to an extraordinary degree. As he did on a whole array of social issues, Clinton found the precise tone of sincere moderation on race that resonated with Reagan Democrats. Wounded by a brief steep recession, the Republican Party could find no effective response to Clinton's careful positioning on race.

1992: THE SETTING

Two strategic realities shaped the 1992 presidential race. First, Bush's unprecedented popularity in the wake of the easy Gulf War victory caused many leading Democratic contenders to stay on the sidelines.

Men such as Mario Cuomo, Bill Bradley, Sam Nunn, and Richard Gephardt, who clearly desired the presidency, evinced no enthusiasm for challenging George Bush, at 90 percent approval just after the mid-point of his term. Because of modern campaign finance rules and the front-loaded primary system, Democrats had to decide whether to run at the apex of Bush's popularity. Consequently, the premier candidates stayed on the sidelines, and Clinton was the presumed front-runner among the group of second-raters who threw their hats in the ring. The second shaping force on the campaign, one that would greatly affect the Republican primaries and the general election, was the sudden drop in economic activity. The 1990–92 recession was instrumental in the victory of Bill Clinton. Had it ended a few months earlier than September 1992, Bush might well have won reelection. The recession was also crucial in permitting Clinton to sublimate the concerns of African Americans under the rhetoric of economic populism.

THE CANDIDATES

George Bush

The Bush administration failed to significantly change the image of Republicans in the black community. Since Bush was elected in part because of his use of racist campaign tactics, this was hardly surprising. However, it did seem to come as a shock to some Republicans. Lee Atwater, newly installed as head of the RNC, hoped that by serving as a trustee of Howard University, the nation's premier black university, he would move toward his goal of 15 percent of the black vote in 1992. After outraged Howard students engaged in protests and sit-ins, leading to national press attention, Atwater realized his past record made it impossible for him to serve on Howard's board. This was the first sign that the memory of Republican tactics of 1988 would linger and effectively end any hope of Republican outreach to African Americans.* Indeed, the mainstream media, as if to apolo-

---

* It may well have been this bruising rejection that produced Atwater's deathbed mea culpa for the Horton campaign. Atwater, who had long defended the use of Horton as legitimate, eventually apologized to Dukakis, as he lay dying of brain cancer.

gize for their role in exacerbating racial tensions through their wide and largely uncritical promulgation of the Horton story, did not hesitate after the election to blame Bush sharply for the dirty campaign of 1988.

Bush did not ignore blacks or their issues entirely during his presidency. In 1991, he replaced legendary black justice Thurgood Marshall with a conservative black activist, Clarence Thomas. However, this appointment did not improve Bush's image in the black community. Although several mainstream black groups reluctantly supported Thomas, his position as a pariah within his own race was solidified by his opposition to color-conscious remedies of all kinds. On domestic policy, Jack Kemp, the head of Housing and Urban Development, was tasked with launching empowerment zones in urban areas. Republicans also hoped to exploit the burgeoning popularity of Colin Powell, who as chairman of the Joint Chiefs during the Gulf War had become a familiar and charismatic figure to many Americans, white and black. Bush also met with black leaders far more frequently than Reagan had. Whatever good these minor measures did for Bush's standing in the black community was erased by his grandstanding on affirmative action. Congress, angered by several Supreme Court decisions reinterpreting civil rights statutes to lessen their effectiveness, passed corrective legislation. Bush twice vetoed the measure, saying, "This bill could lead to more quota hiring of minorities and women. We can't do that at a time when we are working so hard to achieve a color-blind society, a society based on merit, not on race or gender." As the Senate failed to override Bush's veto, former Grand Wizard of the Ku Klux Klan and Louisiana Republican David Duke looked on from the visitors gallery with pride. A month after Bush's first veto of the bill, Senator Jesse Helms was narrowly reelected over a black Democrat. In Helms's race against the moderate black Democrat, his campaign team crafted a TV spot in which a white working-class male gets cheated out of a job by a racial quota. For raw emotionalism and demagoguery, it rivaled the worst of the Horton ads of 1988. It was also highly effective. Some believed that Bush was positioning himself to follow Helms's example and use white antipathy toward affirmative action in 1992.

Finally, the third time the bill passed Congress, moderate Republicans worked out a compromise with Democrats that made marginal changes in the legislation, which Bush now signed. The largely cosmetic changes could not explain the shift in Bush's position. Rather, the heat from civil rights groups, as well as the prospect of a successful veto override because of Republican defections, forced Bush's hand. Bush had thus given away his best issue with which to appeal to the forces of racial conservatism and, with the death of Atwater, lost his most able and ruthless strategist in racial politics. And while Bush might have reaped a harvest of goodwill among blacks by signing the civil rights bill the first time it was passed, two vetoes erased that chance. Signing the bill after twice demonizing almost the exact same legislation as inimical to a color-blind society won Bush no friends among racial conservatives or African Americans. Instead, it again raised the question of whether Bush had any principles at all on racial matters.

Bill Clinton

William Jefferson Clinton was raised in a segregated Arkansas environment, and some of his closest relatives were burdened with a belief in black inferiority. However, like his fellow southerner Jimmy Carter, Clinton early on began to favor civil rights for African Americans. Though Clinton avoided much direct participation in the civil rights movement, he did take part in an emergency relief effort during the nights of rioting in D.C. following the assassination of Martin Luther King and had worked to integrate a swimming pool in Arkansas. Yet Clinton's instincts on racial politics, as on most issues, were aimed at compromise and conciliation, not confrontation.

Throughout his career, Clinton would take advantage of his ease and familiarity with African Americans, which distinguished him from almost every other national Democrat. When the young Clinton arrived at Yale Law School in the early 1970s, he casually broke the informal color line that separated the "black" table in the cafeteria. Clinton's formidable personal magnetism seemed to be color-blind.

Clinton's first exposure to national politics came in the McGovern campaign of 1972, in which he was responsible for the state of Texas. Clinton saw firsthand both how important the black vote was to Democratic success and how McGovern had positioned himself too far to the left on a host of issues to win a national election. From that experience, Clinton also learned "the lesson of not being caught too far out on the left on defense, welfare, crime. From then on he would take steps to make sure those were marketed in a way to appeal to conservatives and moderates." Still, Clinton was popular with the black community in each of the many contests he entered in Arkansas. Black counties produced the bedrock of his support against Democrats in primaries and Republicans in the general elections, often providing more support than his hometown.

In 1980, Clinton lost his bid for reelection as governor in part because of the adroit exploitation of racial fears. The Carter administration had placed thousands of Cuban refugees at a military base in Arkansas. Largely Afro-Cubans with criminal records, these were very different refugees from the first waves of anti-Castro immigrants. When they rioted, it produced weeks of crisis in Arkansas, for which Clinton was ill prepared. His opponent, Frank White, used grainy images of the rioting black Cubans in an aggressive and blunt television ad that played to white fears. Although Clinton accused White of trying to "redneck" the issue of Cuban refugees, the campaign hurt Clinton tremendously. Clinton's later behavior on race and any number of other social issues cannot be understood outside the context of this deeply personal rejection, which drove Clinton into the depths of despair.

Clinton's two years in the political wilderness ended with his triumphant return to the governor's mansion. His 1982 primary victory saw him run to the racial right against one competitor, Jim Guy Tucker, by falsely accusing him of liberalism on welfare. In the runoff primary against another Democrat, Clinton supporters distributed ugly and false rumors in the black community that alleged that Clinton's opponent was antiblack. Payments were made to black ministers, lawyers, and funeral parlor owners. "It was simply taken for granted that in some communities, particularly in the Delta, black votes were for sale and had been bought." In one black precinct,

Clinton's opponent failed to get a single vote. In his general election rematch with White, Clinton again relied heavily on the black vote. Black voters, angered by White's alliance with the former governor, segregationist Orval Faubus, turned out in record numbers for Clinton. "No one in the Arkansas political annals locked up the black vote the way Clinton did in 1982."

By many measures, Clinton was the best governor Arkansas blacks ever had. More blacks were placed on commissions and boards during Clinton's tenure than in all of Arkansas history. He sent his daughter, Chelsea, to a public school that was 60 percent black, an important gesture in a state where some school districts were still imperfectly integrated, to put it mildly. Black leaders generally felt that Clinton gave them access and influence in ways that they never had had before. Yet Arkansas, after twelve years of Clinton in power, was one of only two states without a civil rights law, and it lacked even a human rights commission. Clinton was also sued by the NAACP's Legal Defense Fund (LDF), and refused to take a public stand in favor of black plaintiffs victimized by local voting rules. In one of the counties defended by Clinton, white officials had moved polling places ten times in as many elections, often without prior notice, in an obvious scheme to reduce black turnout. Clinton professed to "love" the LDF attorneys, while opposing them on matters of substance and pandering to white sensitivities. Clinton made education the signature issue of his governorship, but he seldom attacked the regnant racial discrimination in the Arkansas schools. On another issue with clear racial overtones, the death penalty, Clinton shifted from his idealistic McGovern-era opposition to enthusiastic support. He guarded his image as a "tough on crime" governor and initiated policies that resulted in a jump in the incarceration of blacks. Overall, Clinton as governor would speak out in favor of racial harmony, while avoiding mention of race-specific solutions to discrimination, a pattern described as "classic Clinton."

THE BUBBA TACTIC EMERGES: THE DEMOCRATIC PRIMARIES

> The most tell-tale sign of the impact of the racial conservatism of the Reagan-Bush era lies in the fact that Democratic candidates and nominees made no major speeches or concessions to the African American community during the entire 1992 presidential campaign.
>
> POLITICAL SCIENTIST HANES WALTON JR.

Jesse Jackson, who had dominated the politics of race in America since 1984, was still the fulcrum around which the Democratic nomination fight would turn in the early goings. Jackson gave mixed signals about whether he would enter a third consecutive race for president. As in 1983, a Chicago mayoral election played a role in Jackson's decision. In 1983, Jackson had shared in Harold Washington's successful revolt against the white Democratic power structure. However, in 1989 Jackson supported a third-party black challenger, who lost to Daley's son. Daley was supported by moderate black leaders such as Jackson's own former top aide, Ron Brown. Jackson, for whom third-party flirtation had been a common tactic in his political negotiations with Democrats since 1972, had been badly defeated in his hometown. Brown, the new head of the Democratic Party, pressed Jackson to sit out the 1992 race. Finally, Jackson opted not to throw his hat in the ring. As political scientist Lucius Barker argued, Jackson's decision was crucial to Clinton's later success:

> Jackson's decision helped to subordinate, if not suppress, race as an issue, making it easier for Clinton to hold on to the black vote without jeopardizing the moderate-centrist image believed necessary to recapture Reagan Democrats and appeal to whites generally.

The initial expectation was that Jackson's announcement would most benefit another black candidate, Douglas Wilder, the governor of Virginia. Wilder, who had entered the race in March of 1991, long before Jackson's decision, was touted as "a candidate who happened to be black" as opposed to Jackson, who had always been "the black candidate." The first black elected governor of any state since Reconstruction, Wilder ran as a social moderate and a fiscal conservative. As more candidates entered the contest, it appeared that Wilder's race was hurting him. Many Democrats, told of his positions, favored him as just the candidate they were looking for. When they found out his race, his numbers dropped. Wilder changed strategies following Jackson's announcement; he abandoned his "deracialized" appeals, hired a former Jackson staffer as his manager, and began to move left on race and economics. He even attacked Clinton, his primary rival for black support, for distancing himself from minorities.

Clinton responded swiftly to the strategic opportunity presented by Jackson's departure. He flew to Washington to meet privately with Jackson and discussed how Jackson would behave during the primaries. Jackson made it clear that he would not be supporting Wilder, whom Jackson disliked, not only on policy grounds, but also for Wilder's prior refusal to let Jackson campaign for him in his Virginia election. From Jackson's perspective, Wilder threatened Jackson's position as the most prominent black American. Clinton was also the only white Democrat in the race who could challenge Wilder for black votes, placing Jackson in a difficult position. If Jackson moved against Clinton, Wilder might sweep the black vote, and Jackson would be replaced as the titular leader of black America. If Clinton won anyway, Jackson would be similarly weakened since he could not deliver the black vote. If he endorsed the comparatively conservative Clinton, however, he would appear to have lost his principles. In the end, Jackson informally agreed to remain neutral in the race. This was the most significant result of the brief Wilder candidacy, which died stillborn before a single ballot was cast.

Throughout the election, Clinton treated Jackson with "tough love," respecting his power but focusing instead on a number of other black leaders. Unlike Dukakis in 1988, Clinton had long-established connections with blacks, not just in Arkansas, but also with Congressmen John Lewis, Mike Espy, Bobby Rush, and Bill Jefferson. Clinton also counted on the support of moderate black leaders such as Ron Brown and Vernon Jordan. Through associating with black officials of a more mainstream character, Clinton indirectly attacked Jackson's authority as a kingmaker in the Democratic Party. Clinton's black supporters were either politicians who understood electoral politics in a way that Jackson never had or minor figures who needed Clinton as much as he needed them. Vernon Jordan, for one, had been almost entirely eclipsed by other black leaders before Clinton brought him back to national prominence. None of them had the independent stature or penchant for grandstanding that Jackson did. Thus empowered, Clinton did not need Jackson as badly as Dukakis had in 1988.*

Clinton had long before realized the importance of handling Jackson. As early as May 1991, Clinton had excluded Jackson from a convention of moderate Democrats, the beginning of the "bubba" tactic, the deliberate snubbing of Jackson in pursuit of racially conservative whites. Unlike 1988, when Gore's unprecedented attacks on Jackson seemed to pay no electoral dividend, Clinton's support among whites grew while he remained popular in the black community. During the primaries, even when black politicians attacked Clinton for his failure to address black issues, Clinton reaped a harvest of black votes that hurt the reputations of those black leaders who were not yet supporting him. Just as Carter had in 1976, Clinton spoke over the heads of local black leaders, such as Mayor White of Cleveland, directly to the black voters. Without the unifying force of a Jackson candidacy, the black electorate responded to Clinton's deracialized populism and emphasis on economic renewal by making him their choice for nominee.

Clinton's deliberate distance from Jackson was only one of the ways in which he played the politics of race differently. In addition to stressing the need for welfare reform, refusing to advocate large new urban aid programs, and keeping silent about most traditional civil rights issues, Clinton adroitly used the death penalty to insulate him-

---

* Of course, Jackson remained a top consideration of Clinton's; when it was erroneously reported that Jackson had endorsed another candidate, Clinton was caught on videotape launching a stream of obscenities in a tirade against Jackson's duplicity.

self against the expected crime assault by Bush. In the midst of the New Hampshire primary, with the attention of the nation focused on allegations of Clinton's adultery and draft dodging, he returned to Arkansas to preside over the death of a convicted black cop killer. The execution of Ricky Ray Rector was difficult to justify even for proponents of the death penalty. Brain-damaged in a suicide attempt after he was convicted of killing a white police officer, Rector gave little evidence of understanding his situation. A few days before he was killed, he was heard to say how he intended to vote for Clinton, the man scheduled to kill him. He saved the dessert of his last meal "for later." Clinton, a former death penalty opponent, made sure the media was well aware of his actions in killing Rector. As an editorial in the *Houston Chronicle* observed, "Never . . . has a contender for the nation's highest elective office stepped off the campaign trail to ensure the killing of a prisoner." Rector was dying not merely for his own sins, but also for the electoral sins of Lee Atwater. In killing Rector, Clinton was exorcising the ghost of Willie Horton from the Democratic Party.*

The endgame of the contest was never much in doubt once Clinton had at least temporarily put to rest questions about his character. The final showdown came in the New York primary, in which Clinton confronted the last remaining contender, former California governor Jerry Brown. Brown, running a quixotic insurgent candidacy against the establishment Clinton, tried to shake up the race by announcing that Jackson was his favored pick for running mate. The reaction among New York's Jewish voting bloc was instantaneous and negative and helped seal Clinton's nomination. If Clinton had any remaining doubts that Jackson had to be handled gingerly, surely the outcry that followed Brown's comment removed them. Clinton countered Brown's move toward Jackson by transporting busloads of black supporters from Arkansas to New York churches prior to the primary, living proof of Clinton's black popularity.

---

* During the southern primaries, supporters even distributed a brochure showing Clinton chatting to a white prison warden in front of a group of black prisoners. Had any Republican done that, one can just imagine the response from the civil rights establishment.

Clinton now sailed toward the nomination, winning the nod earlier than any Democrat since Johnson in 1964. The removal of Jackson allowed Clinton to get the early victory, and with it crucial months to plan for the general election. But the absence of Jackson, along with Clinton's deracializing strategies, clearly had an effect on black turnout. In almost every state, black primary participation was significantly lower than in 1984 or 1988, sometimes by as much as 75 percent. If that trend continued, Clinton would have to either do better among whites than any Democrat had since 1976 or find some way to reignite enthusiasm among African Americans.

THE FIRES THIS TIME: THE L.A. RIOTS

Racial politics pushed into the 1992 campaign in April when the nation experienced the worst domestic rioting since 1968. The unrest erupted in Los Angeles following the verdicts in the Rodney King police brutality trial. King, a young black male, had been viciously beaten by a gang of white cops. Unlike many other beatings in Los Angeles, this one was videotaped by a bystander. As Americans watched the prolonged brutal beating by police of an unarmed, unresisting man, expectations of a guilty verdict grew. However, a suburban white jury acquitted the four officers on almost all charges and failed to convict on any. Within hours, south central Los Angeles was in flames. In an eerie parallel to the King video, cameras captured black rioters pulling a white man from his truck and bludgeoning him to the edge of death. When the police were finally able to contain the rioting and looting, 60 were dead, 2,500 were injured, and over $850 million worth of property had been destroyed.

For a president who had been depicted as uncaring and out of touch with domestic issues, this was a rare opportunity to demonstrate concern and involvement. However, the White House was divided over how to respond. A gifted speechwriter, Tony Snow, authored a plea for racial harmony in the wake of the riots. More cautious voices within the administration argued for a law-and-order theme, while Bush's internal polling told him that white males between the ages of forty-five and sixty-five were in no mood to spend more money on "those people." The confusion within the White House became obvious to the public. Immediately after the verdict, Bush gave an unqualified endorsement of the verdict. "The court system has worked. What's needed now is calm, respect for the law." The next day, he sternly condemned the riots but remained unclear about how he felt about the brutal beating that led to the uprising. Finally, on Friday, Bush conferred with black leaders at the White House and grasped that perhaps he should come out against a vicious police assault on an American citizen. That night, in his eighth pronouncement in forty-eight hours, Bush labeled King's beating "revolting" and suggested the verdict was "not the end." He promised that federal authorities would investigate bringing civil rights charges against the police. Both Bush and Clinton went to Los Angeles to see the devastation firsthand:

> The candidates and their handlers have toured Los Angeles, and they agree on almost nothing except the fact that the events there will dominate this year's battle for the White House . . . the campaign to define the images they hope will linger is under way with a vengeance.

Bush's team, despite keeping their itinerary secret, were nonetheless shadowed by demonstrators shouting, "Go home!" and, "No justice!"

Both candidates had to answer two questions—what caused the riots, and what would be done in response? During his tour of the riot scene, Bush argued that a decline in moral fiber and values was behind the riots. In a similar vein, Bush's press secretary immediately laid the blame for the riots on the Great Society of LBJ. Clinton responded that the riots reflected twelve years of urban neglect under Bush and Reagan, although he was careful not to defend the actions of the looters. Clinton argued the riots justified his domestic agenda, an impressive mix of neoconservative reforms and traditional liberal spending: earned income tax credits, community financial institutions, child support enforcement, welfare reform, drug treatment on demand, national service, apprenticeship training programs, and community policing. Clinton linked all of them to the deracialized economic rhetoric that had become his trademark: "It has become increasingly clear that the economic future of whites is tied inextricably to that of minorities. From now on, we all rise or fall together, economically as well as morally." Bush, under pressure to prove that he also cared about the inner city, showered new attention on his HUD secretary, Kemp. Kemp had long pushed Bush to do more for urban areas and to reach out to black voters, but he had faced a White House actively hostile to innovative ideas in domestic policy. Kemp's plans to sell public housing to its tenants and to aggressively expand urban enterprise zones were quickly dusted off and made to seem new.

But there were those within the White House who saw the riots as an opportunity not for domestic policy action, but for political gain. Some Bush aides speculated that the bloody footage of the white trucker being assaulted during the riots would appear in a fall ad, with a voice-over reminding whites of the dangers of lawlessness. Some in the media anticipated that the widely distributed images of black looters "running from stores, their arms laden, demonic grins on their faces" would be used in the fall, because the Republicans were "past masters at exploiting the revulsion such travesties spark." A White House aide chortled to a reporter that the L.A. riots would force Clinton to come out with new spending plans for urban areas:

> We'll hit him for supporting the conventional Democratic response of throwing money at the problems. The people who vote, the middle-class swing voters, hear "city" as a code word for blacks and decay, for everything they've run to the suburbs to avoid. They're upset with the King verdict, sure, but they're more upset about their being the next white victim when they drive through the areas they've mortgaged their lives to escape from.

Clinton's response to this expected Republican onslaught was his most cunning use of racial politics yet.

Clinton was invited to address a conference on the riots sponsored by Jackson's Rainbow Coalition. Among the other speakers was a previously unknown rap singer, Sister Souljah, who had made a comment endorsing the killing of whites.* Clinton, by now the presumptive Democratic nominee, attracted much attention when, in his speech to Jackson's organization, he attacked Souljah, comparing her statement to Ku Klux Klan racism. As political scientist and Jackson associate Ron Walters remembers the moment:

> The mood in the room was incredulous ... this son of a bitch ... here he was. ... As though to prove that, again, he was standing up to the left of his party. ... And then come to find out that it was absolutely deliberate ... they interviewed the campaign staff and found out that it was a dedicated strategy. Oh, it worked. No question about the fact that it worked ... Jackson was a convenient symbol. ... By that time he had run twice for president and was the only really acknowledged black leader in the party. ...

Clinton chose to make his highest-profile response to the L.A. riots not a plea for greater social justice or less police brutality, but an assault on black radicalism. In attacking Souljah at the Rainbow Coalition, he once again diminished Jackson. His comments were directed not so much at the black audience present, but at whites nationwide. The sound bite was broadcast widely and was much praised in the press, for both the content of the statement and the refusal to kowtow to a special interest. Clinton's attack on Souljah, or "woofing for the benefit of white folks," paid dividends in establishing Clinton as a racial moderate who was not afraid of challenging black leaders on their home territory.†

Ultimately, the flurry of interest in racial issues that had emerged so quickly in the wake of the L.A. fires went away almost as fast.

---

* Souljah's comment: "I mean if black people kill black people every day, why not have a week and kill white people?"

† Like much of Clinton's strategy in 1992, the "counterscheduling" tactic of offending the immediate audience in pursuit of a larger, more moderate audience, was one that Clinton had honed in his Arkansas elections. Typically, Clinton rebuked groups "who had fallen out of public favor."

Because of Bush's inability to choose a consistent message, and Clinton's calculated move to the middle on the question of responsibility for the riots, "the race issue quickly dropped from the electoral screen." A Republican campaign official felt that Clinton's Souljah attack made it very difficult to launch a "values" argument on matters of race. However, Jesse Jackson was so angered by Clinton's disrespect that he again began to contemplate his November options. And unlike most years, in the spring of 1992 it suddenly seemed that a viable independent candidate might be on the ballot: H. Ross Perot.

PEROT AND "YOU PEOPLE . . .": THE FAILED THIRD OPTION FOR BLACKS

A billionaire businessman from Texas, Ross Perot was from the start an unusual vessel in which to place the hopes of African Americans. Up to 1992, Perot's political interests had involved military affairs, lucrative government contracting, and school reform. He had once suggested that a perimeter be manned around the barrios and ghettos of Dallas, along with house-to-house searches for contraband, stances hardly likely to please black voters. Still, some black leaders such as Ron Walters suggested that blacks should look to Perot in 1992. For a brief period in the spring of 1992, Perot was running well ahead of Bush and Clinton in national polls, although not among blacks. Perot traveled to Harlem and received the endorsement of Calvin Butts, one of the most politically influential clergymen in America. Perot promised to economically develop the inner cities, support civil rights, and expand job programs. He even suggested that he might name a black woman as his running mate. Also, in the immediate aftermath of the Souljah slight, Jackson was reported to be flirting with Perot, in response to Clinton's Machiavellian maneuvers on race. The presence of Perot in the race could force Clinton to work harder for black support, since they would have a more palatable option than voting Republican.

However, Perot quickly removed himself as a viable choice, sparing Clinton the trouble. In a highly publicized speech to the NAACP convention, Perot continually referred to blacks as "you people."

Audible gasps were heard from the deeply offended audience. The phrase was one, according to an NAACP branch director, that "white folk have used when they don't want to call us 'nigger' but they don't want to treat [us] like an equal." The rest of the speech demonstrated Perot's blatant ignorance of black concerns. The press criticism was searing. Perot seemed particularly bothered that his folksy populism and homespun truisms, well received by many white audiences, had been so misinterpreted. Shortly after the NAACP debacle, Perot removed himself from the race.* When he later returned to the campaign, Perot's movement remained almost entirely white. Perot's presence in the campaign ultimately had three effects on the racial politics of 1992. First, his insensitivity to black concerns gave Clinton the ability to continue with his deracialized appeals. If Perot had been an option for blacks, it would have forced Clinton to make more substantive concessions to black concerns. The second effect Perot had was in absorbing much of the media and public attention. The L.A. riots would have lingered longer if the unpredictable Perot had not been the biggest story of the 1992 election. Finally, Perot contributed to a deep split in the white vote, which greatly aided the election of Bill Clinton.

RON BROWN'S TRIUMPH: THE DEMOCRATIC CONVENTION

The Democratic convention in New York City was a perfect metaphor for Clinton's deracialized campaign. Ron Brown, a moderate black who had become a high-powered lobbyist, crafted a convention that avoided the disputes that had beleaguered many previous Democratic gatherings. In a sense, Brown was merely reaping the fruits of his successful campaign to keep Jackson out of the primaries for the first time since 1980. Jackson's reduction in stature, to which Clinton had also contributed greatly, allowed the nominee to avoid

---

* The NAACP experience was so disturbing that Perot did not speak to another black group and, indeed, avoided speaking to anyone but his own supporters from then on.

the tortuous preconvention summits with Jackson that had so damaged Mondale and Dukakis. Clinton refused to consider Jackson for the vice presidency or even to actively consult him about the choice. Jackson again made noises about sitting out the fall campaign or possibly running as an independent. He mentioned working with Perot. Jackson's threats, which had worked very well in 1984 and 1988, failed in 1992. Clinton, secure in his own black base of support, simply ignored Jackson's public and private sniping. This once again had the effect of lessening Jackson's influence. The Clinton forces also avoided floor fights over issues such as affirmative action, busing, welfare reform, or urban aid in the wake of the L.A. riots. Without a slate of Jackson delegates to trumpet these issues, the need for compromise or even discussion was greatly attenuated. Clinton, who had weeks before told the NAACP that the civil rights issue of the 1990s was "economic empowerment," succeeded in keeping civil rights from becoming a major issue at the convention.

When Clinton chose Gore as his running mate, the snubbing of Jackson was complete. Gore, who had been anathema to much of Jackson's staff in 1988, was brought onto the ticket without consultation or explanation. The question now became, what would Jackson do? How would he respond to Clinton's careful and deliberate mistreatment? Jackson's choices were again unpleasant. If he ran as an independent, he would surely become little more than a spoiler, who might fail to carry a fraction of the black vote but would probably ensure the reelection of Bush. If he sat out the election, the black leaders whom Clinton had brought to national prominence would continue to gain in stature at his expense. Shortly before the Democratic convention ended, Perot's candidacy self-destructed, removing any possibility of a third option, had Jackson been serious in his flirting. Ultimately, Jackson decided to take the path of least resistance and lowest risk and endorsed Clinton with feeling and seeming sincerity. Clinton had succeeded in keeping Jackson in the party, while diminishing his image and influence. He left Jackson with no choice but to become a statesman.

The convention also served as an advertisement for racial harmony. The speakers at the podium represented great diversity in ethnicities, if not in views. Clinton's Arkansas pattern of wooing black votes with appointments and not policies was seen in the mixture of a platform with many neoconservative elements combined with black speakers who avoided radical or even liberal appeals that might have divided the electorate. A personal triumph for Ron Brown, who now became a prominent national figure, the convention was unquestionably a success. In the wake of Perot's departure, one poll had Clinton up by twenty-seven points over Bush.

BUCHANAN AND THE TOLERATION OF INTOLERANCE

As far back as January, Bush's reelection hopes had been rapidly diminishing. The first bad news was the surprisingly strong challenge from conservative television commentator Pat Buchanan. Buchanan, an open admirer of George Wallace, had been part of the racial right wing of the Nixon administration. He had urged Nixon to make ever more strident attacks on busing and affirmative action. Not surprisingly, in 1992 he attacked Bush for his waffling on affirmative action and for ultimately signing the civil rights bill the previous year. Not only did Buchanan accuse Bush of endorsing quotas, but Buchanan also referred to his slave-owning ancestors "in a naked bid for . . . the old-line 'seg' vote." Buchanan's anti-Bush ad in several southern states combined his animus against blacks and gays by showing excerpts from a government-supported video depicting nude black gays dancing together. Buchanan's statements were laced with the assumption that America was a white nation:

> Why are we more shocked when a dozen people are killed in Vilnius than a massacre in Burundi? Because they were white people. That's who we are. That's where America comes from.

A widely quoted Buchanan column argued that it would be far wiser to accept white immigrants from England than black immigrants from Africa, because of the difficulty of assimilating Africans into American culture. Combined with Buchanan's well-known penchant for anti-Semitic statements, these public stances put Buchanan on the far right of racial conservatism.

Bush's first strategic response to Buchanan's challenge was to ignore it. The president and his staff blithely assumed that the Republicans of New Hampshire would never support a man who combined nativist sentiments with a complete lack of electoral experience. However, Buchanan stunned Bush by almost winning New Hampshire. Much of Buchanan's vote was simply a protest against Bush's remarkable lack of compassion for those suffering in the recession. It is unlikely that many Buchanan voters endorsed Buchanan's racial views. However, Bush now had to decide how to handle the angry white male challenge of Buchanan. Bush ultimately relied on the strength of the Republican establishment in the later primary states to rescue his candidacy. But rather than attacking Buchanan as a racist, Bush treated him as an annoyance who would inevitably be defeated. Bush also took a number of moves to quell dissent among cultural conservatives and stepped up his rhetoric against racial quotas. In the end, Bush defeated Buchanan handily, as the commentator lacked the stature and the funds to unseat an incumbent president, even during a recession. However, once Bush's victory was assured, the White House sought to placate Buchanan in any way possible. At the convention in Houston, Buchanan was given a prime-time speaking slot from which to spout his nativist and culturally conservative views. In his speech, Buchanan highlighted the L.A. riots as a vivid example of the cultural war in America and praised the National Guardsmen who had restored order.* The contrast that Buchanan drew between the anarchy of the looting and the heroism of the armed men who put it down did not require him to mention the races of the looters and the soldiers. This was the type of campaign that some had feared Bush would run after the L.A. riots. Buchanan's ability to rally a segment of the Republican primary vote showed that there was still a portion of the party enthusiastic for an heir of George Wallace. Moreover, just as Nixon had hesitated

---

* As humorist Molly Ivins observed, the Kulturkampf speech of Buchanan "sounded better in the original German."

to criticize Wallace for racism in 1968 for fear of offending Wallace voters, Bush did not launch a frontal assault on Buchanan's outrageous views on immigration and race. Instead, Bush allowed Buchanan to set the tone for his convention, one memorable for its exclusionary rhetoric. Some believed that exclusion of blacks was the central message of the 1992 Republican convention, and surely putting Buchanan's views in the spotlight was crucial in that development. With his coddling of Buchanan, Bush made certain that few blacks would vote Republican. A party that would give Buchanan so much prominence sent a message to black voters as clear as a Willie Horton ad.

THE GENERAL ELECTION: DERACIALIZATION COMES TO FRUITION

By the time the Republican convention ended, and the two candidates launched their general election campaigns, the racial politics of 1992 had been largely established. There would be no sudden outreach by Bush to blacks. Similarly, Clinton continued to downplay race. Clinton had begun his march to the presidency by emphasizing his status as a "New Democrat" who believed in responsibility as well as rights. He advocated a "New Covenant" politics, in which a caring activist government would demand that welfare recipients work while government provided training and support. As he put it in the spring, "If we help train you and you still refuse to work, then no more welfare." This rhetoric served him well in the primaries, and it continued to do so in the fall. The first television ad run by Clinton in the general election declared that he would force welfare recipients to work for their benefits, which some black leaders correctly saw as an appeal to white conservatives. Clinton also continued to keep his distance from some black leaders and much of the black agenda, such as affirmative action and urban aid. Harlem congressman Charles Rangel compared Clinton to "a woman who gives you her hotel room key but doesn't want to be seen with you in the lobby." But postelection studies suggested that the positions that Clinton would have had to take to ignite fervor among blacks would have cost him votes among Reagan Democrats. Clinton appeared to be willing to trade enthusiasm among blacks in return for taking white votes from Bush. As political scientist Ross Baker observed:

> Clinton's task, then, was to hold onto his black support without seeming to appear overly submissive to it and to reach out to white Reagan Democrats without gratuitous offense to African Americans.

The Clinton staff knew that white males had formed the core of the Reagan coalition and that to appeal to them, they would have to distinguish themselves from Mondale and Dukakis. Stan Greenberg, Clinton's most influential pollster, had conducted focus groups of white Reagan Democrats, finding that one after another perceived blacks as demanding unearned benefits. Instead of defending welfare as earlier Democrats had done, Clinton appeared to loathe the current system as much as the Republicans did.

In addition to Clinton's strategic positioning, several other factors allowed his deracialization tactics to succeed. The poor economy continued to dominate election coverage and allowed racial tensions to be sublimated beneath pan-ethnic populist rhetoric. Clinton also used his ease and familiarity with blacks to rally support without making commitments. And he found issues that would not arouse white conservatives, such as attacking the Bush policy on returning Haitian immigrants, rank discrimination to many blacks compared to the treatment of Cubans. Bush also contributed to the deracialization of the election by hardly mentioning any racial topics. He did not emphasize either the L.A. riots or affirmative action, the two issues that many had anticipated would be the Willie Hortons of 1992. This may have been because reporters seemed far more vigilant for coded racial appeals. When Vice President Quayle launched a bizarre attack on a sitcom character for having a baby out of wedlock, several reporters quickly labeled this as a racial issue. No lesser scribe than Lance Morrow of *Time* felt that Quayle had metaphorically transformed "old Willie Horton into a beautiful blond fortyish WASP." The contrast was extraordinary—the media that had been largely blind to the obvious racial messages of the Horton campaign in 1988 now saw racism in far more innocuous Republican moves. The atmosphere seemed to chasten Bush. While he did on one occasion attack "the whole rotten infrastructure of reverse discrimination," he seemed to be much more hesitant to use race in 1992. Postelection, conservative activist Clint Bolick lamented that Bush had "fumbled away the quota issue," thereby sacrificing a winning Republican strategy.

CONCLUSION: THE POLITICS OF RACIAL SILENCE

> In 1992 . . . race was a dog that did not bark, noteworthy for its relative absence as an issue in the campaign.
>
> POLITICAL HISTORIAN WILSON CAREY MCWILLIAMS

On election day, Clinton won a plurality victory over Bush and Perot. Perot, receiving more of the vote than any third-party candidate since Roosevelt in 1912, basked in his success, while Bush, only the second elected president rejected since Hoover in 1932, went down to a punishing defeat. Clinton's success was certainly a product of his brilliant campaigning, as he was easily the most attractive and charismatic Democrat to win the nomination in decades. Still, Clinton's victory was possible only because of his strong support in the black community, as Bush won a plurality of the white vote.* The most racially conservative Democrat to run since Kennedy had won a victory based on black voters, but it had been a campaign premised on winning back white Reagan Democrats. Clinton had spent much of the primary period insulating himself from Republican attacks on race. The consistency with which he did so is quite clear in hindsight. To prevent a Horton-style attack, he executed a brain-damaged black man. To insulate himself on welfare, he bluntly advocated putting

---

* A split in the white vote caused by the Perot candidacy was a key factor in Clinton's victory. Particularly in states with higher black population levels, Perot took enough votes from Bush to allow Clinton to eke out a win.

welfare mothers to work. To insulate himself on the L.A. riots, he attacked a radical black as if she, and not the Rodney King beating, were somehow the cause of the deaths and fires. To prevent Bush from running an affirmative action campaign, Clinton never talked about affirmative action except when pressed, and he worked to keep the issue off the agenda. Adroitly using the economy as a unifying cause, Clinton preached a color-blind politics, while very quietly advocating a continuation of color-conscious policies. Finally, and perhaps most important, Clinton set out to diminish the position and legitimacy of Jesse Jackson, the albatross of Democratic presidential hopes in years past. His success in so doing was based on his gamble that if he called Jackson's bluff, the reverend would not bolt the party or sit out the election. Each of these moves was designed to send a message to white voters that he was not a racial liberal. Reasoning that black voters would have nowhere else to go, Clinton focused on issues that would burnish his image as a racial moderate.

While Clinton did win the overwhelming majority of votes cast by blacks, black turnout was affected by Clinton's tactics. African American turnout dropped from 8.3 million to 8.1 million, an even larger drop as a percentage of the overall electorate given the sharp rise in white turnout. Had Clinton lost narrowly, surely many would have pointed to his failure to rally more blacks to the polls. As it was, the message of the 1992 election for the Democratic Party was that they could win the White House only by appealing to white racial moderates and conservatives. Just as Carter had brought back many white southerners to their ancestral party, Clinton and Gore had managed to win a few key southern states from Bush.

For the Republican Party, the messages of 1992 were less clear. They had managed to win an election in 1988 with an ugly and barely veiled appeal to white animus and fear. In 1992, with race off the agenda as it had not been in years, thanks to Clinton's adroit positioning, the Republicans had lost by a fairly large margin. Bush had failed to make any effort to reach out to blacks and had sent an emphatic message by tolerating Buchanan. In the general election, Bush could not pierce Clinton's racial insulation on welfare, crime, and the L.A. riots. He scarcely made the attempt. Twelve years of

Republican rule had failed to bring any appreciable number of African Americans into the GOP. The black leadership that Reagan's conservatives had hoped to develop had failed to attract a following in the black community. Without the White House, and facing the first unified Democratic government since 1980, the Republican Party was confused and leaderless on race, as it was on a great many issues.

Still, the potential for strategic opportunities on race abounded for Republicans looking ahead to 1996. Would Clinton be able to continue to draw the nation's attention away from race and to trans-racial issues such as economic renewal? Or, as with Kennedy in 1960, would he eventually have to come down on one side or the other on tough issues loaded with racial baggage, such as welfare reform, affirmative action, and urban spending? Running a deracialized campaign was one thing; avoiding the politics of race while governing would be a far greater challenge.

CLINTON RESURGENT
The Status Quo Racial Politics of 1996

The 1996 presidential election demonstrated that the Republicans had failed to devise a successful response to Clinton's careful racial moderation. In the aftermath of the 1994 Republican revolution, in which conservative Republicans swept to power in Congress for the first time in forty years, Clinton tacked his sails back toward the middle on matters such as welfare and affirmative action. The Republican nominee, Bob Dole, emulated Bush in 1992 and failed to make even token appeals to black voters. At the same time, racial issues were seldom prominent during the election. Although Dole did make a late attempt to ignite white fervor against affirmative action in the crucial state of California, his efforts were inept and unavailing. Clinton, who had appeared to be a lame duck in November of 1994, would once again show himself to be the "comeback kid" of American politics. Clinton's adroit handling of affirmative action and welfare reform allowed him to once again construct a deracialized coalition that helped keep the White House in Democratic hands.

1996: THE SETTING

The most important strategic difference from four years before was the state of the economy. Most Americans perceived that economic conditions had improved and that Clinton deserved some of the credit. Yet two years before the 1996 election, Clinton had appeared to be supremely vulnerable. He had failed to deliver on key campaign promises, such as a middle-class tax cut and welfare reform. Most significant, the centerpiece of his domestic agenda, national health care, had turned into a memorable debacle. In response to many of the missteps by Clinton and Democrats in Congress, Newt Gingrich and the House Republicans crafted a brilliant and unprecedented national campaign to retake the House from Democratic control. The stunning tsunami of pro-Republican voting at all levels of government rocked Clinton. It also attracted a covey of strong Republican challengers and even tempted some Democrats to contemplate a primary challenge to Clinton. The Republican surge also threatened to bring greater attention to race, as from January of 1995, many in the GOP focused on a crusade against affirmative action. Would affirmative action become central to a presidential campaign for the first time since 1972?*

THE CANDIDATES

Bill Clinton

Clinton owed his 1992 election in large degree to his ability to sublimate racial tensions within his party and the nation. Yet in return for relative silence during the campaign, many racial liberals expected that Clinton would deliver policies to their liking. Similarly, Clinton's moderate supporters, such as his former colleagues at the Democratic Leadership Council (DLC), expected that Clinton would govern as he campaigned, as a New Democrat. The first move that Clinton made reversed a campaign promise he had made to African Americans: to treat Haitian refugees with fairness. The blatant injustice of treating "whiter" Cuban immigrants so much better than Haitians had been a source of increasing anger in the black community. Although Clinton had labeled Bush's policy immoral on the cam-

---

* The public's attention was also riveted by the O. J. Simpson trial, a grueling and protracted affair that exposed sharp differences in black and white attitudes about crime, police conduct, and the criminal justice system. However, as opposed to 1992's Rodney King trial, the Simpson criminal trial produced no rioting following its controversial outcome and thus even less electoral impact.

paign trail, he adopted that policy almost immediately. The difficulty of maintaining his deracialized coalition was more directly exposed in the nomination of law professor Lani Guinier to be assistant attorney general for civil rights. Many on the liberal wing in the administration saw Guinier's nomination as a substitute for policy concessions to black America. On the right, Guinier was labeled a "quota queen," and the nomination received extraordinary media attention. Several of Guinier's writings suggested that she was open to innovative and unprecedented electoral solutions to combat racial bloc voting. Some Jewish Democratic fund-raisers also opposed Guinier in back-channel communications to the White House, threatening to expose that fault line in the Democratic coalition yet again. When Clinton ultimately withdrew Guinier's nomination before she was even granted a hearing before the Senate, many of Clinton's black supporters were outraged at this apparent betrayal. The Congressional Black Caucus and Jesse Jackson were particularly strident in their criticism of Clinton. At the same time, centrist Democrats believed that "the brouhaha over Guinier's views and Clinton's tacit support of them continued to send an Old Democratic, culturally liberal message to the public."

Clinton's administration was extremely diverse in terms of minorities and women in executive and judicial positions.* As he had in Arkansas, Clinton repaid his black supporters with appointments but did not often address race as a policy question. Mary Francis Berry, the head of the Civil Rights Commission, observed bitterly:

> Clinton's approach to race is reminiscent of Malcolm X's statement that all that happened when African Americans elected some politicians was that some Negroes who already had jobs got good jobs in government.

---

* However, at least during the first term, the Clinton cabinet was largely a white male preserve at the upper reaches of decision making. The black appointees in particular were kept out of positions of power, relegated to such comparatively minor cabinet positions as Energy and Commerce. The top White House staff also remained remarkably white and male. In an administration that "looked like America," important decisions were usually made by a much less diverse group.

Clinton's greatest demonstration of fealty to black concerns came when he proposed welfare reform in the summer of 1994. Republicans and DLC Democrats had been advocating strict time limits on welfare payments, and surely limits were consonant with the rhetoric of Clinton's 1992 campaign. Yet in the face of strong liberal objections, many of them from black lawmakers, Clinton proposed a very mild version of welfare reform that lacked time limits. Indeed, the crucial and ultimately fatal decision to put health care before welfare reform on the administration's agenda was a product of Clinton's sensitivity to the concerns of liberals. Yet waiting on welfare reform and refusing to include time limits were the racial politics of omission, acts that did not draw attention to race but rather kept it off the agenda.

The shocking victory of Gingrich and his conservative troops in the midterm elections of 1994 forced Clinton back to the New Democratic positions he had run on. Many of Clinton's ideological soul mates among moderate Democrats had been defeated, and some blamed Clinton for tarring them with his liberal image. The president was forced to defend his relevance to the policymaking process in the days after the election, a moment unprecedented in the post-FDR era. Clinton's allies in the DLC also moved in response to the rise of Gingrich. Previously uneasy about affirmative action, they now came out firmly against any "governmental consideration of Americans as members of separate ethnic, religious, and linguistic groups." The DLC was responding to the new mood on affirmative action in Washington. The media explanation for the Democratic disaster of 1994 was a swelling backlash among "angry white males" who were disturbed at Clinton's cultural liberalism on sexuality, spending, and race. Conservative strategist Bill Kristol predicted that affirmative action would become the wedge issue that would destroy the Democratic coalition entirely. Evidence mounted that the Republicans intended to use affirmative action in 1996. Many liberal Democrats were concerned that Clinton would abandon affirmative action in pursuit of reelection. Others agonized that if he did defend it, he could well be defeated in 1996; and still others, such as DLC member Senator Joseph Lieberman, argued that racial preferences were "patently unfair" and should now be abandoned. Clinton could no longer ignore affirmative action, as he had during his campaign and during his first two years. Largely as a reaction to the Republican surge, he launched a full-scale review of affirmative action and put his top domestic adviser, George Stephanopoulos, in charge.

In the meantime, Clinton sought to assuage the angry white male sector of the electorate by several symbolic gestures. In addition to learning how to properly give a military salute, adjusting his sartorial informality (particularly avoiding unflattering jogging shorts), and rearranging his White House staff, Clinton removed one of his highest-profile black nominees. In firing Surgeon General Jocelyn Elders, Clinton demonstrated, as he had in the Guinier affair, that he had little loyalty to a strong, independent-minded black appointee. In the end, it is difficult to disagree with the observation of political scientist Hanes Walton Jr., who concluded:

> Once in office, President Clinton only responded to racial issues raised by Republicans or which evolved from conflicts in racial relations. He neither made nor took any bold legislative initiate [*sic*] except the abandonment of welfare. . . . Thus the New Democrat could combine the past with the future minus one central issue—race. Removing race from the old New Deal agenda might carry the country . . . into the Democratic column in the future.

As the Democratic primaries approached, the crucial question was whether any Democrat would take up the banner of liberalism, particularly racial liberalism, and challenge Clinton for the soul of the party.

Bob Dole

The eventual winner of the Republican nomination was a man with a long and largely positive civil rights record. Placed in the context of the previous twenty years of Republican nominees, Dole marked a return to the midwestern racial moderation of Gerald Ford, with whom Dole had run for the White House in 1976. Reagan, who had been an opponent of all civil rights laws, had been succeeded by Bush, who had been on both sides of many civil rights questions. Dole, however, had seldom wavered in his support of mainstream legislation to redress racial inequalities. Dole had stood up to the Reagan White House in the 1982 fight over renewing the Voting Rights Act and had fought to make Martin Luther King's birthday a federal holiday. Up until the 1994 Republican revolution, Dole had been one of the stronger supporters of affirmative action within the Republican congressional caucus, although it was not an issue on which he sought a high profile.

The initial explanation for Dole's stances on race must be geographic. A native of Kansas, where John Brown's radical abolitionism first saw light, Dole inherited the older GOP tradition of favoring black rights. Additionally, Dole is often credited with greater sensitivity to minorities than many Republicans, as he not only grew up poor, but experienced life as a "minority" as a result of his horrific injuries in World War II. Dole, an authentic war hero, struggled for years to repair his body and to achieve success competing with the able-bodied. Dole had also lamented the failure to reach out to black voters during the 1976 election. In his previous national campaigns (1976, 1980, 1988), Dole had neither sought nor received support from the forces of racial conservatism within the Republican Party. Yet Dole was also largely unchanged from the man he had been in 1976 in regards to racial issues. Generationally, he was socialized into a world in which blacks were second-class citizens and raised in an area in which blacks were not prominent socially and politically. Dole did not have an affinity or following in the black community, and he had no high-ranking black staffers. For a candidate who hoped to take on Clinton, these were notable weaknesses.

THE DEMOCRATIC NONCONTEST: CLINTON AMENDS, BUT DOESN'T END, HIS OUTREACH TO RACIAL CONSERVATISM

The Democratic primaries were nonevents in 1996, as a result of careful positioning on racial matters by Clinton. The first issue that Clinton had to handle was affirmative action. Long before the Iowa caucuses, Clinton had to decide whether to defend affirmative action or to agree with Republicans and some moderate Democrats and end it. The Republicans were drawing attention to some egregious cases of abuse of federal contracting set-asides and quotas, such as the no-risk multimillion-dollar windfall for a group of wealthy black lawyers who acted as fronts for a white billionaire in a broadcast deal. As the administration went through a massive review of the myriad federal programs, Clinton reflected privately on the political costs: "The definition makes all the difference: preferences we lose; affirmative action we win." A leak before the final report was released claimed that the administration's goal was to cut some affirmative action programs while saving others, for political gains. "We want black businessmen to scream enough to let angry white males understand that we've done something for them," said the anonymous Clinton adviser. In the midst of the administrative review, the Supreme Court came down with a decision, *Adarand* v. *Pena*, that greatly constrained federal affirmative action programs. The debate within the administration was intense. Political consultant Dick Morris, the secret consigliere of centrism who had been advising Clinton on an almost daily basis since the start of 1995, advocated praising the decision. Morris predicted that if Clinton came out against affirmative action, not only would it be a popular move, it would also bring a primary challenge from Jesse Jackson. Morris salivated at the prospect of a Jackson candidacy, since it would give Clinton the chance to reestablish his New Democrat credentials by soundly defeating an avatar of traditional liberalism. However, blacks in and out of the administration wanted Clinton to attack *Adarand*. Clinton released a statement that split the difference on *Adarand*, and the review within his administration continued.

The possibility of a Jackson challenge was inextricably linked to Clinton's affirmative action policies. Two top White House aides made a pilgrimage to Jackson at his D.C. headquarters. Sitting beneath a huge map of the United States, marked with each state's deadline for filing as a candidate, Jackson made it clear that if Clinton made any move beyond *Adarand* against affirmative action, Jackson would have no choice but to run. Even before the latest controversy over affirmative action, Jackson had been dissatisfied with the Clinton record on matters such as Guinier, Elders, and spending. As in every election year since 1980, Jackson in 1994 publicly threatened to run for president:

> Those of us who voted for racial equality and workers' rights and economic stimulus and education equity as keys to reduce pain and hardship are sadly disappointed. The option of running is open and the option of running in a general election deserves as much attention as running in the primary.

Boasting that he had a database of five hundred thousand supporters, Jackson promised to run against Clinton in the general election if the party became nothing more than "Demopublicans."

Following the internal review of all affirmative action programs, Clinton pledged to "mend it, not end it" in a moving speech in June of 1995. He attacked those who would eliminate all affirmative action but promised to end policies that went too far and became quotas. In the end, very few programs were altered as a result of the Clinton review, particularly if one considers that *Adarand* had already changed the law. The speech did help prevent a challenge from the Left. Yet affirmative action was not the only issue that Clinton had to monitor as he looked ahead to the primaries; he also had to consider welfare reform.

Clinton had run as an opponent of the current system in 1992, much to the consternation of some of his liberal supporters. The new Republican majority in Congress now sent Clinton two welfare reform bills in sequence, each containing the kinds of tough terms that echoed Clinton's rhetoric from the 1992 campaign trail. In addition to being harsher than Clinton wished on various points, they were also linked to cuts and changes in Medicare and Medicaid. Thus, Clinton could veto them and still claim to be a supporter of welfare reform. Moreover, had Clinton signed either of the bills in 1995; he would have faced a left challenger in the Democratic primaries, if not Jackson, then another liberal paladin or even the iconoclastic Daniel Moynihan. Republicans in Congress, reluctant to allow Clinton to run for reelection as the author of welfare reform, were perfectly content to send Clinton welfare reform bills with the poison pill amendments on health policy that precluded him from signing.

As the Iowa caucuses approached, the deadlines for entering various primaries expired, with no Democratic challenger to Clinton emerging. In the current presidential finance system, if a candidate has not raised vast sums of money by January 1 of the election year, it is almost impossible to run for president. Clinton's careful balancing on welfare and affirmative action allowed him to do what no Democrat had done for almost fifty years: sail to the nomination without a fight. This long period of intraparty calm was crucial in Clinton's eventual victory. Clinton, with Morris's cagey assistance, could focus his attacks on Gingrich and Dole, while the Republicans were turning their knives on one another in a bitter battle for the nomination.

Then Republicans in Congress had a sudden change of heart. As Clinton's prospects for reelection brightened, and much of the conservative agenda stagnated on Capitol Hill, congressional Republicans began to think that they'd rather come to the electorate in November with welfare reform as a prominent accomplishment. In the summer of 1996 they sent Clinton a tough welfare reform bill that lacked the Medicare/Medicaid sections that Clinton abhorred. The welfare reform bill still contained elements Clinton disagreed with, particularly a $24 billion cut in food stamps and removal of legal immigrants from eligibility. As Clinton put it during the long internal debates over the bill, "This is a decent welfare bill wrapped in a sack of shit." Even the aspects of the bill that Clinton supported were objectionable to many liberals in Congress and in the administration. The decision before Clinton was seen by both wings of the Democratic Party as a defining moment for the party and the president. If Clinton signed, it would reverse sixty-one years of social policy by ending the federal guarantee of poverty assistance and return responsibility for poverty policy to the states. The debate came to a head on July 31, 1996, just before the convention. In a move that split Clinton from a number of his closest aides, he signed the bill, while arguing that the objectionable aspects could be fixed later. Among the most influential voices on the decision was Clinton's pollster, Morris, who convinced the president that his reelection would be at risk if he did not sign. The dismay of many liberals was immediate. Peter Edelman, assistant secretary for Health and Human Services, resigned, while his wife, Marian Wright Edelman, a longtime friend of the Clintons', called the welfare bill "a moral blot on his presidency." Politically, the timing of Clinton's betrayal of his liberal and black allies could not have been better. The delay in signing had allowed Clinton to avoid a primary challenge, and even an independent candidacy would have little time to get off the ground.

All Clinton now had to do was manage to keep the anger of the liberals off the television screens at his convention. The two most prominent critics of the welfare policy, Mario Cuomo and Jesse Jackson, were kept out of prime-time speaking positions. This was yet another Clinton slight of Jackson, who had riveted earlier conventions with his moving oratory. As one convention planner put it: "Before nine PM, we're running the 1984 convention. After nine PM, we're running the Clinton convention." Even when Jackson and others at the podium did criticize Clinton's signing of the welfare bill, the criticism was flavored in every case with an overall endorsement of Clinton's politics. Clinton had found the triangulated position between the GOP and racial liberals. Clinton could not have gone any further toward racial conservatism without causing an open breach in his party, nor could he have gone much further toward racial liberalism without giving the GOP an issue in the fall. Clinton's renomination could have been a disaster similar to Carter's 1980 race against Ted Kennedy, which resulted in Carter limping into the general election atop a fractured party. Instead, Clinton's careful balancing of party factions on racial issues and the party's overall fear of the Republicans pulled the Democrats together. The Republican Party, by contrast, was behaving far more like the Democrats of 1972, 1984, or 1988, engaging in protracted contested primaries in which the political heirs of George Wallace and Eisenhower continued their internecine warfare well into the spring.

BUCHANAN SCARES VOTES TOWARD DOLE: THE REPUBLICAN CONTEST

Bob Dole was the front-runner from very early on in the Republican race, but he was a Mondale front-runner rather than a Reagan front-runner. He was the establishment candidate, lacking in ideological distinctiveness and without an identifiable base beyond the party regulars and military veterans. Dole did not ignite fervor, nor did he scare off competition. Dole's age and his lack of resonance with the Republican revolution of 1994 raised fundamental questions about the viability and desirability of his candidacy. Very quickly the Republican field became crowded with candidates, drawn by the breathtaking triumph of Gingrich in Congress as well as the obvious weakness of Clinton, who languished low in the polls until the summer of 1995. Among the Republicans who entered the race at some point were Senators Phil Gramm and Arlen Spector, California governor Pete Wilson, former Reagan State Department official Alan Keyes,* publisher Steve Forbes, former Tennessee governor Lamar Alexander, and, reprising his 1992 campaign, commentator Pat Buchanan.

Looming above every other Republican in many public opinion polls was the former chairman of the Joint Chiefs, General Colin Powell. Powell was the strongest candidate the Republicans could put forward; according to most surveys, he would easily defeat Clinton. Such polls are notoriously unreliable, particularly with an untested candidate such as Powell, but the novelty of a moderate black Republican military hero with charisma running for president drew a national "draft Powell" campaign. There was even talk of Powell running as an independent. No other candidacy scared Clinton as

---

* Keyes, an African American, could have represented an important turning point in Republican politics if he had not been widely acknowledged as a gadfly. A minor figure in Reagan's State Department, Keyes had run two sacrificial lamb candidacies for the Senate in heavily Democratic Maryland. Keyes was caught in a conundrum: his only real qualification for the presidency was his skin color, but he was personally opposed to affirmative action and a member of a party emphatically against racial preferences.

much. Even the front-runner in the Republican contest had to respect Powell's stature. Dole made a personal visit to Powell's home in January of 1995 to find out if the general intended to make the race. Ultimately, Powell withdrew from consideration in November of 1995, citing family concerns and a lack of enthusiasm for the contest. The primary campaign would have been bitter, as Powell differed from his party in supporting not only affirmative action, but also abortion rights. With Powell's withdrawal, the prospect of the Republicans nominating a strong defender of affirmative action was ended.

Among the remaining candidates, three made opposition to affirmative action central to their campaigns: Pete Wilson, Phil Gramm, and Pat Buchanan. Dole had also been moving on affirmative action. Previously a supporter of it, he introduced legislation to end all federal affirmative action programs, because they had produced "quota tokenism." Some of Dole's supporters among moderate Republicans strongly cautioned Dole that he risked looking extreme and racist if he tried to run for president by attacking affirmative action. In separate meetings, three northeastern senators pleaded with Dole to reconsider. All advised that if Dole went too far on affirmative action, there would be electoral consequences. Perhaps because of such advice, Dole remained far less emphatic in his opposition to affirmative action than Wilson, Gramm, and Buchanan. The difference between Dole and these men was not one of policy, as all opposed racial preferences, but in how prominent affirmative action was in their rhetoric and in their campaigns.

Dole's status as front-runner came under severe assault in the New Hampshire primary, when Buchanan won a shocking victory. The "angry white males" of 1994 had seemingly chosen their spokesman. The trembling among mainstream Republicans was similar to that which shook the Democrats in 1988 when Jackson triumphed in Michigan. The media began to focus more attention on the less savory aspects of Buchanan's past. A 1990 column in which he had questioned the existence of gas chambers at Treblinka, and indeed the entire scope of the Holocaust, was uncovered, as was his advocacy of annexing some Canadian provinces to preserve white demographic dominance in America. Buchanan was also taken to task for his associates. One campaign worker was revealed to be a regular attendee at neo-Nazi and white supremacist meetings and reluctantly took a leave from the campaign. Another associate, whom Buchanan also refused to repudiate, had a long history of opposition to interracial marriage and advocated a white pride philosophy. Fresh from his victory in New Hampshire, Buchanan flew to South Carolina, where he pledged fervent allegiance to the Confederate flag as a symbol of southern defiance. Campaigning in Arizona, Buchanan emphasized his plan for an impregnable wall along the border with Mexico and his support for English-only legislation. In southern speeches, Buchanan continued to hit affirmative action hard. It also now emerged that an important victory over Gramm in the early Louisiana caucus had been possible only through the assistance of white supremacists, whom Buchanan belatedly disavowed. For all these reasons, when Buchanan trumpeted his slogan "We're going to take back America!" there was little doubt about for whom and from whom Buchanan intended to take back the country. Yet even as the media was highlighting Buchanan's reprehensible racial views and associations, Dole did not bluntly charge Buchanan with racism, for fear of offending his supporters, although a prominent Dole ally, Senator Alfonse D'Amato, did attack Buchanan for bigotry in forthright and bold language.

The rise of Buchanan eventually led Dole to victory. It gave his purposeless and visionless candidacy a reason for existence: the preservation of mainstream Republican ideology from the assault of America-first nativism. Buchanan's strength also prevented Gramm and Wilson from emerging from the Republican pack. If either man had done so, the Republicans could have chosen a more palatable representative of the anti–affirmative action movement as their nominee. The horrifying prospect of a Buchanan victory pushed sensible Republicans into voting for Dole, even though he lacked charisma, clarity, and, on occasion, coherence. While Dole had to struggle hard against Forbes, Buchanan, and Alexander, after Super Tuesday it was obvious that Dole would take the nomination. Buchanan, the angry outsider, had forced Republicans to pick the avatar of the Republican establishment as its nominee. Yet in defeating Buchanan, Dole had put at least as much emphasis on Buchanan's opposition to free trade as on his opposition to integration and his white supremacist attitudes and associations. Dole gave little indication that he would address black concerns in the general election. After sewing up the nomination, he refused to address the NAACP at its convention, a symbolic snub that reverberated widely. Dole claimed that because the NAACP was led by a liberal former Democratic congressman, the invitation was a "setup" designed to embarrass him.

The Republican convention would witness more than the anointing of Dole as the nominee; Dole's campaign would use the convention to make three moves toward racial moderation. Although opposition to affirmative action was expected to be highlighted, Congressman J. C. Watts, the most prominent elected black Republican, convinced the Republican leadership not to make affirmative action a crucial issue at the convention. Watts had also almost single-handedly stopped congressional legislation aimed at ending racial preferences. Had Watts failed in either of these efforts, affirmative action would have been far more salient in the fall campaign. The leadership was ready for Watts's message. The Republicans, mindful of the scholarly and media criticism of the 1992 convention as an orgy of exclusion, attempted to craft a more inclusive convention. Although only 52 of 1,990 delegates were black, these numbers were boosted by "auxiliaries," nonvoting blacks affiliated with the party who were brought in to occupy seats in the convention hall so that the convention would appear more integrated on television. The GOP also removed Pat Buchanan from any prominent role, thus silencing the loudest voice for white supremacy in the party. As Republican chairman Haley Barbour described the aim of the convention: "We needed to let the public understand that we are not a party of just seventy-year-old white men."

The nearly seventy-year-old white man who was about to take the nomination of the GOP now had to pick his running mate. Dole, who had been hoping that Powell could be convinced to run even at this late date, ended up selecting perhaps the only national Republican with any credibility in the black community, former Housing and Urban Development secretary Jack Kemp. Dole's campaign, in addition to emphasizing Kemp's youth, Reagan connections, and supply-side economics, also highlighted his connection to minority communities. "He's one of the few people in our party who has spoken in union halls and at NAACP conventions and has been applauded," said a top Dole adviser. "The main rap on this party is that we exclude people. Jack Kemp is the best antidote to that," said former Secretary of Education William Bennett. In choosing Kemp, squelching Buchanan, and submerging affirmative action, the Republican convention suggested that Dole might be contemplating an appeal to black voters in the fall. At the very least, Dole would not be able to easily run hard against affirmative action, since he had allied with the most prominent defender of the policy in the party, after Colin Powell.

THE "EPIDEMIC OF TERROR": REPUBLICAN RHETORIC BURNS BLACK CHURCHES?

Even though the conservative Republican majority in Congress had given up on its plans to attack affirmative action, and even after Dole presided over a far more inclusive convention than in 1992, there were those who still argued that conservatism was tantamount to racism. Many African American leaders linked a series of suspicious fires at black churches to the tone and spirit of Republican ideology. A liberal interest group held a press conference in March to announce that black churches were being burned at an alarming rate throughout the South, as part of "a well-organized white supremacist movement." In testimony before Congress, Deval Patrick, a top Justice Department official, called the attacks "chilling. . . . We are facing an epidemic of terror." Later, Patrick was one of many Democrats to accuse Republicans of fomenting the attacks with their ugly rhetoric:

> I feel like we're reaping what we've sown. . . . If you listen to talk radio, if you listen to some of the rhetoric in Congress . . . you can begin to see ways in which civic leadership in this country is not encouraging people to see their stake in each other's struggle.

Jesse Jackson labeled the church burnings "a kind of anti-black mania, a kind of white riot." When evidence emerged that no conspiracy was behind the attacks, Patrick found that "even worse," since it suggested that racism was widespread and not limited to a single group. Gore chimed in, stating that for many of the fires, "the conspiracy is racism itself." Visiting Auschwitz, Hillary Clinton had the chutzpah to compare the church burnings to the Holocaust.

In June, Clinton responded with a moving radio address, which promised immediate federal action, including a national task force, a toll-free telephone number to report tips, visits by federal law enforcement agents to black churches, and new legislation to ease federal prosecution of racially motivated church arsonists. While Clinton reluctantly conceded, "We do not now have evidence of a national conspiracy," he hastened to add that "it is clear that racial hostility is the driving force behind a number of these incidents." Clinton visited the site of one burning and made several references to the church burnings in other speeches in the fall. By July, over 2,200 articles had been written about the attacks, with over 100 stories in *The New York Times* alone. Yet in truth, there was very little evidence that black churches were burning at a higher rate than white churches or that many black churches were being burned by racists, organized or unorganized. Not only were church arsons declining for the most part, the tick upward in 1995–96 seemed to be a result of better record keeping. As when Carter brought the Klan into the campaign discourse in 1980, or when McGovern did the same in 1972, the Clinton administration's flimsy conclusion that the church burnings were the product of a racist epidemic brought about by Republican policies helped rally black support by raising black fears. If the Democrats did not directly say that Newt Gingrich was spending his free time kindling fires at black churches, they did assert that his conservative rhetoric was gasoline on the flames. As the head of the liberal interest group that first raised the issue put it, "There's only a slippery slope between conservative religious persons and those that are really doing the burning." When the Christian Coalition, a conservative religious group largely supportive of Republican candidates, held a press conference to announce efforts to help rebuild black churches, some civil rights leaders were vicious in their criticism. The Reverend Joseph Lowery of the Southern Christian Leadership Conference accused the coalition of cynically using the church burnings to boost its standing in the black community while promulgating the conservative rhetoric that fueled the climate of bigotry behind the fires. Apparently, only Democrats were allowed to exploit burning churches for political gain. Although Dole tried to match Clinton's outrage, and Republicans in Congress unanimously voted for the entirely symbolic legislation against racist arson at churches, there was no way to combat the impression that conservative Republicans were somehow responsible for the fires.

DOLE'S CALIFORNIA CONVERSION: THE GENERAL ELECTION

The Dole campaign limped into the general election without much of a convention bounce and unable to dent Clinton's formidable lead in the polls. If Dole had planned to use Kemp's selection as a preface to an outreach to minorities, the prospects vanished immediately. Kemp was forced by Dole's campaign to fudge his differences with Dole on affirmative action. This damaged Kemp's credibility in the black community; apparently, his fervor for racial outreach did not outweigh the need for congruence with his running mate. By the time Kemp and Gore met for the vice presidential debate, Gore was able to damn his opponent with carefully worded praise as a "lonely voice in the Republican Party" who had fought for affirmative action. But Gore noted with "sadness that . . . the day after he joined Senator Dole's ticket, he announced that he was changing his position . . . to adopt Senator Dole's position to end all affirmative action." Kemp also attracted criticism when he praised Louis Farrakhan's "wonderful" philosophy of self-help. This surprising move toward the most controversial figure in the black community did not redound to Kemp's benefit with blacks and angered some Jewish voters. Perhaps because of his shift on affirmative action, there seemed little enthusiasm in the black community for Kemp. In truth, Kemp had never been a well-known figure in the black community; he was merely the only national Republican who seemed to give a damn about attracting black votes. The importance of that diminished when Kemp was competing not with his fellow Republicans but with Democrats with long histories of support for black causes and records of consistent and successful outreach to black voters. It would take more than an NFL jersey and empowerment zones to beat Bill Clinton in the black community in 1996.

Race continued to be largely unaddressed by either campaign. As journalist Joe Klein observed:

> Race, the abiding agony of American politics, appears to be sliding off the table in the 1996 presidential election. . . . Clinton's response has been a combination of nursery rhymes ("mend it don't end it") and passive resistance . . . the policy is demagoguery by omission . . . and so the Republicans have drifted into a rather pregnant silence on affirmative action. It could be resurrected as a "wedge" issue . . . if California becomes a battleground state.

Analysts had long predicted that California's anti–affirmative action Proposition 209 would inject race into the campaign. By early October, these expectations had not been met; Dole had put no emphasis on the issue. Kemp had publicly forsworn any use of Proposition 209, although he now joined Dole in quietly supporting it. "We are not going to campaign on a wedge issue. . . . We are not going to let this issue tear up California," said Kemp. Then Dole decided to contest California in the waning days of the campaign and changed tactics, perhaps because 209 was ahead in the polls, but he trailed Clinton by twenty points. In a four-day trip to California in late October, Dole began to attack Clinton on immigration and on affirmative action, with an emphasis on Proposition 209. Asked to explain the change by reporters, Dole confessed that Proposition 209 was just a useful wedge issue. Dole's frank admission took away any principled explanation for his sudden shift in tactics and called into question the sincerity of his 1995 conversion to the anti–affirmative action camp.*

---

* Dole's shift didn't help him in California. Exit polls confirmed that 209 was not an important issue in the presidential race. Proposition 209 won handily, while Dole was crushed.

CONCLUSION: YOU CAN'T BEAT SOMEONE WITH NO ONE

By 1996, the Democratic Party was the entrenched "incumbent" choice of African Americans. In congressional races, where the power of incumbency is strongest, political scientists have found that in order to defeat an incumbent, a challenger needs to present the electorate with a reason to vote against the incumbent, a reasonable alternative to the incumbent, and the resources to get those messages out. Bill Clinton had surely given the black community reasons to vote for someone else, such as his abandonment of Guinier, reversals on welfare reform legislation and Haitian immigration, revisionism on affirmative action, and failure to integrate the top cabinet positions. However, on most of those issues, Dole was far from a credible alternative. Moreover, Dole committed almost nothing to black outreach, and Kemp was simply not popular enough or given enough policy autonomy to compete with Clinton-Gore in the black community.

Yet Dole did not make a clear appeal to the forces of racial conservatism in American politics. With the exception of his cynical and blatantly tactical pandering on Proposition 209 in the last two weeks of the campaign, Dole did not reach out symbolically or substantively to racial conservatives. Dole did not even reach out geographically. The Dole-Kemp ticket was only the second Republican slate since 1964 to ignore the South, and the previous one, the Ford-Dole ticket of 1976, had been equally unsuccessful. Since the South remained the regional home of the largest number of white racial conservatives, Clinton-Gore had an extraordinary advantage. Two sons of the modern South running against a Yankee from New York and a prairie state senator was no contest culturally. The 1996 Dole campaign did not test how powerful race remained in American politics, nor did it test the depth of black loyalty to the Democratic Party. The Republicans had played the race card with great success in 1988 and had largely ignored it in 1992 and 1996. It had been almost four decades since they had appealed to black voters on issues. In the face of two successful deracializing campaigns by Bill Clinton, the Republican Party had two choices: to "reracial-ize" politics by appealing to white animus or to revolutionize the party coalitions by reaching out to black voters. The message of 1992 and 1996 was that Democrats won when race was kept off the agenda.

THE INCORRIGIBLY WHITE REPUBLICAN PARTY

The Resilient Racial Politics of 2000

The 2000 presidential election demonstrated the resilience of the black affinity for the Democratic Party, as well as the renewed ability of Republicans to win the White House without black support. As election season loomed, it seemed that the Republican Party had resolved to challenge the racial status quo of American politics. Their presumptive nominee, Texan George W. Bush, had received a relatively high level of black support in his gubernatorial race of 1998. By contrast, it appeared that the Democrats would nominate vice president Al Gore, a New Democrat whose record in the black community was spotty. Many Republicans hoped that 2000 would be the year in which black bipartisanship at the presidential level became a reality, for the first time since 1956. These hopes would be dashed yet again.

2000: THE SETTING

Heading into the 2000 election, a crucial question was the legacy of Bill Clinton. Clinton retained high approval ratings for his job performance, while many voters disapproved of him as a person. In his historic clash with the Republican Congress over impeachment, blacks had been his firmest supporters, both in the public and among politicians. Clinton reached out in particular to Jesse Jackson at the height of the scandal. Jackson's lenient attitude toward Clinton's sexual misconduct and subsequent perjury was emblematic of the response of the black community as a whole.

Clinton's presidency coincided with extraordinary economic growth, both for the nation and for African Americans specifically. The crime rate also declined significantly, although many black leaders complained that the incarceration rate for African American males skyrocketed during Clinton's watch. Clinton successfully maintained most federal affirmative action programs, although at the state level, affirmative action was in retreat, typically at the behest of Republicans. The GOP's image in the black community was also hurt when it was revealed that two top congressmen, including Senate Majority Leader Trent Lott, had long-standing relationships with a group of rabid segregationists, although Lott unconvincingly claimed that he had known nothing about the group's odious antiblack views. In the midterm elections, black voters showed no evidence of moving toward the GOP. The status quo of racial politics seemed as firm as ever.

THE CANDIDATES

Al Gore

Al Gore, groomed since birth for the presidency by his father, a prominent southern moderate senator, was no stranger to the politics of race. Growing up in Washington, D.C., and in Carthage, Tennessee, Gore witnessed the cost segregation exacted on his family's black servants. His father had been one of the few southern congressmen to refuse to sign the Southern Manifesto of segregation. And it was liberalism on race, among other issues, that resulted in his father's painful loss in 1970, a loss that many felt shaped his son's political sensibilities throughout his career. In his 1988 run for the nomination, Gore had made little secret of his desire to reach out to conservative whites, by attacking Jackson's qualifications and Dukakis's weakness on crime. Gore, like Clinton, was a New Democrat, but unlike Clinton, Gore never had a reservoir of good feeling in the black community. His speaking style was hardly one that would resonate with those raised in the tradition of the black church. Ideologically, Gore had never been the kind of white liberal likely to attract the affection of the Congressional Black Caucus or other national black leaders. Gore had been far from the first choice of black leaders in 1992 when Clinton put him on the ticket. Although Gore worked hard during the eight years of the Clinton presidency to woo black leaders to his cause, he also advocated getting rid of affirmative action in federal procurement contracts as part of his Reinventing Government initiative. While he lost that battle, Gore nonetheless aggravated many black federal employees who felt "reinvention" worked against black interests. A group of them released a scathing report attacking Gore's pet initiative: "Reinventing has been generally silent about fairness and equality issues . . . and has had a devastating impact on federal workers, particularly racial minorities." These incidents were not widely known, however, and Gore hoped to rally blacks in the primaries. Through personal outreach to black leaders, Gore had garnered numerous endorsements in the months leading up to the primaries. Gore's strong black support was a key part of his perceived "inevitability" as the Democratic nomination fight began.

George W. Bush

On race, as on a host of national issues, George W. Bush was something of a cipher in 1999. While he had no substantial following in the black community in his initial run for governor in 1994, he had received a relatively high fraction of the black vote (28 percent) in his 1998 reelection. Although his black support was probably a product of the overall weakness of his opponent, Bush touted it widely, as evidence of his status as a new kind of Republican. Bush also seldom brought up affirmative action, which distinguished him from many southern Republicans. When a federal appeals court outlawed affirmative action in admissions for state universities, Bush did not gloat or engage in triumphalism. Perhaps his most significant act as governor that had a racial component was his reaction (or, rather, nonreaction) to a horrific lynching in a small Texas town. As opposed to his behavior in other state tragedies, Bush did not travel to the scene to express his sorrow and dismay at this act of racist murder. When Democrats attempted to use the lynching as a means of strengthening Texas's hate crimes law, Bush quietly helped the bill die. Even though Bush's legislative inaction had more to do with the bill's inclusion of gays and lesbians, it was a decision that would come back to haunt Bush in 2000. Similarly, Bush's failure to symbolically demonstrate how seriously he took a lynching in his home state was a costly example of moral blindness.

A NOT-SO-DIFFERENT KIND OF REPUBLICAN: THE GOP PRIMARIES

As in every presidential primary since 1980, the preprimary campaign of fund-raising and name recognition proved vital to success in 2000. In their efforts to gain advantage during that period, some of the dark horses in the Republican race tried to use affirmative action to rally white conservatives to their campaign. For example, Lamar Alexander of Tennessee stated flatly that "government should stop making distinctions based on race. No discrimination, no preferences." Similarly, publisher Steve Forbes and former Vice President Dan Quayle took strong positions against affirmative action. By contrast, Bush, the front-runner, downplayed his opposition to affirmative action, refusing to even comment on anti–affirmative action referenda. Bush's brother, the governor of Florida, joined with other national leaders to keep affirmative action off the Florida ballot in 2000, as did Bush supporters in Michigan. The fear articulated by many Republicans was that this issue would hurt in the general election. If it were on the ballot in November, or the focus of the Republican general campaign, it would do little to move white voters and would enthuse minority voters against Republicans. It would also hurt Bush's effort to portray himself as a "new kind of Republican" who would finally reach out to the minority community in a way that no Republican had done since Nixon in 1960. Indeed, Bush supporters cited his appeal to Hispanics and blacks in Texas as strong reasons for Republicans to nominate him. A Republican who could take 28 percent of the black vote while winning half the Hispanic vote would cakewalk to the White House, according to these supporters.

First, though, Bush had to win the Republican nomination, and thanks to Arizona senator John McCain, that was no cakewalk. McCain, running as a populist outsider, won New Hampshire by a strong margin, stunning the Bush forces. Reeling, Bush's campaign now faced the next contest in South Carolina. At this juncture, the "new kind of Republican" showed that he knew how to appeal to, or at least appease, white racial conservatives. Two symbolic racial issues unexpectedly became part of the campaign discourse: the Confederate flag and interracial dating. South Carolina's state politics had been roiled for more than five years by the flying of the Confederate flag over the state capitol. Blacks perceived it as a direct attack on the civil rights movement. Many whites saw it as a tribute to the honor and valor of the Confederate South. The fact that it first appeared atop the statehouse during the acme of white resistance to black equality (1962) did not matter to many white Carolinians. The debate became extremely bitter in the midst of the presidential primary. A local Bush supporter, state senator Arthur Ravenal, attacked the National Association for the Advancement of Colored People, which had been leading a national boycott of the state over the issue. Ravenal labeled the group the "National Association for Retarded People" and then apologized the next day for offending retarded people by associating them with the NAACP. Bush labeled the remarks "unfortunate" and waited days to call for an apology. Bush also refused to give his opinion on the flag controversy, saying it was up to South Carolina. When first asked, McCain stated that the flag was a symbol of "racism and slavery," then the next day reverted to echoing Bush's stance that it was a states' rights question and that it was also "a symbol of heritage."

Also in the week before the crucial South Carolina voting, Bush made a trip laden with racial symbolism when he agreed to speak at Bob Jones University. The school had a long record of opposition to civil rights and was founded by men who fervently believed in divine white superiority, segregation, and the evils of Catholicism and Mormonism. More recently, it had admitted blacks but still maintained that interracial dating was against God's will.* While Bush's speech at Bob Jones did not contain any explicit or implicit references to racial issues, the visit was widely interpreted as an appeal to cultural conservatives in the South Carolina primary. McCain's record on race also came under its tightest scrutiny in South Carolina. A liberal interest group attacked McCain for hiring Richard Quinn, the editor of *Southern Partisan,* a magazine that lamented the defeat of the South in the Civil War and argued that slavery had not been so bad for blacks. Quinn himself had called Nelson Mandela a "terrorist," attacked Martin Luther King as a fraud, and advocated voting for former Ku Klux Klansman David Duke. McCain refused to fire Quinn, though Bush's campaign joined the media in criticizing the decision. So salient was race during the South Carolina campaign that McCain was even attacked for using the word "gook" to refer to his Vietnamese captors during his years as a POW. By the time of the balloting, both Bush and McCain had shown a surprising tolerance of modern racism, as manifested in their supporters Ravenal and Quinn, as well as their great deference to the Confederate flag. Bush, now running as a true conservative, not a new kind of Republican, won a strong victory in South Carolina.

The swing to the racial right did not come without its costs. Bush's appearance at Bob Jones caused a moderate New York congressman to switch to McCain (more because of the school's record of strident anti-Catholic rhetoric than its record of racism). Faye Anderson, a longtime black GOP activist, resigned from the party in bitter anger over Bush's appearance at the school. Anderson, whose resignation attracted national media attention, was also offended that Bush apologized to Catholics but not blacks. In Michigan, black voters organized to vote in the Republican primary for McCain, although probably not because they perceived McCain as more friendly to black interests. Following South Carolina, race almost disappeared

---

* After the national media furor in 2000, the university ended its ban on interracial dating, although students interested in cross-racial romance would have to get letters from their parents granting permission. Regardless, the head of the school still maintained on *Larry King Live* that interracial sex was part of a move toward the one-world government of the Antichrist.

from the Republican primaries as an issue. However, during those few days when race dominated the campaign coverage, Bush had shown a great dexterity with racial politics and a willingness to appeal to white backlash voters when necessary.

BRADLEY FUMBLES THE RACE CARD: THE DEMOCRATIC PRIMARIES

Gore's only challenger for the nomination was former New Jersey senator Bill Bradley. Bradley, a northeastern liberal, made racial equality a fundamental part of his campaign from the very start. He talked about racial issues frequently, such as racial profiling and preserving affirmative action. This was part of Bradley's attempt to run to Gore's left and appeal to the Democratic base. However, Bradley was singularly unsuccessful; much of Gore's preprimary lead in states such as Maryland was a product of his huge advantage among blacks. Even when Bradley beat Gore among whites, the black preference for Gore put him ahead. Still, Bradley continued to press Gore substantively and symbolically on race. Bradley met publicly with the Reverend Al Sharpton and sought his support. Sharpton, whose record included using the fake rape story of Tawana Brawley to inflame racial tensions in New York, as well as ugly comments against Koreans and Jews, was now "mainstreamed" by Bradley's outreach. Gore, who had avoided Sharpton up to this point, was forced to meet with the controversial leader, although Gore at first tried to do so in secret, while his campaign dissembled about the meeting. Bradley met again with Sharpton and even hired his former campaign manager as his top deputy. Bradley and Gore both recognized the importance of the black vote when, for the first time, a debate was held before a largely black audience designed to address black concerns. However, the first question at the debate was thrown out by Sharpton, allowing McCain to attack Gore and Bradley for their cozy relationship with one of the nation's "agents of intolerance."

As Bradley's campaign floundered, he put even more emphasis on race, flying to Florida to defend affirmative action and to South Carolina to attack the Confederate flag. He tried to outdo Gore in his indignation at Bush's and McCain's silence on the flag issue. But in the end, Gore's black support remained firm, and when Super Tuesday ended with Bradley resoundingly rejected in every state, he withdrew. Why did Bradley fail to rally black supporters with his strong rhetoric on racial profiling, social justice, and affirmative action? Gore benefited immensely from his strong connection with Clinton, a heroic figure in much of the black community. Bradley also failed to connect with many black Democrats. Indeed, Bradley was one of the few campaigners who could make Gore seem comparatively exciting. Bradley also failed to attract a single black elected official to his banner, a tribute to Gore's careful work gathering IOUs from mayors and members of Congress. The prominent black supporters Bradley did have were primarily sports stars, such as Michael Jordan. As Richard Nixon, Gerald Ford, or Ronald Reagan could have told Bradley, the black community has a long record of ignoring the political preferences of its star athletes. The main effect of the Bradley challenge on race was to deny Gore a "Sister Souljah" moment, an opportunity to demonstrate to conservative white voters that he was not a captive of black "special interests." Bradley, in forcing Gore to the left on race, had pushed Gore into the arms of Sharpton, who otherwise might have provided Gore with an opportunity to emulate his mentor, Clinton.

A REPUBLICAN "MINSTREL SHOW" AND SOOTHING MAXINE: A TALE OF TWO CONVENTIONS

The conventions of 2000 both featured controversies over race. The Republican convention came under attack for tokenism, as had the Republican conventions of 1972, 1976, 1980, and 1984. This echoed the earlier criticism of Gore campaign manager Donna Brazile, who had said that Republicans "would rather take pictures with black children than feed them." Liberal columnist Bob Kuttner attacked the convention as a cynical "minstrel show" in which "there were more blacks as token entertainers than there were black delegates." A speech by Colin Powell did forthrightly defend affirmative action in terms that offended some Republicans:

Some in our party miss no opportunity to roundly and loudly condemn affirmative action that helped a few thousand black kids get an education, but hardly a whimper is heard from them over lobbyists who load our federal tax codes with preferences for special interests.

Still, the Republican platform did not agree with Powell, and the loud cheers that greeted him came in spite of his views on affirmative action rather than because of them. In giving prominence to Powell, Bush foreign policy adviser Condoleezza Rice, and many other minority Republicans, the party was trying desperately to avoid the exclusionary image projected by the conventions of 1992 and 1996. The media even examined the musical choices of the party, trying to divine whether the inclusion of black and Hispanic musical stars qualified as "outreach." Bush, in his acceptance speech, praised the civil rights movement and said that "racial progress has been steady, if still too slow." However, he did not offer many policy positions likely to appeal to blacks or other minorities.

The Democratic convention in Los Angeles was a demonstration of black political power and progress. Clinton in his farewell speech to his party took credit for the lowest black unemployment in history. The video of Clinton's achievements featured Clinton with blacks, and the only other politician given a speaking part in the movie was Jesse Jackson. The irony was palpable; Clinton, who deliberately stiff-armed Jackson in 1992 to aid his quest for the White House, now ended his time in office by embracing Jackson. The burning of black churches, racial profiling, and the need for hate crimes legislation were all highlighted in Clinton's farewell. He took a dig at the Republican convention, pointing out that his cabinet resembled the Republican stage in Philadelphia, only minorities had real power in his administration. Gore's acceptance speech also made much of black progress under the Clinton administration and promised more. The contrast in podium presence was also vivid. While the Republicans elevated minor black Republicans (such as a state representative) to speaking positions, the list of minority Democratic speakers included very powerful members of Congress, governors, and cabinet officers.

Perhaps the most important function performed by modern conventions is the announcement of the nominee for vice president. The Republicans, in nominating Dick Cheney of Wyoming, had not helped themselves with minorities. Not only had Cheney been one of the only members of Congress to vote against a bill calling for Mandela's freedom, he also had no record of outreach to minorities at all. A number of other Bush choices would have offered dividends with minorities. Rumors abounded throughout the primary season that the nomination was Colin Powell's, if only he would take it. In choosing Cheney, a Republican from one of the whitest states in the country who had never had to campaign among blacks in his life, Bush belied his own rhetoric about outreach.

Gore's nominee for the vice presidency would attract even greater attention: Senator Joseph Lieberman of Connecticut. The choice induced extraordinary excitement in the Jewish community nationwide and, indeed, around the world. At the same time, Lieberman inflamed opposition among blacks. Black anti-Semitism explained some of the reaction, particularly in the case of the head of the Dallas NAACP, who advocated suspicion toward "any partnerships with Jews at that level," particularly because Jews were concerned only about money. Louis Farrakhan resurfaced to suggest that as a Jew, Lieberman was a "dual citizen of Israel" and should be questioned about his loyalty. But the larger uneasiness in the black community had little to do with Lieberman's ethnicity and much more to do with his issue positions.

Lieberman had in the past opposed affirmative action, with language similar to Bush's relatively muted opposition. In 1995 he had said, "You can't defend policies that are based on group preferences as opposed to individual opportunity," and labeled racial preferences "patently unfair." He had spoken out in favor of California's Proposition 209, although he now said that later court decisions made a national version unnecessary. "I wanted to ban quotas, and I think that's basically happened," Lieberman now explained. Unfortunately for Lieberman, both the proposition and the later court decisions were anathema to leading black Democrats. Although Lieberman averred that he now favored affirmative action, and had supported

Clinton-Gore's "mend it, don't end it" position on affirmative action, the unease among many black Democrats was obvious. Leading the charge was California congresswoman Maxine Waters. She told reporters that she might not endorse the ticket because of Lieberman's opposition to affirmative action, his support of school vouchers, and his tough stance on crime. In a dull convention's most dramatic moment, Lieberman was called before the Black Caucus to defend his record or, rather, to retreat from it bashfully. He now felt racial preferences were necessary "because history and current reality make it necessary. . . . I was for affirmative action, am for affirmative action, and will be for affirmative action!" Lieberman's retraction of his earlier views on affirmative action and other issues mollified Maxine Waters and other Black Caucus members, but analysts predicted that Lieberman would depress turnout among blacks. In addition to his other tension points with blacks, Lieberman had been one of the most caustic critics of Clinton's sexual misconduct, a stance offensive to many blacks.

BUSH'S RECORD OUTREACH: THE EARLY GENERAL ELECTION

> . . . he would surround himself by black babies, but would not go to speak to black adults, it really tipped his hand to what he is all about—trying to convince white swing voters that he is a different kind of candidate.
>
> FORMER GOP ACTIVIST FAYE ANDERSON, ON GEORGE BUSH IN 2000

> I haven't had a chance to prove my heart to people.
>
> BUSH ON HIS OUTREACH TO BLACKS

The 2000 presidential election saw the largest commitment of resources to black outreach in the modern history of the Republican Party. The GOP spent well over a million dollars on radio ads targeted directly at the black community. The radio ads touted Bush's support of school vouchers, an issue that had some appeal to urban blacks. Republicans also utilized a "New Majority Council," formed in 1997, to reach out to blacks, Asians, and Hispanics. Perhaps most important, Bush went to the NAACP convention and apologized for the party's past mistakes on civil rights. In so doing, Bush became the first Republican nominee to appear at the NAACP since Reagan in 1980. Unlike his father in 1988 and 1992, or Robert Dole in 1996, Bush actually campaigned in black areas. Yet some believed that Bush's campaign was intent not on winning black votes, but rather on convincing moderate whites that Republicans were not opposed to black equality.

It is difficult to say how much Bush's stance on the Confederate flag or his speech at Bob Jones University hurt his outreach to blacks, but surely these acts resonated far beyond South Carolina. Bush's image may also have been damaged by his reputation as the governor with the most executions to his name since the return of the death penalty in 1976. Blacks are far less supportive of the death penalty, for obvious reasons. Not only was the death penalty used in a blatantly discriminatory fashion during much of American history, there is also evidence that the current system still places a far higher value on white life than black life. In June, the case of Gary Graham, a convicted murderer on death row in Texas, briefly entered the campaign. Graham, a black man, had been convicted on the basis of one eyewitness's shaky testimony. Although Bush did little to publicize this case, the international anti–death penalty movement made it a cause célèbre in May and June. That Bush's Texas also had a record of executing blacks and Hispanics whose lawyers were asleep during their trials also did not help his outreach to those communities. Yet the fact that the Clinton/Gore administration had greatly expanded the federal death penalty mitigated any broad attack on Bush's death penalty record.

GORE'S INITIAL RESTRAINT ON RACE

Gore was advised early on by black leaders that he needed to campaign hard in the black community. However, the emphasis of the Gore campaign was on keeping centrist whites in the Democratic fold, because they had allowed Clinton to beat the Republicans twice. Some blacks complained they were being ignored in favor of the white vote and, to a lesser extent, the Hispanic vote. Gore gradually increased his focus on race as the campaign went on. In September, speaking at Howard University, Gore highlighted a local incident that he linked to racial profiling.* Still, Gore was not highlighting racial issues on the scale that Bradley had in his campaign. A *Washington Post* article argued that many blacks were supporting Gore as the "lesser of two evils" and compared Gore unfavorably to Clinton, still a heroic figure in much of the black community.

Yet while Gore was not electrifying black audiences or speaking to their issues with great frequency early in the campaign, some felt that he had not gone far enough to reach out to white voters. Senator John Breaux, a moderate Democrat, argued that Gore needed "a Sister Souljah moment" to repeat Clinton's calculated insult to Jesse Jackson. Unlike Clinton, or Jimmy Carter, Gore made no public stands against symbols of black extremism or against any component of the black agenda. Indeed, Gore very quietly endorsed the proposition that blacks might receive some form of reparations for slavery, a very unpopular idea with whites.[†]

Gore's reluctance with racial topics was much commented on by African Americans following the first debate. Black radio host Tom Joyner raised the issue with Gore in a postdebate interview:

> We've got these people registered to vote, we've got people fired up ... but last night during the debate, neither one of you addressed issues for us, for African Americans. . . . I didn't hear anything about affirmative action ... we didn't hear about racial profiling, we didn't hear about reparations ... all these things that affect us we heard nothing about.

Gore blamed the absence of black issues on the moderator and promised to bring up the topic directly in the second debate. However, it was in the third debate when the issue came up most dramatically.

---

* Gore's link was puzzling, as the officer and the victim were both black.
[†] The Republican restraint on race in 2000 is amply demonstrated by their failure to run an antireparations campaign. Gore's support for legislation to consider reparations could have been used against him to devastating effect by the Republicans. Surely the late Lee Atwater would not have let it go without comment.

While opposing quotas because "they're against the American way," Gore strongly endorsed affirmative action. Bush, pressed by Gore aggressively to state his position, came out in favor of affirmative "access" but opposed affirmative action if it involved quotas. Gore almost blocked Bush's stance. No candidate had ever been so strident in his endorsement of affirmative action in a fall presidential debate. This move signaled a shift in Gore's strategy. The last month of his campaign would emphasize race to a much greater degree.

ENDGAME: THE DEMOCRATS TURN UP THE HEAT ON RACE

The tone of the last month of the presidential race was set by a new force in presidential politics: an aggressive national ad campaign by the dean of civil rights groups, the NAACP. Under the leadership of former Democratic congressman Kweisi Mfume, the civil rights organization ran radio and television ads of unprecedented emotionalism and rhetoric. One radio ad featured an announcer invoking the police dogs and water cannons used against civil rights demonstrators. The NAACP ad that received the widest attention was a television spot featuring the daughter of the black man lynched by racist whites during Bush's tenure as governor of Texas. The victim, James Byrd Jr., had been dragged behind a pickup truck by a chain until he died. The television ad featured scary black-and-white footage of a pickup truck dragging a chain through Texas back roads, while on the voice-over the daughter almost accused Bush of killing her father a second time.

> I'm Renee Mullins, James Byrd's daughter. On June 7, 1998, in Texas, my father was killed. He was beaten, chained and then dragged three miles to his death—all because he was black. So when Governor George W. Bush refused to support hate crimes legislation, it was like my father was killed all over again. Call George W. Bush and tell him to support hate crimes legislation. We won't be dragged away from our future.

The NAACP arranged for Mullins to speak to black audiences across the country, weaving the terrible story of her father's murder into an implied plea to vote for Gore. Republicans cried foul, but the raw emotionalism and the exploitation of tragedy should have reminded them of their own Willie Horton campaign of 1988. Mullins's speaking tour against Bush mirrored the speaking tour of Horton's victims in 1988. Republicans tried desperately to counter the Byrd ads with facts, such as Bush's endorsement of earlier hate crimes legislation and the fact that two of the three killers were sentenced to death and the third to life in prison. But as in 1988, when Democrats had argued that the Republicans were distorting the Horton case and Massachusetts's furlough program, the facts were immaterial. The NAACP ads allowed Gore to whip up fear and fervor among his black base, without looking mean, as Carter had in 1980.

While the inflammatory television ad received the most coverage in the media, the NAACP also launched its largest, and most transparently partisan, voter registration and turnout drive in U.S. history. At the same time, the Democratic Party began to run ads on black radio stations touting Gore's record on affirmative action and his plans for addressing racial profiling. Yet despite these activities, there remained a distinct lack of enthusiasm for Gore, particularly when compared to the reverence many blacks had for Clinton. A community activist in Chicago told a reporter that it seemed as if the Democrats' focus was on scaring blacks with the idea that if Bush wins, "all hell is going to break loose." Similarly, a national black political commentator, Tavis Smiley, said, "As far as I'm concerned Bush . . . is nothing more than a serial killer. But we can't expect that much more from Gore."

Perhaps in response to such attitudes, Gore himself turned up the rhetoric. Gore refused to criticize* the NAACP ads that accused Bush of condoning lynching; instead, he emphasized that the lynching had occurred in Bush's home state, as if that somehow made the governor culpable. Then three days before the election, speaking in a black church, Gore launched the harshest racial rhetoric of his campaign, again linking Bush to the lynching and to the Confederate flag in South Carolina. He accused Bush of employing code words to disguise his intent of turning back the clock on black progress. Gore

---

* Some principled Democrats, such as Senator Bob Kerrey, did criticize the NAACP's lynching ad as race baiting.

implied that if Bush won, the Supreme Court would again consider blacks "three fifths of a human being." In the last weekend of the campaign, Gore even appeared at a rally with James Byrd's sister, who described in graphic detail her brother's dismemberment and falsely claimed that Bush "doesn't think that's a hate crime!" Bush personally did not respond to Gore's attacks, although surrogate Republicans continued to insist that the attacks were unfair.

CONCLUSION: BLACKS REFUSE TO JUDGE BUSH ON HIS "HEART"

> I know the current wisdom, "Well, he's a Republican, a white guy Republican, and therefore he has no chance to get the African American vote." You know they may be right, but that's not going to stop me. So you'll find me in neighborhoods the Republicans normally don't go to.
>
> GEORGE W. BUSH, 2000

When election day ended, the outreach to African Americans that Bush had made so much of was a tremendous failure. Nationwide, Bush received 8 percent of the black vote, a stunning rejection. Bush failed to achieve the anemic support levels of his father or even the much-disliked Ronald Reagan. In his home state of Texas, Bush did even worse, getting just 5 percent of the black vote, a fifth of his state-wide total two years before. Why did the black vote remain so resolutely Democratic?

One explanation was Bill Clinton. Clinton remained the most popular politician, black or white, among black voters. Moreover, he had presided over a golden age of economic growth for African Americans. Black and Hispanic unemployment in the last year of Clinton's presidency was the lowest ever recorded. The growth in household income among blacks was impressive and sustained during much of Clinton's presidency. Some even suggested that Clinton's problems, which had caused "Clinton fatigue" in many white Americans, actually contributed to his popularity among blacks. So many black leaders, from Adam Clayton Powell to Martin Luther King Jr., had been investigated by federal officers and attacked for sexual improprieties that Clinton's problems were a call to arms rather than a time for judgment. Even though Gore limited Clinton's role in the campaign, Clinton was wisely deployed to some black areas in the last month of the campaign. Another explanation was the NAACP campaign and the hard-biting rhetoric of Gore's last weeks of campaigning. As with the 1996 "epidemic" of church burnings, the Republicans were damaged in 2000 by accusations of racial violence and racial insensitivity.

Black loyalty and black mobilization were also involved in the riveting deadlock in Florida that made 2000 the longest wait for a winner since the presidential election of 1876. Black turnout in Florida rose an astonishing 65 percent from 1996 levels and accounted for 16 percent of the state's electorate, up from 10 percent in 1996. Bush received only 7 percent of that newly enlarged black vote in Florida. Why did black turnout skyrocket in Florida? Jackson, who had campaigned hard for Gore in Florida, kept linking George Bush to Jeb Bush, his brother, the governor of Florida, with his simple slogan "Stay Out [of] the Bushes!" But Jackson had been in Florida long before the campaign season. When Jeb Bush had presided over a retreat on affirmative action, Jackson and other black leaders had promised to "remember in November!" The extraordinary jump in turnout in Florida, along with higher levels of Democratic loyalty than even the beloved Clinton had experienced, demonstrated that blacks in Florida had indeed remembered. Without that surge in black support for Gore, Bush would have won Florida without the help of the Supreme Court.

It was also widely alleged that there were racial patterns to some of the voting irregularities that occupied the attention of the nation for the month of November. Not only were black voters far more likely to vote at precincts with error-prone voting machines, blacks had been aggressively struck from the rolls in the year before the election. Florida had hired an outside vendor with Republican ties to remove felons from its rolls. At least eight thousand names were unlawfully deleted, disproportionately minorities. Jackson, Sharpton, and the NAACP's Mfume all claimed that even more blatant disenfranchisement of blacks had occurred and called for a federal investigation. By the time a deeply divided Supreme Court stopped the counting in Florida and effectively gave the presidency to Bush, the allegations of large-scale disenfranchisement of blacks were widely believed in the black community. Surveys showed a racial divide in acceptance of Bush's victory, with blacks by overwhelming majorities believing that Bush had stolen the election. Thus, the 2000 presidential election, which had at first seemed so promising for Republican outreach to blacks, ended with the party more alienated from African Americans than at any time since the Goldwater campaign of 1964.

One bright spot for the GOP was the rise in Hispanic and Asian support the party experienced in 2000. Bush captured 31 percent of the Hispanic vote, proving that not all outreach to minorities was fruitless for the GOP. Yet even the leader of the New Majority Council worried that the message for many Republicans might well be that the black vote was simply unreachable. The last time the Republicans had conducted serious outreach to blacks and been rejected, 1960, had ended with the leader of the GOP saying "the hell with them [blacks]." Would Bush take a similar position? Forty years after Kennedy's phone call to Mrs. King, the first election of the new millennium suggested that the post-1960 status quo in racial politics was as firm as ever.

THE FUTURE OF RACE IN PRESIDENTIAL CAMPAIGNS

The prejudices of centuries die hard, and even when they wane, the institutional frameworks that sustained them are bound to linger.

SOCIOLOGIST ORLANDO PATTERSON

This study began at a moment of great tension in the New Deal coalition, with both blacks and racially conservative whites wavering in their allegiance to FDR's party. For the next forty years, presidential candidates had to structure their campaigns with a keen cognizance of the power of race in American elections. Democratic candidates who were not nimble on racial politics were defeated without exception, sometimes by landslide margins. Certain Republican candidates, such as Bush in 1988 or Nixon in 1968–72, demonstrated that appeals to white fears and racial animosities were an effective aid to White House hopes. Jimmy Carter and Bill Clinton, the only Democrats to win the White House since the second Reconstruction of 1964–65, were distinguished from all other Democratic nominees by their strong black support and understanding of black political culture. Both men also carefully insulated themselves on racial matters by reaching out to white racial conservatives and muting their appeals for racial policy shifts. The defeat of Al Gore in 2000 resulted in part from his new image as an Al Sharpton Democrat, who made no overture to racial conservatism. Many other issues affected these eleven presidential elections, and race was often tertiary compared to foreign and domestic issues. But race always mattered, particularly when the primary campaigns are also considered.

From the moment that John F. Kennedy picked up the phone and called Coretta Scott King, black voters joined their political fate to the Democratic Party. Kennedy's symbolic act of sympathy signaled the end of the black flirtation with the GOP that had characterized the 1956 presidential election. After LBJ signed the 1965 Voting Rights Act, no Democrat won a clear victory among white voters, although Clinton came quite close.* These core realities of racial politics remained unchanged throughout the eleven elections examined in these pages. That they could remain unchanged while the substantive questions of racial policies underwent vast and rapid shifts is impressive. As Kennedy and Nixon toured the nation in 1960, the second-class citizenship of African Americans, even in the supposedly enlightened North, was an inescapable reality. There was no constitutional right to racial equality and nondiscrimination in housing, voting, jury duty, or even marriage. While the right to racial equality in education had been recognized by a Republican-led Supreme Court in 1954, it remained an unfulfilled promise for decades. African Americans languished far behind white Americans in every measure of wealth, health, education, and status. Both candidates had to be careful not to get too close even to the moderate black leadership, for fear of alienating those whites openly disdainful of blacks as a race. The majority of African Americans were not participants in the election, greatly attenuating their worth as coalition partners.

When Al Gore and George Bush campaigned in the fall of 2000, African Americans were in positions of influence, as a bloc of voters and as political leaders. Both parties went to great lengths at their conventions to demonstrate their openness to the black community. A black man, Colin Powell, could have had the vice presidential nomination in either party merely by expressing an interest. The debate over racial equality under the law was long over. Neither pro-

---

* Some surveys suggest Clinton narrowly won the white vote in 1992 but lost in 1996, while others suggest the opposite. The national exit polls, however, give Republicans a narrow victory among whites in 1992 and a four-point margin among whites in 1996. The outcome of the 2000 election suggests in any case that the crucial factor in both 1992 and 1996 was the presence of Perot as a divider of the white anti-Democratic vote.

ponents nor opponents of affirmative action, hate crimes legislation, or laws against racial profiling could credibly claim that any of these issues were of the scope or importance of the great civil rights battles of the sixties. Although Jesse Jackson and others would label each modern cause the new Selma, the comparison was laughable. While the new issues touched on important questions of fairness and black-white equality, they were not, in the end, arguments about black humanity itself. There remained, of course, inequalities between blacks and whites, in many fields of endeavor and by many social indicators. Yet the advances in black economic and political power were vast. Thus, the changes in racial politics were both substantive, in terms of the issues addressed, and procedural, in terms of the role blacks played in the political system and the degree of respect that presidential candidates had to extend to them.

The Republican strategy of neglecting the black vote and, in some elections, exploiting America's racial divide has been quite successful measured by the near lock Republicans had on the White House from 1968 to 1992. Only the combination of Watergate, Carter's own moderation on race, and Ford's refusal to cater either to racial conservatives or to black voters permitted the sole Democratic victory during that period. Republicans took from the 1960 campaign the lesson that the black vote was rigidly Democratic. This prophecy became self-fulfilling following the Goldwater debacle, in which the party learned to avoid the rabid racism of many of Goldwater's southern supporters. As a result of Nixon's southern strategy of 1968–72, the Republican Party became increasingly dominated by southern whites, many of them former segregationists such as Jesse Helms, Strom Thurmond, and Trent Lott. In raw political terms, trading the 30–40 percent of the black vote that the Republicans won in 1956–60 for the far larger white southern and northern backlash voting blocs was brilliant. The great triumphs of modern American conservatism, such as the Nixon landslide of 1972, the Reagan victories of 1980 and 1984, and the Gingrich revolution of 1994, have been almost all-white affairs as a result. Race was far from the only issue uniting the incorrigibly white coalition of the Republican Party, and it could be argued that each victory had less to do with race than the one that preceded it. Yet race remains salient, if only in the hard-nosed calculations of political operatives of both parties, who make assumptions about turnout and loyalty among the races that continue to structure campaigns.

Still, racial animosities and fears are not as effective at motivating white voters as they were in the fevered atmosphere of 1968–72 or even 1988. Republicans have not repeated their Willie Horton campaign in any subsequent election. With the exception of a few statements against racial preferences in 1992, and Dole's bizarre and brief shift in tactics at the end of the 1996 campaign, Republican candidates have largely avoided racial issues since 1988. Perhaps there has been a sudden upsurge in electoral morality in the upper echelons of the party. Far more likely, however, is that polling data and political instincts have told them that such appeals to white voters will backfire, as Reagan's pollster Richard Wirthlin believes. Why else have general election Republican nominees downplayed affirmative action since Nixon in 1972? Not only is it an issue on which the Republicans are on the side of the vast majority of white Americans, it is also one that can be easily simplified for public consumption in the age of the sound bite and the thirty-second TV spot. Yet there has been no general election ad campaign linked to a Republican presidential candidate on affirmative action, even as Republicans have used it successfully in statewide and congressional elections. It is of course possible that the good economic times of the recent past have led to a kinder, gentler white electorate and that an economic reversal could again make appeals to white fears and prejudices politically profitable. Alternatively, perhaps Republicans are so deeply associated with racial conservatism in the minds of white voters that they do not need to stress the issue. While both of these explanations have merit, it seems incontrovertible that racial appeals are becoming less effective at rallying whites to the GOP.

While racial issues and tactics have declined in importance as wedge issues aiding Republican hopes among whites, Democrats still retain the loyalty of African Americans on the basis of the past behavior of the two parties. The legacy of the anti–civil rights positions of Goldwater and Reagan, the white backlash sloganeering of Nixon and Agnew, and the cynical exploitation of racial fears by G.H.W. Bush has helped cement the overwhelmingly Democratic tendency of the African American electorate. Clinton was able to woo Reagan Democrats back to the party, in part by careful positioning on race, while retaining landslide support levels among blacks, because blacks did not see the Republican Party as a realistic option. Even when Republicans tried some measure of outreach, as they did in 2000, the vast majority of blacks remained convinced that the Republicans were still the party of Nixon and Reagan. Republican candidates for the White House start out every presidential election more than ten points behind because the campaign tactics and governing policies of the Republican presidents who preceded them deny them any significant black support. How long will blacks remain nearly monolithic in their loyalty to Democrats in presidential elections?

THE INEVITABILITY OF BLACK BIPARTISANSHIP?

> Sometime before the end of this century, a very substantial minority, if not a majority, of African Americans are going to begin identifying with political conservatism rather than political liberalism.
>
> CONSERVATIVE ANALYST ADAM MYERSON, 1994

For forty years, some Republicans, black and white, have predicted that a large group of black voters would defect to the GOP. Each election, those hopes have been dashed; blacks remain the most loyal members of the New Deal coalition. Yet such a singular devotion to a party by a social group is unlikely to persist over time. Because of the nature of America's competitive two-party system, several forces will eventually test and overcome the Democratic loyalty of blacks. The danger for African Americans in persisting in Democratic allegiance has always been that they will be ignored or demonized by the Republicans and taken for granted by the Democrats. Since 1960, all the Democrats had to do was be marginally more sensitive to black concerns than the Republicans, a task made quite easy by the modern Republican Party. The strategic impetus for Republicans to woo blacks away from the Democrats is obvious. Had Republicans received even one in four black votes in 1976 and 1992, they would have held the White House for almost thirty years. Blacks are now the essential core of the Democratic coalition, without whom victory is inconceivable. This helps explain the tactics adopted by some Democrats to ensure continued black loyalty. Both parties have learned to play the race card with vicious brutality. The Willie Horton ads of 1988 were answered by linking Republicans to church burnings in 1996 and to the Byrd lynching in 2000. Because of these tactics, and because of the stubborn unwillingness of Republicans to offer even a modicum of compromise to blacks on issues such as affirmative action, racial profiling, or urban spending, black loyalty to the Democratic Party increased in 2000, despite the superficial outreach of George Bush. To all appearances, the black center of the Democratic coalition remained as firm as ever.

The decay in that loyalty is difficult to perceive at this point, but it will come. Consider two historic examples. No group was more loyal to the Democratic coalition in the post–Civil War era than white southerners. Political scientists considered the South to be a one-party system, in which a Republican victory was virtually inconceivable. Yet the region now features a competitive two-party system, tilted toward the Republicans in presidential elections. This transformation has been produced by sharp differences on policy matters, most importantly race. It is possible that a similar issue could emerge to divide blacks from white Democrats. More likely, however, would be a gradual realignment similar to that which occurred among many Catholics during the same period. At the turn of the century, ethnic whites in urban centers were a bulwark of the Democratic coalition. Because of the legacy of the great urban machines and the lingering antipopery of some Republicans, these voters were almost as loyally Democratic as white southerners. Beginning with the Eisenhower elections, and accelerating with the Nixon and Reagan victories, Catholics began to abandon their Democratic allegiance. There was no single dramatic issue or moment, although again, race was a major issue pushing urban white Catholics toward the GOP. But one key to Catholic bipartisanship was a lessening of societal prejudice against them. A group that is threatened by the majority is more likely to vote as a bloc. A minority group that has seen its members rise to the highest positions in corporate and political life may eventually become more bipartisan. Social prejudice against Catholics, a significant political barrier in 1960, has now been relegated to the uttermost fringes of American public life. Just as the victory of Kennedy and the doors to Catholics that it opened eventually made it easier for Catholics to vote Republican, the lessening of racial prejudice and the extraordinary economic and political progress of blacks during the Clinton years will contribute to black bipartisanship in the near future. Indeed, another cause of the decline in Democratic loyalty among Catholics was economic and educational progress, which helped break the urban machines. Although there is little evidence of conservatism among upper-income blacks at present, if societal prejudice lessens, wealthier blacks will be far more likely to emulate wealthier whites and vote GOP.

A third historic example also suggests itself: the sudden movement away from the GOP seen among nonsouthern blacks in 1932–36. Blacks had favored the party of Lincoln in elections from 1868 to 1932, and many blacks had strong emotional ties to Republicans. The Republican Party, for all its flaws, was seen as the only one that had ever lifted a finger for Negroes. Most significant, most southern white supremacist politicians were Democrats. Thus, for many blacks, registering as a Democrat in the 1920s "was a form of heresy practically unknown and unpractised . . . like announcing one had typhoid." Yet the crushing nature of the Great Depression pulled blacks toward FDR's nonracial policies, which took the side of lower-class Americans against entrenched economic interests. Since blacks were overwhelmingly poor, they became part of the great New Deal realignment, although FDR made little outreach to their community. However, a change along those lines is unlikely because the increasing diversity of black America has lessened the nonracial connections among African Americans. Compared to 1932, the distinctiveness of blacks beyond the mere fact of skin color has been greatly reduced. One possible exception is the higher rates of religiosity among blacks. The black church is a far more influential social and political force in its community than is the "white church" among whites (indeed, the ease with which the "black church" is discussed hints at the far more uniform acceptance of a certain archetype of Christianity in the black community). The Bush administration is already attempting to use religion as a wedge issue, to peel off blacks from the Democratic Party, as seen by Bush's inclusion of an array of black religious figures in two major policy meetings at the White House in his first fifty days in office. Such attempts will increase, particularly because one of the best predictors of vote choice in 2000 was frequency of attendance at religious services. The Republicans will focus their attention on upper-class blacks and the more religious members of the community over the next few years.

George W. Bush, despite his notable failure to win black votes in 2000, could be the pivotal figure in returning a sizable number of black voters to the party of Lincoln. In gubernatorial elections, many Republicans have failed to get black votes in their initial elections, but done much better in their reelection drives, if they put political capital behind outreach during their first term. This pattern charac-terized Bush's own success with black voters in his gubernatorial elections. The early signs are that Bush intends to try to heal the deep racial wounds of the 2000 campaign. In the months following his tortuous victory, Bush reached out to black religious leaders and met with the Congressional Black Caucus. He phoned Jackson, still the de facto leader of black America, to express his support as the rev-erend was embroiled in a sex scandal. While this act of sympathy hardly had the resonance of Kennedy's phone call to Coretta Scott King forty years previous, it did signify Bush's personal interest in bridging the racial divide. One cannot imagine any previous Republi-can president making a similar call to Jackson.

Of course, the black electorate is hardly likely to be seduced by mere superficial outreach. Ford launched a similar charm offensive in the early months of his presidency but then failed to propose policies that matched his talk. In 1980 Reagan campaigned harder in the black community than any Republican since Henry Cabot Lodge in 1960, but he reaped little reward at the polls because of his far right social views and his opposition to the civil rights movement. Bush may also find many blacks unwilling to forget his father's cynical use of race in 1988, and there are lingering tensions over the Florida vote that are far more significant in the black community than in the nation as a whole. To move his black support much above the anemic 8 percent he received in 2000, Bush must offer at least one high-profile policy proposal designed to appeal to blacks—perhaps a strong defense of affirmative action or a plan to force local police agencies to monitor and combat racial profiling.* Each of these would exact a political cost on Bush, but those disturbed by these moves would have nowhere to go politically, since Democratic support for both measures would be high. The only other hope for Bush to steal a sizable fraction of the black vote from the Democrats in 2004 would be running with a black vice presidential nominee. The historic grandeur of the move would go a long way toward repairing the Republican image among blacks. If some black organizations and individuals felt compelled to rally around Supreme Court nominee Clarence Thomas in 1991, despite his weak civil rights record, similar forces would work in the election of 2004, particularly if the nominee were not as conservative as Thomas. The obvious candidate, Colin Powell, polls far higher among whites than blacks. Yet to be successful in disrupting the Democratic hopes for victory, Powell would need to receive only 20 percent of the black vote, surely a reachable goal given his moderate record. The exuberance and enthusiasm of the Jewish community in response to the nomination of Joseph Lieberman in 2000 was as nothing compared to the excitement that would be produced by the major-party nomination of a black for the second highest office in the land.

The razor-thin margin of Bush's victory will force Republican strategists in 2004 to compete for black votes as they have not since 1960. Aiding in that effort will be the relative silence on racial issues that characterized Republicans in 1992–2000. With the disappearance of Pat Buchanan's white nativism from Republican politics, yet another obstacle to black outreach has vanished. Still, even with a black nominee on the ticket, the Republicans will not find it easy to get much more than a fifth of the black vote. Not only does the

---

* In August 2001, Bush's Justice Department filed a brief supporting a contentious set-aside program for highway contracting. Although many conservative groups were unhappy with the move, it did signal that the Bush administration is open to putting black outreach ahead of conservative purity.

Democratic Party have a far better record on civil rights questions since 1965, but also the vast majority of black elected officials are Democrats. In addition, the social costs of becoming a Republican can be quite high for many blacks. A *Washington Post* headline even asked whether Colin Powell was a "black man or a Bush man," as if Republicanism were somehow incongruent with blackness. Social ostracism and challenges to racial authenticity will not disappear anytime soon. The NAACP's anti-Bush ads of 2000 also demonstrate that forces within the Democratic coalition will not hesitate to emulate Lee Atwater in their cynical exploitation of racial incidents, if it serves to maintain the nearly monolithic character of black partisanship. If Republican outreach to the black vote is sustained, sincere, and promising, the response of Democratic campaign strategists might well be even more extreme than the lynching ads of 2000.* The battle for the black vote in 2004 could be surprisingly intense.

STRATEGY FOR AN EVOLVING COLOR LINE: THE FADING OF BLACK AND WHITE CAMPAIGNS

> We cannot remind ourselves too often that the concept of "race" as it is used in commonsense, everyday language to signify connectedness and common characteristics in relation to type and descent is a relatively recent and absolutely modern invention.
>
> SOCIOLOGIST PAUL GILROY, 2000

The true test for campaign strategists of both parties in the twenty-first century will be to address the evolving nature of race itself.

---

* Frightening a minority group into continued partisan loyalty has a long history in American politics. In the 1920s, the scoundrel-hero of Boston Irish politics, Mayor James Curley, had associates burn crosses on hilltops before his campaign speeches. By simulating bravery in the face of Ku Klux Klan activism, Curley made voting for him a test of Catholic pride. As with Catholics, black voters will be less influenced by fear campaigns as black political and economic power grows. Thus, Republican hopes for black bipartisanship rest on ending the remaining social barriers to black progress.

Racial politics in America is undergoing a paradigm shift unprecedented in American history. The first sign came in early 2001, when Hispanics replaced African Americans as the largest minority group. The politics of black and white, always a simplification, now and forever will be the politics of black and brown and yellow and red and white, a politics of a mosaic of ethnicities competing and allying one with the other. The demographic dominance of whites will be greatly reduced in the next hundred years, thanks to differing birthrates and the diversity of recent immigrants. While it is unlikely that whites will lose majority status in the next hundred years, they could become a plurality in many of the largest states, such as California, New York, and Texas. Many of the accepted truths about racial politics will have withered by then. The party that responds effectively to the new complexity of America's racial politics stands to gain a tremendous electoral advantage.

In the long term, instead of racial groups allying and competing with one another, the clear lines dividing them will begin to fade. Race as a category is undergoing a subtle but vitally important shift. By the end of the twenty-first century, most Americans will realize that race is a social construct, of little meaning or utility in and of itself. The 2000 census was the first in which respondents were allowed to pick more than one race, resulting in 126 combinations and categories. The Census Bureau made this change in response to thousands of complaints from descendants of interracial relationships, who resented having to put one parent's heritage over the other's. While the multiracial vote will be too small and divided to matter much in any presidential election in the near term, the number of multiracial citizens is growing exponentially. Moreover, the official recognition of multiraciality will foster the consciousness of the multiracial as a group, and simultaneously erode the more established categories, by exposing the arbitrary nature of the racial classifications themselves.

The increasing influence of Hispanic culture will also affect the way Americans think about race. The conception of race in Puerto Rico, and throughout much of Latin America, is one of skin shade, of tone, of nuanced and often unspoken gradations between white and black. It is a conception corrosive of the American black-white divide as currently understood.* While this may seem odd to other Americans, it is in fact the traditional American racial categories that are unusual by global standards. Americans define race differently from any other nation on earth. Many people considered black in this country are not so considered when they travel abroad. Colin Powell, currently the most likely "black" occupant of the White House, and the first "black" to guide our foreign policy, would not be considered black in his ancestral homeland of Jamaica. Nor would he be black in Africa. Seventy-five percent of African Americans have some white ancestry; as the diversity of America increases, the idea that anyone with any visible black heritage is African American will be more openly challenged. The "one drop of blood" rule of blackness is already fading as the echoes of slavery and Jim Crow grow fainter.

The process of globalization will also cause Americans to see their similarities and ignore their diminishing racial differences. The cultural values shared between a black American and a white American will be far more compelling than the racial similarities that the one shares with a Nigerian and the other with a Croat. As a response to Anglo cultural hegemony, the black pride movement of the 1960s correctly sought out the regnant examples of cultural affinity between African Americans and Africans. Many cultural differences between white and black Americans remain. Yet through the Internet, television, trade, and travel, the ties that bind Americans and distinguish us from other cultures and nations will be emphasized. The dismay and shock that black intellectual Cornel West felt when a Latin American scholar labeled him an "Anglo" because of his cultural values will become a far more common experience, and the dis-

---

* Of course, the Hispanic conception of race is no ideal. Throughout Latin America, wealth is concentrated among whiter citizens, while poverty is overwhelmingly darker and more Afro-Indian. Governments throughout the region deny that race is a problem for their countries, but social discrimination by skin shade is an accepted practice, if one that is seldom discussed. The assumption throughout much of Latin America is that it is "denigrating to marry someone much darker than oneself." As a black leader in Latin America noted, "Brazil is the most successful racist system in the world," because black disempowerment is hidden behind the myth of racial equality. Intermarriage alone will not defeat racism; it certainly has not in Latin America.

may will be replaced by agreement over time. Even advances in medical technology, such as organ transplants and magnetic resonance imaging, will serve to deemphasize skin color in favor of our shared humanity. Would Louis Farrakhan turn down a Jewish liver? Would even David Duke reject a kidney from a black donor?*

To proclaim that race will be fundamentally altered in the next hundred years is to say that America will lose what has been a dominant theme of the entirety of its history as a nation. From the earliest appearance of English colonies on the American continent, firm racial categories allied with the systematic oppression of African Americans have been fundamental to the American story. White hegemony has been a constant, if often denied or ignored, challenge to America's decency, humanity, and justice. When Jefferson argued that all men were created equal, he lived a life of luxury made possible only through the ownership of other humans. When Madison promised that his new system of constitutional government had solved the problem of majority faction, he must have known that his extended republic would permit the white majority faction to oppress and enslave the black minority faction. There were no coalition partners ready to compromise on the question of white dominance, and there would not be for almost a hundred years. When Lincoln led a war over slavery, he still defended white superiority and political supremacy. In America's long and illustrious history, every white politician shared to a lesser or greater degree in the crimes of

---

* The terrorist attacks of September 11 took place after this book was nearly completed. The sense of national purpose and unity that followed was occasionally depicted as evidence that Americans were moving beyond race and "hyphenated-Americans." During previous periods of national crisis, advances in race relations have certainly occurred, although they were typically followed by reassertion of white dominance. A prolonged war against terror could contribute to the diminishing significance of race in the new century. The military as an institution is among the most integrated in America; as it rises in public esteem and prominence, this may tend to ameliorate existing levels of prejudice. And the conflict has served to highlight the cultural and political distinctiveness of Americans, thus implicitly contributing to a sense of common values that unite Americans of all races. Finally, engaging in equal status interactions with shared goals is the classic method for reducing intergroup tension and prejudice, according to the "contact hypothesis" that motivated the integration movement.

the nation against its black residents and citizens. Not even those who in moments of mingled courage and political expediency took brave moves for black equality were free of the unearned benefits of white privilege: not Lincoln, not FDR, not Kennedy, Johnson, or Clinton.

Thus, to suggest that white privilege and the color line that made it possible will fade in the next hundred years might sound hopelessly naive or even be perceived as a malicious attempt to ignore existing racial inequalities. Yet would it have been any more difficult to convince Teddy Roosevelt and Woodrow Wilson at the dawn of this century that a hundred years later a black man would serve as secretary of state? That a black man could rank ahead of all competitors in the hearts of his white compatriots as a presidential candidate? Roosevelt and Wilson, antipodes in so many ways, were united in their belief in white supremacy; neither man could even imagine social and political equality for the "inferior" race. Today, our minds are as tied to our current racial categories as theirs were to the rank ordering of those categories. The American categories, unique in the world, are products of a particular moment in history, and they will undergo tremendous stress in the twenty-first century. The implications of this change for the future of American politics are as significant as the consequences of the invention of white identity in America in the seventeenth and eighteenth centuries.

Only a Pollyanna would soon anticipate a day in which race will not matter in presidential politics, but only one locked in the past would fail to see that race will decline in importance. Indeed, that process is outlined in the preceding chapters. Though race was not a central issue in the 1960 campaign, that was merely the quiet before the storm or, indeed, the eye of the hurricane of racial politics, a period of deceptive calm following the cataclysm of war and Reconstruction. Beneath the surface of the electoral politics of 1960, racial tensions were gathering tremendous force. Race moved to the fore of the nation's agenda in 1964–72 because it was essential to bring African Americans into the nation's political, social, and economic life. That process, still incomplete, had progressed so far by 2001 that blacks had been the deciding vote in two of the last three presidential elections. Yet racial issues were not prominent in these elections; indeed, it was part of Clinton's brilliance that submerged race as an issue during the 1990s. Race mattered in recent presidential elections, but it mattered less, and in different ways, than it had earlier.

Du Bois proclaimed in 1903 that the color line would be the dominant motif of the twentieth century; his bold prognostication was amply justified by ensuing events, including the effect of racial politics on presidential campaigns. The fading of that line will not be the dominant story of the next hundred years of American life, because history is written about appearances, not fadings; about presences, not absences. But the receding of the color line can already be glimpsed. We will not enter the color-blind utopia of some conservatives, in which white norms and values will be adopted wholesale. Nixon's hope of "assimilation" as a solution to our racial crisis will not be realized. The entirety of American politics and culture will become far more integrated, as American worksites, churches, and, yes, political parties and families become far more integrated. Campaigns that are structured around starkly divided races will simply become ineffective.

If race diminishes as an organizing principle of our politics, this will signal the revitalization of class in American politics. Robert Huckfeldt and Carol Kohfeld, among many other political scientists, have argued convincingly that Republican appeals to racial prejudice and white fears undermined the class politics of the New Deal. Lower-class whites were brought into the GOP coalition, putting their cultural and racial identity over their economic interests. As race declines in significance, many of these whites may return to the Democratic fold (although the emerging religiosity divide in American politics will keep some in the GOP). Similarly, some wealthier and/or socially conservative blacks will stop voting by race and see the GOP as representing their interests. As racial categories decay, economic inequalities between blacks and whites will not magically disappear. But a new emphasis on class will draw the lines of policy debate with increasing clarity; the problems of the urban underclass, left largely untouched by affirmative action and other current racial issues, may be more easily addressed as race evolves and fades.

As the black-white divide becomes less omnipresent, the racial strategies of the presidential campaigns of 1960–2000 will become inconceivable, relics of a bygone era. For the forty-year period of this study, the color line undergirded the strategies and tactics that provided many of the most dramatic moments in presidential campaigns. When Johnson fought for the Civil Rights Act against the brewing white backlash, both he and those who hated him accepted "race" as an existential truth of American life. Busing, which roiled the campaigns of 1972, was obviously premised on being able to count black children and white children, on the meaningfulness of counting and categorizing. Bill Clinton worked hard to submerge affirmative action as an issue in 1992 and 1996 while preserving it as a policy, but how will affirmative action operate as the population of multiracial Americans skyrockets? The number of issues in American politics that have direct relevance to race has been declining since 1972, and this process will continue. Put differently, many issues that have been perceived as racial, such as welfare reform or urban poverty, will be more likely to be framed as class issues, with whites and blacks on both sides.

The declining significance of race in presidential politics does not mean that race will disappear as a consideration in campaigns. Even if blacks become more bipartisan in presidential elections, a nearly unified black voting bloc will be quickly reassembled if there is a major gap in sensitivity to black concerns between any two candidates. Just as Jewish Americans are distinctive in their voting behavior despite their economic success and the lessening of social prejudice against them, African American identity, shaped by the struggle of centuries, will remain politically salient. The symbols and shibboleths of the brave fight against discrimination will remain significant for decades to come. It was probably a political mistake for George W. Bush to equivocate on the Confederate flag during the South Carolina primary. Bush's hard right turn in 2000, and Reagan's quota attacks during the 1976 primaries, were politically viable only because the Republican contests were almost entirely white affairs. If black bipartisanship materializes in any significant measure, these tactics will certainly lose their efficacy. The coded appeals of Nixon's

1968 and 1972 law-and-order campaigns, and the Horton campaign of 1988 will also lose their potency in general elections, if they have not already. The evolution of race as a social and political construct will increase the penalty for appearing at all intolerant. Campaign tactics that rely, even implicitly, on racial prejudice are today as likely to backfire as those that would use anti-Semitism or anti-Catholicism.

Still, race continues to divide Americans with far greater force than religion does. In 2001, a Harvard study found that public school systems throughout the country had resegregated at an alarming pace throughout the 1990s. Heavily minority schools were also far more likely to be underfunded and underachieving. The ongoing inequalities in access to educational and social opportunity will work to maintain the relevance of race in public life and in political campaigns. There remain issues upon which the races are deeply divided, and surely politicians will seek to find ways to exploit these questions for political gain. The newest racial issue in presidential politics, reparations, could become quite divisive. Reparations to the descendants of slaves strikes most white Americans as an impossible attempt to rectify the sins of long-dead ancestors. They raise procedural and substantive obstacles to any reparations plan: Who is to get the payments? Why should recent immigrants who arrived after 1865 or their descendants pay? What about descendants of other groups who suffered oppression, here and abroad? At the same time, many African Americans see the justice of the idea, particularly given that the legacy of slavery and de jure discrimination (at least) persisted well into the lifetime of a middle-aged black citizen. Similarly, affirmative action remains a point of contention between whites and blacks.* Whites and blacks also differ greatly on the question of how much discrimination is present in modern American life. While polls of blacks show frequent brushes with discrimination, many whites

---

* A grand compromise on affirmative action and reparations does suggest itself. Since affirmative action is retreating in many states, and under assault from a conservative judiciary, while reparations are far from politically viable given the opposition of many whites, a cunning policy solution would be to trade set-asides and racial preferences in hiring for a uniform onetime reparations payment, probably in the form of a tuition credit for blacks under thirty.

believe the era of widespread racial discrimination is long over. A portion of the white public even contends, despite the evidence of continuing economic and social inequality, that blacks enjoy more opportunities than whites do in modern American society. The differing perceptions and opinions of most whites and most blacks on these specific topics will remain opportunities for campaign operatives intent on using race for political gain. But as the penalties for tactics that appear racial increase, and the payoffs diminish, campaigns will be increasingly hesitant to exploit them.

Presidential campaigns could also directly challenge the evolution of race as a concept. The Republican Party could be a key institution attempting to redefine whiteness for the twenty-first century. Instead of race declining in significance through the social forces depicted above, white privilege could be extended to Asians, lighter-toned Hispanics, and the elite of black America. It has happened before. As historian Noel Ignatiev outlined in his brilliant book, *How the Irish Became White,* the nineteenth-century idea of Anglo identity expanded to include the previously denigrated Irish Catholics over a few decades at the turn of the century. The Republican Party would remain incorrigibly "white," but whiteness would be defined solely as "not black" or, indeed, "not black underclass." If white privilege were successfully reshaped in this fashion, race would only appear to diminish in force in our presidential politics but would linger beneath the surface of our campaigns and our institutions. On the other side of the partisan fence, black political figures will probably resist any weakening of the existing racial categories. As sociologist Orlando Patterson has pointed out, among the firmest defenders of the fraying color line in American life are black leaders,* some of whom have even opposed interracial adoption as an attack on black identity. Ironically, those adhering rigidly to current racial categories and those who will attempt to reapply white privilege to select groups will in effect work as allies in the coming battle over the concept of race. Ultimately,

---

* Patterson also blames the media, as well as academics who are "intellectually terrorized by the fear that any report of a decline in racism exposes them to the charge of racism. . . ."

the forces of intermarriage, globalization, class politics, and demographic diversity will prove stronger, but more than a few presidential campaigns could be won by opponents of the new order in the interim.

Changes in the American conception of "race" will eventually make their way into presidential campaigns, just as the clash over racial equality finally pushed into the campaigns of 1960–72. Once American elites began to find widespread racial intolerance morally abhorrent, or at least internationally embarrassing, it was only a matter of time before presidential campaigns were forced to address race. Kennedy and Nixon had to structure their campaigns around the existence of widespread white racism and the fervent aspirations of African Americans for equality; the victor was the man who through bold action and cunning calculation led both factions to perceive him as sympathetic. Today the Kennedy straddle on race appears morally questionable, but such balances are the essence of successful presidential politics. So too with Clinton's execution of Rickey Ray Rector and his carefully calibrated diminishing of Jesse Jackson. The electorate ultimately judges whether the act was too politically expedient to be morally wise, to paraphrase King. Fortunately for presidential aspirants in the new century, it is unlikely that racial politics will require such ugly choices. Instead, the presidential candidates of the twenty-first century will have to straddle the divide between those citizens who still adhere to firm racial categories and those more in tune with the evolving conception of race described above. As Kennedy well knew, the nation cannot be taken too far too fast, even if a candidate is sure, as it appears Kennedy was, that racial discrimination would eventually wither away.

In the near term, current racial categories carry enough cultural force to remain highly salient politically. As these words are written, Cincinnati is entering its fifth day of rioting. The black community is outraged that police have killed fifteen blacks in five years and no whites. In the most recent incident, an unarmed black man attempting to flee from a traffic summons was murdered by a white police officer. Racial tensions will not disappear anytime soon, as long as segregation characterizes many of our neighborhoods, as long as racial profiling remains a problem in so many police departments, as long as some whites believe, openly or secretly, in black inferiority, and as long as racial preferences inflame racial animosities. The racial politics of 2004 could be very similar to the racial politics of 2000, unless President Bush takes aggressive action to combat (or, cynically speaking, to appear to combat) some or all of these ills. Even so, Republicans in 2004 will have to labor mightily to gain any significant support among blacks. The Democratic nominee will surely try to emulate Clinton's tactical deracialization, and a new fear campaign to rally black support is not improbable. The color line around which forty years of presidential campaigns were fought will remain vital to our politics until the surging tide of history washes it away. In 1964–65, Lyndon Johnson courageously removed the evil hierarchy of race from American law; in the process, Johnson also shaped the racial politics of presidential campaigns for decades. At some point in the twenty-first century, an American president will acknowledge fundamental changes in our conception of race itself, signaling the end of an era in presidential campaigns.

NOTES

ADAH George Wallace Collection, Alabama Department of Archives and History, Montgomery, Alabama
DDE Dwight David Eisenhower Presidential Library, Abilene, Kansas
FCPC Fair Campaign Practices Committee Records, Lauinger Library, Georgetown University, Washington, D.C.
GF Gerald Ford Presidential Library, Ann Arbor, Michigan
GP Senator Barry M. Goldwater Papers, Arizona Historical Foundation, Hayden Library, Arizona State University, Tempe, Arizona
JC Jimmy Carter Presidential Library, Atlanta, Georgia
JFK John F. Kennedy Library, Boston, Massachusetts
LBJ Lyndon Johnson Library, Austin, Texas
MHS Hubert Humphrey Papers, Minnesota Historical Society, St. Paul, Minnesota
MP Senator George McGovern Papers, Mudd Library, Princeton University, Princeton, New Jersey
NP Nixon Project, National Archives and Records Administration, Bethesda, Maryland
RMN Richard Nixon Library, Yorba Linda, California
RR Ronald Reagan Presidential Library, Simi Valley, California
OH Oral history collections

CHAPTER 1: THE IMPORTANCE OF RACE IN PRESIDENTIAL ELECTIONS

3 "The problem of the" *The Souls of Black Folk* (New York, 1982 [1903]), 78. Du Bois was of course referring not only to the racial dilemma in the United States, but also the global fight against colonialism.
3 Much of the battle For solid treatments of the presidency and race relations in history, see Russell L. Riley, *The Presidency and the Politics of Racial Inequality* (New York, 1999), and Kenneth O'Reilly, *Nixon's Piano* (New York, 1995).
4 had shifted to Roosevelt in 1936 FDR never brought up race as an issue in any of his campaigns, understanding that it would decimate his coalition if he did. Nancy J. Weiss, *Farewell to the Party of Lincoln* (Princeton, 1983), 204–5. Henry Sirgo's chapter in *Blacks and the American Political System,*

Huey L. Perry and Wayne Parent, eds. (Miami 1995), 74–79, makes much the same point.

8 Yet there is persuasive   The Bush election and campaign effects generally are discussed in Thomas M. Holbrook, *Do Campaigns Matter?* (Thousand Oaks, 1996).

8 collapse of the New Deal Democratic coalition   Among a great many books on the crucial role race played in the decline of the Democratic majority: Tom Edsall and Mary Edsall, *Chain Reaction* (New York, 1993), Kevin Phillips, *The Emerging Republican Majority* (New York, 1969), Richard Scammon and Ben Wattenberg, *The Real Majority* (New York, 1970), Earl and Merle Black, *The Vital South* (Cambridge, Mass., 1992).

CHAPTER 2: A TALE OF TWO STRADDLES

9 "can be morally wise"   quoted in Chris Matthews, *Kennedy & Nixon* (New York, 1994), 173.

9 "A key to the new strategy"   *Daily Defender* (Chicago), July 25, 1957.

10 lose the northern black vote   Theodore H. White, *The Making of the President 1960* (New York, 1961), 203.

10 "[t]he Negro vote is"   Quoted in Stephen Ambrose, *Nixon* (New York, 1988), 434.

10 estimates ranging   Herbert S. Parmet, *Richard Nixon and His America* (Boston, 1990), Fawn M. Brodie, *Richard Nixon* (New York, 1987). The National Election Study has Eisenhower receiving only 39 percent, still a post-Hoover high for Republicans.

10 A majority of black   Parmet, *Nixon,* 294–95.

10 "What have the two"   *New York Times,* October 16, 1960.

11 would be counterproductive   Stephen B. Oates, *Let the Trumpet Sound* (New York, 1982), 160.

11 "as Kennedy entered"   White, *Making,* 354.

12 "never said a word"   Thomas C. Reeves, *A Question of Character* (Rocklin, Calif., 1992), 136.

12 too much profile   Reeves, *Character,* 140.

12 "Kennedy had no"   Belford V. Lawson, January 11, 1966 (OH, JFK).

12 "I'm going to sing"   Reeves, *Character,* 136.

13 The NAACP rebuked   Matthews, *Kennedy & Nixon,* 120–21.

13 attacked Kennedy's vote   Robinson to JFK, May 25, 1959, JFK.

13 In 1959–60, Kennedy's   Marjorie Lawson, October 25, 1965 (OH, JFK).

13 There was even   Matthews, *Kennedy & Nixon,* 120–21.

13 "the friends and the foes"   Arthur M. Schlesinger Jr., *Robert F. Kennedy and His Times* (New York, 1978), 224.

13 Contemporary press   *Arkansas Gazette,* June 8, 1957.

14 emphatically denies   Theodore C. Sorenson interview, July 26, 1999.

14 "I have met you"   Barham to JFK, May 15, 1959, JFK.

14 "I am not in Jackson" Jackson, Mississippi, speech, October 17, 1957, JFK.

14 Kennedy also won Faubus to Hynes, October 30, 1959, JFK.

14 how little thought Belford and Marjorie Lawson (OH, JFK).

14 moderate on racial matters James McGregor Burns, *John Kennedy* (New York, 1960), 220.

15 a "very bleak record" Jackie Robinson, *I Never Had It Made* (New York, 1972), 149–50.

15 "compromise basic principles" David J. Garrow, *Bearing the Cross* (New York, 1986), 138–39.

15 Lawson tracked Lawson to RFK, November 20, 1959, JFK.

15 "to be manipulated" Marjorie Lawson (OH, JFK).

15 "consistent in his denunciation" Ambrose, *Nixon*, 614–15.

15 In law school Jonathan Aitken, *Nixon* (Washington, 1993), 72. Richard M. Nixon, *In the Arena* (New York, 1990), 106.

16 "not one person" Ambrose, *Nixon*, 395–96.

16 given him a reputation Ambrose, *Nixon*, 396.

16 Nixon was a member Matthews, *Kennedy & Nixon*, 120–21.

16 cagey advice Lawson to JFK, October 22, 1958, JFK.

16 At a crucial point Ambrose, *Nixon*, 434–36, Matthews, *Kennedy & Nixon*, 121.

17 "dauntless courage" MLK to RMN, August 30, 1957, RMN.

17 So prominent Ambrose, *Nixon*, 438.

17 "absolute sincerity" Garrow, *Cross*, 118–19.

17 close personal friends Ambrose, *Nixon*, 411–13.

18 "morally right" Ambrose, *Nixon*, 414–15.

18 "demagoguery and prejudice" Ambrose, *Nixon*, 589.

18 Nixon was even known Parmet, *Nixon*, 269.

19 civil rights only faintly Arthur M. Schlesinger Jr., *Kennedy or Nixon* (New York, 1960).

19 "slightly soft" Schlesinger was so disturbed about the story that he wrote to JFK, alleging he had been misquoted. Whatever the truth of the matter, an attentive progressive like Schlesinger surely saw that Kennedy had cut corners on civil rights, at least in the 1957 vote. Schlesinger to JFK, May 25, 1960, JFK.

19 Kennedy's outreach to the South *Washington Post* and *Times Herald*, October 24, 1958.

19 "antagonized the mass of Negroes" "Here's What They Say About Kennedy," ND, Republican pamphlet, JFK.

20 "rather be right morally" Robinson, *Made*, 148.

20 "high-minded moderate" Reeves, *Character*, 139.

20 Humphrey brought in Jackie Robinson Robinson, *Made*, 148.

20 an amplified phone Marjorie Lawson (OH, JFK). This may have been the first appearance of the modern technique of speaking to unpopular political groups from a technological distance, as seen when President Reagan would speak to pro-life groups over the wires from the White House to the Mall.

20 "muffling the issue" Marjorie Lawson (OH, JFK), 10–15.

20 "a code word for blacks" Carl Solberg, *Hubert Humphrey* (New York, 1984), 205.

20 Lawson scheduled Marjorie Lawson (OH, JFK).

21 former Ku Klux Klansman Schlesinger, *Robert F. Kennedy*, 225.

21 "any self-respecting Negro" *New York Post*, June 3, 1960.

21 "I packed up" Marjorie Lawson (OH, JFK), 22.

21 give the black vote to Nixon G. Mennen Williams to JFK, June 25, 1960, JFK.

21 "some people will wonder" Marjorie Lawson (OH, JFK).

21 uneasy with Kennedy Charles V. Hamilton, *Adam Clayton Powell, Jr.* (New York, 1991), 333.

22 "muffled oars" Speech to NAACP, July 10, 1960, JFK.

22 Members of Kennedy's Schlesinger, *RFK*, 225–26.

22 The record of that night Jeff Shesol, *Mutual Contempt* (New York, 1997), 43–56; Reeves, *Character*, 178–80.

22 "sellout" Shesol, *Mutual*, 51.

22 This reaction was Hamilton, *Powell*, 333.

23 Yet it was a sign Parmet, *Nixon*, 372.

23 "doomed him with the right" Parmet, *Nixon*, 381–83.

24 The intent was clear White, *Making*, 203.

24 Among the planks White, *Making*, 195–98.

24 The deputy attorney general Lawrence Walsh interview, June 24, 1999.

24 They were impressed Parmet, *Nixon*, 388.

24 The response among many White, *Making*, 199–202.

24 "sweeping antisegregation laws" Parmet, *Nixon*, 389.

24 Following the election White, *Making*, 203.

25 Nixon argued in Richard M. Nixon, *Six Crises* (Garden City, N.Y., 1962), 317–18.

25 The southern delegates Herbert J. Muller, *Adlai Stevenson* (New York, 1967), 250.

25 As segregationist Alabama John Patterson, May 27, 1967 (OH, JFK).

26 "extreme legislation" *New York Times*, October 15, 1960.

26 "the price of Southern comfort" *New York Post*, August 10, 1960.

26 "Republican political trickery" Kennedy Statement, August 9, 1960, JFK.

27 Both parties had Patterson (OH, JFK), 29.

27 He frequently accused Syria Mosque Speech, October 10, 1960, JFK.

27 His speeches in Michigan Jacksonville Speech, October 18, 1960, JFK.

27 In northern speeches Speeches in Battle Creek, Mich., October 14, 1960, Wittenberg College Stadium, Springfield, Ohio, October 17, 1960, American Legion Convention, Miami, October 18, 1960, JFK.

27 The clearest example Counterattack Sourcebook, Kennedy Campaign Materials, JFK.

28 "some bigoted Democrats" Bruce L. Felknor, *Dirty Politics* (New York, 1966), 62–63.

28 "I think it is clear"   Speech at State House, Columbia, S.C., October 10, 1960, JFK.

29 "I want to ask you"   Harris Wofford, *Of Kennedys and Kings* (New York, 1980), 82; Harris Wofford 1988 (OH, JFK).

29 When Wofford conceded   Wofford, *Of Kennedys*, 28.

29 Kennedy also canceled   Wofford (OH, JFK), 85.

29 Kennedy's personal involvement   Harlem Speech, October 12, 1960, JFK.

30 While we cannot   Burns, *Kennedy*; Sorensen interview.

30 When Richard Nixon   Tom Wicker, *One of Us* (New York, 1991), 238–39.

30 Nixon's campaign throughout   White, *Making*, 272.

30 The trip south   White, *Making*, 271.

30 Lodge spent   Earl Mazo and Stephen Hess, *Nixon* (New York, 1967), 230.

30 Nixon refused   Robinson, *Made*, 151.

31 "The Nixon-Lodge ticket"   *New York Times*, October 16, 1960.

31 NEGRO IN CABINET   *New York Times*, October 13, 1960.

31 As Lodge met   *New York Times*, October 14, 1960.

31 Nixon's fury   David Broder interview, December 31, 1998. Nixon's unhappiness at Lodge was even the subject of song parodies among the reporters on his plane.

31 So deep was   *New York Times*, October 15, 1960.

31 On the very   Ambrose, *Nixon*, 580.

32 Nixon and Lodge were   William J. Miller, *Henry Cabot Lodge* (New York, 1967), 325.

32 civil rights leaders   David Levering Lewis, *King: A Critical Biography* (New York, 1970), 120.

33 King's imprisonment   *New York Times*, October 26, 1960.

33 While in prison   Stephen B. Oates, *Let the Trumpet Sound* (New York, 1982), 163–65.

33 Three southern governors   White, *Making*, 322.

33 Wofford and Louis Martin   Garrow, *Cross*, 146–47.

33 "impulsive, direct"   White, *Making*, 322.

34 "You bombthrowers"   Schlesinger, *RFK*, 227–28.

34 Robinson's efforts   Matthews, *Kennedy & Nixon*, 172.

34 Much later   Nixon, *Crises*, 362–63.

34 Morrow was told   Garrow, *Cross*, 146.

34 Walsh tried numerous   Walsh interview.

35 "No Comment Nixon"   Wofford (OH, JFK).

35 There were some signs   *New York Times*, October 29, 1960.

35 In *Time*   *Time*, November 7, 1960.

35 "The entire episode"   White, *Making*, 323.

35 "take off your Nixon"   Oates, *Trumpet*, 164–65.

36 "milder than expected"   *New York Times*, October 30, 1960.

36 "I don't know what"   Oates, *Trumpet*, 160.

36 "The finest strategies"   Wofford, *Of Kennedys*, 27.

36 In a campaign   White, *Making*, 323, 354.

37 "took everything relating" *Time,* October 17, 1960.

37 Voters watching the debates Sidney Kraus and Raymond G. Smith, eds., *The Great Debates* (Bloomington, Ind., 1962), 306–7.

37 Finally, civil rights Powell threatened to spread false rumors that King and Rustin were engaged in a homosexual relationship. Garrow, *Cross,* 137–39.

38 He grew up learning Burns, *Kennedy,* 12–13, 58–59.

38 "strange and repugnant" Burns, *Kennedy,* 13.

38 "always really worried" Wofford (OH, JFK), 85.

39 "to be emotionally" Burns, *Kennedy,* 264.

39 When King came Oates, *Trumpet,* 166.

39 "wanted to win" Wofford (OH, JFK), 85.

39 Kennedy's straddle Sammy Davis Jr., *Sammy* (New York, 2000).

CHAPTER 3: LBJ WINS DESPITE CIVIL RIGHTS

40 "If we have to get" July 24, 1964, #4328 (Tape Collection, LBJ).

40 As such Carmines and Stimson, *Issue Evolution* (New York, 1989); Edsall and Edsall, *Chain.*

41 That race could dominate "Some Indications of Public Opinion at the Close of 1963," January 1964, GP.

42 The eventual delivery Had Kennedy been assassinated in November of 1962, instead of a year later, he would not be remembered as a strong proponent of civil rights. Many black leaders had been alienated by the breaking of Kennedy's campaign promise to integrate public housing on his first day in office. Kennedy had also appointed a number of racist judges in the South to appease southern senators. Andrew Young, June 18, 1970 (OH, LBJ), 3. Even after 1963, some never agreed with Kennedy's image as a defender of black equality; Bayard Rustin, architect of the 1963 March on Washington, considered the Kennedy administration's civil rights record "horribly overrated." Bayard Rustin, June 17, 1969 (OH, LBJ), 16.

42 "See the Japs" "Progress Report #2," September 1963, GP.

42 As one of his key A. Leon Higginbotham Jr., October 7, 1976 (OH, LBJ), 20.

43 Yet his selection Rustin (OH, LBJ); John Lewis, *Walking with the Wind* (New York, 1998); Higginbotham (OH, LBJ); James Farmer, October 1969 (OH, LBJ).

43 For example Robert A. Caro, *Means of Ascent* (New York, 1990), xvii–xviii.

43 One of the favorite Harry McPherson, *A Political Education* (Boston, 1972), 140; Doris Kearns, *Lyndon Johnson and the American Dream* (New York, 1976).

43 Later, as a New Deal Democrat Robert A. Caro, *The Path to Power* (New York, 1990), 364.

43 And much later Robert Dallek, *Lone Star Rising* (New York, 1991), 367.

43   To adhere   McPherson, *Political,* 143–44.

44   With a nearly   Dallek, *Lone Star,* 390–91.

44   Johnson understood   McPherson, *Political,* 144–45.

44   He believed   McPherson, *Political,* 142–43.

44   "Until justice is blind"   Vaughn Davis Bornet, *The Presidency of Lyndon Baines Johnson* (Lawrence, Kans., 1983), 96–97.

44   One of the few   Kearns, *Johnson;* Shesol, *Contempt,* 85–87.

44   "straight in the face"   Shesol, *Contempt,* 101–2; Bornet, *Presidency,* 110.

44   In the first two   Lyndon Baines Johnson, *The Vantage Point* (New York, 1971), 29.

45   He signaled to Congress   Yet so deep was the distrust among certain liberals of Johnson's shift on civil rights, that a popular joke extending well into his presidency had him shouting "nigger" at midnight in the middle of nowhere to release his allegedly pent-up racism. Kearns, *Johnson,* 230.

45   Growing up in Arizona   Goldwater did have, from an early age, a very pronounced affinity for another oppressed minority, Native Americans, with whom he had sustained contact. Lee Edwards, *Goldwater* (Washington, D.C., 1995), 246.

45   "Throughout his life"   Robert Alan Goldberg, *Barry Goldwater* (New Haven, Conn., 1995), 34.

45   He worked for   Edwin McDowell, "Goldwater: A Portrait in Words and Pictures," *Human Events,* January 25, 1964.

45   As late as   Gilbert A. Harrison, *New Republic,* March 27, 1961.

45   "We ought to forget"   *Washington Post,* November 26, 1961.

46   He also supported a segregationist   *New York Times,* November 19, 1961.

46   At least up   Goldberg, *Goldwater,* 154.

46   "When I spoke"   Barry M. Goldwater, "The GOP Invades the South," *Saturday Evening Post,* 1963.

46   It is difficult   Gilbert A. Harrison, *New Republic,* November 23, 1963.

47   Wallace sat at   George C. Wallace, May 15, 1969 (OH, LBJ), 5.

47   Wallace began hinting   Dan Carter, *The Politics of Rage* (New York, 1995), 200.

47   Wallace entered his first   Carter, *Politics,* 203; William Lulloff, *An Analysis of Selected Issues in the 1968 and 1972 Presidential Campaigns,* master's thesis, University of Wisconsin–Eau Claire (1974).

47   Yet in Indiana   White, *Making 1964,* 223–24.

48   "Alabama is coming"   May 13, 1964, #3450 (Tape Collection, LBJ).

48   The success of Wallace   So worried was the White House that they prepared four different DNC press releases on the eve of the Maryland primary—one each for Wallace scoring under 30 percent, between 30 and 40 percent, between 40 and 50 percent, and for the nightmare scenario of Wallace winning a majority of the vote. Moyers Files, Box 40, LBJ.

48   Johnson avoided commenting   *Public Papers of LBJ,* 246, 256, 316, Washington, D.C., May 20, 1964, #3480 (Tape Collection, LBJ); Johnson did encourage Reedy to see if Maryland newspapers could surreptitiously be

given information damaging to Wallace in time for the primary. May 13, 1964, #3451 (Tape Collection, LBJ).

48 Moreover, Johnson's narrow   Carter, *Politics*, 214.

48 Yet even as   The only concession that Johnson made to southern sensitivities was that his southern speeches are devoid of direct references to the upcoming civil rights bill, while his northern speeches do refer explicitly to the ongoing legislative battle (*Public Papers*, 330, 321, 334).

48 Far from moderating   *Public Papers*, 357.

48 In nearly daily   Johnson, *Vantage*, 37.

48 In a seminal   That a higher percentage of Republicans voted for the CRA bill in both the House and the Senate is a fact that even top scholars have forgotten. In a recent work on racial politics, Sapiro and Canon attribute passage to a Democratic Congress defeating Republican opposition. Given that Republican leaders marshaled more of their troops to vote for Johnson's bill than Humphrey was able to on the other side, this is unsustainable even as rhetoric. So deafening was the symbolism of Goldwater's anti-CRA vote that it has drowned out the fact that congressional Republicans were more pro–civil rights than the Democrats. See Sapiro and Canon's chapter in Campbell and Rockman's *The Clinton Legacy* (New York, 2000), 171.

49 Johnson intimate   July 23, 1964, #4322 (Tape Collection, LBJ).

49 "If they just"   July 23, 1964, #4323 (Tape Collection, LBJ).

49 When hundreds of   White, *Making 1964*, 235.

49 With the exceptions   Lewis, *Walking*, 276–77; White, *Making 1964*, 236; Kearns, *Johnson*, 192.

49 "If they have"   July 23, 1964, #4322 (Tape Collection, LBJ).

50 They held a primary   Lewis, *Walking*, 277–82.

50 If Alabama and Mississippi   July 23, 1964, #4320 (Tape Collection, LBJ). LBJ asks Connally how the Texas delegation looks in terms of diversity. Connally answers that his delegation "got more niggers than we got Mexicans," which captures the hard-edged flavor that Johnson brought to his discussions of racial politics in private. July 23, 1964, #4320 (Tape Collection, LBJ).

50 "You got Wagner"   July 24, 1964, #4328 (Tape Collection, LBJ).

50 "an unnecessary affront"   White to LBJ, August 12, 1964, LBJ.

50 As the convention opened   White, *Making 1964*, 236; DeLoach to LBJ, August 19, 1964, LBJ; White to LBJ, August 19, 1964, LBJ.

50 Johnson had the FBI   Lewis, *Walking*, 281.

50 So damaging   Lewis, *Walking*, 280.

51 "we won a victory"   August 25, 1964, #5193 (Tape Collection, LBJ).

51 With his three   August 25, 1964, #5210 (Tape Collection, LBJ).

51 He told another   August 25, 1964, #5208 (Tape Collection, LBJ).

51 "I think the Negroes"   August 24, 1964, #5165 (Tape Collection, LBJ).

52 "Please, please"   July 23, 1964, #4320 (Tape Collection, LBJ).

52 Johnson's selection   Lewis, *Walking*, 280.

52 the head of the Republican National Committee   Stephen Hess and David Broder, *The Republican Establishment* (New York, 1967), 341.

53 The party also   "FACT Book," 1964, GP.
53 Yet at the   Karl A. Lamb, "Under One Roof" (unpublished manuscript), GP, 18–30.
53 Whatever the practicality   The most disgusting example of a fawning attempt to appeal to African Americans was certainly an RNC pamphlet entitled "Who Is George Lewis?"(ND, GP). The text and photos show blacks happily laboring at the nerve center of Republicanism. The implication is that blacks hold positions of high responsibility within the RNC, but the star of the pamphlet is the head of the library, scarcely a policy position. Other featured blacks directed the printing operations and worked as secretaries. The gaping lacuna of blacks as committee members or elected officials is not mentioned. A more transparent effort at tokenism can scarcely be imagined.
53 During the brief   "Automation, Unemployment, and the Paycheck," May 7, 1964, GP.
53 Early supporters distributed   Hess and Broder, *Establishment*, 336–37.
53 "I hate to win"   Harrison, *New Republic*, November 23, 1963.
54 Indeed, one of   Rockefeller's open checkbook for controversial black groups dismayed his campaign staff. "[H]is counselors moaned that even an abolitionist running for President would not go as far as Rockefeller went. If there were to be any hope of peeling off Southern delegates from Goldwater at the convention, why, why did he have to encourage the Negro revolution of 1963 in the South just at that time?" White, *Making 1964*, 74.
54 In Georgia   *Macon Telegraph News*, May 3, 1964.
54 In some states   Edsall and Edsall, *Chain*, 43.
54 In a moment of   Carter, *Politics*, 218.
54 It was this vote   Broder interview.
55 "The structure of"   Speech in Columbus, Ga., May 1, 1964, GP.
55 "Where are the states"   National Goldwater Rally, Madison Square Garden, New York, May 13, 1964, GP.
55 His strong showing   White, *Making 1964*, 196. Goldwater, however, did not consistently endorse states' rights. Indeed, on a nationally televised program in May, he retreated from his earlier opposition to federal intervention in school desegregation and criticized Johnson's administration for not pushing harder on the issue (*Issues and Answers*, ABC transcript, 1964, GP).
55 "a very able man"   *Life*, July 24, 1964.
55 Ultimately, Wallace gave   Carter, *Politics*, 220–22.
56 A number of prominent   "Remarks by Henry Cabot Lodge, Committee on Resolutions," July 8, 1964, GP; Garrow, *Cross*, 339–40.
56 "the unspoken watchword"   Rowland Evans and Robert Novak, *Washington Post*, July 15, 1964.
56 "Finally, consistent with"   "Laird Group" file, GP. The Democratic platform echoed that sentiment, in less fulsome language. "True Democracy of opportunity will not be served by establishing quotas based on the same false distinctions we seek to erase, nor can the effects of prejudice be neutralized by the expedient of preferential practices."

56 As was seen   Given the extraordinary irregularities in the 1960 election, it should have been expected that the Republicans would recruit poll watchers and seek to combat vote fraud. However, overzealous ballot security focusing on black areas is a tactic to reduce black turnout.

56 "A truly national"   *Life,* July 24, 1964.

57 As he told   July 20, 1964, #4286 (Tape Collection, LBJ).

57 Johnson suspected   July 23, 1964, #4320 (Tape Collection, LBJ).

57 "It's not our"   July 20, 1964, #4286 (Tape Collection, LBJ).

58 "He came in"   July 25, 1964, #4337 (Tape Collection, LBJ).

58 "they don't want"   Remarks Before the National Democratic Committee, Atlantic City, N.J., August 28, 1964.

58 "The so-called backlash"   Buford Ellington to LBJ, August 10, 1964, LBJ.

59 "The racial issue"   Johnson, *Vantage,* 109.

59 Similarly, the highest-profile   Rustin (OH, LBJ); Young (OH, LBJ).

59 On his way   Johnson, *Vantage,* 105–6.

59 As the election neared   T. W. Benham, "1964 Presidential Campaign Base Survey," August 1964, GP.

59 "Black Bird Go Home"   *George,* August 1999.

60 "the less said"   Frank Givney to LBJ, 1964 (ND), LBJ.

60 "civil . . . constitutional . . . settling"   Bill Moyers to Jack Valenti, October 9, 1964, LBJ.

60 "Now the people"   Remarks at a Dinner in the Jung Hotel, New Orleans, La., October 9, 1964, LBJ.

60 Far from soft-pedaling   Johnson did soft-pedal civil rights on occasion, such as his delicate treatment of southern delegations at the convention. A similar event occurred in the closing weeks of the 1964 campaign; King won the Nobel prize, but Johnson failed to send a congratulation, though many foreign leaders did. King believed that Johnson was trying to avoid offending white southern sensibilities. Garrow, *Cross,* 357.

61 The few other issues   "Strategy Analysis of Campaign Survey," NA, ND, GP; Benham, "Survey"; "Midwest Poll Results," NA, August 28, 1964, GP.

61 "There is considerable evidence"   "Illinois," NA, ND, GP.

61 "the pull of"   "Characteristics of the 'non-voter,'" NA, September 1, 1964, GP.

61 The general election   "HHH Notebook," RNC, September 24, 1964, GP.

61 In his speech   Speech in St. Petersburg, September 15, 1964, GP. Goldwater did attack civil disobedience in this speech.

62 In a speech in October   Speech in Houston, October 15, 1964, GP.

62 "I will not"   Statement in Phoenix, July 18, 1964, GP.

62 One is that   Goldberg, *Goldwater,* 215.

62 The central theme   "Choice," 1964 campaign video, GP. Seen by the modern viewer, it looks like a campaign video directed by a prejudiced Frank Capra. It sells a vision of a halcyon America, before pornography, illegitimacy, riots, and the decay of values among our precious youth. Even the soundtrack juxtaposes the evils of jazz versus the positive influence of Sousa. The schmaltz becomes intolerable when John Wayne appears near the

end to encourage the saving of America through the election of Goldwater. If Goldwater hadn't objected to the racist imagery, he might well have rejected the film on the grounds of bad taste.

62 Goldwater deemed Goldberg, *Goldwater,* 231.
63 On the eve William Scranton to Goldwater, July 12, 1964, GP.
63 At a unity conference Goldberg, *Goldwater,* 220.
63 "Senator Goldwater and I" "Statement of John M. Bailey," August 2, 1964, LBJ.
63 "It's all right" Speech to Pennsylvania Union League Club, October 13, 1964, GP.
64 Yet scarcely a month Speech in Wilmington, Delaware, September 19, 1964, GP.
64 Finally, Miller went Lamb, *Roof,* 69.
64 The confusion among Republicans "Miller Hits Restrictive Clause in Johnson Land Sale," RNC press release, September 15, 1964, GP; "GOP Chairman Says Party Welcomes Sen. Thurmond Because 'He Practices His Principles,'" September 16, 1964, GP.
64 If Goldwater was Goldberg, *Goldwater,* 217–19.
64 "The way things" "Georgia," NA, ND, GP.
65 The campaign, credited *St. Louis Dispatch,* November 3, 1964.
65 Seventy-five percent Edsall and Edsall, *Chain,* 35.
65 The Goldwater effect Goldberg, *Goldwater,* 235.
66 "idolatry . . . wilder" Dick Thompson to Pam Rymer, ND, GP.
66 Goldwater's staff "Tennessee," NA, ND, GP.
66 An editorial in *St. Petersburg Times,* August 11, 1964.
66 "Backlash . . . was a" White, *Making 1964,* 233–34.
66 In a July Goldberg, *Goldwater,* 196–97.
67 But for the White, *Making 1964,* 328.
67 Goldwater, like Johnson This speech confirms the contemporary insight of Arthur Schlesinger Jr., who, while opposing Goldwater's politics on nearly every point, sees him as a libertarian and not racist. Arthur Schlesinger interview, September 9, 1999.
67 "even a hint" Hess and Broder, *Establishment,* 401–3.
67 "If the Republicans" White, *Making 1964,* 383.

CHAPTER 4: THE BULLETS, THE BALLOTS, AND THE BACKLASH

69 "People are terrified" Ambrose, *Nixon,* 124.
70 Even Vietnam was Theodore H. White, *The Making of the President—1968* (New York, 1969), 26–27; David Halberstam, *The Unfinished Odyssey of Robert Kennedy* (New York, 1968), 79.
71 "The single issue" Marvin Watson to LBJ, January 12, 1967, LBJ.
71 In 1967, several *Report of the National Advisory Commission on Civil Disorders* (New York, 1968), 38–107.
71 The percentage of McPherson, *Political,* 450.

72 "I'm gonna bomb" Adam Fairclough, *To Redeem the South of America* (Athens, Ga., 1987), 316–18.

72 Leaders who had Lewis, *Walking,* 370–74.

72 "If a white. . . . When you talk" White, *Making 1969,* 239.

72 "From the day" White, *Making 1969,* 32–33.

72 Democratic mayors complained Sam Yorty to LBJ, May 27, 1967, LBJ.

72 Sargent Shriver James Gaither to Joseph Califano, July 27, 1967, LBJ; James Gaither to Joseph Califano, October 17, 1967, LBJ.

72 ". . . a white, lower-middle-class" John P. Roche to LBJ, July 6, 1967, LBJ.

73 White Americans did Roy Wilkins, April 1, 1969 (OH, LBJ), 18–20.

73 Even before the Kearns, *Johnson,* 304.

73 As the election Warren Christopher to Joseph Califano, January 15, 1968, LBJ.

73 "How is it" Halberstam, *Odyssey,* 83; Kearns, *Johnson,* 304.

73 "to investigate, coordinate" "Memorandum for the Record," NA, July 15, 1967, LBJ.

73 "It simply wasn't" Kearns, *Johnson,* 305.

74 "just do . . . just killed . . . bought . . . the hell" "Memorandum for the Record," December 28, 1960, DDE.

74 "dropped his long-time" Hess and Broder, *Establishment,* 167–68; Jules Witcover, *The Resurrection of Richard Nixon* (New York, 1970), 72–73.

74 It was Nixon's Ambrose, *Triumph,* 57.

74 Nixon did help Hess and Broder, *Establishment,* 51–52.

74 "Unlike Rockefeller" Hess and Broder, *Establishment,* 180–81.

75 "for the Northern" Ambrose, *Triumph,* 88–89.

75 Polls showed that *Los Angeles Times,* February 26, 1968.

75 "would act as" Marvin Watson (?) to LBJ, January 12, 1967, LBJ.

75 A year before Stephen Lesher, *George Wallace* (New York, 1994), 392.

75 His announcement on Lesher, *Wallace,* 389–90.

75 For some Americans Lesher, *Wallace,* 402.

76 "it was very" Schlesinger interview.

76 "offset . . . the bad" Barbara Currier to John Stewart, May 15, 1968, MHS.

76 Johnson's Pyrrhic victory Arthur M. Schlesinger, *Robert F. Kennedy and His Times* (Boston, 1978), 843–57.

77 As attorney general Schlesinger interview.

77 Improbably, Kennedy was Halberstam, *Odyssey,* 12.

77 In most homes Schlesinger, *Kennedy,* 845.

77 ". . . he was the Liberator" White, *Making 1968,* 202.

78 Even McCarthy conceded Eugene J. McCarthy, *Year of the People* (Garden City, N.Y., 1969), 164.

78 King had broken *Philadelphia Inquirer,* April 25, 1967; *Christian Science Monitor,* August 9, 1967.

78 The idea disturbed Fairclough, *Redeem,* 364; Schlesinger, *Kennedy,* 873; *Baltimore Sun,* February 3, 1968.

78 He called on Halberstam, *Odyssey.*

78   Kennedy was one   Schlesinger interview.

78   In the aftermath   White, *Making 1968*, 243–44.

78   "[t]he rednecks would"   Halberstam, *Odyssey*, 89.

79   As a crowd   Halberstam, *Odyssey*, 91; Schlesinger, *Kennedy*.

79   Troops had to   Ben W. Gilbert, *Ten Blocks from the White House* (New York, 1968).

79   Some reporters traveling   Halberstam, *Odyssey*; Schlesinger, *Kennedy*; White, *Making 1968*, 206.

79   "coon-catcher"   Halberstam, *Odyssey*, 93.

79   "So far in"   Halberstam, *Odyssey*, 95.

79   When he was subsequently   Halberstam, *Odyssey*, 187.

79   These ludicrous ads   McCarthy, *Year of*, 164.

80   The appeal to   Eugene McCarthy interview, April 6, 2000.

80   "I used to be"   Halberstam, *Odyssey*, 197; McCarthy, *Year of*.

80   Even before King's death   Fairclough, *Redeem*, 364.

80   The administration pondered   Matt Nimetz to Joseph Califano, April 25, 1968, LBJ.

80   The initial response   Joseph Califano to LBJ, May 16, 1968, LBJ. All major cabinet secretaries were required to submit documents for Abernathy's review, outlining how their specific agency was responsive to his concerns.

80   At its peak   Gilbert, *Blocks*, 197.

80   Almost immediately   Matt Nimetz to Joseph Califano, May 28, 1968, LBJ.

80   He attempted to play   John Stewart to HHH, May 20, 1968, MHS; Barbara Currier to John Stewart, May 15, 1968, MHS; HHH to LBJ, June 12, 1968, MHS.

81   The PPC symbolized   It is difficult to argue with the judgment of Bayard Rustin that the PPC "ended ignominiously" Rustin (OH, LBJ). "Whoever cleared us out, may have done us a favor," said Andrew Young. Fairclough, *Redeem*, 388.

81   Humphrey was the preferred   White, *Making 1968*, 316, 332.

81   "We have all"   *Meet the Press*, April 28, 1968, MHS.

82   On his right   White, *Making 1968*, 40.

82   "Reagan's strength derives"   Joe McGinnis, *The Selling of the President* (New York, 1969), 170.

82   "who could possibly"   Watson (?) to LBJ, June 6, 1967, LBJ.

82   Romney had received   White, *Making 1968*, 41–42.

82   Rockefeller, a longtime   White, *Making 1968*, 272–73.

83   Law and order   White, *Making 1968*, 152.

83   He also pledged   White, *Making 1968*, 160–61.

83   Some saw in Wallace   Hess and Broder, *Establishment*, 358.

83   Nixon wooed the South   *Boston Globe*, August 8, 1968.

83   Nixon's criticism   *The State* (Columbia, S.C.), August 9, 1968.

84   had risen to national prominence   Ambrose, *Triumph*, 162–63.

84   Jackie Robinson   "Response to Nixon-Agnew Ticket," NA, MHS.

84   Agnew was also expected   *Philadelphia Inquirer*, August 9, 1968.

85 In April, his support   Lesher, *Wallace*, 413.

85 "Wallace, Daley"   Witcover, *Resurrection*, 409.

85 "scum of the earth"   *Washington Star*, September 12, 1968.

85 "There has been more violence"   "George Wallace: A Rebel and His Cause," Wallace brochure, MHS.

85 He also attacked   *Issues and Answers*, June 16, 1968, ADAH.

85 Wallace was masterful   *Issues and Answers*, June 16, 1968, ADAH; *Issues and Answers*, November 3, 1968, ADAH.

85 "Some militants have charged"   *Issues and Answers*, June 16, 1968, ADAH.

85 A Wallace supporter   Speech by John J. Synon, October 19, 1968, ADAH.

85 Another supporter   Jim Johnson telecast, April 3, 1968, ADAH.

86 "We don't have riots"   Carter, *Politics*, 366.

86 "I wish I was"   Mike Royko, *Boss* (New York, 1971), 144.

86 "We have tried"   Lulloff, *Analysis*, 26.

86 LBJ's pollster believed   McPherson, *Political*, 377–79.

87 "American policemen are"   "George Wallace: A Rebel . . . ," MHS.

87 "There's nothing wrong"   Lesher, *Wallace*, 395, 405.

87 "an eighth-grade education"   Hubert Humphrey, KDKA Interview, September 14, 1968; Hubert Humphrey to Pittsburgh-Area College Newspaper Editors, WTAE-TV, September 13, 1968, MHS.

87 "People will not live"   *Denver Post*, September 13, 1968.

88 Humphrey's lectures on federalism   "Vice President's Press Conference on the Beach," September 13, 1968, MHS.

88 Humphrey protested that   "KRON-TV," September 26, 1968, MHS.

88 The most memorable   McGinnis, *Selling*, 251–53.

88 This ad, like others   McGinnis, *Selling*, 125.

88 "this hits it"   McGinnis, *Selling*, 23.

88 "good, mean. . . . Wouldn't that"   McGinnis, *Selling*, 101.

88 With Wallace on   Carter, *Politics*, 350.

88 Thus, in a year   White, *Making 1968*, 220.

89 "These people are"   McGinnis, *Selling*, 225.

89 "tempting target"   McGinnis, *Selling*, 236.

89 The black community   Rustin (OH, LBJ), 242.

89 One of the largest   *Washington Star*, August 11, 1968.

89 The numerous black endorsements   "Response to Nixon-Agnew Ticket," NA, MHS; *Washington Post*, August 12, 1968.

89 Nixon and his running mate   Witcover, *Resurrection*, 321, 397.

89 Nixon's welfare policy   Ambrose, *Triumph*, 124.

90 All Nixon could offer   Ambrose, *Triumph*, 158.

90 Nixon was also unlikely   Lesher, *Wallace*, 403.

90 A camera crew   McGinnis, *Selling*, 98.

90 Surprisingly, it was Humphrey   White, *Making 1968*, 352.

90 Humphrey also faced   Edgar Berman, *Hubert: The Triumph and Tragedy of the Humphrey I Knew* (New York, 1979), 199, 203–4.

90 In refusing to compete   The Humphrey campaign at least contemplated attacking Nixon in the South for endorsing civil rights earlier in his career. In

a lengthy compendium of quotes in a campaign attack book, under the heading "For use by us in the South," Nixon's quotes prior to 1961 in favor of sit-ins and school integration, as well as his attacks on Maddox, Faubus, Bilbo, and Talmadge, are listed. Never again would a Democratic campaign even consider using pro–civil rights stances against a Republican nominee. "Summary of Views," NA, ND, MHS.

90 Also, Humphrey had put   Halberstam, *Odyssey,* 164.

91 In a later visit   Berman, *Hubert,* 199.

91 "beneath contempt"   "Memorandum on Wallace Impact," NA, ND, MHS.

91 "those 1.1 million"   Bob Klein to John Stewart, ND, MHS.

91 Humphrey's decision to go   Based on handwritten notation on file copy in Humphrey papers.

91 "It is as if"   *New York,* October 7, 1968.

91 "People are always"   *New York,* October 7, 1968

92 The unions launched   White, *Making 1968,* 434.

92 Humphrey may have had   Lesher, *Wallace,* 423.

92 His forbearance   *St. Louis Post-Dispatch,* October 8, 1968.

92 The Republicans knew   Carter, *Politics,* 347.

92 Humphrey then attacked   Carter, *Politics,* 363.

92 In the closing weeks   *Atlanta Constitution,* October 24, 1968.

92 Ads arguing that   Carter, *Politics,* 363.

92 Wallace had memorably promised   *St. Louis Post-Dispatch,* October 8, 1968.

93 "I'm not going"   *Minneapolis Star,* October 8, 1968.

93 He focused   White, *Making 1968,* 386.

93 The percentage of Americans   The disastrous nomination of General Curtis LeMay as Wallace's running mate was the cause of much of Wallace's late decline in support. White, *Making 1968,* 425.

93 "I think that"   "Press Conference of Vice President Humphrey En Route to Las Vegas," October 24, 1968, MHS.

93 Accusing Nixon of insincerity   Whites who hoped Nixon was mouthing racial platitudes to get elected had some evidence for the case. In a speech to southern delegates at the convention that was secretly taped and later leaked to the media, Nixon said that he was actually against open housing legislation but had supported it to keep it off the agenda at the convention (Witcover, *Resurrection,* 343–44). This could only lead many white southerners to believe that Nixon would not be much of a martinet on civil rights once his electoral pressures were removed.

94 The contest had been   White, *Making 1968,* 466–67.

CHAPTER 5: NIXON BUSES TO VICTORY

96 "we must realize"   Harry Dent to RMN, October 13, 1969, NP.

97 Nixon, who had promised   Theodore White, *The Making of the President 1972* (New York, 1973), 323.

97   In 1968, 68 percent   Richard M. Nixon, *RN: The Memoirs of Richard Nixon* (New York, 1990), 443.

97   Even critics of Nixon   Schlesinger interview.

97   Nixon directed his   Ken Cole to Harry Dent, September 29, 1969; Dent to RMN, July 8, 1969, NP.

98   But when asked   White, *Making 1972*, 65.

98   "It just may be that"   "Commentary for Post Newsweek Broadcasting," July 15, 1969, NP.

99   Nixon was careful   Nixon later claimed that he was an "ultraliberal" on race, but that his personal feelings about integration could not overcome his opposition to forced integration, Nixon, *RN*, 444. The record, however, shows differently. See Carter, *Politics*, 372.

99   the author of a memo   James Farmer, *Lay Bare the Heart* (New York, 1985), 325.

99   Moynihan allegedly brought up   Farmer, *Lay Bare the Heart*, 325.

99   Moynihan today denies   Daniel Moynihan, private communication to the author, December 10, 2001.

99   "You are not going to"   William Safire, *After the Fall* (New York, 1975), 237.

99   Nixon was also criticized   Edsall and Edsall, *Chain*, 84.

100   "meddling in racial matters"   Robert S. Byrd to Spiro Agnew, May 29, 1969, NP.

100   "Nixon had to be hauled"   Ambrose, *Triumph*, 407.

100   A staffer would later   White, *Making 1972*, 338–39.

101   While McGovern in   George McGovern, *Grassroots* (New York, 1977), 144–49.

101   Muskie, Humphrey's running   Theo Lippmann and Donald C. Hansen, *Muskie* (New York, 1971), 25.

101   Muskie appeared to be   Stanley S. Scott to Ken Khachigian, September 21, 1971, NP; *Jet*, October 21, 1971; *Washington Afro-American*, September 21, 1971.

102   "a libel on the American"   *New York Times*, September 17, 1971.

102   Republicans suggested   *Atlanta Daily World*, September 21, 1971.

102   The RNC's internal   "Muskie Summary," October 3–10, NP.

102   In an analysis leaked   *Jacksonville Times Union*, October 4, 1971.

102   On the eve of the primaries   Edsall and Edsall, *Chain*, 88.

103   "That busing problem"   *Washington Post*, February 15, 1972; Edward Muskie, *Journeys* (New York, 1972), 121; White, *Making 1972*, 83.

103   Humphrey, Chisholm, Lindsay   White, *Making 1972*, 89–92.

103   Pat Buchanan, a Nixon   Carter, *Politics*, 433.

103   Wallace's secret alliance   Lesher, *Wallace*, 437.

103   Following Wallace's   A January 1972 White House memo indicates interest in "buying off" Wallace, to prevent a 1972 run as an independent, Buchanan, cc Khachigian, January 24, 1972, NP.

103   "shows that some of the worst"   Lesher, *Wallace*, 475.

104 The Wallace voters were "Attention Must Be Paid," Milwaukee, Wisc., Speech by McGovern, March 23, 1972, MP.

104 "voted to give away millions" *New York Times,* February 20, 1972.

104 "They're a-hemming" *New York Times,* February 26, 1972.

104 Wallace had no compunction "Wallace Stand," 1972 campaign LP (transcript), ADAH.

104 The same month that *Washington Post,* March 13, 1972.

104 Liberal Democrats in the House *Washington Post,* February 16, 1972.

104 In Wisconsin, Wallace White, *Making 1972,* 109.

105 "Humphrey's Michigan managers" *Washington Post,* May 12, 1972.

105 The battle lines were *New York Times,* May 15, 1972.

105 But now even McGovern "Response of Senator George McGovern to Booth Newspapers Questionnaire," April 28, 1972, MP.

105 In April, when Michigan Carter, *Politics,* 431–32.

106 Organized labor indicated "The McGovern Record: A Critical Appraisal," ND, NP.

106 Humphrey, who had during Lesher, *Wallace,* 486–89.

106 It was at the convention White, *Making 1972,* 185.

106 "There's only one Italian" Royko quoted in White, *Making 1972,* 174–75.

107 "non-negotiable demands" *Washington Post,* June 2, 1972.

107 The National Black Political McGovern to Charles C. Diggs, Richard C. Hatcher, and Imamu Amiri Baraka, June 23, 1972, MP.

107 The threat to McGovern's *Washington Post,* June 16, 1972.

107 McGovern had earlier endorsed *Amsterdam News,* March 4, 1972. McGovern's comments on reparations were given little attention beyond the black media.

107 "providing federal appointments" McGovern to Diggs et al., June 23, 1972, MP.

107 McGovern forces voted *Evening Star,* July 12, 1972.

107 McGovern was so far left George McGovern interview, September 20, 1999.

108 Nixon was briefly flanked *Washington Post,* February 10, 1972.

108 At the same time *U.S. News,* February 14, 1972.

108 "Let me say candidly" "The Ship of Integration Is Going Down," Pat Buchanan to RMN, ND, NP.

108 Within the White House Safire, *Fall,* 236–41.

108 Buchanan pushed hard for Ed Harper to John Ehrlichman, March 20, 1972, NP.

109 "poisonous" "GOP Leadership Meeting" (Buchanan notes), March 28, 1972, NP.

109 McGovern, however, responded *New York Times,* March 20, 1972.

109 However, Nixon's speech Dana Mead to J. Stanley Pottinger, October 26, 1972, NP.

109 Some staffers now advised Harper to Ehrlichman, May 10, 1972, NP.

109 Moreover, Republican operatives   Khachigian to Buchanan, March 30, 1972, NP.

109 Still, the White House strategists   "Opposition Research Meeting Notes" (Khachigian, ND); Buchanan to RMN, April 3, 1972, NP.

109 Buchanan suggested running   Buchanan and Khachigian to John Mitchell, March 14, 1972, NP.

109 Republicans also forged   *New York Times,* October 15, 1972.

109 Agnew had built upon   *Time,* July 17, 1972.

110 "Political operatives have"   *Washington Post,* July 16, 1972.

110 "we will automatically surrender"   Buchanan to RMN, August 2, 1972, NP.

110 Rather than adopting quotas   "Cabinet and GOP Leadership Breakfast" (Buchanan notes), August 13, 1972, NP.

110 In Nixon's two convention films   "Nixon: A Portrait of a Man for a Half Hour Film" (Wolper Productions script), May 17, 1972; "Nixon, The Presidential Years" (Keogh script), May 18, 1972, NP.

110 Harry Dent, Nixon's   Dent to Rogers Morton, August 22, 1969; Dent to Clarke Reed, November 12, 1969, NP.

111 "basically a stranger"   Clarence L. Townes to Jimmy Allison, May 5, 1970, NP.

111 "[I]nstead of sending the orders"   Buchanan to Ehrlichman, H. R. Haldeman, and Charles Colson, September 23, 1972, NP.

111 "There is a legitimate grievance"   Buchanan to RMN, April 3, 1972, NP.

111 A Nixon campaign ad   *Washington Post,* October 9, 1972.

112 As pollster Sam Lubell   *Evening Star,* September 18, 1972.

112 The bishops publicly   "AME Bishops Say 'No' to Anti-Black President's Offer for Them to Dine at White House," DNC press release, September 21, 1972, MP.

112 The few prominent black Nixon   *Washington Post,* October 17, 1972.

112 The White House prepared   "Sargent Shriver and the Blacks," August 31, 1972, NP.

112 The campaign also tried   "Campaign Strategy Meetings" (Khachigian notes), September 9, 15, 23, 1972, NP.

112 Local Republicans   "What Has McGovern Done for the Blacks?", NA, ND, NP.

112 Consequently, McGovern never   McGovern interview.

112 "The black community is"   *U.S. News,* October 16, 1972.

112 Internal memos   Hillary Rodham to Don O'Brien and William Clinton, ND, MP.

113 "You can stand against"   "Statement by Senator George McGovern, Meeting with Black Ministers," October 6, 1972, MP.

113 The Republicans were, in fact   Buchanan to Clark, MacGregor, Haldeman, and Colson, August 1, 1972, NP.

113 "the Nixon Administration has"   "Draft for Los Angeles Black Leadership Luncheon," October 27, 1972, MP.

114 As the majority of   Certainly, Nixon's appeal in the South had myriad nonracial components, as discussed in Ambrose, *Triumph,* Black and Black, *Vital South,* Lesher, *Wallace.*

114 Yet the South   Leon Panetta, *Bring Us Together* (Philadelphia, 1971).

114 Six Justice Department   "Six Justice Department Attorneys Resign Over Civil Rights Enforcement," May 10, 1972, MP.

114 When Nixon visited Atlanta   *Newsweek,* October 23, 1972.

114 McGovern continued to be unpopular   *Christian Science Monitor,* May 5, 1972.

114 Other Democratic officeholders   *New York Times,* August 13, 1972.

114 In the end, Nixon won   Black and Black, *Vital South,* 305.

115 "This Family Shall"   *Daily News,* October 19, 1972.

115 In a national ad   *Washington Post,* August 16, 1972.

115 The White House coordinated   "Campaign Strategy Meetings," September 20, October 9, 1972, NP.

115 A foreign policy speech   Colson to Buchanan, Dwight Chapin, and David Gergen, October 3, 1972, NP.

115 "with increasingly little heart"   *Newsweek,* July 10, 1972.

116 No one could mistake   "Busing—Myths and Realities," NA, ND, MP.

116 McGovern never regretted   McGovern interview.

116 "The idea of quotas"   White, *Making 1972,* 32.

117 Hyman Bookbinder, of   *Washington Post,* September 2, 1972.

117 In his reply, Nixon   "Office Memorandum No. 73-17," October 19, 1972, NP.

117 While rejecting rigid   McGovern to Phillip E. Hoffman, August 16, 1972, MP.

117 Returning to California   *Baltimore Sun,* September 11, 1972.

117 "justify retrenchment"   "Statement on Quotas," October 4, 1972, MP.

117 In the end, Nixon   White, *Making 1972,* 371.

118 "open fags"   White, *Making 1972,* 188.

118 "as popular as a crab"   Nixon, *RN,* 437–38.

118 More certainly, however   *Washington Post,* September 19, 1972.

118 "Now that they have made"   "Clark Blasts Nixon Civil Rights Record," October 11, 1972, MP.

118 While blue-collar workers were   *New York Times,* October 12, 1972.

118 Nixon had succeeded in   Buchanan to Haldeman, June 18, 1972, NP.

119 The Nixon campaign was even   "Assault Strategy," June 8, 1972, NP.

119 "apartheid"   *Congressional Record,* Thursday, May 11, 1972.

119 Later, McGovern would explicitly   "Speech to National League of Cities," June 20, 1972, MP.

119 "break the tight ring"   "Assault Book," ND, NP.

119 On the eve of the election   *New York Times,* October 28, 1972.

119 White ethnic coolness   *Washington Post,* September 29, 1972.

120 "George McGovern talks about blacks"   *Washington Post,* September 26, 1972.

120   "Ethnic Heritage Studies"   "Nixon Administration Shows No Concern for Ethnic Groups, McGovern Says," October 28, 1972, MP.

120   "American symphony"   "Melting Pot Did Not Happen, Sargent Shriver Says," October 30, 1972, MP.

120   "McGovern, who supports"   "Assault Book," NP.

122   Nixon argued repeatedly   *New York Times,* October 22, 1972.

122   As a young ambitious   Lesher, *Wallace,* 491.

CHAPTER 6: FORD GIVES UP ON BLACKS

124   The opposition to busing   *Washington Star,* November 13, 1974.

124   Pollster Louis Harris   "Presentation by Louis Harris, Pollster, Chicago Democratic Conference," March 13–14, 1975, JEC.

124   The Congressional Black Caucus   *Washington Post,* August 20, 1975.

125   He had supported the civil   "Fact Sheet: Ford's Record on Key Bills," ND, GF.

125   "no worse than"   *Washington Post,* August 16, 1974.

125   When Boston erupted   Edward Levi interview with James Reichley, January 24, 1978, GF.

125   In his first few weeks as   Stan Scott to Ford, October 23, 1974; Scott to Robert T. Hartmann, September 12, 1974, GF.

125   Ford immediately increased   "Highlights of Administration Initiatives in Civil Rights and Related Social Programs," February 1975, GF; *Chicago Defender,* May 31, 1975.

126   "empty-handed"   *The Chronicle* (Charleston, S.C.), July 12, 1975.

126   "massuh"   Kandy Stroud, *How Jimmy Won* (New York, 1977), 123.

126   As a member of the local   "Carter and Blacks," NA, ND, GF.

126   As late as the spring of   James Wooten, *Dasher* (New York, 1978), 330.

127   "out-and-out racists"   Stroud, *Jimmy,* 48.

127   "aimed at the instincts"   Wooten, *Dasher,* 336.

127   Julian Bond, a prominent   Julian Bond, "Why I Don't Support Jimmy Carter," *The Nation,* April 17, 1976.

127   Carter supporters circulated   Martin Schram, *Running for President 1976* (New York, 1977), 48; Benjamin Stein, "If You Liked Richard Nixon, You'll Love Jimmy Carter," *Penthouse,* November 1976.

127   "The sound of Lester Maddox's"   John Dennis, "Casing the Democrats," *The Nation,* May 17, 1975.

128   "mistakes of the past"   "Issue Development for 1974 Democratic Party Campaign," October 27, 1973 (handwritten comments on copy from Rafshoon papers), JC.

128   In his announcement letter   "Letter to Friends," December 4, 1974, JC.

129   Ultimately, the convention   Jules Witcover, *Marathon* (New York, 1977), 129–30.

129   Almost all the candidates,   Witcover, *Marathon,* 181.

129   He condemned abortion   Witcover, *Marathon*, 207.

129   Similarly, Carter could   *Capital Times* (Madison, Wisc.), April 1, 1976.

129   Carter also would include   *Face the Nation* transcript, March 14, 1976, GF.

130   Critics charged that   Gerald Pomper, ed., *The Election of 1976* (New York, 1976), 12.

130   As late as January   *Newsweek*, January 12, 1976.

130   Issues such as abortion   "George C. Wallace Has the Courage America Needs Now," pamphlet, 1976, ADAH.

130   The new Wallace even   *Michigan Chronicle*, August 30, 1974; *Atlanta Journal*, September 19, 1975.

130   Carter blamed his defeat   Witcover, *Marathon*, 244.

131   Some, including civil rights   Jonathan Moore and Janet Fraser, *Campaign for President* (Cambridge, Mass., 1977), 94; Julian Bond, "Why I Don't Support Jimmy Carter," *The Nation*, April 1976.

131   For the first time   Moore and Fraser, *Campaign*, 91–94; *Minneapolis Tribune*, April 13, 1976.

131   "black intrusions"   Stroud, *Jimmy*, 278–80.

131   While Hosea Williams   *Los Angeles Times*, April 14, 1976.

132   "race baiting"   *Wichita Eagle*, April 15, 1976.

132   Ford himself attacked   "Black Americans," April 13, 1976, GF.

132   Some reporters believed   Stroud, *Jimmy*, 280–81.

132   A Republican pollster   Gergen to Richard Cheney, April 12, 1976, GF.

132   Coleman Young, the fiery   Wooten, *Dasher*, 357.

132   The irony was that Udall   *Congressional Quarterly, Candidates '76* (Washington, D.C., 1976), 72–77.

133   Thanks to strong black   *Washington Post*, May 20, 1976.

133   In a gesture to conservatives   John Osborne, *White House Watch* (Washington, D.C., 1977), 98.

133   In a twenty-nine-page campaign   Jack Calkins and Gwen Anderson to Ford, April 28, 1976, GF.

133   In a state-by-state   "The President Ford Committee Campaign Plan," August 29, 1975, GF.

134   In the Illinois showdown   Joint Center for Political Studies, *The Black Vote: Election '76* (Washington, 1977).

134   Black Republicans were particularly   Larnie G. Horton to Bob Marik, February 27, 1976; Robert L. Mitchell Sr. to Ford, February 24, 1976, GF.

134   Black turnout in   John Calhoun to Bill Baroody, May 27, 1976, GF.

134   Ford even ran ads   Moore and Fraser, *Campaign*, 105.

134   Reagan could not even   Robert J. Keyes to RR, September 17, 1975, GF.

134   During the campaign, Reagan even   Witcover, *Marathon*, 95.

134   Ford's pollster found   Malcolm D. MacDougall, *We Almost Made It* (New York, 1977), 48.

134   As Wallace's candidacy was throttled   *Newsweek*, May 17, 1976.

134   Reagan's campaign sent out   *Washington Star*, April 29, 1976.

134   Even after eighty-eight members   Don Young to Ford, October 3, 1975, GF.

135 Ford's opposition to busing   "Statement by the President," May 29, 1976; "Remarks of the President and Question and Answer Session at the Chamber of Commerce Breakfast," February 20, 1976, GF.

135 In many ways, Ford's   George Van Cleve to Gergen, June 4, 1976, GF.

135 A conservative group ran   *Baltimore Sun,* April 23, 1976.

135 Reagan linked declines   "Reagan and Busing," NA, ND, GF.

135 In a nationwide telecast   "Text of Governor Ronald Reagan's Nationwide Television Address, NBC," March 31, 1976, GF.

135 "we have adopted legislation"   "Text of Governor Ronald Reagan's Nationwide Television Address," July 6, 1976, GF.

136 Reagan supporters in North Carolina   *Wichita Eagle,* April 15, 1976.

136 Even Ford's advocacy   *Chicago Tribune,* May 12, 1976; Osborne, *Watch,* 345.

136 In this pressurized situation   *Wall Street Journal,* June 10, 1976; Jim Cannon to Ford, June 22, 1976, GF.

136 Although short of a ban   "Fact Sheet: The School Desegregation Standards and Assistance Act of 1976," June 24, 1976, GF.

136 "practically running our school"   *United Press International,* June 22, 1976.

136 Carter's campaign had succeeded   *Chicago Tribune,* July 14, 1976.

137 "cracker lovers"   *Chicago Tribune,* July 13, 1976.

137 Jackson tried to influence   *Chicago Tribune,* July 13, 1976.

137 "Mr. Busing"   *Newsweek,* July 26, 1976; *Congressional Quarterly,* July 24, 1976.

137 "it symbolized for blacks"   Henry A. Plotkin, "Issues in the 1976 Presidential Campaign," Pomper, *Election,* 44.

137 The platform committee   *Meet the Press* transcript, May 30, 1976, GF.

138 Hamilton Jordan   *Meet the Press* transcript, June 20, 1976, JC.

138 "compensatory opportunity"   *Newsweek,* July 26, 1976.

138 "mediocrity"   Chicago *Sun-Times,* October 15, 1975.

138 "goals and timetables"   *National Journal,* June 26, 1976, 902.

138 Blacks did not have   Pomper, *Election,* 30–31.

139 Blacks had played almost   *Observer Newspapers,* August 19–25, 1976.

139 "find issues"   "Special Voter Groups," Presidential Campaign Task Force, ND, GF.

139 Ford's chief of staff   James A. Reichley to Cheney, June 5 and June 25, 1976, GF.

140 Although a coordinated campaign   Mimi Austen to Bo Calloway, November 7, 1975, GF.

140 By the time James Baker   Ed DeBolt to James Baker, September 8, 1976, GF.

140 The "Black Desk"   Martin L. Dinkins to Mary Louis Smith, September 29, 1976, GF.

140 "State Coordinators"   "President Ford: We Can Depend on Him," brochure, 1976, GF.

140 The conversion of   Elly Peterson to Dinkins, October 7, 1976, GF.

140 When the Black Desk held   "Black Desk: First Progress Report," October 2, 1976, GF.

140 The deceptive ads were   *The Sun,* October 21, 1976.

140 "Shimmy Jimmy"   "Black Clergy Warn Against Carter Cunning," Independent Clergy Campaign Committee, October 27, 1976, GF.

140 The campaign failed to target   MacDougall, *Almost,* 233.

140 Ford's top media consultant   Moore and Fraser, *Campaign,* 139–40.

140 Some in the Ford campaign   MacDougall, *Almost,* 219, 233.

141 Ford continued in his   *Chicago Tribune,* July 14, 1976.

141 "I would like as many"   "Black Americans," April 13, 1976, GF.

141 "tight pussy"   Ron Nessen, *It Sure Looks Different from the Inside* (Chicago, 1978), 280–83, Osborne, *Watch,* 404–6.

141 The Black Desk at the Ford   "Butz statement response," NA, ND; Dinkins to Keyes, October 2, 1976, GF.

141 The Butz affair received   *New York Times,* October 10, 1976.

141 "given up on the black vote"   MacDougall, *Almost,* 233.

142 "secret"   William Coleman interview with James Reichley, December 19, 1977, GF.

142 "The cadences with which he speaks"   *Minneapolis Tribune,* April 13, 1976.

142 "The current welfare system is"   "Meeting with Stu Eizenstat, Re: Campaign Issues," July 31, 1976, JC.

142 Only Jesse Jackson   *Newsweek,* July 19, 1976.

143 In the Democratic attack/response   "Carter and Mondale on the Issues," Democratic Presidential Campaign Committee, JC.

143 When Vernon Jordan, president   "The State of Black America," January 28, 1976, GF.

143 Unlike McGovern, who   *Newsweek,* July 19, 1976.

143 "secret of his success"   Stroud, *Jimmy,* 170–71.

143 Carter's outreach to black churches   *Los Angeles Times,* August 11, 1976.

144 "To watch Jimmy Carter"   Michael Novak, *Washington Star,* May 9, 1976.

144 Although both Ford and Carter   *Christian Science Monitor,* April 12, 1976.

144 "Jimmy Carter grew up with black"   *New York,* July 19, 1976.

144 In addition to the early organizing   *New York Times,* August 14, 1976.

145 "Ford's busing"   "Quotes from Carter on Busing," ND, GF; *Atlanta Constitution,* May 18, 1976.

145 Ford's advisers were confused   "Carter vs. Ford on Busing," David Gergen, June 8, 1976; "Quotes from Carter on Busing," GF.

145 Ford finally did reluctantly   Plotkin, in Pomper, 45.

145 Similarly, his running mate   "Dole/Mondale Vote by Vote Comparison," ND, GF.

145 when Ford spoke   *Public Papers of Gerald R. Ford* (Washington, 1979), 1565–69; "President's Remarks Before the American Jewish Committee" (Gergen draft), May 13, 1976, GF.

145 Another Jewish magazine   *National Jewish Monthly,* September 1976; *Jewish Week and American Examiner,* September 5–11, 1976.

146 During a visit to Buffalo   Cannon to Cheney, October 30, 1976; Pat Rowland to Jack Marsh, October 28, 1976, GF.

146 In his remarks, Ford   *Public Papers,* 998.

146 That same week, Ford's   *Washington Post,* October 28, 1976.

146 His attorney general, Edward   Levi interview.

146 Some in the campaign saw   "Preliminary Media Plan for President Ford Campaign," August 21, 1976, GF.

146 "the problems in running a major busing"   "Special Voter Groups," GF.

147 Had Ford been less circumspect   David Treen interview with James Reichley, October 5, 1977, GF.

147 "the code word for racism"   *Meet the Press* transcript, May 30, 1976, GF.

147 "staked his political fortunes"   *Christian Science Monitor,* June 30, 1976.

147 "using the busing issue"   *Boston Globe,* June 3, 1976.

147 "does not quite suit my"   *Meet the Press* transcript, May 30, 1976, GF.

147 Black voters made the difference   Joint Center, *The Black Vote.*

147 Without the black vote,   Pomper, *Election,* 62.

148 "We utterly failed"   MacDougall, *Almost,* 169.

148 The Ford campaign considered   "Carter and the Blacks," GF.

148 A bold foray into   Michael Raoul-Duval to Cheney and Jerry Jones, October 19, 1976; "Presidential Visit to Bedford-Stuyvesant," October 1976, GF.

148 In the end, neither Ford   *St. Louis Post-Dispatch,* September 12, 1976.

148 Political historian Wilson   Wilson Carey McWilliams, in Pomper, *Election,* 161.

149 Dole, Ford's running mate   Robert Dole interview with James Reichley, September 9, 1977, GF.

149 "fulfills the easy task"   "Initial Working Paper on Political Strategy," December 10, 1976, JC.

CHAPTER 7: CARTER AND THE POLITICS OF FEAR

150 "It's going to be all right to kill"   Richard Hardwood, ed., *The Pursuit of the Presidency* (New York, 1980), 286.

150 "After you get through booing"   *Newsweek,* March 10, 1980.

151 Fewer intercounty busing plans   *U.S. News,* September 15, 1980.

151 By the start of the general election   *Time,* September 15, 1980.

152 Reagan grew up in a world   Lou Cannon, *President Reagan* (New York, 1991), 519; Ronnie Dugger, *On Reagan* (New York, 1983), 195.

152 Throughout his public life   Edwin Meese interview, March 6, 2000; Richard Wirthlin interview, November 20, 2000.

152 "You can't guarantee"   Dugger, *Reagan,* 197.

152 The press coverage was   Lynn Nofziger, *Nofziger* (Washington, 1992), 38–40.

152 Throughout his career, Reagan   Cannon, *Reagan*, 519–21.

153 "In the backlash context"   Dugger, *Reagan*, 199–200.

153 As governor, Reagan would   Nofziger, *Nofziger*, 244.

153 Reagan, who had opposed   Dan T. Carter, *From George Wallace to Newt Gingrich* (Baton Rouge, 1996), 55–56.

153 "The greatest proof"   Dugger, *Reagan*, 197.

153 "a great tragedy that began"   Dugger, *Reagan*, 200.

153 "heartless know-nothing foe"   Hardwood, *Pursuit*, 263.

154 Some might have seen   Cannon, *Reagan*, 519–20.

154 "learning how to gain"   Hanes Walton Jr., *African American Power and Politics* (New York, 1997), 20; Wayne Greenshaw, *Elephants in the Cottonfields* (New York, 1982), 9–14.

154 "young buck"   Nofziger, *Nofziger*, 177.

154 "welfare queen"   Cannon, *Reagan*, 518–19.

154 So hurt was Reagan   Nofziger, *Nofziger*, 244.

155 An "insensitive" joke   Dugger, *Reagan*, 199.

155 Many of his closest associates   Martin Anderson interview, January 2000; Meese interview, Wirthlin interview.

155 "think in terms of race"   Nofziger, *Nofziger*, 244.

155 "bigotry and prejudice"   "Town Meeting of the World," video, May 15, 1967, RR.

155 The number of black federal   Lois B. Moreland, in David and Everson, eds., *The Presidential Election and Transition, 1980–1981* (Carbondale, Ill., 1982), 103.

155 From its earliest moments   "Minority Appointments Profile, Compiled for Hamilton Jordan," March 16, 1977, JC.

156 Racial balance in key   "Memorandum for the President from Jack Watson," December 1, 1979, JC.

156 "figureheads"   Gerald Rafshoon to Louis Martin, October 20, 1978, JC.

156 On affirmative action   Theodore H. White, *America in Search of Itself* (New York, 1982), 131.

156 "moved the government out"   "The First Two Years," December 21, 1978, JC.

156 "private Christian schools"   *Washington Post*, December 12, 1978; *New York Times*, December 8, 1978, and August 1, 1980.

156 A memo from Carter's top   Steven M. Gillon, *The Democrats' Dilemma* (New York, 1992), 206.

156 Carter demanded Young's resignation   *Washington Star*, August 16, 1979.

156 The civil rights leadership   "Statement of Black Leadership Forum," August 16, 1979, JC.

156 "decided to sacrifice Africa"   *New York Times*, August 16, 1979.

157 In his resignation letter   Andrew Young to JEC, August 14, 1979, JC; *St. Louis Post Dispatch*, August 16, 1979.

157 "is going to assure a Republican"   *Washington Star*, August 16, 1979.

157 By the time he became the front-runner   Richard Bond interview, September 6, 2000; Doug Bailey interview, November 13, 2000; Wirthlin interview.

158   Unlike Reagan, Bush endorsed   *Newsweek,* February 4, 1980.

158   Bush, however, never sought   Bond interview.

158   Similarly, when Reagan attacked   *Newsweek,* February 25, 1980.

158   When Bush and Reagan met   "April 4th Debate in Houston, Texas, between George Bush and Ronald Reagan," video, RR.

158   Anderson, Bush, and Reagan split   Moreland, in David and Everson, *Presidential,* 99–100.

158   Although Reagan met with   Charles O. Jones, in Austin Ranney, ed., *The American Elections of 1980* (Washington, 1981), 94.

158   Only 55 of 1,993   Moreland, in Davis and Everson, *Presidential,* 99.

158   In choosing a running mate   *Newsweek,* July 28, 1980.

158   The Republican convention and platform   Michael J. Malbin, in Ranney, *American,* 100–101.

158   One sign that blacks   Paul T. David, in David and Everson, *Presidential,* 73.

159   "one of the bloodiest fronts"   *Richmond Times Dispatch,* December 16, 1979.

159   The Carter forces carefully   Martin to Phil Wise, January 17, 1980, JC.

159   "He is really sweating"   Martin to JEC, January 30, 1980, JC.

159   "an accommodation"   "Why We Need a Third Political Force?" People United to Save Humanity, December 26, 1980, JC.

160   "least desirable"   "An Interview with Senator Edward Kennedy," transcript, November 1, 1979, JC.

160   Only in Illinois did   Moreland, in David and Everson, *Presidential,* 99–100.

160   Carter's campaign worried   Rick Rendon to Tom Donilon, July 14, 1980, JC.

160   But Carter's black support remained   "Statement by Coretta Scott King," ND, JC.

160   The key may have been   Hardwood, *Pursuit,* 72.

161   Much more attention   "This is a first cut at a general election strategy," ND, JC.

161   When Carter's political brain trust   Richard Moe to Hamilton Jordan, September 28, 1979; "Themes, Draft One," ND (1979?), JC.

161   Following the Kennedy defeat   Eizenstat to JEC, May 31, 1980, JC.

161   In a postconvention Caddell   Pat Caddell to JEC, August 17, 1980, JC.

161   "our 'affirmative' actions may provoke"   "Initial Working Paper on Political Strategy," December 10, 1976, JC.

161   Of course, Carter's campaign   Rafshoon to Carter, 1979, JC.

161   They reminded him that   Moreland, in David and Everson, *Presidential,* 103.

162   What, then, had blacks   *Congressional Record,* December 12, 1980.

162   Before Carter met with   Frank Moore and Eizenstat to JEC, June 7, 1980, JC.

162   The top issues were   *Newsweek,* March 10, 1980; *U.S. News,* October 13, 1980.

162   "Many blacks view the campaign"   *U.S. News,* September 29, 1980.

162 "[b]lack dissatisfaction with Carter's" *U.S. News,* October 13, 1980.

162 "There are even those who say" "Address of Senator Edward M. Kennedy, 71st Annual Convention of the NAACP," July 2, 1980, JC.

163 "I have a secret weapon" White, *America,* 380.

163 So ably and eloquently Mark Bisnow, *Diary of a Dark Horse* (Carbondale, Ill., 1983), 64–65.

163 By some accounts Harwood, *Pursuit,* 218–19.

163 "There is a very strong" "Black Vote," June 28, 1980, JC.

163 Indeed, Anderson's campaign manager Bisnow, *Diary,* 166.

163 The Anderson-Lucey platform *Atlanta Journal-Constitution,* October 21, 1980.

164 Anderson spoke to national black *Amsterdam News,* August 9, 1980; *Cleveland Plain Dealer,* August 9, 1980.

164 He accused Reagan "Anderson-Reagan Debate" video, September 21, 1980, RR.

164 Reagan entered the election Wirthlin interview.

164 The goal of the campaign White, *America,* 381.

164 "A speech by Jerry Ford" *Newsweek,* August 18, 1980.

164 "I can't do a damn thing" Harwood, *Pursuit,* 270; *Newsweek,* August 18, 1980; Wirthlin interview.

165 "turned the event into a major" Nofziger, *Nofziger,* 256–57.

165 Reagan also had a public shouting match "Political News Summary," May 22, 1968, MHS.

165 "anti-poor, anti-black" "Address by the Honorable Ronald Reagan to the Annual Convention of the National Urban League," August 5, 1980, RR.

165 Reagan also met with Jesse Nofziger, *Nofziger,* 257.

165 Jackson, who had publicly toyed *St. Petersburg Times,* July 21, 1980.

165 "I think we have opened communications" *U.S. News,* August 18, 1980.

166 "poor Ralph" *Atlanta Journal-Constitution,* October 21, 1980.

166 Even Jackson praised "An Analysis of the Remarks of the Honorable Ronald Reagan Before the Urban League Convention," Jesse Jackson, August 1980, JC.

166 Reagan's central focus Harwood, *Pursuit,* 281; Wirthlin, Bond, Anderson interviews.

166 Even when Reagan did *Newsweek,* April 14, 1980.

166 In speeches directed at "Speech by Governor Ronald Reagan, Green Bay, Wisconsin," October 2, 1980; "Speech by Governor Ronald Reagan, Wheaton College," October 8, 1980, RR.

166 "I recognize the need to offer *U.S. News,* October 6, 1980.

167 "I stood . . . in the South Bronx" "Reagan Reports" transcript, October 12, 1980, RR.

168 Reagan had no need Wirthlin interview.

168 Incensed at Wirthlin's refusal Wirthlin interview.

168 "Carter hoped to increase" Albert R. Hunt, in Ranney, *Elections,* 160.

168 "an erroneous but widespread belief" "Black Vote," July 28, 1980, JC.

169   Democrats hoped to use   *Time,* September 1, 1980.

169   "Isn't it time we laid off"   "Debate Background Materials," September 13, 1980, JC.

170   However, now that Reagan   *New York Times,* August 1, 1980; Hunt, in Ranney, *Elections,* 149–50.

170   "You've seen in this campaign"   Hunt, in Ranney, *Elections,* 155.

170   In August, Carter's administration seized on   "Rising Klu [*sic*] Klan Activities Pose Threat for Nation. President Carter Clamps Down on Justice Department," press release, August 15, 1980, JC; see also coverage in the *Times Herald Record* (Middletown, N.Y.).

171   Carter's managers later argued   Jonathan Moore, *The Campaign for President* (Cambridge, Mass., 1981), 209–11.

171   The effort was intentional   James Reston, *Dayton Daily News,* September 23, 1980.

171   When the managers   Moore, *Campaign.*

172   "just wanted to show"   White, *America,* 385; Wirthlin interview.

CHAPTER 8: THE AGE OF JACKSON

173   "Run! When you run"   Peter Goldman and Tony Fuller, *The Quest for the Presidency, 1984* (New York, 1985), 104.

173   "It's not so much white drift"   Harold W. Stanley, in Robert P. Steed et al., *The 1984 Presidential Election in the South* (New York, 1986), 316.

174   The victory against de jure   Lucius J. Barker and Ronald W. Walters, eds., *The 1984 Presidential Campaign of Jesse Jackson* (Chicago, 1985), 21.

174   The great majority of blacks   William Crotty, in Barker and Walters, *Jackson,* 68.

174   While Americans continued to   "Americans Favor Affirmative Action Programs," January 28, 1982, RR.

174   Busing, the least popular   "Majorities Oppose Many 'Moral Majority' Positions," March 15, 1982, RR.

174   Still, as many as seventeen   "Busing as a Remedy in School Desegregation Cases," April 2, 1982, RR.

174   Even following the campaign   Michael J. Robinson, in Austin Ranney, ed., *The American Elections of 1984* (Durham, N.C., 1985), 186.

174   Ironically, it was only on   "A Perceptual Analysis of the Presidential Candidates," February 1984, RR.

175   The administration sponsored   Ronald Walters interview, October 24, 2000.

175   Reagan and his supporters   Ronald Reagan, *Speaking My Mind* (New York, 1989), 160–63.

175   Within the administration, however   Anderson interview.

175   This angered many true   Kenneth Cribb to Craig Fuller, July 23, 1981, RR.

175   Reagan also faced pressure   Jerry Falwell to RR, March 15, 1983, RR.

175 Racial conservatives and modern defenders   Lott was crucial in bringing the Bob Jones case to Reagan's attention. Cannon, *Reagan,* 520–22.

176 Reagan angered some on   *Washington Post,* October 18, 1983; *Newsweek,* October 10, 1983.

176 "In one sentence"   *Newsweek,* October 31, 1983.

176 "a black, a woman"   Richard Brookheiser, *The Outside Story* (Garden City, N.Y., 1986), 10–11.

176 "While no single category of"   Edwin L. Harper to RR, March 5, 1982, RR.

177 "the elimination of Reaganism"   *Newsweek,* September 5, 1983.

177 "biggest contribution is staying"   *Washington Post,* October 19, 1983.

177 Ed Meese, the leading voice   Edwin Meese, *With Reagan* (Washington, 1992), 316–18.

178 "totally false image"   *Public Papers of the President* (Washington, 1983), 1098–1100.

178 "a crusader for civil rights"   *New York Times,* July 16, 1981.

178 Civil rights was one of the key   Gillon, *Democrats',* 24–25.

178 "morally correct and politically shrewd"   Gillon, *Democrats',* 69.

178 Working directly for LBJ   Finley Lewis, *Mondale* (New York, 1980), 132–36.

178 "five most dramatic"   Gillon, *Democrats',* 88.

178 "Decent housing does not"   Gillon, *Democrats',* 106–8.

178 "Mr. Busing"   *Congressional Quarterly, Candidates '84* (Washington, 1984), 114.

179 "the sickening truth"   Lewis, *Mondale,* 194.

179 He also angered   Gillon, *Democrats',* 126, 134.

179 Mondale chose a middle path   Gillon, *Democrats',* 137–41.

179 Mondale's rhetoric on busing   Lewis, *Mondale,* 223.

179 Mondale, like many wealthy   Gillon, *Democrats',* 144.

179 "favored son"   Lewis, *Mondale,* 9.

179 "how many blacks I want"   Gillon, *Democrats',* 175–76.

179 Mondale privately believed   Gillon, *Democrats',* 190–92.

179 "a political signal of the"   Gillon, *Democrats',* 193–94; Brookheiser, *Outside,* 53–54.

180 In a meeting with the prime   Lewis, *Mondale,* 253–54.

180 "No one anointed"   Bob Faw and Nancy Skelton, *Thunder in America* (Austin, Tex., 1986), 30.

180 Among the factors pushing   Walters interview.

180 Jackson, who claimed   Ron Walters, in Barker and Walters, *Jackson,* 38–40.

181 Against the explicit   Faw and Skelton, *Thunder,* 234–35; *Congressional Quarterly, Candidates,* 92–93.

181 "flashy trespasser"   Goldman and Fuller, *Quest,* 107.

181 To many, it seemed   Barker, in Barker and Walters, *Jackson,* 10–11; Walters interview.

181 "Run, Jesse, Run!" Walters, in Barker and Walters, *Jackson*, 39–44.

181 "You can't teach Jesse" Faw and Skelton, *Thunder*, 13.

181 Jackson's chances were also *Newsweek*, September 26, 1983.

182 By running, Jackson *Playboy*, July 1984.

182 "being the party concubines" Faw and Skelton, *Thunder*, 10–11.

182 Some states still had Faw and Skelton, *Thunder*, 33–39.

182 A record number of states Crotty, in Barker and Walters, *Jackson*, 80–82.

183 When he succeeded *Time*, January 16, 1984.

183 Jackson, who had already Robinson, in Ranney, *American*, 180.

183 "beat up on" *Time*, January 16, 1984.

184 "conspiracy" "crucifixion" Faw and Skelton, *Thunder*, 49.

184 He had even compared Faw and Skelton, *Thunder*, 63–64.

184 "I am sick and tired" Only later did the exact quote come out: "It's about time American Jews stopped putting Americans on a guilt trip about the Holocaust." Faw and Skelton, *Thunder*, 66–68.

184 "fuck the Jews" Faw and Skelton, *Thunder*, 49.

184 The tardy speech Goldman and Fuller, *Quest*, 119–21.

184 The first question aimed Brookheiser, *Outside*, 88.

184 Up until this point Brookheiser, *Outside*, 83–85.

186 Indeed, Hart even encouraged Goldman and Fuller, *Quest*, 159.

186 Not only were his main interests *Congressional Quarterly, Candidates*, 74.

186 "white primary" Goldman and Fuller, *Quest*, 156.

186 Many of them felt eclipsed Walters interview.

186 With such inflammatory statements Goldman and Fuller, *Quest*, 159–62; Faw and Skelton, *Thunder*, 128–32.

186 In Philadelphia, Mondale's campaign Goldman and Fuller, *Quest*, 178.

186 Hart's campaign contemplated Goldman and Fuller, *Quest*, 101.

187 For Mondale, Jackson was Goldman and Fuller, *Quest*, 182.

187 "the sun of thunder" Faw and Skelton, *Thunder*, 152.

187 "We picked their cotton" *U.S. News*, December 19, 1984.

187 A poll among Democrats *Time*, February 20, 1984.

187 "If any candidate" *Newsweek*, May 7, 1984.

187 For Jackson, this was Gillon, *Democrats'*, 352.

188 Black registration went up Faw and Skelton, *Thunder*, 153, 205; Glen E. Thurow, in Peter W. Schramm and Dennis J. Mahoney, eds., *The 1984 Election and the Future of American Politics* (Durham, N.C., 1987), 48.

188 "dirty religion" *Newsweek*, July 9, 1984.

188 Mondale quickly attacked Gillon, *Democrats'*, 125.

188 The threat was taken seriously Faw and Skelton, *Thunder*, 110–14.

189 "Jesus repudiated the politics" Faw and Skelton, *Thunder*, 115–17.

189 Jackson could not afford Walters interview.

189 "World War III" Gillon, *Democrats'*, 350.

189 "last significant politician" Goldman and Fuller, *Quest*, 222–23.

189 "ghettoized" Weekly News Summary, CBS, July 15, 1984, RR.

190 "This is the best conversation" Goldman and Fuller, *Quest*, 227.

190 Of the remaining seven   Brookheiser, *Outside*, 154–56.

190 "pandering"   Goldman and Fuller, *Quest*, 206.

191 The quota issue deeply   Robert G. Newby, in Barker and Walter, *Jackson*, 172.

191 "verifiable measurements"   Thurow in Schramm and Mahoney, *Election*, 51; Goldman and Fuller, *Quest*, 234.

191 Jackson forces won their   Curtina Moreland-Young, in Barker and Walters, *Jackson*, 156–57.

191 "a bit unwashed"   Newby, in Barker and Walters, *Jackson*, 164–66.

192 "black eunuchs"   Goldman and Fuller, *Quest*, 223–24.

192 As the victor   Walters interview; Faw and Skelton, *Thunder*, 187.

192 "wait for his signal"   Weekly News Summary, ABC, July 7, 1984, RR.

192 "can disrupt the convention"   Faw and Skelton, *Thunder*, 190–91.

192 Yet one group was immune   Goldman and Fuller, *Quest*, 28–33.

193 "Of course, civil rights is"   Wirthlin interview.

193 Reagan's campaign knew well   "Reagan Campaign Action Plan," October 27, 1983, RR.

193 Although Reagan had spoken   *Washington Times*, October 18, 1983.

193 "looked like a GOP Rainbow"   Brookheiser, *Outside*, 225, 210–11.

194 Yet away from the podium   Charles O. Jones, in Ranney, *American*, 98.

194 The platform, like Mondale's first   Jeffrey Douglas and Dennis Teti, in Schramm and Mahoney, *Election*, 65–66.

194 "your vote may already be"   Stanley, in Steed et al., *Presidential*, 311–12.

194 "Jackson helped me with the turnout"   Faw and Skelton, *Thunder*, 214–15.

194 "we can assess more clearly"   "Reagan Campaign Action Plan," 141, October 27, 1983, RR.

195 "a beautiful stroke"   *Time*, February 20, 1984.

195 While Charlotte had been   Jack Fleer, in Steed et al., *Presidential*, 259.

195 "It was very embarrassing"   Gillon, *Democrats'*, 372.

196 Rather than taking his grievances   Gillon, *Democrats'*, 372.

196 From that point on, Jesse Jackson   Goldman and Fuller, *Quest*, 274.

196 "the last day of the primary"   *Newsweek*, September 10, 1984.

196 "'Jesse's got to have his self-respect'"   Faw and Skelton, *Thunder*, 246.

197 More than a quarter of   Gillon, *Democrats'*, 389.

197 "How would Democrats convince"   Gillon, *Democrats'*, 309–10.

197 "He inspires and he scares"   Gillon, *Democrats'*, 349.

198 "a great deal of underlying racism"   Alexander P. Lamis, in Steed et al., *Presidential*, 65.

198 "George Bush was in Mobile"   Stanley, in Steed et al., *Presidential*, 316.

198 Mondale's racial liberalism hurt   Steven Rosenstone, *Brookings Review*, Winter 1985.

199 "Nobody wanted to admit"   Faw and Skelton, *Thunder*, 39.

199 Similarly, whites saw Reagan's   Crotty, in Barker and Walters, *Jackson*, 69–71.

199 Mondale did succeed in convincing   William Schneider, in Ranney, *American*, 218.
200 The report was so damning   Gillon, *Democrats'*, 395.

CHAPTER 9: FURLOUGH FROM THE TRUTH

201 Estrich and Atwater quotes, David R. Runkel, ed., *Campaign for President* (Dover, Mass., 1989), 113–17.
202 Reagan had abjectly failed   *Newsweek*, March 7, 1988.
203 During the Reagan presidency,   Michael Dawson, in Hanes Walton Jr., *African American Power and Politics*, 149.
204 Bush, raised in a tradition   Herbert Parmet, *George Bush* (New York, 1997), 65–66.
204 "He told his crowds"   Parmet, *Bush*, 108–9.
204 Bush said that what   *Newsweek*, October 19, 1987; Parmet, *Bush*, 102.
204 Bush met with black leaders   Parmet, *Bush*, 120–32.
204 In the 1980 Republican   Bond interview; Carter, *Wallace*, 73–74.
206 After Hart's candidacy was derailed   Kenneth Wald, in Emmet Buell and Lee Sigelman, eds., *Nominating the President* (Knoxville, Tenn., 1991), 126–27.
206 "When they close down"   *Congressional Quarterly, Candidates '88* (Washington, 1988), 211.
206 Jackson spoke in the white   Marshall Frady, *Jesse* (New York, 1996), 381.
206 Jackson even visited   Lesher, *Wallace*, xvii, 504–6.
207 "whitening his message"   *Newsweek*, February 8, 1988.
207 The most prominent black supporter   *Newsweek*, December 1, 1987.
207 "the five star general"   *Time*, April 25, 1988.
207 Sharpton and his associates   *Newsweek*, March 7, 1988.
207 "'84 was a crusade"   Frady, *Jesse*, 378.
207 "If it's seen that the nominee"   *Newsweek*, March 7, 1988.
208 He even echoed   Christine Black and Thomas Oliphant, *All By Myself* (Chester, Conn., 1989), 82.
208 Even though Dukakis had   Buell and Sigelman, *Nominating*, 28.
209 Now Jackson had won   *Newsweek*, April 11, 1988.
209 Unable to stay on the   Buell and Sigelman, *Nominating*, 30–31.
209 Dukakis also defeated Jackson   *Newsweek*, April 11, 1988.
210 Surprisingly, the candidate   *Newsweek*, April 18, 1988.
210 "lies under stress"   *Time*, May 2, 1988.
210 For the five days leading   Bill Turque, *Inventing Al Gore* (New York, 2000), 210.
210 "we're not choosing a preacher"   *Newsweek*, April 11, 1988.
210 Second-tier candidate Senator Paul Simon   Black and Oliphant, *Myself*, 121.
210 Simultaneously, Dukakis sympathizers   *Time*, April 18, 1988.
210 Dukakis did not campaign   *Time*, May 2, 1988.

213 Moreover, many other states   Black and Oliphant, *Myself,* 218–19.

213 "Here's [Bush's] first ad"   Black and Oliphant, *Myself,* 143.

213 The message was immediately apparent   Turque, *Inventing,* 210–11.

214 Atwater was also the Bush staffer   John Joseph Brady, *Bad Boy* (Reading, Mass., 1997), 183.

214 "the easy-to-digest tale"   Brady, *Bad Boy,* 148.

214 Along with Dukakis's   Haynes Johnson, *Sleepwalking Through History* (New York, 1991), 395–97.

214 In another focus group   Runkel, *Campaign,* 117.

214 "it was the only way"   Carter, *Wallace,* 75.

215 "voters seem to judge"   Frady, *Jesse,* 404.

215 Although Dukakis went out of   *Time,* June 20, 1988.

215 Dukakis was afraid   *Time,* August 1, 1988.

215 "keep hope alive"   Buell and Sigelman, *Nominating,* 237.

215 Dukakis headquarters was   Frady, *Jesse,* 405–7; Black and Oliphant, *Myself,* 167.

215 "I'm going to push him"   *Time,* June 20, 1988.

215 "equal standing"   Frady, *Jesse,* 403.

216 "he'd been treated like a nigger"   Frady, *Jesse,* 407.

216 Dukakis, who had wanted   *Time,* July 18, 1988.

216 Jackson continued to jet   Frady, *Jesse,* 405–6.

216 Jackson's negotiators shot back   *Time,* July 18, 1988.

216 Dukakis staffers pressured   Black and Oliphant, *Myself,* 166–68.

216 Dukakis seemed to think   Frady, *Jesse,* 408–9.

216 Dukakis eliminated Gore from consideration   Turque, *Inventing,* 215; *Time,* July 18, 1988.

216 surprisingly strong record   *Time,* July 25, 1988.

216 But Jackson found out   Black and Oliphant, *Myself,* 164–66.

217 "It is too much to expect"   Stephen Holmes, *Ron Brown* (New York, 2000), 152.

217 "I will never surrender!"   Black and Oliphant, *Myself,* 166–69.

217 Some in the press   *Time,* July 25, 1988.

217 The mood of the crowd was   Frady, *Jesse,* 409.

217 Thus, on the eve   Black and Oliphant, *Myself,* 166–68.

217 DUKAKIS GIVES JACKSON NOTHING   Buell and Sigelman, *Nominating,* 34; Frady, *Jesse,* 410–11.

218 "the press will burn you"   Holmes, *Brown,* 154.

218 "any measurably overt moves"   Bond interview.

218 The general public   Buell and Sigelman, *Nominating,* 233–39.

219 "The only question is whether we"   *Time,* August 22, 1988.

219 "come to symbolize"   Kathleen Hall Jamieson, *Dirty Politics* (New York, 1993), 134.

219 The Bush team shot   Jamieson, *Dirty,* 34.

219 "every suburban mother's"   Stephen Wayne and Clyde Wilcox, eds., *The Quest for National Office* (New York, 1992), 230.

219 Another PAC spent Stephen Wayne, *The Road to the White House* (New York, 1992), 219; Jamieson, *Dirty,* 25–30.

219 Cliff Barnes, the fiancé Black and Oliphant, *Myself,* 226–27.

219 Some state Republican Gerald Pomper, ed., *The Elections of 1988* (Chatham, N.J., 1989), 86; Jack Germond and Jules Witcover, *Whose Broad Stripes and Bright Stars* (New York, 1989), 11–12.

220 "the faintly hollow ring" Peter Goldman and Tom Matthews, *The Quest for the Presidency* (New York, 1989), 359.

220 This was emphatically encouraged Black and Oliphant, *Myself,* 225.

220 Once it aired Wayne and Wilcox, *Quest,* 232.

220 The media bought Tali Mendleberg, "Public Norms and White Response to Covert Racial Appeals," a paper presented at the 1995 annual meeting of the American Political Science Association.

221 Even the refusal Black and Oliphant, *Myself,* 225–26.

221 In a postelection investigation Parmet, *Bush,* 352–53.

221 "single most effective" Germond and Witcover, *Whose,* 410.

221 Horton was as well-known Thomas Patterson, *Out of Order* (New York, 1993), 163.

221 And those who had seen Darrell West, *Air Wars* (Washington, 1993), 114.

221 "leniency to criminals" Martin Wattenberg, *The Rise of Candidate-Centered Politics* (Cambridge, Mass.).

222 In an early June campaign memo Black and Oliphant, *Myself,* 147.

222 but pressure from local Black and Oliphant, *Myself,* 185–86.

222 Dukakis seldom campaigned Black and Oliphant, *Myself,* 318–19.

222 "grudgingly and reluctantly" *Time,* October 31, 1988.

222 Jackson once again complained *Time,* November 21, 1988.

222 Dukakis's staff had *Time,* October 31, 1988.

222 Jackson also complained directly Holmes, *Brown,* 158–59.

222 Only in the last two weeks *Time,* October 31, 1988, November 21, 1988.

223 "Dukakis of course might" *Time,* November 14, 1988.

223 After all, Dukakis reasoned Black and Oliphant, *Myself,* 153.

224 Far more graphic than Black and Oliphant, *Myself,* 255.

224 Atwater told reporters Black and Oliphant, *Myself,* 225.

224 "He can't vote" Patterson, *Order,* 164; Jamieson, *Dirty,* 31.

224 "lies" Black and Oliphant, *Myself,* 302–4.

225 However, Dukakis's factual Germond and Witcover, *Whose,* 2–12.

225 "While race has been" James Glaser and Ewa Golebiowska, "White Attributions for Racial Inequality and Campaign Sway," a paper presented at the 1996 annual meeting of the Midwest Political Science Association.

225 Lee Atwater even made Runkel, *Campaign,* 117.

225 Even if some voters Glaser and Golebiowska, 1996.

227 "all of the white men in America" Black and Oliphant, *Myself,* 284.

227 "the attitude among the white" Holmes, *Brown,* 149.

228 "I watched him" Holmes, *Brown,* 158–59.

CHAPTER 10: FORGETTING ABOUT RACE

229 "Let's forget about race"   *Newsweek*, March 23, 1992.
229 "The day he told off that fucking"   Carter, *Wallace*, 100.
231 Bush also met with   Walton, *African American*, 138.
231 "This bill could lead"   Kweisi Mfume, *No Free Ride* (New York, 1996), 297.
231 Some believed that   Michael Kinsley, "Hortonism Redux," *New Republic*, June 24, 1991; Kevin Phillips, *Boiling Point* (New York, 1993), 238.
232 Rather, the heat from civil   Mfume, *Ride*, 302.
232 When the young Clinton   Roger Morris, *Partners in Power* (New York, 1996), 145.
233 "the lesson of not being"   David Maraniss, *First in His Class* (New York, 1995), 285.
233 Black counties produced   Hanes Walton, *Reelection* (New York, 2000), 151–52.
233 "redneck"   Maraniss, *First*, 393; Morris, *Partners*, 241–42.
233 His 1982 primary victory   Maraniss, *First*, 401.
233 "It was simply taken for granted"   Morris, *Partners*, 284–85.
234 Black voters, angered   Steed et al., *Presidential*, 183.
234 "No one in the Arkansas political"   Maraniss, *First*, 403.
234 Yet Arkansas, after   Maraniss, *First*, 453.
234 In one of the counties   Lani Guinier, *Lift Every Voice* (New York, 1998), 11–12, 54.
234 Clinton made education the   Morris, *Partners*, 456.
234 "classic Clinton"   *National Journal*, December 12, 1992.
235 "The most tell-tale sign"   Walton, *African American*, 28.
235 Daley was supported by   Holmes, *Brown*, 201–2.
235 pressed Jackson to sit   Anthony Corrado, in Daniel Shea and John Green, eds., *The State of the Parties* (Lanham, Md., 1994).
235 "Jackson's decision helped"   Lucius J. Barker, "Limits of Political Strategy," *American Political Science Review*, 1994, 6.
235 "a candidate who happened"   Walton, *African American*, 299.
236 He even attacked Clinton   Walton, *African American*, 301–2.
236 He flew to Washington   George Stephanopoulos, *All Too Human* (New York, 1999), 44.
236 "tough love"   Stephanopoulos, *Human*, 44.
237 Vernon Jordan, for one   Walton, *African American*, 319.
237 Of course, Jackson remained   *Newsweek*, March 9, 1992.
237 "bubba" tactic   Morris, *Partners*, 459–60.
237 During the primaries, even when   Walton, *African American*, 318.
238 "Never . . . has a contender"   Morris, *Partners*, 465.
238 During the southern primaries   Theodore Rueter, ed., *The Politics of Race*, (Armonk, N.Y., 1995), 389.
238 The reaction among   Charles T. Royer, ed., *Campaign for President* (Hollis, N.H., 1993), 85–87.

238 Clinton countered Brown's   Samuel J. Eldersveld and Hanes Walton, *Political Parties in American Society* (New York, 2000), 237.

239 In almost every   Gerald Pomper, ed., *The Elections of 1992* (Chatham, N.J.: 1993), 102–3.

240 "those people"   *Newsweek*, August 24, 1992.

240 "revolting"   *Time*, May 11, 1992.

240 "The candidates and their handlers"   Michael Kramer, *Time*, May 18, 1992.

240 "Go home!"   *Time*, May 18, 1992.

240 Clinton responded that   John Hohenberg, *The Bill Clinton Story* (Syracuse, N.Y., 1994), 27.

241 "It has become increasingly clear"   *Time*, May 18, 1992.

241 "running from stores, their arms laden"   *Time*, May 18, 1992.

241 "We'll hit him for supporting"   *Time*, May 18, 1992.

242 Souljah's comment   Carter, *Wallace*, 99.

242 "The mood in the room was incredulous"   Walters interview.

242 "woofing for the benefit"   Peter Goldman et al., *Quest for the Presidency 1992* (College Station, Tex., 1994), 275.

242 Like much of Clinton's   Morris, *Partners*, 348.

243 "the race issue quickly dropped"   Carter, *Wallace*, 98.

243 A Republican campaign official   Royer, *Campaign*, 201.

243 Still, some black leaders   Walton, *African American*, 138.

243 Perot traveled to Harlem   Walton, *African American*, 289–91.

243 Also, in the immediate aftermath   *Time*, June 29, 1992.

243 The presence of Perot   *Time*, June 1, 1992.

244 "white folk have used when"   Walton, *African American*, 288–89.

244 The press criticism was searing.   Myron Levine, *Presidential Campaigns and Elections* (Itasca, Ill., 1995), 267.

245 Jackson again made noises   James Ceaser and Andrew Busch, *Upside Down and Inside Out* (Lanham, Md., 1993), 23, 74–76.

245 "economic empowerment"   Walton, *African American*, 319.

246 "in a naked bid for"   *Newsweek*, March 9, 1992.

246 "Why are we more shocked"   *Newsweek*, January 27, 1992.

248 Some believed that   Edsall and Edsall, *Chain*; Louis Bolce et al., "The 1992 Republican 'Tent,'" *Political Science Quarterly*, 1993, 269.

248 "If we help train you and"   *Time*, May 4, 1992.

248 "a woman who gives you her"   *National Journal*, December 12, 1992.

248 But postelection studies suggested   Pomper, *Elections of 1992*, 103.

249 "Clinton's task, then, was"   Pomper, *Elections of 1992*, 62.

249 Stan Greenberg, Clinton's most   Carter, *Wallace*, 98.

249 This may have been because reporters   Carter, *Wallace*, 93, 96.

250 "old Willie Horton into a beautiful"   *Time*, June 1, 1992.

250 "fumbled away the quota issue"   *National Journal*, December 12, 1992.

250 "In 1992 . . . race was a dog"   Quoted in Pomper, *Elections*, 203.

250 A split in the white vote   Mayer, "Critical Mass," 1996, Georgetown University, Ph.D. dissertation.

CHAPTER 11: CLINTON RESURGENT

254 The Republican surge also threatened   Stephanopoulos, *Human*, 361.
255 Some Jewish Democratic   Elizabeth Drew, *On the Edge* (New York, 1994), 202.
255 "the brouhaha over"   Kenneth Baer, *Reinventing Democrats* (Lawrence, Kans., 2000), 213.
255 "Clinton's approach to race"   Rueter, ed., *Politics*, 392.
256 Yet in the face of strong liberal   Baer, *Reinventing*, 216–17.
256 "governmental consideration of Americans"   Baer, *Reinventing*, 235.
256 "patently unfair"   Stephanopoulos, *Human*, 361–65.
257 "Once in office, President Clinton"   Walton, *Reelection*, 234–35.
258 Dole had also lamented   Robert Dole interview with James Reichley, September 9, 1977, GF.
259 "We want black businessmen to scream"   Stephanopoulos, *Human*, 361–65.
259 Morris salivated at   Dick Morris, *Behind the Oval Office* (New York, 1997); Stephanopoulos, *Human*, 366–68.
259 Sitting beneath a huge map   Stephanopoulos, *Human*, 370.
259 Even before the latest controversy   James Ceaser and Andrew Busch, *Losing to Win* (New York, 1997), 49–51.
260 "Those of us who voted"   Robert Shogan, *The Fate of the Union* (Boulder, Colo., 1998), 245.
261 "This is a decent welfare bill wrapped"   *Time*, August 12, 1996
261 In a move that split   *Time*, November 4, 1996.
261 Among the most influential   Morris, *Behind*, 301–4.
262 "a moral blot on"   *Time*, August 12, 1996.
262 The two most prominent   Ceaser and Busch, *Losing*, 109.
262 "Before nine PM, we're running"   Shogan, *Fate*, 276.
264 Dole made a personal visit   *Newsweek*, July 1, 1996.
264 In separate meetings   Bob Woodward, *The Choice* (New York, 1996), 100, 225–30.
264 A 1990 column in which   *Newsweek*, March 4, 1996.
265 Another associate, whom Buchanan   *Newsweek*, February 26, 1996.
265 It also now emerged that   *Newsweek*, March 4, 1996.
265 "We're going to take back America!"   *Newsweek*, March 4, March 11, 1996.
266 "setup"   Ceaser and Busch, *Losing*, 98.
266 Congressman J. C. Watts, the most   Walters interview.
266 "auxiliaries"   *Time*, August 26, 1996.
266 "We needed to let"   Larry Sabato, *Toward the Millennium* (Boston, 1997), 95.
266 "He's one of the few people"   *Time*, August 19, 1996.
267 "chilling. . . . We are facing an epidemic"   *Washington Post*, May 22, 1996.

267   "I feel like we're reaping"   *Washington Post,* June 12, 1996.

268   Visiting Auschwitz   Michael Fumento, "Politics and Church Burnings,"
      Commentary, October 1996.

268   "We do not now have evidence"   Jill Dougherty, "Clinton sounds call to
      stop church burnings," CNN, June 8, 1996.

268   Not only were church arsons   Michael Fumento, *Wall Street Journal,* July 8,
      1996.

268   The Reverend Joseph Lowery   *Washington Post,* June 19, 1996.

269   "lonely voice in the Republican"   Sabato, *Millennium,* 135.

269   "wonderful"   *U.S. News,* October 14, 1996.

270   "Race, the abiding agony of American"   *Newsweek,* June 24, 1996.

270   "We are not going to campaign"   Bruce Cain and Karin McDonald, *Race
      and Party Politics in the 1996 Presidential Election* (Berkeley, Calif., 1997),
      2–3.

270   Asked to explain the change   Cain and McDonald, *Race,* 2–3.

CHAPTER 12: THE INCORRIGIBLY WHITE REPUBLICAN PARTY

275   advocated getting rid of affirmative action   Stephanopoulos, *Human,*
      208–9.

275   "Reinventing has been generally"   Alexander Cockburn and Jeffrey
      St. Clair, *Al Gore* (New York, 2000), 185.

276   "government should stop making"   *Washington Post,* January 23, 1999.

276   By contrast, Bush   *Washington Post,* May 15, 2000.

277   "unfortunate"   Jesse Jackson, "Pandering to Racism," *Los Angeles Times,*
      January 19, 2000.

278   "gook"   *Washington Post,* February 18, 2000.

278   The swing to the racial right   *Washington Post,* February 21, 2000.

278   Anderson, whose resignation   *Washington Post,* June 13, 2000.

278   In Michigan, black voters   *Washington Post,* February 21, 2000.

279   Even when Bradley beat   *Los Angeles Times,* February 9, 2000; Jeremy
      Mayer and Alexander Sarapu, "Bradley's Failure and McCain's Michigan
      Success," *Political Chronicle,* Fall 2000.

279   Gore, who had avoided Sharpton   Michael Kelly, *Washington Post,*
      February 16, 2000.

279   "agents of intolerance"   *Washington Post,* March 7, 2000.

279   He tried to outdo Gore   *New York Times,* February 9, 2000.

280   "would rather take pictures"   *Bloomberg News,* March 28, 2000.

280   "minstrel show"   *Boston Globe,* December 10, 2000.

281   "Some in our party miss no"   *Washington Times,* August 2, 2000.

282   "any partnerships with Jews"   *Los Angeles Times,* August 10, August 11,
      2000.

282   "dual citizen of Israel"   *Los Angeles Times,* August 12, 2000.

282   "You can't defend policies that"   *New York Times,* August 9, 2000.

282   "I wanted to ban quotas"   *Los Angeles Times,* August 14, 2000.
283   "because history and current reality"   *New York Times,* August 9, 2000.
283   Anderson and Bush quotes from *Washington Post,* June 13, 2000.
283   "New Majority Council"   Rene Amoore, director of New Majority Council, interview, December 7, 2000.
284   Some blacks complained they were   *Washington Post,* October 29, 2000.
285   Gore's link was puzzling   *Los Angeles Times,* September 16, 2000.
285   "a Sister Souljah moment"   *Washington Post,* May 15, 2000.
285   "We've got these people"   Joyner interview transcript, October 4, 2000 (www.tomjoyner.com).
286   While opposing quotas because   *Washington Times,* October 20, 2000.
286   The NAACP arranged   Amoore interview.
287   While the inflammatory television   *Washington Post,* October 21, 2000.
287   "all hell is going to break loose"   *Washington Post,* October 29, 2000.
288   "three fifths of a human being"   *Washington Post,* November 5, 2000.
288   "doesn't think that's a hate"   *National Review,* November 6, 2000.
288   "I know the current wisdom"   *New York Times,* September 16, 2000.
289   Black turnout in Florida rose   *Los Angeles Times,* December 8, 2000. The figures on black turnout have been challenged recently.
289   "remember in November!"   *Boston Globe,* December 10, 2000.
289   At least eight thousand names   Tim Palast, "Florida's Flawed 'Voter Cleansing' Program," *Salon,* December 4, 2000.
290   Surveys showed a racial   *Los Angeles Times,* December 17, 2000.
290   Yet even the leader of the New Majority   Amoore interview.

CHAPTER 13: THE FUTURE OF RACE IN PRESIDENTIAL CAMPAIGNS

291   "The prejudices of centuries"   Orlando Patterson, *The Ordeal of Integration* (Washington, 1997), 15.
295   "Sometime before the end"   *Policy Review,* Spring 1994.
297   "was a form of heresy"   Weiss, *Farewell,* 4.
300   "We cannot remind ourselves"   Paul Gilroy, *Against Race* (Cambridge, Mass., 2000), 30–31.
301   The conception of race in Puerto   Peter Winn, *Americas* (Los Angeles, 1999), 270–78.
302   "denigrating to marry someone"   Julian Pitt-Rivers, in John Hope Franklin, ed., *Color and Race* (Boston, 1969), 278.
302   "Brazil is the most successful racist system"   Winn, *Americas,* 296–99.
302   Many people considered   James Davis, *Who Is Black?* (University Park, Penn., 1991), 11–12.
302   The dismay and shock   Earl Shorris, "Our Next Race Question," *Harper's,* April 1996.
304   products of a particular   For an extraordinary tracery of the rise of race as an idea, see Ivan Hannaford, *Race* (Baltimore, 1996).

305   Lower-class whites   Robert Huckfeldt and Carol Kohfeld, *Race and the Decline of Class in American Politics* (Urbana, Ill., 1989).

307   a Harvard study found   Gary Orfield, *Schools More Separate: Consequences of a Decade of Resegregation.* Civil Rights Project Report, July 2001.

308   A portion of the white public   *Washington Post,* October 8, 1995.

308   even opposed interracial adoption   Patterson, *Ordeal,* 48.

SELECTED BIBLIOGRAPHY

BOOKS

Abrahamson, Paul R., John H. Aldrich, and David W. Rohde. 1998. *Change and Continuity in the 1996 Elections*. Washington: CQ Press.

Ambrose, Stephen E. 1988. *Nixon: The Education of a Politician*. New York: Touchstone.

———. 1989. *Nixon: The Triumph of a Politician*. New York: Simon & Schuster.

Baer, Kenneth S. 2000. *Reinventing Democrats*. Lawrence, Kans.: University of Kansas Press.

Barker, Lucius J., and Ronald W. Walters, eds. 1985. *The 1984 Presidential Campaign of Jesse Jackson*. Chicago: University of Illinois Press.

Black, Christine M., and Thomas Oliphant. 1989. *All By Myself: The Unmaking of a Presidential Campaign*. Chester, Conn.: Globe Pequot Press.

Black, Earl, and Merle Black. 1992. *The Vital South: How Presidents Are Elected*. Cambridge, Mass.: Harvard University Press.

Buell, Emmett H. Jr., and Lee Sigelman, eds. 1991. *Nominating the President*. Knoxville, Tenn.: The University of Tennessee Press.

Burns, James MacGregor. 1960. *John Kennedy: A Political Profile*. New York: Harcourt, Brace & Co.

Campbell, Angus, Phillip E. Converse, Warren E. Miller, and Donald E. Stokes. 1960. *The American Voter*. New York: Wiley.

Cannon, Lou. 1991. *President Reagan: The Role of a Lifetime*. New York: Simon & Schuster.

Carmines, Edward, and James Stimson. 1989. *Issue Evolution: Race and the Transformation of American Politics*. Princeton, N.J.: Princeton University Press.

Caro, Robert A. 1982. *The Path to Power*. New York: Knopf.

———. 1990. *Means of Ascent*. New York: Knopf.

Carter, Dan T. 1995. *The Politics of Rage*. Baton Rouge, La.: Louisiana University Press.

———. 1996. *From George Wallace to Newt Gingrich*. Baton Rouge, La.: Louisiana University Press.

Ceaser, James, and Andrew Busch. 1993. *Upside Down and Inside Out: The 1992 Election and American Politics*. Lanham, Md.: Rowman & Littlefield.

———. 1997. *Losing to Win: The 1996 Elections and American Politics*. New York: Rowman & Littlefield.

Cockburn, Alexander, and Jeffrey St. Clair. 2000. *Al Gore: A User's Manual.* New York: Verso.

Dallek, Robert. 1991. *Lone Star Rising.* New York: Oxford University Press.

Davis, James F. 1991. *Who Is Black? One Nation's Definitions.* University Park, Pa.: Pennsylvania State University Press.

Du Bois, W. E. B. 1982 (1903). *The Souls of Black Folk.* New York: Signet.

———. 1995. *W. E. B. Du Bois: A Reader.* David Levering Lewis, ed. New York: Henry Holt & Co.

Dugger, Ronnie. 1983. *On Reagan.* New York: McGraw-Hill.

Edsall, Thomas B., and Mary D. Edsall. 1992. *Chain Reaction: The Impact of Race, Rights and Taxes on American Politics.* New York: W. W. Norton & Co.

Eldersveld, Samuel J., and Hanes Walton Jr. 2000. *Political Parties in American Society,* 2nd ed. New York: Bedford/St. Martin's.

Fairclough, Adam. 1987. *To Redeem the South of America: The Southern Christian Leadership Conference and Martin Luther King, Jr.* Athens, Ga.: University of Georgia Press.

Farmer, James. 1985. *Lay Bare the Heart.* New York: Arbor House.

Faw, Bob, and Nancy Skelton. 1986. *Thunder in America.* Austin, Tex.: Texas Monthly Press.

Felknor, Bruce L. 1967. *Dirty Politics.* New York: W. W. Norton & Co.

Fox, Geoffrey. 1996. *Hispanic Nation: Culture, Politics, and the Constructing of Identity.* Secaucus, N.J.: Birch Lane.

Frady, Marshall. 1996. *Jesse: The Life and Pilgrimage of Jesse Jackson.* New York: Random House.

Franklin, John Hope, ed. 1968. *Color and Race.* Boston: Beacon.

Fraser, Steve, and Gary Gerstle, eds. 1989. *The Rise and Fall of the New Deal Order.* Princeton, N.J.: Princeton University Press.

Garrow, David J. 1986. *Bearing the Cross.* New York: William Morrow & Co.

Germond, Jack W., and Jules Witcover. 1989. *Whose Broad Stripes and Bright Stars: The Trivial Pursuit of the Presidency 1988.* New York: Warner Books.

Gillon, Steven M. 1992. *The Democrats' Dilemma: Walter F. Mondale and the Liberal Legacy.* New York: Columbia University Press.

Gilroy, Paul. 2000. *Against Race: Imagining Political Culture Beyond the Color Line.* Cambridge, Mass.: Belknap.

Goldman, Peter, Thomas M. DeFrank, Mark Miller, Andrew Murr, and Tom Matthews. 1994. *Quest for the Presidency, 1992.* College Station, Tex.: Texas A&M University Press.

Goldman, Peter, and Tom Matthews. 1989. *The Quest for the Presidency: The 1988 Campaign.* New York: Touchstone.

Greenberg, Stanley B. 1995. *Middle Class Dreams.* New York: Random House.

Greenshaw, Wayne. 1982. *Elephants in the Cottonfields: Ronald Reagan and the New Republican South.* New York: Macmillan.

Halberstam, David. 1968. *The Unfinished Odyssey of Robert Kennedy.* New York: Random House.

Hannaford, Ivan. 1996. *Race: The History of an Idea in the West*. Baltimore: Johns Hopkins.

Hess, Stephen, and David Broder. 1967. *The Republican Establishment*. New York: Harper & Row.

Holbrook, Thomas M. 1996. *Do Campaigns Matter?* Thousand Oaks, Calif.: Sage.

Holden, Matthew Jr. 1986. *The President, Congress, and Race Relations*. Ernest Patterson Memorial Lecture. Boulder, Col.: University of Colorado Press.

Holmes, Stephen A. 2000. *Ron Brown: An Uncommon Life*. New York: John Wiley & Sons.

Holt, Thomas C. 2000. *The Problem of Race in the Twenty-first Century*. Cambridge, Mass.: Harvard University Press.

Huckfeldt, Robert, and Carol Weitzel Kohfeld. 1989. *Race and the Decline of Class in American Politics*. Urbana, Ill.: University of Illinois Press.

Ignatiev, Noah. 1995. *How the Irish Became White*. New York: Routledge.

Jamieson, Kathleen Hall. 1993. *Dirty Politics*. New York: Oxford University Press.

Johnson, Haynes. 1991. *Sleepwalking Through History: America in the Reagan Years*. New York: W. W. Norton & Co.

Johnson, Lyndon Baines. 1971. *The Vantage Point*. New York: Holt, Rinehart, & Winston.

Jordan, Winthrop D. 1968. *White over Black*. Kingsport, Tenn.: University of North Carolina Press.

Kearns, Doris. 1976. *Lyndon Johnson and the American Dream*. New York: Harper & Row.

Lesher, Stephen. 1994. *George Wallace: American Populist*. New York: William Patrick.

Lewis, David Levering. 1970. *King: A Critical Biography*. New York: Praeger.

Lewis, Finlay. 1980. *Mondale: Portrait of an American Politician*. New York: Harper & Row.

Lewis, John, with Michael D'Orso. 1998. *Walking with the Wind*. New York: Simon & Schuster.

Maraniss, David. 1995. *First in His Class*. New York: Touchstone.

Matthews, Christopher. 1994. *Kennedy & Nixon: The Rivalry That Shaped Postwar America*. New York: Simon & Schuster.

Mayer, Jeremy D. 1996. "Critical Mass: The Effect of Black Population Levels on White Voting Behavior in the 1988 and 1992 Presidential Elections." Georgetown University, Ph.D. dissertation.

Mazo, Earl, and Stephen Hess. 1967. *Nixon: A Political Portrait*. New York: Harper & Row.

McCarthy, Eugene J. 1969. *The Year of the People*. Garden City, N.Y.: Doubleday.

McGinnis, Joe. 1969. *The Selling of the President*. New York: Trident.

McGovern, George. 1977. *Grassroots*. New York: Random House.

Miller, William J. 1967. *Henry Cabot Lodge: A Biography*. New York: Heinemann.

Morris, Roger. 1990. *Richard Milhous Nixon: The Rise of an American Politician.* New York: Henry Holt & Co.

———. 1996. *Partners in Power.* New York: Henry Holt & Co.

Muskie, Edward. 1972. *Journeys.* Garden City, N.Y.: Doubleday.

Nixon, Richard M. 1962. *Six Crises.* Garden City, N.Y.: Doubleday.

———. 1990. *In the Arena.* New York: Simon & Schuster.

———. 1990. *RN: The Memoirs of Richard Nixon.* New York: Touchstone.

Nofziger, Lynn. 1992. *Nofziger.* Washington, D.C.: Regnery.

Oates, Stephen B. 1982. *Let the Trumpet Sound.* New York: Harper & Row.

O'Reilly, Kenneth. 1995. *Nixon's Piano: Presidents and Racial Politics from Washington to Clinton.* New York: Free Press.

Panetta, Leon E. 1971. *Bring Us Together: The Nixon Team and the Civil Rights Retreat.* Philadelphia: Lippincott.

Parmet, Herbert S. 1997. *George Bush: The Life of a Lone Star Yankee.* New York: Scribner.

———. 1990. *Richard Nixon and His America.* Boston: Little Brown & Company.

Patterson, Orlando. 1997. *The Ordeal of Integration.* Washington, D.C.: Civitas Counterpoint.

Patterson, Thomas. 1993. *Out of Order.* New York: Knopf.

Perry, Huey L., and Wayne Parent, eds. 1995. *Blacks and the American Political System.* Miami: University Press of Florida.

Phillips, Kevin. 1969. *The Emerging Republican Majority.* New Rochelle, N.Y.: Arlington House.

———. 1993. *Boiling Point: Republicans, Democrats, and the Decline in Middle-Class Prosperity.* New York: Random House.

Polsby, Nelson W., and Aaron Wildavsky. 1991. *Presidential Elections,* 8th ed. New York: Free Press.

Ranney, Austin, ed. 1981. *The American Elections of 1980.* Washington, D.C.: American Enterprise Institute.

———, ed. 1985. *The American Elections of 1984.* Durham, N.C.: Duke University Press.

Reeves, Thomas C. 1992. *A Question of Character.* Rocklin, Calif.: Prima.

Riley, Russell L. 1999. *The Presidency and the Politics of Racial Inequality: Nation-Keeping from 1831 to 1965.* New York: Columbia University Press.

Robinson, Jackie. 1972. *I Never Had It Made.* New York: Putnam.

Rueter, Theodore, ed. 1995. *The Politics of Race: African Americans and the Political System.* Armonk, N.Y.: M. E. Sharpe.

Runkel, David R., ed. 1989. *Campaign for President: The Managers Look at '88.* Dover, Mass.: Auburn House.

Sabato, Larry J., ed. 1997. *Toward the Millennium: The Elections of 1996.* Boston: Allyn & Bacon.

Safire, William. 1975. *Before the Fall.* Garden City, N.Y.: Doubleday.

Scammon, Richard M., and Ben J. Wattenberg. 1970. *The Real Majority.* New York: Coward McCann.

Schlesinger, Arthur M. Jr. 1960. *Kennedy or Nixon: Does It Make Any Difference?* New York: Macmillan.

———. 1978. *Robert F. Kennedy and His Times.* Boston: Houghton Mifflin.

Schram, Martin. 1977. *Running for President 1976.* New York: Stein & Day.

Shesol, Jeff. 1997. *Mutual Contempt.* New York: W. W. Norton & Co.

Snowden, Frank M. 1983. *Before Color Prejudice: The Ancient View of Blacks.* Cambridge, Mass.: Harvard University Press.

Solberg, Carl. 1984. *Hubert Humphrey: A Biography.* New York: W. W. Norton & Co.

Sorensen, Theodore C. 1965. *Kennedy.* New York: Harper & Row.

Steed, Robert P., Laurence W. Moreland, and Tod A. Baker, eds. 1986. *The 1984 Presidential Election in the South.* New York: Praeger.

Stephanopoulos, George. 1999. *All Too Human.* New York: Little Brown & Company.

Stroud, Kandy. 1977. *How Jimmy Won.* New York: William Morrow & Co.

Turque, Bill. 2000. *Inventing Al Gore.* New York: Houghton Mifflin.

Walton, Hanes Jr. 1997. *African American Power and Politics: The Political Context Variable.* New York: Columbia University Press.

———. 2000. *Reelection: William Jefferson Clinton as a Native-Son Presidential Candidate.* New York: Columbia University Press.

Wattenberg, Martin P. 1991. *The Rise of Candidate-Centered Politics: Presidential Elections of the 1980s.* Cambridge, Mass.: Harvard University Press.

Wayne, Stephen J., and Clyde Wilcox, eds. 1992. *The Quest for National Office.* New York: St. Martin's Press.

Wayne, Stephen J. 1992. *The Road to the White House: The Politics of Presidential Elections.* New York: St. Martin's Press.

Weiss, Nancy J. 1983. *Farewell to the Party of Lincoln: Black Politics in the Age of FDR.* Princeton, N.J.: Princeton University Press.

White, Theodore H. 1961. *The Making of the President 1960.* New York: Atheneum.

Wicker, Tom. 1970. *JFK and LBJ.* Baltimore: Penguin.

———. 1991. *One of Us: Richard Nixon and the American Dream.* New York: Random House.

Witcover, Jules. 1970. *The Resurrection of Richard Nixon.* New York: Putnam.

———. 1977. *Marathon: The Pursuit of the Presidency, 1972–1976.* New York: Viking.

Wofford, Harris. 1980. *Of Kennedys and Kings: Making Sense of the Sixties.* New York: Farrar, Straus, Giroux.

Woodward, Bob. 1996. *The Choice.* New York: Simon & Schuster.

Wooten, James. 1978. *Dasher: The Roots and the Rising of Jimmy Carter.* New York: Summit Books.

JOURNAL ARTICLES

Barker, Lucius J. 1994. "Limits of Political Strategy: A Systemic View of the African American Experience." *American Political Science Review* 88:1, 1–13.

Bolce, Louis, Gerald De Maio, and Douglas Muzzio. 1993. "The 1992 Republican Tent: No Blacks Walked In." *Political Science Quarterly* 108:2.

Mayer, Jeremy D., and Alexander Sarapu. 2000. "Bradley's Failure and McCain's Michigan Success: The Preprimary Campaigns of 2000." *Political Chronicle* (Fall).

INDEX

ABOUT THE AUTHOR

JEREMY D. MAYER grew up in Arlington, Virginia, and received his undergraduate degree in political science from Brown University in 1990. After two years in Japan, he pursued graduate studies in politics at Oxford and Georgetown, receiving his Ph.D. from Georgetown in 1996. He is a visiting assistant professor of government at Georgetown.

ABOUT THE TYPE

This book was set in Sabon, a typeface designed by the well-known German typographer Jan Tschichold (1902–74). Sabon's design is based on the original letterforms of Claude Garamond and was created specifically to be used for three sources: foundry type for hand composition, Linotype, and Monotype. Tschichold named his typeface for the famous Frankfurt typefounder Jacques Sabon, who died in 1580.